The Guardian Year '95

Introduction by **Fay Weldon**
Edited by **Georgina Henry**

FOURTH ESTATE • *London*

First published in Great Britain in 1995 by
Fourth Estate Limited
6 Salem Road
London W2 4BU

A catalogue record for this book is available from
the British Library.

ISBN 1–85702–371–4

Typeset by CentraCet Limited, Cambridge
Printed in Great Britain by Bath Press

Contents

Bodies politic
....

World views
....

Fond farewells
....

Culture
....

Not forgetting . . .

Sporting life

Fay Weldon
Introduction

Take some small comfort from the fact that the worse the world gets, the better the journalism which relates to it seems to become. A particularly bad year leads to a particularly stunning overview of what's been going on, at home and abroad. Let Patrick Wright report on page 116 of *The Guardian Year '95*, in despair, that 'Middle England is no longer a stable and virtuous place. It is seething with confusion, moaning and insecurity' – but other *Guardian* correspondents will detail that confusion, moaning and insecurity with certainty, style and aplomb. Nothing like a flaky politician to inflame Steve Bell's wit and fury; the idiocy of the common man will do as much for Austin. By its cartoonists the flavour of a newspaper is known.

The *Guardian* continues to field as good a collection of columnists as the world has to offer, providing a running commentary on matters horrendous, significant and merely diverting. Simon Hoggart, wicked on the subject of John Major; Duncan Campbell wry and sparky on Ronnie Kray's funeral; Suzanne Moore,[1] both forgiving and censorious on Gay Outing. Look around and the world gets altogether bleaker: though to read Lawrence Donegan on the tragic deaths of a family in Rhyl would shake any of us out of complacency, or any notion that evil is something that happens somewhere else.

The Guardian Year replaced *The Bedside Guardian* as a title a year ago – and just as well. The latter, by implication, suggested a world in which at a proper hour *Guardian* readers would put out the cat, set the breakfast oats to soak, and have a soothing read in bed before switching off the lamp and going to sleep. (Chance would be a fine thing!) That you could expect to find within its covers a collection of gentle musings, crosswords and country notes, reflecting a mythical fifty-ish Middle England which was indeed stable and virtuous. Through its pages feather-footed the questing vole, as at home here as in the plashy fen. I quote of course the egregious William Boot, who wrote the *Lush Places* column for *The Brute*, in Evelyn Waugh's novel *Scoop* before he was sent (by mistake) to learn reality in Africa. What happened to William Boot has now happened to all of us; we have learned reality, and a painful business it is. To read Chris McGreal on the massacres in Rwanda and Clive Stafford Smith on the details of death by official electrocution will lull no one to sleep.

The world itself may not have changed so much – terrible and dreadful

---

[1] She of the fuck-me stilettos, *vide* Germaine Greer: who does *not* appear in these pages. Well, Germaine resigned, as the Editorial Board haughtily observed, so what did she expect but banishment from the annual Round-up? Pity, though, murmurs this reader: such a good writer, and whoever said feminists were meant to be sweet?

things have always happened: evil is like a balloon; reduce its girth here and it swells out there – but our apprehension of it has. Our capacity for empathy has, alas for us, increased. Newspaper and TV editors, insisting on 'human interest', if only in the pursuit of circulation and ratings, have obliged us to see the victims of massacre and disaster as human beings, not just pawns in political, military or empirical games. The consensus of opinion has become that even if we can sleep we don't deserve to. What is more, the suggestion is, the slumber of blissful ignorance is dangerous. If we don't look out, what happened in Rwanda will happen here: we are all tribal creatures at heart: civilisation is under threat: the bad times are getting nearer. Consider Srebrenica. If death in the electric chair is not described in hideous detail, we'll have Death Row over here as well as over there. It's almost a superstition. Therefore, and rightly, *The Guardian Year* in its present form; *The Bedside Guardian* ceases to exist.

The danger of all this, of course, is the relish the reader may find in the easy contemplation of death and destruction; we may travel too easily to the far side of empathy, begin to take the side of the oppressor not the victim, if identifying with the victim becomes too painful. We may find an appetite in ourselves for the drama of carnage; we may suffer a remarkable blunting of our sensibilities as we view yet another pile of dead bodies. And, of course, as ever, take great pleasure in disapproving of others the better to approve of ourselves.

The greater danger, to date, remains ignorance and complacency, but only, I suspect, by a margin. The world knows all too much about Rwanda: but ethnic cleansing in Srebrenica still happens. Martin McGuinness of Sinn Fein – 'all dead, all dead', said the caption – carries the coffin of yet another IRA volunteer to its grave. His face shows anguish, but McGuinness still won't renounce violence, for all he is so profoundly knowledgeable about its results. The end, he continues to believe, justifies the means. Theoretical notions of 'freedom' – so much the obsession of young men and middle-class intellectuals – cause dreadful distress all over the world, to women and children who just want to get on with their lives.

The camera is there to catch the scene, new printing technology brings us the moment in all its gritty truth – fantastic portrait; brilliant photograph! – but, what then? To what purpose, all this excellence? To what end this surfeit of information, when all we ever required was wisdom?

We seemed to conduct ourselves better as nations when news came by messenger, on a forked stick. When our leaders spoke not to the cameras, not for sound bites, but to each other. The rot began, I daresay, with the first telegram, as reported in Alfred Austin's poem on the illness of the Prince of Wales:

> Flashed from his bed, the electric message came,
> He is not better; he is much the same.

A newspaper, by definition, gives us the short view: who is there left to put things in their longer perspective? The church? Too self-absorbed. Academics? Too intent on being right. And politicians see no further than the next election. Technology dooms us to live in an over-explicit present. I daresay at the century's end we'll get a 100-year overview from the newspapers, but only till 3 January 2001. After that the twentieth century will be old hat, over. Forget it. And us.

But this is ungracious carping. There are really good encouraging moments, too, here in *The Guardian Year*. The Arts, of course; the very essence of civilisation: those solid barriers of culture keeping barbarity at bay, no matter how it batters at the walls crying 'let me in!' Painting, literature, fashion, sport – antidotes to the news. James Wood, who keeps the *Guardian*'s literature columns properly stringent, makes a feisty defence of James Kelman, who so stubbornly, and to such good effect, uses the profane Glaswegian dialect as the folk poetry it is. Mark Lawson is appropriately funny and brilliant on the novelist-as-personality phenomenon, in relation to brilliantly funny Martin Amis; whose teeth seem to loom more importantly in the national psyche than his excellent book. Good reading, good fun.

The information superhighway, by the way, promises us a future in which our own personalised newspapers feature – your computer will print it out for you first thing in the morning, colour pictures and all. You won't even have to walk as far as your letter box. Instead of studiously by-passing Sports, say, or Party Politics, the text you don't want just won't be there any more. If you can't stand Art, the future will spare you the misery of getting so much as a glimpse of the Turner Prize short-list; you can avoid the pain altogether. Your new meta-intelligent digital fibre-optic computer will sieve out anything which might upset or discommode you or, worst of all, bore you. I know this because I was recently in the offices of *Wired* and suffered a conversion to the new Metaverse. *Wired* is the new layperson's magazine for the Internet – which, since I am in the business of recommending, I recommend to even the most sceptical of *Guardian* readers. If you want to know what's going on *next*, not just now, *Wired* becomes compulsory reading: this may well be the retreat into virtual reality, into the future out of the real year, and on into the unhappened next, but it seems altogether reasonable in the face of the confusion, moaning and insecurity we find in the present. No more future shock when we find that the cat we once so blithely put out into the night, before we took up our *Bedside Guardian*, is no longer a pet but an animal companion, as likely to suffer from cold and fear as we are, and that anthropomorphism is all the rage. That we would be wiser to use bottled water than tap, and that old habits of frugality must go – and so on? And who at bedtime reads any more anyway? TV, sex or exhaustion is more likely to set in. Yesterday, *The Bedside Guardian*; today, *The Guardian Year*, tomorrow we're *Wired*.

Introduction

Mind you, to censor your own reading can be a mistake, let alone allow a computer to do it for you. Certainly, the computer can weigh up your earlier choices, and decide in the light of those what new novel, say, you'd like to buy, and organize for payment and delivery, and very nice too. Let it read the reviews. Bad enough to do one's own selection: but wouldn't this inhibit change, 'personal growth' (if one's to acknowledge such a thing even exists) – in machine terms, cut out the random, the inadvertent mutation, which might lead one's taste to improve. Your new PC might well be possessed of artificial intelligence, even good judgement, but aesthetic sensibility? 'All in good time,' they say at *Wired*, 'all in good time!'

The great benefit of *The Guardian Year*, as with our proposed new personalised newspapers, is that it allows the reader to expand his comprehension without too much rustling and wasted newsprint – to try a little sport, a little local politics, say, though in the ordinary habit of *not* reading certain parts; often, indeed, taking pleasure in the time wasted in conscientiously avoiding them. The 'pah!' and 'pah!' again of Disgusted, Tunbridge Wells.

At the end of *Scoop* William Boot – wiser and rendered grateful by his experiences – gets back safely to his column, *Lush Places*. 'The wagons lumber in the lane under their golden glory of harvested sheaves; maternal rodents pilot their furry brood through the stubble . . .' William Boot, as Waugh observed, made no reference to the owls which hunted the maternal rodents. May such a safe and happy return happen for all of us. ●

Brightlingsea 1995

Garry Weaver

Home thoughts

••

4 February 1995

Catherine Bennett
The human factor

A ndrew Blake suffers from Friedreich's ataxia, an incurable disorder of the central nervous system. Understandably, he campaigns for the continuation of medical research requiring experiments on animals. In consequence he receives many letters from animal lovers. From Rose Cottage, for example, a lady animal lover writes: 'Your horrible face portrays your evil soul, you awful man.'

Her pastel writing paper announces that it is 100 per cent recycled, and comes from 'a supporter of the League Against Cruel Sports'. A picture of a baby fox lies beneath her neat rows of maledictions: 'You are not just sick in body but sick in mind. May the rest of your life be a misery and I wish you all the suffering that you are wishing to inflict on animals.' A pretty reciprocity.

The most passionate animal lovers prefer anonymity. One, describing him or herself as 'An Animal Lover and Ugly Scum Hater', has sent Andrew Blake a nicely typewritten message on notepaper printed with a picture of a rat, beneath the slogan 'Rats Have Rights'.

'To the Ugly Bastard in the Wheelchair,' the rat-fan begins. 'I'm so glad you're in a wheelchair, you don't deserve to live on this earth. If I had my own way, I would stick a blazing tyre round your neck and laugh as your ugly, evil face melts off.' Another nameless writer informs Blake: 'I think spastics like you should be banished off to a land of your own, your wheelchairs are no better than pushchairs – you're in the fucking way you ugly loser.'

Some, stressing that they are not violent, animal liberationist types, offer him health tips. 'Why don't you do these experiments on yourselves?' asks 'Animal Lover'. 'I am not an Animal Rights Extremist,' stresses another moderate, adding: 'People like you should be Put Away, you are IGNORANT and Disgusting and EVIL.' Then there are shorter missives, scrawled capital letters scored into lined paper torn from notebooks: 'Giving your support to vivisection makes you a target. You have been warned.'

Anyone who becomes publicly identified with experiments on animals receives similar correspondence. If a sufferer from a hereditary disease receives such treatment, you can imagine what professional scientists get. If they are particularly prominent, or vociferous, they may also receive obscene telephone calls, death threats, graffiti, parcels of razor blades, or bombs. They will have to check under their cars, request ex-directory telephone numbers, install intruder alarms and automated lights around their homes. Sometimes this is not enough. Colin Blakemore, Oxford's Waynflete Professor of Physiology, thought he had kept his address a secret, until he came home one evening in

December 1993 to find his children had taken delivery of a Post Office mailing tube. 'If the plastic plug had been pulled out of the end, then it would have gone off – half a pound of explosive with needles in it. It was very big and potentially lethal.'

Blakemore and his family have suffered for his willingness to speak openly in defence of his experiments on the eyes and brains of cats and monkeys, for which he has, on the other hand, been acclaimed by ophthalmologists, and awarded a medal by the American Academy of Optometry. In 1987, a leading animal welfare group, Animal Aid, made him the target of a personal campaign, which began with a legal challenge. 'As soon as an attack on an individual becomes public, however reasonably it's done, then the extremists will tag on to it,' Blakemore says. 'Whether they're just harmless loonies, who just write horrid letters, or serious ALF members who would contemplate killing or carrying out some material damage – there's no way of distinguishing from the hate mail. I get lots of unsigned mail, usually on purple-coloured lined paper, saying we're going to kill you, or kidnap your children or whatever. The police were particularly worried about kidnap, and they kept our kids under constant surveillance for about a two-month period.'

Max Headley, a phsysiologist at Bristol University, was lucky to survive when his car was blown up in 1990. He was not a public figure and had received no prior threats or warning, both facts which carried an obvious message to other scientists: it could happen to *you*, any day. In a recent review of animal rights extremist activity, the Research Defence Society (RDS) counted over 100 'anti-personnel' attacks between October 1993 and '94, compared with around 25 in the preceding 11 years. These attacks included the 13 tube bombs sent out before Christmas in 1993, one of which was addressed to the RDS office in London. The more violent attacks have dwindled recently, but there is no reason to believe they will not be revived. From the prison where he is now serving a 14-year sentence for an assortment of terrorist activities, Keith Mann told the *Guardian*: 'What they have done is put the bullet in the gun. For a long time people in our movement have been talking about killing vivisectors, and the vivisectors know that. Eventually, someone's going to get shot.'

Not all intimidation is so direct. Some activists work as undercover technicians, hoping to expose malpractice in laboratories, or break into research institutions where they 'liberate' mice, rabbits and dogs. More moderate protesters may confine their protests to affrighting volunteers in cancer and heart research charity shops, superglueing locks, or writing abusive letters to known researchers. And the majority of animal rights activists are, of course, decent, peaceful citizens who prefer to argue rather than fight their cause. Richard Ryder, for example, is the Westminster lobbyist for the Political Animal Lobby. What does he think about the intimidation of scientists? 'Well, I deplore, obviously, violent tactics,' he says. 'But I don't know whether these scientists are really expressing a realistic fear, or whether somehow it is an expression of their guilt.'

Well, Blakemore's fears were realistic enough, weren't they? Max Headley's bomb really did go off, injuring a passing baby. 'Look,' Ryder says, 'the history of violence in this movement shows quite clearly . . . there hasn't been any vivisector or other animal exploiter killed, or indeed seriously wounded. But the other way around. There have been very many animal campaigners and indeed Green campaigners who have been killed and seriously wounded in the last 20 years. The serious violence has come from the other side!'

Who are these homicidal vivisectors? 'I'm talking in general terms about the violence of the animal user,' Ryder said. 'I'm not saying any vivisectors have used it, but it tends to be a bit of a cliché to assume that the animal rights movement is violent, and that all the fault lies on their side.'

The degree of violence and threats in animal rights activity has been enough to reduce most researchers to a cowed silence, and to turn laboratories into grim-looking, windowless bunkers, bristling with security cameras, locks, entry points and infra-red alarm systems. Inevitably, the spectacle of such intense security further inflames and inspires animal rights activists, who make comparisons with concentration camps, and redouble their efforts to expose the torturers within. 'Direct intimidation is pretty effective,' says Ian Hart, Dimbleby Professor of Cancer Research at London's St Thomas's Hospital. 'It's been effective in South Africa and Soviet Russia over the years. There's no reason why it shouldn't work at this level, and I think it has worked, in as much as it's made us very reticent about going out to the general public and saying, these are the benefits that have accrued from animal experiments.'

In short, bullying has worked, with the rhetorical advantage obviously going to anti-vivisectionists. After all, few emotional appeals *for* vivisection can be made. Even scientists themselves dislike experimenting on animals, and the reasons for having to do it sound dull. Perhaps only the ill, who could hope to benefit, could make an emotional appeal. Even then, a cancer sufferer is less televisual than a beagle. We don't like to think about the ill, and we don't think of ourselves as ill until we actually are.

Since 1975, when Richard Ryder produced *Victims of Science* and Peter Singer published *Animal Liberation*, the peculiarly British zeal for animal protection and horror of vivisection have revived and intensified, launching scores of new pressure groups and bringing new life to venerable organisations such as the RSPCA, the National Anti-Vivisection Society (NAVS) and British Union Against Vivisection (BUAV). Between 1978 and 1985, BUAV membership alone is said to have risen from 4,000 to 16,000. By 1991, the major anti-vivisection groups had a total of 47,000 members and are now thought to command an annual income of around £3 million. Not much compared to the armies anglers could wield, if they ever got organised, but enough for an effective lobbying group, or guerrilla movement. Such impressive growth in organised activity has been matched by widespread change in public attitudes, particularly among women and the tender young.

In his recent book *Animals, Politics and Morality*, Robert Garner quotes a 'remarkable' poll conducted for *Sky* magazine in 1989, in which one in four of those aged between 16 and 19 said they supported the Animal Liberation Front's terrorist campaigns, and 40 per cent said they did not approve of animal experiments under any circumstances. In 1991, a Mintel poll showed that animal testing appalled more people than any other ethical or environmental issue.

What makes all experiments on animals indefensible? At first, the new generation of animal advocates argued very much like Jeremy Bentham: 'The question is not can they *reason*, nor can they *talk*, but can they *suffer?*' Both Singer and Ryder based their case on the idea of 'sentience', the ability to feel pleasure and pain, and Ryder coined the expression 'speciesist' to describe those who feel that the sentience of an animal is of less importance than the sentience of a human being. Like racism and sexism, the expression struck a tremendous chord with well-meaning liberals, even if it seemed to equate women and blacks with mice and hamsters. 'It's very difficult to find rational grounds for distinguishing between human and non-human animals, 'Ryder says now. Not rational? This is a widely accepted point, but you need to be human to think it. 'The suffering of a dog or a cat is of equal validity, in my opinion, as the suffering of human animals,' Ryder continues. 'I'm against all of it.' Presumably, then, he believes the evil of Auschwitz is utterly dwarfed by the activities of Dewhurst's.

An American, Tom Regan, took the argument further by investing animals with rights. To him, the question of suffering was subordinate to the argument that using animals – even in the Pony Club – is a form of injustice. This was not an approach ever fully endorsed by Peter Singer, though he happily adopted the expression. 'The language of rights is a convenient political shorthand,' he explained. 'It is even more valuable in the era of 30-second TV news clips than it was in Bentham's day; but in the argument for a radical change in our attitude to animals, it is in no way necessary.'

This slogan appealed mightily to animal protection activists, who were pressuring the government to reform and extend the 1876 Cruelty to Animals Act. Their arguments revolved around the moral status of animals. 'We got commitment to new legislation in 1979,' says Ryder, 'and we used almost entirely the ethical argument.' In 1986, Parliament passed the Animals (Scientific Procedures) Act, widely considered to be the most stringent piece of legislation on animal experimentation in the world. Its effect was none the less to polarise the animal protection movement, setting animal rights absolutists against animal welfare moderates.

Groups such as FRAME (Fund for the Replacement of Animals in Medical Experiments) and the British Veterinary Association were prepared to accept the new act as a genuine, if limited advance in reducing the suffering of laboratory animals. Radical anti-vivisection groups labelled the act a 'vivisector's charter', and formed a coalition, 'Mobilisation Against the Government White Paper', to fight its progress. Nowadays the three main participants, BUAV, NAVS and a younger group, Animal Aid, are no longer a coalition – in fact they seem unwilling to work together – but all three groups have spent the last decade devotedly opposing the 1986 act and campaigning for total abolition of animal research.

'Vivisection' means cutting up a living animal. The word conjures up images of struggling, agonised dogs, pinioned to tables before a rapt huddle of male scientists. Nowadays most experiments do not involve cutting up the animal and those which do require the animal to be anaesthetised. For obvious reasons, the word is more often used by animal rights campaigners than it is by scientists. There are similar difficulties when the animal rights groups use words like 'torture' and 'cruel', where the scientific community prefers 'procedure' or 'severe'. But this does not explain why dialogue between the two sides has all but died out.

The reason for that can be found in the leaflets and literature distributed by the main anti-vivisection groups. 'Take Animal Experiments: The Facts', published by NAVS. Illustrated with a sad-eyed beagle, it declares: 'Our research indicates that not only are animal experiments misleading, they can actually hold up medical progress.' The leaflet, which makes no mention of ethical notions like animal rights, sentience or speciesism, relies entirely upon an argument which has dominated radical animal rights campaigns since the late 1980s, a tactic variously known as 'practical anti-vivisection', 'species difference' or 'the invalidity argument'. Crudely, it goes: a mouse is not a man; ergo, there is no scientific justification for experimenting on mice to find out things applicable to people.

In the NAVS head office, a substantial house in west London, I asked the director, Jan Creamer, what was wrong with limited, regulated experiments on animals. Immediately she said they were useless.

'Underpinning the whole thing, is our belief that animal experiments are unjustified, they don't work, and we need to move towards a better system of medical and scientific research.'

So, how would she study the spread of cancerous tumours, other than by observing them in an animal model, as Professor Hart is now doing with mice?

'It's still in a mouse, isn't it?' she objected. 'Everything that's flowing through it belongs to a mouse, not a person. The results that he gets at the end of that experiment will tell him about mice, it won't tell him about people.'

None the less, Professor Hart has applied for permission to conduct human trials of a gene therapy for malignant melanoma, which has already proved effective in animal tests. If you believe the BUAV, these tests were quite irrelevant. 'Animal experiments not only give the wrong answer,' the organisation claims, in a leaflet called 'Health with Humanity', 'but they also divert attention and resources away from other more relevant sources of information.' BUAV recommends complementary medicines, such as homoeopathy, as an alternative: 'These are known to be safe and effective and treat a person as a whole instead of like a disconnected assortment of parts.'

At Animal Aid, Gillian Egan also offers a vague, yet confident speech on scientific shortcomings: 'In forms of research when they're looking at certain things, you'd be better off tossing a coin, quite frankly, than using animals. Because the amount of times that they correlate with anything to do with humans, it just doesn't work.'

Asked to elaborate, all three organisations produce lists of diseases which, they say, were conquered by improvements in public health rather than by drugs. This may be true, but when you have the disease you may not be content with preventive medicine alone. They mention Thalidomide and Opren, drugs which were tested on animals, yet produced catastrophic side-effects in humans. Asked how they would proceed without animals, they sing the praises of tissue culture, computer modelling or epidemiology.

Stripped of vogueish scientific jargon, their argument is nothing new. When ethical opposition failed to achieve abolition, Victorian campaigners also moved on to deny the utility of vivisection, opposing vaccination, for example, on the grounds both that it degraded human beings (by injecting them with diseased animal matter) and that it obscured the primacy of vice and filth in spreading infectious diseases. 'Provided it's sincerely offered, I suppose it's politically fair game,' comments Richard Ryder, who prefers to argue on ethics. 'It's just that I don't actually believe that all their arguments are true.'

But invalidity appears to be an argument that appeals to the general public, baffled by complex ethical dilemmas. It's often repeated in letters from outraged animal lovers, such as this: 'Don't work, does it, vivisection – go back to the Stone Age, dickhead.' Anti-vivisection groups say they receive constant enquiries from people who don't want accidentally to give money to charities that conduct experiments on animals. The better to starve them of funds, NAVS has produced a *Good Charities Guide*, in which the 'Bad Guys' are marked by a cross. Bad Guys include the British Heart Foundation, the Cystic Fibrosis Research Trust, the Imperial Cancer Research Fund (ICRF) and the Muscular Dystrophy Group.

Nick Wright is Scientific Director of the ICRF, Professor of Pathology at Hammersmith Hospital, and chairman of the Research for Health Charities Group, a group of 14 of Britain's largest medical research organisations founded five years ago to combat the anti-fund-raising efforts and adverse publicity flooding from anti-vivisectionist groups. Plainly exasperated, he says that only 2 or 3 per cent of their funds are spent on animal experiments; in any case, these very charities have helped develop 'alternatives', such as tissue culture and population studies which anti-vivisectionists accuse them of ignoring. 'The main contribution to tissue culture in the 1940s and 1950s was in *this* institution. They talk about epidemiology – we have major epidemiological laboratories, we do research on human beings, we have many laboratories just to do research on human tissue simulation, we do computer simulation, we're the people that actually *make* the alternatives. Most of the advances which have stopped the use of animals have actually come from orthodox scientists.'

What does he say to the claim that reductions in infectious diseases were entirely related to improvements in living standards?

'Okay. Let's talk about 1958, when living standards in this country were pretty high compared with the rest of the world. Then the polio vaccine was introduced. We had 150 cases of deaths from poliomyelitis. Within two or three years this was down to seven deaths a year. Are you telling me that this had nothing to do with that?' Wright bangs the table: 'They say *yes*, it had nothing to do with it!'

He describes the use of animals in organ transplantation, in the discovery of insulin, anaesthetics, canine distemper – all medical advances which are now claimed by anti-vivisectionists to have owed nothing to animal experiments. 'If you were knocked down, broke your leg and you were taken to hospital, you might need a blood transfusion, with immunology that was animal-based; you'd need an anaesthetic, that came from animal experimentation; you'd need antibiotics, again tested on animals; and if you had surgery, the techniques were probably tested on animals as well. So if you said I want nothing to do with animals, you'd have to sit there and die.'

Would Jan Creamer sit there and die? Would she refuse anaesthetic? 'It would depend really,' she said. 'Because original anaesthetics came about not as a result of animal experiments, but because of experiments on people.'

But not modern anaesthetics, surely? How can she bring herself to accept most of contemporary medicine? 'I would then say,' Creamer responded, with the air of one producing a clinching rebuttal, 'if you were in favour of animal experiments, then you should refute everything that *hasn't* been brought about as a result of animal experiments.'

This is a sad step away from logic, isn't it? Scientists are not trying to ban non-animal experiments. They don't shun computers. 'It's just as valid,' she insisted. 'If a member of the opposition is saying we can't have any medical progress without animal experiments, then if they feel that strongly, they shouldn't be taking anything that has been developed without animal experiments.'

In an attempt to restore some common sense to the debate, the ICRF occasionally invites visitors, including schoolchildren and animal rights supporters, to tour Clare Hall, its rigorously guarded compound of laboratories just off the M25. Behind the barriers and security cameras are colonies of rodents and toads, and a staff of nervous technicians, some of whom refuse even to show their faces during such visits, for fear of becoming a target. Yet far from being animal fiends, the technicians say they work here because they like animals. One wanted to be a gamekeeper, another a zookeeper, another formerly worked in a veterinary surgery.

How can she both like animals and experiment on them? 'Actually, I found it more upsetting working for a vet than anything I've done here,' she said. 'I think people's cruelty to their own pets is quite amazing.'

Most of the technicians would disapprove of veal-crating and cosmetic-testing on animals, claiming sympathy with much of the animal welfare argument. 'I've never worked in a research place with dogs and cats,' says one. 'I don't think I could. I think the animal libbers have done a lot of good, they've swayed public opinion and probably got the Government to tighten up, which has been a good thing.'

It has not, however, been pleasant for the technicians themselves. 'You can never talk about what you do,' said one woman. 'If someone asks what I do for a living, I just say I work in research.'

Another technician, now working on transgenic mice, used actively to disapprove of animal research. 'Then I got interested in transgenics, and I saw there were questions you could only answer by using animals.'

Transgenics, in which an animal's DNA sequence is altered, allowing the study of a function of a particular gene, now accounts for around 70 per cent of the ICRF's work on mice. If, in mice, researchers can establish how to knock out defective genes which allow cancer to spread, or to introduce healthy genes which inhibit the process, they might, in the future, be able to apply gene therapy to humans. The work is still, the scientists admit, at an exploratory stage, involving a high wastage of mice, and has therefore been singled out for attack by anti-vivisectionists, who claim the research is particularly cruel, misleading and pointless.

'It's not true,' says the transgenics technician. 'It's as simple as that. It's not true. There's a whole range of experiments which can be done, and are done, as steps before producing the mice, but to look at the effect of a gene, not just one cell to another but from one organ to another, from one end of the mouse to another, you can only do that by having the whole animal model there.'

In one laboratory, the homology between mice and humans is employed in experiments on mice which have been injected with human ovarian cancer. A compound developed by British Bio-Technology has proved so effective in 'freezing' tumours in mice that it is now being tested on women with ovarian cancer. 'It's a classic example of how useful mice can be,' says the technician supervising the experiment.

It is his task to feed, water, clean and monitor the mice, taking out the controls which have developed tumours; watching for toxicity or other side-effects in the survivors. 'If we're worried about a mouse, we may check her two or three times a day, constantly watching her, and when we're not happy with the way she's moving, the way she's reacting with her other friends in the cage, then we take her out, she's no use to us. We don't want her to suffer. We humanely kill her. We then go in and look and see what's going on.'

He picks out a seemingly healthy, tumourless mouse from its plastic cage. 'This mouse goes right back to September, so she should be long dead, and if you look, it's basically a healthy mouse, so we see a direct example of the drug working.'

Doesn't he find the work disturbing?

'That's the normal human response, but when we're on an up, it does make our job slightly easier. It's a very hard job this, you know, it's one of the hardest jobs around. But you have to weigh up your personal stress and grievance with hopefully the outcome. And when the results are good, and you can see mice sort of saving human lives, perhaps other animals' lives, you're getting a good result.'

To the anti-vivisectionists, this is not good enough. A mouse is not a man. 'The assumption is that they're very similar,' says BUAV's spokesman, Malcolm Eames. 'That simply isn't true.'

In the face of such intransigence, scientists have begun to retaliate with speakers and literature. The RDS (Research Defence Society), formed in 1908 to answer early anti-science agitation, recently launched a propaganda effort, producing handy lists of diseases whose cure owed much to animal experiments. Confusingly, for the layman, many of the same cures and diseases are mentioned by anti-vivisectionists trying to make the opposite point. Hip replacement is claimed by NAVS as a triumph of 'progress without animals', but advertised by the RDS as a technique practised on dogs, sheep and goats. There are straightforward wrangles over historical fact: NAVS claims that circulation of the blood was a non-animal discovery; the RDS points out that it was discovered by Harvey in 1628, using about 40 different species.

Two years ago Professor John Martin, Professor of Cardiovascular Science in the Department of Medicine at King's College Hospital, decided the anti-vivisectionists were winning the argument. It was time to speak up. 'I felt that if I believed in it, I had to be open about it, and I felt the public had been misled, and that the moral high ground had been taken by the anti-vivisectionists . . . I now feel that because people who really know what they are talking about are starting to talk, it's really moving the other way.'

Martin experiments on rabbits, in an attempt to understand the early cell changes in artery walls which can lead, in man, to strokes and heart attacks. He ridicules the BUAV leaflet, 'Health with Humanity', which instructs him to use alternatives such as tissue techniques – 'I've used that' – or computer modelling: 'I've published on that. It doesn't work, it gives me a very partial answer. What I don't like is the *amateurishness* of all this. It's almost medieval, Luddite – commenting on the reality of something that has data in it, that has means and statistics and a peer-reviewed self-criticism, and then to say, "Oh, that's rubbish because I believe it's rubbish."'

Professor Hart, working in cancer research, has the same problem confronting simple belief with convoluted scientific qualifications. 'I know that, as a scientist, much of that animal experimentation will be useless, in the way that much of scientific work is useless,' he says. 'Because being a scientist is a bit like being a bricklayer on the Great Wall of China ... What you do is you just put in one piece of information into the mass of information. So you can't say, "Well, yes, I cured cancer," or it's very unlikely. You've got to beaver away at these things, and add what little piece of information you can glean without knowing perhaps whether that is going to be useful. That's how science evolves. It's tough to get that over, and it's tough to make it a soundbite. Whereas, "Look at this cat, it's being tortured," hits you in the gut and is a very potent approach to your heart.'

But even if Professor Hart could make a simple, tempting offer: give me 500 mice and I'll give you a cure for colonic cancer, BUAV's Malcolm Eames would not do a deal. 'No. If they said give me 500 orphans from the other side of the planet, somewhere you'd never have to visit, and you won't see, I'd say no as well.'

So he's comparing the life of a mouse to the life of a child?

'Yeah. Because I think those individual people, and those individual animals have a value in their own right.'

How far down does he go? Do individual flies have a value in their own right? 'I'm not convinced that flies experience the conscious world in the same way that we or many other animals do, therefore I wouldn't rank them as a priority in terms of campaigning.' Here, Jan Creamer of NAVS would disagree. Fly life must be respected. 'We don't support anything like that. No.' At Animal Aid, Gillian Egan concurs. 'We're complete abolitionists, we want to see an outlaw of all of them.'

So why don't insects feature on any of the three groups' publicity material? Doesn't Animal Aid's emphasis on monkeys, dogs and mice imply that they, too, are speciesist, or at least, fur-ist?

'I wouldn't say there's a hierarchy,' says Egan. 'But when you're trying to get a message across to the public, you have to attract them to your message in some way, you have to make them realise these creatures do feel pain. It's the same with the whole live export thing; it's much easier for people to get emotive about a veal calf than it is about a broiler chicken. Bring out something about veal calves and, because they're cute and fluffy, people immediately go, "Oh, that's terrible, they're suffering terribly." I mean, that's what humans are about.'

British humans, anyway. It is Andrew Blake's aim to remind them that humans can suffer terribly too. In 1990 he founded a group called Seriously Ill for Medical Research, and now tours schools, reminding children to look beyond the pictures of caged dogs, cats and monkeys. 'I always say, we've got to look at patients suffering in hospitals, that is where you really want to see suffering. You must look at the balance.'

In schools, with their soaring population of urban, environmentally correct vegetarians, anti-vivisection campaigners have found it easy to engender distrust of scientists. A colourful BUAV leaflet, 'Animal Experiments; A Reference Guide for Schools', plays on childish sentiment, with a caged white bunny on its cover. Inside, the Animals Act of 1986 is travestied as a law which 'protects scientists from being prosecuted for cruelty to animals'.

Dissection has already ceased to be compulsory in school, and scientists fear that talented children are now being deterred from studying science, while a justifiable fear of martyrdom dissuades graduates from undertaking research involving animals. As Blakemore says: 'If I'd known what was going to happen to me, if I'd known that in advance, I'd have found some nice backwater of biochemistry or something to work in, where there are only test tubes.'

Few researchers would deny there are important moral questions to be asked about experiments on animals. Indeed, they are increasingly setting up ethical committees to monitor work in animal houses. They will often concede that there are bad experiments and arrogant scientists, agree that the law could be better policed, and endorse FRAME's objectives of reduction, refinement and replacement. Apart from anything else, animal experiments are costly, difficult to control and an instant security risk. 'I'd be the first to pop the champagne on the day the last animal has to be used for research,' says Blakemore, who is now attempting to encourage dialogue between the two factions.

Underlying this often ignorant, grotesquely violent dispute over dumb animals is an attack on the validity of science itself. From their different corners, the campaigner Richard Ryder and the scientist Stephen Rose, Professor of Biology at the Open University, both recognise that the fervour with which the invalidity argument is expressed reflects the public's suspicion and distaste for science. 'It comes on the crest of a wave of ecological and environmental concern,' says Rose, 'and also at a time when there is a rising anti-science within the population at large, which is partly to do with a *fin de siècle* thing, in which people are happier with Nietzsche than Voltaire, and it's partly, I think, because many of the promises of science are seen to be at best double-edged.'

If the scientists are scared of the extremists, the extremists are scared of science. Transgenic experiments are linked, in their minds, with the nuclear bomb, with Dr Mengele and the abuse of psychiatric patients. Any work without an immediate clinical *raison d'être*, such as Blakemore's early work on the development of the visual system, is condemned outright as 'curiosity-driven'. 'The bottom line here,' says Blakemore, 'is that if we're willing to eat animals for the pleasure of how they *taste*, then what value does society place on knowledge?'

Not as much as one might imagine. 'Not all knowledge is good,' says BUAV's Malcolm Eames.

In what deserves to be an intelligent debate, the level of argument is low. On the one side is wilful nescience, blind faith and emotional overspill. On the other is fear and laborious factuality, also known as scientific research. We might as well accept that the two are never going to get on. ●

10 January 1995

Matthew Fort
The case for killing the fatted calf

What, no Wiener schnitzel, no sauté de veau Marengo? Are we to wave farewell to osso bucco and saltimbocca alla romana? Are vitello tonnato and blanquette de veau to become no more than a distant memory like the songlines of the aborigines? Dear, oh dear. The national diet in the UK, miserable enough already, is now to be shorn of yet another component. No monkey's brain. No bear's paw. No tiger's whiskers. No rhinoceros horn. No suckling pig. No duck's livers. No broiler chickens. And now no veal.

Luckily, we never ate very much of the stuff knowingly in the first place. There was a bit of veal and ham pie about, but it's hardly been a serious mainstay of the national kitchen. It was far too valuable to flog for two and a tanner at old Liver & Lites, butchers to the discerning. Most of it got flogged abroad to satisfy the curious predilections of a set of savages with a taste for prepubescent protein.

And what did we miss? Not that much, if you ask me. Oh, yes, I remember that grilled veal chop with wild mushrooms we had in Milan, all burnt and crunchy on the outside and the mushrooms sort of soft and garlicky and just slipping down the throat. But that was in Italy, and you know the Italians.

Well, all right, and there was the veal stew we had in the Auvergne at Madame Vache's farm, but they were her very own calves. Of course, I said it was absolutely delicious; fragrant and succulent. I didn't know it was veal until she told us how she had fed the calves herself when they had been deserted by their mother. Why, tears came into her eyes. And mine when I had a second helping. Anyway, that was in France, and you know the French.

Naturally, we would not dream of such barbaric practices for palatal paedophilia ourselves. Roast up a leg of New Season's lamb, bumped off when it's scarcely finished suckling? Heaven forfend! Fillet out a slab of salmon grown to 'maturity' in a matter of weeks in a cage off the Scottish coast? Don't be absurd! Rend that grilled poussin, advertised in the supermarket as bargain` of the week, limb from limb? Over my dead body, Pimlott.

The idea that we reserve out fiercest, fiercest outrage for creatures with large liquid eyes and a plaintive noise is patently absurd. Personally, I feel just as strongly about scaly things with cold, wet eyes, and those nasty, dirty, noisy, noxious, nervous, disease-ridden chickens. Lamb? Of course, I am all for the rights of lambs. Calve – sorry, carve me another slice and lead me to the barricades for the herring, the piglet and the baby cauliflower.

All the same, I am not quite clear from the present brouhaha whether people object to the notion of veal in itself, are exercised by the way it is husbanded, or whether we are talking about a bit of a transport problem.

Having been subjected to the rigours of modern transport systems myself recently, I have a good deal of sympathy. The last time I went abroad, I wouldn't have minded being stunned before we were loaded on to train, bus, ferry and aeroplane. I would never have known the sweaty indignities on my way to our holiday destination. And that wasn't much different from an abattoir in Spain. People are right to whip themselves into a frenzy of outrage at the mention of veal, but will they please accord the same sensitivity to the millions of travellers who pass through ports, stations, and airports.

It is obviously quite right that any animal should have the right to a decent standard of travel to its last port of call, as it were, just as it should have the right to decent treatment beforehand. If we have learned nothing else, we should know by now that well-looked-after animals, grown in natural conditions and slaughtered with a minimal amount of distress, produce the best-flavoured and healthiest food. And that animals produced otherwise (*vide* broiler chickens and cows fed on minced-up sheep) produce gastro-garbage. Cheap it may be, but then so is all rubbish. Where will the list of proscribed foods end? Is there anything left that we can eat with a clear conscience? Almost everything seems to be hedged around with health warnings and moral imperatives these days. If it isn't bad for your body, its bound to be bad for your conscience.

But once you assume the pre-eminence of humans in the natural order of things, then the cultivation, use and disposal of animals become natural consequences of it. Naturally, too, with such dominance comes responsibility. At the moment, we seem to be a bit slow to acknowledge the responsibilities and rather too keen to exploit various unsavoury aspects of the dominance.

However, we still accord greater 'rights' to animals than we do to our children. Between 1988 and 1992 – recession years, remember – the only sector of the food industry on which expenditure by the public actually increased was the amount we spent on our pets. We will allow the diet of our children go hang as long as Orlando, or Mungo and Muddle come to that, get fed properly. Quite right, too. We could be eating them any time now. •

Pass Notes

28 March 1995 John Humphrys

Appearance: Box with an aerial, several knobs and an on-off switch.

Profession: Presenter on the *Today* programme.

The one who regularly exposes the vacuity and evasions of the Labour front bench? You must have the wrong man. We're talking about the loathsome apologist for Stalin, Pol Pot and Arthur Scargill who regularly pollutes the airwaves with his 'ego trip interviewing'.

What exactly is ego-trip interviewing? Any interviewing that displeases Jonathan Aitken.

Could you clarify that? That's just the kind of egregious rudeness that Mr Aitken is campaigning to stop.

But: Could I finish what I'm saying? You asked a question and I'm trying to answer it and what I'd really like to say is that money spent on the NHS has actually *tripled* since 1810, and Labour's drip-drip-drip campaign to undermine the privatisation, I mean, improvement of

the health service represents the sort of politics of envy which led to the First and Second World Wars, the winter of discontent, not to mention civil war in Bosnia, global warming . . .

B-but: Look! If you're interested in a future in journalism you might like to consider the fact that Prince Aitken's feelings about sneering, overbearing interviewers are *entirely shared* by John Birt, or 'boy' as we call him.

I just wanted to know how to address Mr Aitken: Your Serene Highness; Your Beneficent Majesty; Your Munificent Pleasantness.

What would his Holiness like to be asked? Is your appearance best described as hunky, or just plain gorgeous? Could you share with us some generous acts you have performed recently? What's your favourite colour?

What did Humphrys ask him? Some wholly irrelevant, impertinent and aggressive nonsense about the public sector borrowing deficit.

But he's Chief Secretary to the Treasury! A comment that could have come straight from the 'Islington Blair band', as John Redwood has so accurately defined the BBC's serried ranks of anarchists.

Does Humphrys live in Islington? That's a blatantly biased question.

It's west London, isn't it? No comment.

And he's a very experienced presenter, isn't he? If that's what you call over 20 years of brainwashing in the Trotskyite sink that passes for the BBC. But would you trust someone who said 'interviewing politicians can be like nailing custard to the wall'?

Yes: Then you can go back to Russia.

Tory politicians say: Bastard.

Labour politicians say: Er, it would be quite unfairly irresponsible and irresponsibly unfair to commit ourselves at this point in time on such a major piece of policy, but our Committee on John Humphrys is working on precisely this question, and should be reporting back in the year 2009.

Listeners say: Nail the bastard, get him, go for it, ask him another! ●

3 June 1995

Roger Cowe
Keeping it in the family

Dear shareholder, I thought it would be useful to write to you now that tempers have had time to cool following the recent controversy, culminating in last month's well-attended annual general meeting. A number of shareholders have subsequently written to me to suggest that the whole exercise was a waste of time. I can say that that is one shareholder proposition with which I am entirely in agreement. The board had made it perfectly clear that proxies under my control amounted to 84 per cent of the total shares, making inevitable the defeat of the resolutions opposing re-election of the directors and auditors, and calling for a 90 per cent reduction in top-executive pay.

Of course, it is your democratic right to have your say, although following the passing of resolution 14 at the meeting, the media will in future be excluded and the chairman will have the right to declare the meeting over once he considers there has been sufficient debate.

There has subsequently been some questioning of the objectivity of the two pension funds which led the institutional support. I can assure you that my brother, who chairs one of them, always exercises the utmost impartiality in these matters, while I ensured that my chairmanship of the other fund did not influence its decision.

Following the annual meeting, the directors considered that our new corporate governance arrangements merited review. But at a brief board meeting last week, the directors unanimously agreed that no changes were necessary.

Concerning my roles as both chairman and chief executive, we concluded once again that it would be inappropriate to bring in a non-family member as a non-executive chairman, and the board persuaded me that the company would suffer if I were to relinquish my executive responsibilities.

I think it was an understanding of just how substantial are those duties which led my colleagues to confirm the executive incentive schemes introduced last year. The chairman of the remuneration committee, cousin Charles, pointed out at the meeting that while the 235 per cent increase in pay appears to be out of line with the rest of the sector, it does in fact represent excellent value for shareholders.

I ask you to bear in mind that pay must be competitive and I have often been induced to leave this company. Indeed, at the AGM, a number of shareholders made suggestions of where I might go.

Crucially, excellent performance deserves excellent reward. Some shareholders have suggested that the £324 million loss recorded last year does not represent excellent performance, but I can assure you that I had to work extremely hard to achieve such a result.

I am writing to explain all this now because these arguments seemed to be obscured in the heat of the AGM, resulting in the unanimous votes against the board on a show of hands.

Thankfully, those misunderstandings have not been allowed to damage our company, due to the 17 million votes in favour. I am grateful to shareholders for that overwhelming support, and look forward to ensuring that the board does not face such ill-founded criticism next year,

Yours sincerely,

Chairman and chief executive. ●

9 February 1995

Hugo Young
Muted grunts are no response to financial gluttony

In the Grill Room at the Dorchester Hotel, London, the most expensive claret, Château Petrus, stands in the list at £960 a bottle. On Christmas Day 1994, a party of six men got through 12 bottles of the Dorchester's Château Petrus at a sitting. Actually, they were unable to manage the last half-bottle, which they graciously left for the wine waiter, although it was his opinion that, had they been interested in the very best rather than the most expensive claret, he could have recommended something rather cheaper, perhaps running to even as little as £500 a bottle. But they did not want to stint themselves. Somebody was prepared to ante up £11,500 for the Christmas meal, and that's without the food.

Some members of the Dorchester party, according to a man who saw them, were Arabs. But this scene strikes me as a story of our own time and country as well. It is currently the most extreme display of conspicuous consumption in a short time that I have to offer: excess on a level which even lottery hysteria hasn't managed to inspire. That it could happen at all is a reminder that, when it comes to the making and spending of money, the scale of acceptable normality at the very top has edged beyond what anyone would have defended even a decade ago, at the height of Mrs Thatcher's crusade against the levellers. It is the secret British disease. We are living in new realms of financial gluttony, to which the response of public people is a doctrine of silence.

The private beneficiaries have been less quiet. That, too, is fall-out from the Thatcher years. Ed Wallis, chief executive of PowerGen, says he's worth every penny when, on top of a fourfold pay rise, he is forced to account for £1.2

million he will gain from share options in a near-monopoly that was once in public hands. Colleagues in the same sector airily dismiss criticism of similar bonanzas by insisting they are *de rigueur*. Sir Iain Vallance, chairman of BT, got stroppy when his £663,000 salary was queried in the Commons, contending, with dubious relevance but memorable effect, that he worked harder than a junior doctor whose monetary value might, in any case, be compared unfavourably with his own.

How much has this to do with government? Quite a lot. Many of the flagrant cases, most shamelessly defended by their culprit-heroes, come, like Wallis's, from the monopolistic utilities. These were handed a low share price by ministers anxious to sell them and now enjoy, through no exceptional effort of their own, the vastly greater share prices that have made a new breed of corporate millionaires. Their bosses have grown wealthy at public expense and very little risk. They are by far the largest beneficiaries of privatisation, exceeding in profit even the ex-ministers who helped put them where they are and then joined their boards.

But that is not the limit of the Government's role. For these new rich are also spared, by official ordinance, embarrassment. They're the exponents of an approved philosophy, fought for by the Tories since 1797. They personify what market capitalism is about. They've done well, and why not? Their success, far from raising questions, is a kind of prize: proof that these old public businesses play big and equal in the private sector. The Prime Minister may sometimes writhe at the more grotesque implications, but he never denounces them. He deflects the problem to shareholders, unconcerned that in PowerGen the government still holds 40 per cent. He is the silent accomplice, as his predecessor was the triumphant prophet of the age of excess.

He will pay his own price for this. The repulsive sight of these self-seeking predators, and the feeble casuistry they are sometimes obliged to venture in their own defence, are not lost on other employees in their businesses, however blithely ministers pass it by. For Labour, such episodes are a gift. Gordon Brown, the shadow chancellor, sometimes makes it sound as though the whole prospective budget deficit implied by his party's spending plans can be covered by an assault on windfall profits from quasi-monopolistic electricity and water businesses.

Quite rightly, he is relentless in calculating the scale of the share-option scams. He suggests, though not with much conviction, that each utility regulator should tame the option-gluttons by limiting the price increases he will countenance. Nobody doubts that Mr Brown speaks for a world which is outraged that Britain should now register more inequality of income distribution than at any time since records began last century, and a greater increase in poverty since 1979 than any other advanced country.

Yet there is something muted about Labour's response all the same. The party is cautious in the promises it makes about what it will do. It is safe to say, I guess, that not a single glass of Château Petrus has been drunk in the

Dorchester Grill by anyone who ever voted Labour, or ever would. But the leadership still sounds more anxious to make the world safe for the Petrus-drinking classes, for fear of alienating the £10-a-bottle brigade, than standing up for an equalisation that would drive an even bigger inroad than £960 a time into their taxed income.

Nobody doubts that top business executives need to be well paid. They may not deserve more than junior doctors. Some may be of less social utility than the teachers to whom Kenneth Clarke is this week applying the same brusque scorn as he did a few years ago when they learned to love him at the Department of Education. But scarcity dictates in rough-and-ready fashion the logic of most executive rewards. Risk and pressure and responsibility and the often huge costs of making bad judgements, define the load that needs to command large financial recompense.

But that's not true of Ed Wallis's share options, and it's not the last word on the policy a party of the left should be promoting. Among the tricks of the age of excess has been to pretend that its critics are as green-eyed as its practitioners. The politics of envy has been made to displace the politics of social justice, and Labour is still not entirely released from the consequent paralysis. The leadership issues pious hints, but will not yet promise to tax heavily incomes and options on the Vallance–Wallis scale. It lets its justified concern for the aspirational middle-class voter impede the scaling down of plutocrats. Yet raising tax against them is not an act born of trifling envy. It would be a new statement of social norms, replacing the indecent conventions that became the texts not just of normality but of virtue in the last decade. Why can't Labour make that statement, loud and proud? •

....

18 July 1995

Nick Davies
Justice amid enveloping air of chaos

Mr Bourke is a magistrate of the gentle school, courteous to the point of deference, rather like the old English character actor Wilfred Hyde White with his air of barely suppressed confusion.

He sits on his high-backed chair, peering over his spectacles at the ceaseless flow of wretches and rogues passing through the dock below him, and from time to time he likes to shake his head and sadly murmur his catch-phrase. 'Well,' he says, more or less to himself, 'so there it is.'

Out on the steps of Clerkenwell court, two long-haired figures with rough hands are tipping lager down their throats. In the foyer, the benches are nearly full: several thick-set young men rubbing the tattoos on their wrists; a tall, elegant black man reading a book on advanced motoring; two women with anoraks and tired eyes; a good-looking young guy who keeps smiling to himself; numerous shuffling groups of solicitors and clients all swapping nods and whispers.

For a little while longer, they are all nameless and shapeless, nothing more than a random collection of men and women, swept off the streets of London, like a sample of ordinary life. For a few minutes longer, they sit and wait, while the security men stand back and watch them with their arms folded across their chests. Then it is 10.30am, and the usher appears at the edge of the room and calls out the name Terrence Brightley, and the elegant black man folds up his book and walks away to see Mr Bourke.

Inside the court, the magistrate nods quietly as the behaviour of Mr Brightley is explained to him. He has been convicted of attacking two police officers, who found him selling jewellery at Camden Market one Sunday morning, and he is here to be sentenced.

Mr Bourke says he is a great believer in hearing what the complainant has to say, and so it is that while Mr Brightley sits staring at the floor of the dock, the statement of two police officers is read out: the swear words he yelled at the policewoman who asked if he had a licence; the fist he threw into the face of the policeman who tried to restrain him; how he screamed abuse at the policewoman and injured her left hand before other officers arrested him. Mr Bourke looks at the sheet of previous offences for dishonesty and sighs.

Then Mr Brightley's solicitor stands up and explains that his client has been trying to put his past behind him. He has not been in any trouble with the law now for five years. He has never in his life been in trouble for any kind of violence. The position simply is that he has been trying to improve himself. At the time of the offence, he was not signing on, he was trying to save money to go to college by selling jewellery, and, since he was surrounded by other people who were doing exactly the same thing, he could not understand why he was singled out by the police.

Despite this trouble, the lawyer explains, he is still trying to improve himself. Even at the court, he has been reading about how to improve his driving skills. He was willing to pay compensation and asked to be given a suspended sentence. Mr Bourke nods towards the lawyer. 'Thank you so much for your help in this matter,' he says, and then he explains that we really can't have people abusing and denouncing police officers who are merely trying to do their duty and he asks Mr Brightley if he would stand up so that he can sentence him to 72 days in prison. 'Well, there it is,' he whispers more in sorrow than in anger, and looks up for the next case.

The defendants start to shuttle through the court at speed. It is like watching snapshots of the secret lives of strangers, the kind of lives that normally warrant no mention in a newspaper because they are too small to be noticed, and as they flash by, several things become clear. One is that even though these are the people who clog the columns of the annual crime statistics, they appear in close-up far more sad than bad.

Here, now, are the two men who were swirling cans of lager on the courthouse steps. As they stand in the dock to hear the complaint about them read, one of them sways back on his heels with his eyes shut, only to snap out of his slumber just long enough to save himself from collapsing, before drifting off again, while the other keeps pushing his hand up, looking for attention like an anxious schoolboy. Mr Bourke would like him to wait his turn while he hears the case against them.

They are charged with theft. It is said that they sat next to a man on a park bench and walked away with his mobile phone.

The man realised what had happened and went to a call box, where he dialled the number of his missing mobile. One of the thieves answered, agreed to sell the man back his property, and volunteered to meet him in Trafalgar Square. There the man turned up with a police officer who arrested the pair of them. The man in the dock is still begging for attention. 'Very well,' says Mr Bourke and asks him what it is that is troubling him. 'Your lordship,' he says, 'we want to say we're sorry.' Mr Bourke grants them bail.

Here, too, is the shoplifter with his bush of curly black hair tied back behind his ears. He steals relentlessly – 20 pieces of steak from Sainsbury's, £23 worth of batteries from Woolworths – but he is constantly getting caught. He is so incompetent that he is causing confusion in the court. He has just been arrested in Sainsbury's, but it turns out that he is already on bail awaiting sentence for three other offences, to which he pleaded guilty three weeks ago, and that, in the meantime, he was arrested last week with his hands full of shop goods in Kentish Town. Mr Bourke watches his clerk, shuffling files and checking dates and peeps over his glasses, and asks: 'Is this a matter of heroin addiction?' It is.

Mr Bourke adjourns the shoplifter and finds another young man staggering out of the jailer's door and into the dock before him. This one has a white cotton shirt, which is liberally smeared with blood and hangs open from his throat to his belly button. There is a fresh gash across his forehead and he sways gently as the jailer lets go of his arm.

'Do please sit down,' says the magistrate, and so he sits, with his arms wrapped around his ribs while Mr Bourke hears how he rode a mountain bike out of a shop in the West End and ran straight into a police car. He is 30 years old, and he has a long list of convictions. He has three other offences outstanding and Mr Bourke – who does not need to ask whether this is another heroin matter – remands him in custody for three weeks.

And that is one more thing that becomes clear as the cases come and go: Mr Bourke is there to hurt people. That is all he can do because that is all that the law wants him to do. If he feels sympathetic, as sometimes he plainly does, the best that he can do is to hurt them slightly less. He tries hard to smuggle some compassion into the proceedings when he comes to deal with the good-looking young man who was sitting outside in the foyer with the little smile on his mouth.

Now, in the dock, he does the same. At first, as the case against him is outlined, it seems that this might be a smile of arrogance, a 'screw you, what do I care?' sort of pose. The prosecution say he was arrested on Euston Station, drunkenly attempting to board a train without a ticket and then threatening to kill the police officer who arrested him, that he was given bail but failed to turn up in court and had to be re-arrested. But the truth about the smile becomes clearer when his solicitor, a small young woman with brown hair, stands up and starts to talk about him. He has been breaking the law since he was a small boy, she says, and now, aged 17, he has just emerged from his first custodial sentence. He is a solitary man, she says; he was taken into care when he was a child. The reason for this, she explains, is that he was being routinely raped by his father. For a moment, the young man drops his head and then, a second later, he looks up again, and now you can see that his smile is not a challenge at all, it is a kind of helpless shrug.

Mr Bourke shakes his head and explains that even though he might like to give this man a chance by suspending his prison sentence, the law does not allow him to do that for an offender of this age. Then he finds a way through: he gives him a conditional discharge, which means he goes free unless he gets into trouble within the next year. 'It has the effect of a suspended sentence,' he says. The young man thanks him and Mr Bourke gently whispers his favourite phrase.

There is one other thing which emerges as the cases come and go. It is a feeling of overwhelming chaos pressing at the door of the courthouse. It is there in the defendants who explain that they missed appointments because they have been chucked out of their homes or lost their papers or been attacked in the street or lost their jobs.

It is there with the authorities: with the jailer who says it's chaos in the cells because Brixton have sent him the wrong prisoner and Wandsworth have sent him one extra; and with the policeman who asks apologetically for an arrest warrant for a prisoner released from the station by mistake.

Even as Mr Bourke tries to finish his list for the morning, more chaos piles in: there's a crack dealer who has just been arrested and swallowed his stash, and a prostitute who is too ill to come into the dock.

On the courthouse steps, one of the men drinking lager turns out to be HIV positive. Down the road, there is a little shop that is really a crack house, a bookshop selling hard porn, phone boxes full of cards offering women for sale, a pub with strippers, a couple of guys selling crack outside the Thameslink station, rubbish lying on the pavement, people lying on the pavement. An English city in 1995. There it is. ●

17 February 1995

Duncan Campbell

Mad Frankie's crime stories charm chapel

They were playing Mad Frankie Fraser's tune. Perhaps it's better known as Hymn 774: 'Freedom give to those in bondage / Lift the burdens caused by sin.'

The place was Wesley's Chapel on City Road in east London and the occasion one of the regular conversations the chapel's minister, the Reverend Paul Hulme, holds there at lunchtimes. Past and future guests include Baroness Williams, Lord Jakobovits and Bishop Hugh Montefiore.

But yesterday's speaker was one F Fraser, free after more than 40 years in jails and borstals and introduced as 'one of the most notorious criminals of this century'.

The reverend had met the former gangster in his local Angel bookshop and, since one of last year's guests had been the director of the prison service, Derek Lewis, 'it seemed it would be a good idea to hear the story from the other side, as it were'.

So was the dapper, besuited little figure in front of the 100-strong congregation the sinner who repenteth? There were, indeed, regrets: 'I attacked nine prison governors. I was really upset,' he said, deadpan. 'I like even numbers – and I could never find a 10th.'

And yes, if he could have lived his life again – he's a sprightly 70 now – he would have wanted things to be different: 'I would have liked to have found a bigger bank with more money in it.' But would he have made changes in his life? 'Yes – I wouldn't have got caught.'

The Reverend Hulme is nothing if not persistent. Did Mr Fraser not feel remorse?

'None whatsoever,' came the reply, sharp as a razor. 'I know that's not a nice thing to say in a chapel but that's the way it is.'

The former altar boy, brought up as a Catholic, shared his memories of Sundays spent in prison chapels. 'You had to go. It was a form of blackmail – forgive me for saying that – because in those days there were no newspapers in prison and after the service the chaplain read the football results.' As for prison chaplains: 'I'll upset you here. They were not regarded as friends.'

Frank, who was with his girlfriend, Marilyn Wisbey, the daughter of great train robber Tommy Wisbey, said he had started his life of crime at the age of eight.

His parents were hard-working and blameless. His heroes were movie gangsters like Jimmy Cagney, Humphrey Bogart and Edward G Robinson and

'Mad' Frankie Fraser at Ronnie Kray's Funeral

he was disappointed to find Wormwood Scrubs was not quite as jolly as jails seemed on screen.

He had retired, he said: 'I can't do a smash and grab job on a jewellers – I don't think I'd be fast enough.' Instead, he had written his memoirs and was happy just to bring Marilyn her morning cup of tea in bed. Asked about one of his nicknames, The Dentist, Frank was adamant it was misplaced: 'I never done fillings. I only done extractions – and they only took place with gold-lated pliers.'

He was resigned to being called 'Mad'. 'I can't really grumble. I have been certified three times,' he said, although he added this was partly due to a performance of which, he felt, Laurence Olivier would have been proud. Afterwards, signing autographs, he said he was delighted by the warm reception. 'They're lovely people, aren't they?'

The congregation returned the compliment. Margaret Whiteman, a regular attender, said: 'I think it shows reconciliation. I found it very interesting. Of course, he's a comedian.'

When John Wesley first preached in the same chapel in 1778, he berated some of the women in the congregation for their elaborate hats because he hated ostentation and affluence. What he would have made of 'Mad' Frank, only the Immortal and Invisible one of Hymn Number 9 can tell. But he would surely refer all doubting Thomases to Jude, chapter 16, verse 15: 'Behold, I came as a thief.' ●

1 March 1995   The Fox

Also known as: Reynard, *Vulpes vulpes, Mr Tod, Macnab*

Appearance: Robin Cook with a long bushy tail.

Personality type: Sadist.

Don't you mean innocent victim? How many victims enjoy killing and maiming blameless mice and rabbits? The fox is also partial to lambskins, fowl and a nice slice of Quorn, lightly grilled.

How do I meet one? Lead a fox hunt to the nearest covert.

What will I need? Scarlet coat, a horse, a horn, 15 pairs of hounds, several terriers, a Master, one huntsman, three whippers-in, grooms, second horsemen, terrier men, earth stoppers, approximately 40 members of the upper class.

Where do I find them? Pick them up for a song outside Baring's Bank.

Then what? Find Mr Tod then chase until he's cornered.

How to greet Mr Tod: Holloa! (a high pitched cry).

What happens next? If you ask nicely, Camilla Parker Bowles will rip him apart with her bare teeth.

How does she dispose of the body? She might present certain trophies such as the brush (tail), mask (head), or pads (feet) to Prince Charles. The remains are thrown to Roger Scruton.

Isn't it a bit cruel? Absolutely not; any decent fox will positively relish sustained aerobic exercise in beautiful countryside, not to mention the chance to be killed by the quality.

No wonder foxes vote Labour And no wonder they're disappointed when they meet Baroness Mallalieu, Lord Donoughue, Melvyn Bragg, David Puttnam and John Mortimer.

Why so? They're all stirrup-cup socialists.

Red in tooth and claw? And politics.

D'they ken John McFall? Only too well. On Friday his Wild Mammals Protection bill will attempt to outlaw vulpicide.

And hedgehog football? Enjoy it while you can.

What next! Fishes, pheasants and grouse are holding their breath.

What about boxers? You don't understand. Banning boxing would solve nothing. Members of the working class would simply have to be snared, poisoned or shot to keep the numbers down.

Not to be confused with: Charles James Fox, George Fox, 20th Century Fox.

Most likely to say: Without us, chickens would devastate the countryside.

Least likely to say: Tally-ho. ●

6 *February 1995*

Lawrence Donegan
Flowers for the forlorn

L es Harker's bingo arcade was the picture of defiance as the Irish Sea lashed the seafront at Rhyl. On the street outside, the caller's smooth delivery could just about be heard over the gale. Inside, five diehards huddled round their numbers boards; the winner could scarcely be bothered to shout 'house'.

Further up the coastal road, Brotherhood of Man – Eurovision Song Contest winners 1976 – are billed to appear at the New Pavilion Theatre on 5 February but, otherwise, the chip shops are closed and the pubs empty. The Tourist Information Office round the corner offers handfuls of pamphlets for attractions that are shut for another month at least.

This is Rhyl in February, where every day is like Sunday; silent, grey, charged with anticipation of events yet to come. In summer, the North Wales resort attracts more than four million visitors. During the rest of the year, most of the country would not know it was even there. This winter has been different.

Firstly, there was the notoriety visited upon local Tory MP Roderick Richards when he called Welsh Labour councillors 'slimy and fundamentally corrupt'. He has since slipped back into obscurity but Rhyl has been catapulted into the headlines again by the death of a young family in a first-floor flat yards from the town's busy High Street.

Tragedy is an overused word but it doesn't come near to capturing the full horror of what happened to Tony and Liz Walker and their 18-month-old son, Michael.

The story starts on 20 December, when 28-year-old postman Tony Walker failed to show up for his shift at the town's Royal Mail sorting office. On 28 December, a colleague was sent round to the Walkers' home at 26 Kinmel Street to find out what was wrong. He was unable to get past the communal entrance to the flat. The Post Office visited four times that week and sent two letters to No 26 but got no reply.

The Walkers moved into the one-bedroom flat just over a year ago. The rent was £62: Social Security paid £50 and they paid the other £12 to Michael Garton, who runs the Sellfast furniture store next door and acts as agent for the Cheshire-based printing company which owns the building.

The couple were irregular payers and Garton thought nothing of it when they failed to drop in with the extra £12. In any case, they had said they would probably be going down south over Christmas to visit Tony's parents in Northamptonshire.

On 20 January, Rhyl police station received a phone call from Tony's relatives asking if someone could check if he still lived at No 26. Officers went round on successive days but couldn't get past the communal entrance. 'Normally, if you go on these sort of calls and there is something wrong, there are tell-tale signs like milk bottles or newspapers,' Superintendent Barry Jones of Rhyl police says.

But there were no such signs and the police left it at that. Four days later Liz's parents, Dennis and Audrey Steventon, came into the Sellfast store. They had gone round to the flat just before Christmas to drop off presents but got no reply and had become increasingly worried when Liz didn't get in touch.

Garton tried to get in using his spare key but it wouldn't go into the lock. He promised the elderly couple he'd get a locksmith and ring them at home later that day. Andrew Gizzi, owner of A and R Locksmiths, recalls: 'The problem was there was a key on the inside of the lock. I went back downstairs and got my tools. I have done lots of these jobs in Rhyl, where the landlord would phone up and say: "People haven't paid the rent, could you go round and see what's happening?" Usually you find the people have done a runner. This time, though, I had a feeling. There had been a terrible smell about the place for a couple of weeks. We thought it was coming from gas cannisters or even a dead rat. The day before all this happened we took a panel out from under the stairs in the shop just to check there was nothing in there.'

Gizzi noticed a children's buggy on the landing as he went back upstairs. 'I took the glass out of the door, put my hand in and turned the key. Normally, I would have walked straight in and checked all the rooms. This time I just knew something was up.'

Dave Edgington, who lives in a bedsit above the Walkers, volunteered to go into the flat first. He checked the bathroom on his left and moved along the hallway towards the sound of a television set. He pushed open the lounge door, briefly noted the Christmas decorations on the wall and looked down to the floor where he saw the bodies of Tony, Liz and Michael Walker. They had been lying there for almost five weeks. 'It was bad, awful,' Edgington says. 'A terrible thing for anyone to see.'

Initially, it was reported the family had died in a 'suicide pact'. This is almost certainly not the case. Inexplicably, both adults were found half-naked and kneeling beside each other, while Michael's body appeared to have been carefully laid out on the floor. Police found a number of syringes and other drug paraphernalia in the flat.

In the only public comment from either family since the deaths, Tony Walker's father admitted his son had dabbled in drugs in his youth: 'We didn't think he was doing that any more.'

An inquest into the deaths, opened and adjourned last week, was told 18-month-old Michael died of a heart attack, probably induced by thirst. Forensic tests to establish the cause of his parents' death will take another six weeks but the local grapevine has already made up its mind – notes attached to the flowers and cuddly toys piled up outside 26 Kinmel Street are addressed mainly to Michael. 'If a couple of junkies want to go and kill themselves, who cares? It's the kid everyone feels sorry for,' said one local resident.

There is an alternative view, however: that the deaths have highlighted the fact that Rhyl has some very serious social problems. This is not a popular thing to say in a town which has invested £24 million in its tourist industry in recent years, which is probably why it was most eloquently expressed by a young pupil at Ysgol Mair primary school in an essay Class Four was asked to write about the 'tragic news'.

'There was a woman, a man and a baby,' wrote the youngster. 'They were very poor. The thing was that nobody missed them for five weeks or more. Just imagine living in a dark, lonely, wet flat not far away from the warm city lights. They must have been very lonely . . .'

Sunny Rhyl, as it is known in the tourist trade, began to prosper as a seaside resort with the construction of the Chester to Holyhead rail link. The railway station was opened in 1848, making the town easily accessible to the industrial workers of the north-west conurbations. Entrepreneurs moved in and by the end of the century the population had risen to around 8,000. Its heyday in the 1930s was followed by another boom immediately after the war. Most holiday-makers came to Rhyl from Manchester, Liverpool and the Potteries. But by the mid-1960s even the most ardent devotee of the Welsh coast couldn't resist the lure of the package holiday abroad.

Many local guest houses lost their trade virtually overnight and, in an effort to regain ground, converted into self-contained tourist flats. This market is only good for five months of the year and it wasn't long before Rhyl's landlords were advertising cheap, year-round accommodation in the major city evening papers. This was an astute piece of marketing aimed at people like Ian King, who visited the town and fell in love.

'I'm originally from the Midlands. Me and a couple of friends were on a trek round Wales for a week when we stopped here. It was wonderful. It was such a relaxed way of life. We eventually came back but the other two couldn't keep their head above water – they're in jail for theft and burglary. I survived.'

King now lives in a two-roomed flat above a tattoo artist's with his girlfriend Denise and their three young children. It's a five-minute walk from Kinmel Street. Their flat has bars across the windows, chicken wire to keep the ceiling in place and the wallpaper he put up two weeks ago has fallen off. 'Eighteen months ago we were told the place was unfit for human habitation,' he says, poking his finger through a damp supporting wall.

Rhuddlan borough council, which takes in the town of Rhyl, has tried to eradicate this type of slum in recent years. In 1987, it launched the West Rhyl Initiative – a seven-year programme aimed at overcoming all of the town's housing problems. 'We've completely refurbished some properties, put new windows in, new doors. We're spending £1.4 million a year,' says the council's chief executive Eddie Lake.

Parts of west Rhyl have clearly benefited from this investment but even Mr Lake would concede there is still some way to go. Local councillor Chris Ruane, who has campaigned against 'houses of multiple occupation' (officialese for bedsits) for years, still has a fat file of press cuttings and letters detailing housing horrors. 'The bedsit business has been excellent for the landlords, who've had a field day making money out of other people's misery, but it's been terrible for Rhyl. It's as if Mrs Thatcher's idea about there being no society "only individuals" has come true. I don't blame people for coming here but we now have this transient population which moves around from flat to flat and town to town; they don't have any network of contacts or friends and are completely lost to officialdom.'

Tony and Liz Walker were not lost to officialdom but their circle of friends seems to have been remarkably small. He used to drink occasionally in the Alexander, she would pop into the newsagents on Bodfor Street to buy sweets for Michael. 'They were very well dressed, always clean and tidy. He had short hair, he was every mother's dream for a daughter to bring home,' says Gareth Lloyd Williams, who rents an office above Sellfast furniture store. But the most frequently used phrase to describe the dead couple is that they 'kept themselves to themselves'.

Michelle Taylor lives next door to the Walkers' old flat with her unemployed boyfriend Paul. She and Liz had a lot in common – they were the same age, brought up on the North Wales coast and both had a child of roughly the same age – yet they never knew each other. Michelle went into the flat at No 26 for the first time last week to let in an environmental health officer. 'It's sad but it didn't devastate us,' says Paul. 'We just didn't know them. In fact, on the day they were found we didn't know anything was wrong for a few hours, until we saw all the television vans and reporters outside the flat.'

A dispute has developed in Rhyl over why the family had lain undiscovered for almost five weeks: was it the police's fault or the neighbours' or Mrs Thatcher's breakdown of society? There has also been the controversy over the town's bedsit population, while the deaths have focused attention on North Wales's drug problem.

Tony and Liz Walker were not known to the authorities as drug users but over 500 others in the region are registered as addicts. Rhyl itself has an 'endemic' heroin problem, according to Dr Daffed Alun Jones, the psychiatrist in drug and alcohol abuse for North Wales. 'It is probably something to do with the fact that it has always been allied to Manchester and Liverpool – both areas with substantial heroin problems. But we have built up a strong network of support and counselling over the years. The problem now is that the number of beds available to us to help these youngsters in North Wales is going to be cut back from this summer. 'I have made myself extremely unpopular because

I've been trying to persuade the local health authorities not to cut back on the service we provide,' he confesses.

This is exactly the kind of publicity Rhyl could do without and Eddie Lake shifts uncomfortably in his chair when asked to comment on the Walkers' deaths. 'It is certainly a tragedy, especially for this youngster, and it brings home the extent of the problems that remain. But it could have happened in any bedsit, in any town in the UK.'

As for the root causes of the tragedy? It's a question for the politicians, he says. 'I'm only the fellow at the council trying to make the regeneration work.'

Undoubtedly, the council suceeded against all the odds in reviving Rhyl's fortunes. Its seafront boasts a new children's village, a state of the art theatre, a sealife centre and the Sun Centre (Britain's first indoor water facility): most will be open for business from March, the same month that an inquest into the death of Tony, Liz and Michael Walker is expected to reopen. •

------

16 March 1995

Suzanne Moore
Straight talking

So Peter Tatchell has finally been 'outed' as a martyr. What a surprise that is. The man has been crucified this week following his organisation's (OutRage!) 'victory' that they got the Bishop of London, the Rt Rev David Hope, to admit his sexuality was 'ambiguous'. Although the news is his 'confession', Tatchell's letter was actually written a while ago.

Tatchell has since been denounced as a hypocrite, a blackmailer, one of the least 'attractive characters in British public life', a fascist, a terrorist and, in the words of the *Sun*, 'an Australian-born Vietnam draft-dodger'. Australian-born, hey, how low can you go? This is a Murdoch paper after all.

The spectacle of the press denouncing outing is a sight to behold, since the business of journalism has become more and more about outing over the past couple of years. Outing adulterous MPs, public figures who cream off private perks, or indeed fumbling footballers and mumbling monarchs. This is not called outing, this is called 'scoops' and newspapers such as the *News of the World* win awards for such endeavours.

Dishing the dirt – it is in the public interest that hypocrisy is revealed, you understand – is part of the growing climate that is pushing towards greater accountability. We all think it is a good thing. Tatchell stands accused of blackmail.

When a journalist says to a public figure we have certain information about you that we will publish if you don't tell us first, no one cries blackmail. When the *Sun* discovered the MP Michael Brown in the company of a young man it ran the story. Later on he decided to be open about the fact that he was gay. This was not called outing but investigative journalism.

Actually, I have never supported outing but I understand where it comes from. In the condemnation of Tatchell no one has mentioned the word Aids, not one person has attempted to explain the history of this kind of activism.

In America it was groups like ACT-UP campaigning around health issues for gay men, for funding and education, which began to use outing strategically. It was always controversial. While many gay people were involved in the long, slow struggle for equality, there were others who felt there wasn't enough time for dainty debate, for polite political discussions. Maybe if you had seen your friends dying, you might feel the same way too.

'Don't die of ignorance', remember? That was the slogan that was used to try and educate us into safer sex. The opposite of ignorance is knowledge, but it still seems many of us would rather not know the truth. It is fine, in fact almost mandatory, for heterosexuals to flaunt their sexuality, but if a man stands up and imparts the knowledge that he is gay he is somehow flaunting something that is best kept behind closed doors. No one could have watched the *Newsnight* interview with Bishop Derek Rawcliffe and not felt unbearably sad that this deeply sympathetic man had spent so much of his life in turmoil. The church talks of love and yet this man had been made to feel bad about those he loved and this is the tragedy.

Most of us believe that some level of acceptance about what we are is healthier than denying it. How we achieve this, as long as homosexuality is regarded as an entirely private affair, is what needs to be debated. Unlike Tatchell, I do believe in grey areas. I think that the odd ambivalent feeling or act is not proof of innate homosexuality.

I don't think it's all so black and white, probably because I do not think homophobia is so black and white either. As we leave the 20th century behind, the clergy is struggling to enter it. Their congregations have long shown that kind of Middle English, middle-class tolerance for what the clergy choose to regard as a human failing. Regarding homosexuality as a human failing may in theory constitute homophobia. In practice I'm not so sure.

I always think of my mum in these matters. When one of my 'uncles' phoned to tell her that he had Aids, her immaculately politically incorrect response was: 'Well, dear, you always were a hypochondriac.' Her actions, on the other hand, told a different story. She immediately went to visit him when others would not and offered to nurse him when the time came.

This is the grey area and this is what most of us inhabit. I dislike outing because it presupposes two options: one is gay or one is straight. The whole point of the queer politics which Tatchell claims to champion is that it liberates us from the strait-jacket of such categories.

A bit of blurring is no bad thing. Besides which any historical or anthropological study of sexuality demonstrates that the idea of a distinct homosexual identity is a relatively new one. It depends entirely on hetero-sexuality being an equally watertight category. In terms of legislation this is a nightmare which when unpicked becomes a nonsense. This is why both Clinton in his muddle over gays in the US military and Cardinal Hume in his recent 'acceptance' of gay Catholics make the distinction between a homosexual identity, which it is somehow OK to have, and a homosexual act, which it isn't. In other words, you can be it as long as you don't do it.

Not only is this entirely unworkable, it misses the point completely. No one actually needs permission to drink cappuccino all day and listen to the Pet Shop Boys. What they need is a world in which their private sexual practices have as much or as little relevance to the other parts of their lives as they do for the rest of us. This is the heterosexual privilege that we take for granted.

The vilification of Tatchell has shown just how far gays are from attaining it. He has been delving into that fragile area – the gap between what is private and what is public. His detractors claim that he has no right to poke his nose into the private lives of priests. Gayness is seen as an essentially private issue in the way that heterosexuality is not. No one says to the adulterous politician: 'How dare you flaunt your private sexual practices in front of us in the form of your wife, your mistress and your two lovely children.' They say: 'Don't say one thing and then do another.' Or they say: 'There should be some correlation between how you live and how you tell others to live.'

The case against Tatchell is that he uses homophobia as a weapon, to lob at those in the closet, and this can and does backfire. The cause is elevated over the individual and the public has far more time for suffering and confused individuals than it does for militant activists. In Tatchell's black and white world 'the gay community' is a necessary myth that will entice these people out of the closet. In practice, even he must know this is not the case. Many members of this community thoroughly oppose his activities. An agenda upon which gay men and lesbians can agree is far off. The priorities are different. The issue of lesbians becoming mothers is a different one to arguing for more research towards helping people with HIV and so on.

Outing is premised on the idea that the personal is political. The reaction, in recent days, has reduced a political argument to personal terms once more, with confused clergy as victims and Tatchell and his gang as persecutors. However ambiguous David Hope may be, he knows a good PR opportunity when it hits him. To be pictured clutching a cross sets him up as some kind of human sacrifice. What is really being sacrificed here is much more than one man's 'right to privacy'; it is the chance to have an open discussion about what we expect from those who set themselves up as our moral guardians. I am not gay, nor militant, nor a supporter of Tatchell, but the refusal of the press to countenance such a discussion strikes me as extremely narrow-minded.

Tatchell may be wrong in his methods but no one that his group has targeted has actually denied the allegations made against them. The pressure that has been used against them is clearly distasteful, although this pressure is daily applied when it comes to matters other than homosexuality. What is distasteful is that while on the one hand the press has encouraged us to think that it is their moral duty to pressurise public figures into revealing their private doings, it will destroy anyone else who does so on a freelance basis. You cannot have it both ways it would appear, unless, that is, you are straight. ●

4 March 1995

Alex Brummer
Don't blame it all on Nick

The irony of Britain's oldest and most exclusive merchant bank being taken over for £1 by a pan-European financial services group, with the present participle for its name, is an appropriate metaphor for the fate of Barings. During an age of globalised financial markets – in which capital is measured in the billions and only the most sophisticated information systems have a hope of assessing risk – Barings was a fossil of the UK's past mercantile greatness. In much the same way as ownership of key British manufacturing industries, such as motor cars, has moved to the Continent, so has that of the City. In case anyone has forgotten, the Queen's other merchant-banking advisers, Morgan Grenfell, already has been swallowed by Deutsche Bank, having been deprived of its dignity in a share-dealing scandal. Trafalgar House, the owners of another Queen – the *QE2* – has chosen to take its merchant-banking business to the Swiss Banking Corporation.

The simple theory that Leeson lost Barings has become less believable with each passing day since the bank's problems emerged. Nick Leeson was the fall-guy who allowed the loss of the bank to take place, in much the same way as Jimmy Carter's presidency of the US is broadly associated with the loss of Iran to the West. The reality is that Barings collapsed for a variety of reasons. First, the failure of those who govern the Western financial system – the G7 finance ministers, the Bank for International Settlements and influential commercial banks' groups like the Group of 30 – to take the very obvious problems which are posed by the derivatives markets seriously.

Second, the Barings management which in search of easier profits failed to properly manage Mr Leeson and chose to make false savings by failing to implement critical compliance advice.

And finally the regulators, including the Bank of England, which in the past has shown such admirable patience in saving a range of industries, projects and companies, including the Chunnel, Leyland-Daf, British Land and even the Stock Exchange settlement – but on this occasion blinked. The reality is that whatever the political flak, the Bank should have acted as lender of the last resort and persuaded Chancellor Kenneth Clarke that it was the right thing to do: in much the same way as Robin Leigh-Pemberton persuaded Nigel Lawson that Johnson Matthey Bank, a far more marginal enterprise, was worth saving.

No doubt, as the experts keep on telling us, the derivatives markets are wonderful places which have brought all kinds of real world trading efficiencies to financial markets, as they have done to commodity markets. But there is strong evidence to suggest that the monster is out of control: making money from these extraordinary trading programmes has in some cases – including that of Barings – become totally divorced from the real-world activities on behalf of clients. Barings was not arbitraging in the Far Eastern markets to assist Inchcape or some other worthy client in the region; it was doing it for itself because it was an easier way of making money than, say, lending to medium-sized businesses in the UK. Why bother with relationship banking, when a 28-year-old derivatives dealer can bring in the profits at far less cost?

Indeed, the monster is so far out of control that it can actually affect the fate of national economies. In the case of Barings, the market damage was relatively limited, because Barings – after all is said and done – is a bit player. But last year when the Federal Reserve tightened interest rates in the US, it set off a derivative programme around the world which pushed bond prices to unacceptably high levels, forced interest rates up in a time of declining global inflation and postponed recovery and relief to high levels of global unemployment. Is this a sensible and efficient way of managing global markets? Hardly. Yet the matter was buried in a waffly inquiry by G10 finance ministers and central banks (the G7 plus the Benelux and Scandinavians) which brought no credible reforms to bear. Now the derivatives markets are hurling brickbats at the US dollar, forcing global central banks into intervention which could potentially damage the monetary stance.

The answer to this global monetary indiscipline, of which the Barings example is more easy to understand because of its focus on one individual and firm, is better regulation – or certainly some means of putting sand in the wheels. Of course, regulation is the enemy of commerce in the lexicon of the Reagan–Thatcher economics of the 1980s and early 1990s. But as the German finance minister Theo Waigel, who lives by a different rule book, noted this week, it couldn't happen in Frankfurt because of tighter controls. Maybe that was a bit self-serving; however, German capitalism had demonstrated itself to be less averse to interfering with the marketplace, when matters as important as systemic risk and monetary policy are at stake. The pity is that the Germans have not been able to exert their influence more strongly in the many global forums which have discussed the derivatives issue.

Of course, it is not clear that any of this might have stopped the Barings imbroglio. What is plain is that better controls are needed at multinational level and at corporate level. In the Barings case, a derivatives department of 180 people was grafted on to an antique merchant bank with neither the systems skills nor the controls to handle what had been created. What was required at Barings, as Bill Acker of the consultants Acker Deboeck & Co has observed, was a better understanding of how innovative techniques were to be integrated. This required Barings to monitor the moral hazard – the risk that Nick Leeson (or someone like him) would pursue his own interests at the expense of the organisation. Or, as Barings has sought to claim, the dealer Nick Leeson did something incompetent. If there was incompetence it was, according to the company's own internal reports, inside the group treasury and risk committee, which failed to put in place recommended compliance procedures.

As for the Bank of England, it no doubt meant well by allowing Barings to go. But Barings was not BCCI. This was a bank at the heart of the City and established networks, where the credibility was beyond reproach. There had been no obvious warnings, as in the case of BCCI, that this was a bank with problems. Far from it; its asset management clients were as blue chip as it is possible to be, from the Prince's Trust to the Church of England and the Wellcome group. Although technically the Accepting Houses Committee – the inner circle of merchant banks – no longer exists, it remained a sort of club to which Barings belonged: the equivalent in financial terms of a Bank of England warrant.

By allowing Barings to go, the Bank has in effect withdrawn a certificate of sea worthiness from what remains of the UK's independent merchant-banking sector. This, as the Governor Eddie George said, was a 'wonderful bank' with an important client list. If ING could have saved it, so should the City of London. ●

. . . .

7 January 1995

David Hare
The new republic

At a conference organised by Charter 88 in May 1993, one of the few people to call outright for the abolition of the monarchy was the playwright David Hare. In a dialogue he has written with a fictional interviewer, he now tries to answer some of the objections which have since been raised.

Interviewer: *What is striking about the Charter 88 debate, even to an imaginary monarchist like myself, is the extraordinary caution with which people still approach the subject.*

Hare: Yes. There certainly was a funny atmosphere. The conference was co-organised by *The Times* newspaper, who asked me to write the keynote piece which would appear the day before the conference. When they got it, they refused to print it. I asked why and they said, well it calls for the immediate creation of a republic. I said, *so?* I mean, what did they expect? Why did they ask me in the first place? Then, at the conference itself, the editor of *The Times* was extraordinarily craven. He said they were having this historic debate only because the Queen herself had said that she now welcomed discussion about her role. The editor was announcing, in other words, that the whole conference was by royal dispensation. The debate was under royal warrant, in fact. He seemed as proud of that as of what was actually said.

Interviewer: *What do you think accounts for this caution?*

Hare: Sheer existentialist terror. The function of the royal family is to give this country a sense of identity. That's their main role. So the terrible question arises: if we are not defined by the royal family, then what the hell are we defined by?

Interviewer: *That's rather a large question.*

Hare: Yes. Obviously, issues of identity are puzzling all nation states at the moment, especially in Europe, where the argument is particularly ferocious. Personally, I find the behaviour of Eurosceptics completely incomprehensible. It's richly satisfying, of course, to watch the Tory Party tear itself apart. Those of us who've always seen Conservatism primarily as an organised conspiracy to keep the rich rich by whatever ideological means lay to hand have been rather bewildered to see some Tories discover something which is apparently more important to them than power. Late in its life, the Conservative Party seems to have stumbled on a principle. But the only thing which actually accounts for the distinctive savagery of the argument is that these people are fighting for something which, to them, is more than politics. They're fighting for the continuing idea of what it means to be British.

Interviewer: *And you think the royal family is bound up in that idea of Britishness?*

Hare: Of course. It has to be. These are people who hanker for an idea of what Britain was like in the 1950s. It's what I call the Miserablist tendency. You know, the people who want interminable Sunday afternoons and to drink warm beer. For anyone who defines Britain by a fantasy of what it once was in the past, the monarchy exists as the supreme troupe of repertory players. They can be wheeled out at any point, wrapped in moth-eaten velveteen, alongside the Beefeaters and MI6 and the SAS. They perform that long-running British hit – *We Do Things Differently Here*.

Interviewer: *But you might say, what's wrong with that? Why shouldn't this country be distinctive in its public rituals? What's wrong with the sense of reassurance the monarchy provides?*

Hare: Well, for a start you have to face the fact that the show is not attracting the paying customers in quite the way it was. I don't think it's the alarming divorce rate which has discredited the royal family as much as the sudden realisation of how mean they are. To maintain the aura of royalty, it is important that there's a mystical aspect to their behaviour. And frankly, being purse-proud is not a very mystical quality. The financial excesses, the lack of accountability are not in themselves so shocking as the underlying attitudes they reveal. This is a monarchy which is more interested in self-preservation than in looking outward to the people.

Interviewer: *But how can they do that? Realistically?*

Hare: I think they've failed to make all the necessary gestures of good faith. Where are the great schools they've built? Where are the hospitals? Where's the land they've given to the country at large? You'd think in 40 years the Queen would have made some inspired intervention to bequeath the people some of her wealth. Not a bit of it. She refuses even to clean the Albert Memorial.

Interviewer: *But why should she? That's not what monarchies are for. They're there to be above the everyday.*

Hare: Yes. That's the central claim. They want it both ways. They want to be both at the centre of the society, the symbol of its life, if you like, yet at the same time they want not to be implicated in its failures. Plainly the most successful countries in the world are republics. On all sides we agree that the post-1950 record of Britain is one of accelerated decline, particularly in our self-respect and in our skill at protecting our neediest citizens. Yet for some reason we want to salvage from this unhappy period the one defining institution which has claimed to be at the centre of our values and affection during these very years.

Interviewer: *But you can hardly blame the monarchy for everything that's gone wrong in Britain in the last 40 years. Historically, all empires have a terrible period of self-doubt and confusion when they come to an end. You might say, compared with some, we're getting off lightly.*

Hare: Yes. But shouldn't empires also disembarrass themselves of elements which once served a purpose and no longer do? All the bowing and scraping, the deference, the absurdly false behaviour, the maintenance of the hereditary principle, the employment of an honours system as an emollient kind of thought police to stop too many middle-class people stepping out of line – doesn't all this belong to a system which is now seen not to be serving this country very well?

Interviewer: *But the royal family themselves admit they have to adapt.*

Hare: Ah, well of course, this is the great myth. Whenever logic compels us towards saying the imperial pantomime is over, and is actually preventing us from re-casting this country's future, there is always some telegenic courtier ready to step forward and use the magic word 'adapt'.

Interviewer: *But that's fair, isn't it?*

Hare: No, it's actually impossible. There isn't any way you can find a balance between the medieval privileges of the old monarchy and the self-conscious mateyness of the new. It can't be done. The monarchy can't be modernised. And if you doubt me, look at the desperate figure of Prince Charles. He is the man who, more than any other, has tried to bring the monarchy up to date. And by his own account, he has been a total failure.

Interviewer: *Why do you think that is?*

Hare: Because he can't actually work out new rules for getting through the day. He wants all the old rights of monarchy – the right to start debates on subjects which concern him, the right to make his views known, the right to damage the livelihoods of individuals by using his unique position to discredit their work – but he then refuses to follow through. You can't answer back. He's not going to take part in a proper debate. And then he actually claims to be hurt when he realises that nobody wants to play tennis with a man who cannot countenance any shot except his own first serve.

Interviewer: *Yes, I can see that his interventions in public life have been desperately unequal.*

Hare: So have his attempts at explaining his own dilemmas. Finally he can't rid himself of the notion of *entitlement*. That he is entitled by birth to behave in a particular way. It's bred in him. That's what a king is, for god's sake. A man who thinks he's entitled. Look, this is a man who is theoretically what they call informal and friendly. But if you are foolish enough to mistake his friendliness for real and put your hand on his back, he's going to think twice about talking to you again. It's only this inbred arrogance, this sense of unreality in all his behaviour that makes him think it's all right to announce to the nation that he never loved his wife when he married her. I mean, what sort of saps does that make of the rest of us? I seem to remember we had a day of national celebration. A lot of poor idiots waved flags in the street. Now he comes along and tells us the whole thing was a dynastic charade. And what's more, he even asks us to feel sorry for him. I mean, you have to laugh, don't you?

Interviewer: *But just because one individual is ridiculous, that doesn't discredit the idea of monarchy. There have been weak kings before, and the family has survived.*

Hare: But I don't think he is weak. Nor is he ridiculous. I think he's honest. Unlike his mother, he's not at ease with the idea of sacrifice. Why should he be? In some part of himself he knows it's an outdated notion to sacrifice your personality in order to be a national symbol. He's in such trouble precisely because he's trying to reconcile the irreconcilable.

Interviewer: *You sound almost fond of him.*

Hare: I think we either have to maintain the monarchy or abolish it. What we can't go on doing is mocking it. Because actually it reflects so badly on *us*. The reason the monarchy is subject to such terrifying abuse at the moment is a function of our own impotence. In our hearts we can sense its day is up, that it's finished. But because we're such cowards we refuse to face the problem head on and devise a peaceful way of removing it. So instead we resort to this shameful practice of trying to torture the individuals involved. It's a form of self-hatred. Because we haven't got the guts to undertake the honest job of establishing a republic, we try and make the royal family feel as miserable as possible. Every day one of Murdoch's papers tries to make them feel a little bit unhappier, yet when Murdoch is asked personally what the point of it all is, and if he actually wants a republic here, he says, 'Oh, I don't know.' That's a contemptible attitude.

Interviewer: *Can you see any disadvantages in a republic?*

Hare: If I'm honest, yes. The Queen's most useful function in this country is to neutralise the incipient lunatic right wing. The military take an oath of loyalty to her, and it means something to them. There's also still a fascist fringe in this country, but we've suffered less from it than if she hadn't been there.

Interviewer: *Do you really think the abolition of the monarchy is practical politics? Can you see an incoming Labour government tackling the issue?*

Hare: Like everyone else, I reserve the right to be surprised by Tony Blair. He appears to be one of those Labour politicians who can always think of a reason for not doing anything, but let's see. The problem is that it's change itself which has been discredited in this country. Because so much change in the last 15 years has been mischievously conceived, and has had such self-evidently disastrous consequences we are going through a numb phase where radicals behave like conservatives. They feel they must fight for what is still left, rather than strike out for what is new.

Interviewer: *But if you're saying we need to recover our passion for change, why start with the monarchy? Isn't it irrelevant, compared with all the work that needs doing on the House of Lords, the judiciary, the NHS, the educational system and so on?*

Hare: We need to close a chapter in our imperial past. This is morally important, for our own self-confidence. Our symbolic institutions should not be bastions of self-interested wealth and snobbery. They should not be full of people we cannot speak to. It's part of the process of growing up, of becoming adult that we say we shall look after our own affairs. We don't need kings any more, because all they represent is an extra layer of self-interest which confuses rather than liberates the workings of democracy. We should define ourselves not by the union flag, but truly as citizens, and by the distinctive way we care for each other as citizens.

To me, abolishing the monarchy is the essential psychological kick-start we need for the 21st century. I love the idea of us starting the next century by saying we're on our own at last. We've pushed Nanny over the cliff. God knows, we can't do worse without her. •

···

11 January 1995

Thomas Keneally
Crown under

To a moderate Australian republican, British republicanism can seem very Jacobin. It isn't quite off-with-their-heads but it is certainly to-hell-with-their-privileges.

I found out through the experience of discussing the issue on British radio that British republicanism is imbued with far more personal animus against the present incumbents than is the Australian version. Robert Hughes, writing of this phenomenon, said the proposed Australian republic 'lies beyond the scandals and transcends matters of celebrity . . . real republicans may have a genuine affection for Elizabeth II'.

While Australian republican feeling is based on constitutional issues and geo-political reality, the British version seems to be more personal. There may in fact well be more affection for the royal family in Australia than in Britain.

Who could have failed to be impressed by the way Prince Charles managed a sad incident in Sydney last year? Very bravely he stood up to an assault with what turned out to be a starter pistol but which could have been the real thing. The weapon was wielded by a Kampuchean refugee, but it raised memories of the wounding at a Sydney harbour picnic in 1868 of Queen Victoria's son, Prince Alfred, the first royal visitor to Australia.

Last year's starter-pistol incident indicated one of the perils of being future or present head of state of remote countries for whose administrative policies you might at any time be blamed. Immediately after the attack Charles gave a gallant speech in which he made it clear that Australia's future direction was its own business. Constitutional changes (including, by implication, an Australian Republic) would not diminish traditional affections.

Charles, therefore, is treated with some affection in Oz as a flawed bloke, like the rest of us, but a good sport. I do not believe that that was the British reaction to him after his memoir-apologia appeared in the press last year. One of the arguments against maintaining the British monarch as head of state of Australia is that she or he is 12,000 miles removed and cannot speak for us. Yet there is an Australian anxiety that British rancour could produce an Australian destiny for the royals reminiscent of Sue Townsend's *The Queen and I*.

British republican sentiment drives the royal family out of the British Isles. They apply for Australian citizenship and settle down companionably in the Antipodes. Charles becomes a ranger on the Barrier Reef, the Queen Mum becomes patron of the Dee Why Bowling Club, the Queen herself spends every Saturday punting a dollar each way at the races in Kerry Packer's box.

All whimsy aside, this matter of our head of state being 12,000 miles offshore is for us not a minor issue – Australia is not part of the European Community and has to make its diplomatic and commercial way in Asia and the Pacific. The fact that it has not yet been forgiven by Asia for the White Australia policy of earlier this century is not the fault of the monarchy.

But it behoves Australia poorly to go forth trying to do business in our region using as our symbols the same ones we employed in the days of Empire. Our neighbours are quite frank in stating that they will see our becoming a republic as a gesture of commitment to the region.

This kind of regional pressure towards a republic does not exist in Britain's case. There are different internal arguments in both cases too. The monarch and her representative, the Governor-General, have extraordinary reserve powers under the Australian constitution. Section 58 permits the Governor-General to reserve any bill passed by the federal parliament for the 'Queen's Pleasure'. Section 59 enables the monarch retrospectively to disallow any law within one year of its enactment.

These powers, of course, have been governed by the so-called Westminster conventions which circumscribe the political powers of the monarch in Britain too. But the question still arises as to what such clauses are doing in the constitution of a country which would like to cast itself as a sovereign state. And the reserve powers were used in 1975 by Governor-General Sir John Kerr to dismiss Prime Minister Gough Whitlam.

The irony is that the monarch herself was not even informed beforehand of Sir John's exercise of power and almost certainly wouldn't have approved of it, correctly perceiving in it inevitable damage to the monarchy in Australia. So the problem was not so much the Crown itself but the powers which had been affectionately accorded it in 1901 under the constitution.

Again, no such republican motivations operate in the British case. But in Britain, by contrast, I sense a belief that the royal family has broken some unuttered contract with the British people.

There was a time when this contract did not exist. The last reckless, swingeing, gambling, hedonist monarch was Edward VII. As a prince he fornicated his way around the Dominions and one of his more renowned paramours was the Marilyn Monroe of his day – Lily Langtry. At least he could not be accused of pursuing average follies.

The monarchy's problem today is that, particularly from the reign of George V onwards, the implied compact has been as follows: the monarchy would be the central symbol of Britishness, and 'King' would continue to be invoked before 'country' in the customary mantra of British duty, but in return the royal family would have to turn itself into the incarnation of the proprieties middle-class and working-class Britons most professed to admire.

The present Queen's father reinforced this contract, appearing in blitzed London during the Second World War with his wife, both of them wearing the same conjugally united and sincere look of shared, sage, parental concern. Their elder daughter, Elizabeth, carried on the tradition both as a child and as a young adult.

But while the monarchy, aided by a then seemly press, was ensuring affection, it was also painting itself into a corner of respectability and taking on roles as living icons. When the icons crumbled, they crumbled not hectically like their forebears but in an average suburban way: adultery, divorce, accusations of parental callousness, unwise telephone calls.

This is what has created the British crisis – surprise and disappointment that the royal family should not prove to be 'above moral lapses' in the way that its members are supposed to be 'above politics'.

Dare I say, as a lad from Sydney commenting on a British crisis, that I feel that some of the present rage is based on the unreal psychic investment the British have put on the monarchy? In choosing the monarchy as their model, the British inevitably opted for the rubrics of privilege over the flawed but robust rubrics of fraternity and equality, which are the better and most persistent angels of a republic.

It doesn't serve any purpose to defend the monarchy by pointing to grievous republics – the Sudan, for example, or Iraq. Good republics may be as remarkable as good marriages but that does not staunch the eminently human desire to attempt or achieve them. For good marriages are a condition geared to human survival and to the future. And so are republics.

People will instinctively hanker for them because of their inherently higher moral possibilities. Against this impulse the dreary cry 'If it isn't broken don't fix it' just does not work. Humans inevitably abandon what is not broken – the horse carriage, the DC3, the four-megabyte computer – for a higher order – the automobile, the 747, the eight-megabyte computer.

What, then, the British have chosen for themselves is that the Queen should be the Good Madonna and the King the Good Father. Under this regime Britons could 'look up to' the monarch instead of looking up to themselves. They would fix their ambitions on achieving excellence according to a Byzantine gradation of imperial honours, generally arranged by class, as subtle in arrangement and weight and as impervious to average understanding as quantum physics. Command performances would be the height of showbiz, and the royal garden party, with its few valued and inane exchanges, the summit of entire careers.

In the 1970s an Australian commentator, A J Marshall, wrote: 'To the bulk of the British people it [the monarchy] is as necessary as aspirin and in a general way serves much the same purpose.' If that is so, many of the British have now lost faith in their key mythic opiate, their wonder drug. Hence their sense of loss and rage, so accentuated by comparison with the Australian phenomenon.

But whether in Australia or in Britain, there are inherent problems that relate specifically to monarchy that do not apply to republics. First, the monarchy discriminates against women in a way a republic would not. A woman can be head of state of Great Britain only if her parents fail to have a son.

Second, though I have no desire to raise sectarian issues, particularly at this stage of history, it has to be acknowledged that the issue is already raised by the Act of Settlement itself. The monarch, her heirs and successors must be Anglicans. I think a British citizen would be entitled to ask how this sits in the New Britain, a Britain in which there are so many Catholics and Islamics; the Britain also of a distinguished Jewish tradition.

There is also the inherent inadequacy in depending upon the genetics of a particular family, instead of more directly upon the will of the people, to produce a head of state. And last of all arises the old argument about what one wants to be, a citizen or a subject.

The idea of subjection to the Crown is seen by many as some sort of harmless fiction of the modern constitutional monarchy. But it is apparent that ministers in the Commonwealth are only too willing to invoke the Crown as a means of justifying inequitable administrative decisions.

The point is that a huge deal of British psychological effort goes into ignoring these dark areas of royalty, energy which would be more creatively invested in institutions more obviously related to the realities of the present and the hopes of the future.

So how will the monarchy fare in this late age? In an age in which I think all of us, Australians and British, could well be debating more constructive issues if our system had not stuck with this unfinished matter.

It seems likely that the monarchy will disappear from Australia and New Zealand, perhaps within the next 10 years. In Australia, people speak increasingly of the Sydney Olympics of 2000 as the likely date for us. (The young are already asking who will open the games – the monarch or an Australian head of state?) And Mr Bolger, National Party leader of New Zealand, has already projected a New Zealand republic.

The monarchy is probably at its strongest in Canada, where it serves as a device Anglophones can use both to assert their Britishness over the Québecois and to distinguish themselves from the Americans. Ultimately, Anglophones will have to find some distinguishing mark from amongst themselves rather than borrow Britain's. But for the moment the loyal toast is frequently and heartily drunk in Canada.

As for Britain, it is likely that in the short term the monarchy will adapt itself to this new crisis through an agreed-upon shrinkage of the civil list and the institution of a more matey, 'democratic' sort of monarchy like the kind seen in Scandinavia.

If, however, at some stage the British move by popular will towards a republic in the shared unambiguous unity of Britons, there will no doubt be a huge, positive cultural and psychic fall-out.

For our metaphors and symbols both define us and give us our opportunities. Over 200 years or more the Australians were cargo-cultists, receiving in penal-colony days their rations, in the 20th century their validity and sovereignty, shipped in over huge distances from Britain.

The liberating concepts and images of the republic are ones untested as yet in either modern Britain or Australia, but now it is a possibility frankly discussed. It appears that Australia will grasp its unexplored but valid republican opportunity. As for the British, the decision is your business and none of mine. I know that in the end, however, we all need to stop playing tea parties. ●

12 October 1994

Tony Harrison
Deathwatch danceathon

In the first of a series of poems on current themes written for the *Guardian*, Tony Harrison explores the parallels between the destructive amatory activities of the deathwatch beetle and the alleged royal lovers unmasked by Anna Pasternak.

Six centuries of insect sex
make hallowed rafters hollow wrecks,
the high and holy upheld by
oak-beams gnawed to casks of ply,
and their *Totentanz* tattoos
percussive in half-empty pews
are sex-sex-sex, the tapping crown
of cruising bug brings churches down.

How many houses of the Lord
has the knock-for-nooky squatter gnawed?
Carved escutcheon-, scuncheon-squatters
more bug cloggies than gavotters,
rafter-feasters, roodscreen-wreckers
send morse-a-mate from mite maracas.
In oak as old as Robin Hood
the midnight maters knock on wood.

The male bug's tappings telegraph to
every female in the rafter,
11 times per second beat
the insect 42nd St,
and oak-feasters' Easter Parade's
booming in old balustrades.
And the sick man in the bed below
hears the knock-tease to and fro.

The mortal patient in the bed
hears their mating call with dread.
He hears the termite dancers tapping
tattoos that terminate in tupping,
the Deathwatch Beetle like Blind Pew
groping towards his rendezvous,
and that dry staccato sound
brings old institutions to the ground.

Beetle bonkers in the beams
spell the end of old regimes.
Down come beams and joists and doors
to the foreplay of the xylovores,
ancient truss and cruck
cracked by fronsaphonic fuck.
Bluntly put the bugger's fucked yer
entire infested infrastructure!

Devourer of dead wood supports
of mansions, palaces and courts,
each fat white grub will have gnawed a
good few yards of Old World Order.
The rat-a-tat-tat of rafter roaches
tapping their sexual approaches,
a frolic of phallic infestation
expected in a monarch nation.

Old palaces, old churches, courts
with rotting tap-schools for supports,
sex-mad rafter-hopping hordes
in chapel panel, west wing boards.
In the end the bug brings down
the bedpost carved with shield and crown
and goes on dining and makes fall
the portrait-laden palace wall.

Other lives get nourished by
the sick man who's about to die.
As *On Ilkla Moor Baht'at*
declares: man's himself a habitat
where worm and duck and fellow Tyke'll
help complete the foodchain cycle.
So don't imagine it's all gloom
to hear the deathwatch in the room.

The mortal summons in the wall's
some other creature's mating calls,
sending a rhythm along the beams
that spells the end of old regimes.
And the fruitful female bears
a future horde of new Astaires,
each a tuneful tapping trouper
part Gene Kelly, part Gene Krupa.

Gilt cherubs once with chubby cheeks
look down now like noseless freaks.
Like stuffing from a teddy bear
their wooden innards fill the air,
little motes of carven oak
with brief puffs of a golden smoke,
golden *putti* tiny specks
of oak confetti for mite sex.

The wooden saintling wondreth whither
cometh the knock-knock-knock come hither,
from his brain or from his heart
or from some other uncarved part.
Sawdust created by no saw
but sexaphonic xylovore,
their friable physique now floats
as dancing, dull or golden motes.

The momentum of this very verse
drums up the stretcher and the hearse,
a beat that comes from long before
the King-beheading Civil War
divided still divided Britain
and Andrew Marvell's poem got written –
(though now he'd say that at his back
trotted ghost-writer Pasternak!)

So 'never send' and 'had we but'
And such like thoughts sublimely put
by poets who've used the tolling bell
to cast an otherworldly spell,
or 'time's wingèd chariot' as a ploy
to make a mistress act less coy.
Put less ornately 'we're soon dead,
my sweetest darling, come to bed!'

So lovers lie, listening to taps,
part copulation, part collapse,
the mortal summons in the wall
that's just some creature's mating call –
Eros/Thanatos a pair
like Ginger Rogers/Fred Astaire,
one figure fleshless and one full,
the dancing duo, cheek to skull.

The very verse the poet employed
to make the virgin see the void
and be thus vertiginously sped
into Andrew Marvell's bed,
is the beat whose very ictus
turns smiling kiss to smirking rictus,
the urgent beat that wipes away
the urgency of what poems say.

Like the car and house alarms
that lovers in each other's arms
hear going off and left to bleep
the neighbourhood from love and sleep,
piercing, pulsating throbbers
disturbing everyone but robbers.
Everywhere there is a measure
heard or unheard of our pleasure.

Two pulses slightly out of synch,
flexi-phials of coursing *Quink*,
the metred couplet with its rhyme
revels in and coasts on time
we haven't got enough of – there
beneath the gently lifted hair
the artery that keeps repeating
life and its ending in one beating.

And in a palace's four-poster where
deathwatch dustmotes fill the air
in the densest dancing cloud
the beetle's drumming is most loud.
In Kensington he makes a killing,
the Deathwatch Beetle, drumming, drilling,
head in and out the polished oak
leaves one last prick-hole as they poke –

Their 'grubby' passion, his and hers
spurned, pampered Princess, squire in spurs,
and as fourposter bedposts rock
we hear the deathwatch: knock . . . knock . . . knock . . .
and though too gentle for the axe
quicker than Anna Pasternak's,
I think, with Andrew Marvell, I can hear
the gavel of the auctioneer . . .

[The Deathwatch geigering for fucks
leaves the bookworm to the books!] ●

Making news

....

3 *November* 1994

Simon Hoggart
Dish of day turns out to be a flounder

Tory MPs gathered yesterday for a feeding frenzy, with the *Guardian*'s editor as *plat du jour*. Unfortunately something had gone wrong in the kitchens. Like Timon of Athens's unhappy guests, they were served only dishes of lukewarm water. (Not even a cod fax.)

No wonder famished MPs kept talking about food. Roger Gale (C. Thanet N) called Mr Preston a 'gamekeeper whose coat pockets are stuffed with stolen pheasants', adding that other newspapers now had 'egg on their faces', then tacking on a flourish about turkeys voting for Christmas.

Possibly Mr Gale has been on hunger strike, which can have a damaging effect on the synapses. At one point he said of Mr Preston that he was a Guardian angel who had 'turned into the whore from Hell'.

(Or possibly a horse from Hull. Either way, it's not language you expect from a former *Blue Peter* producer. 'Now, here's a whore I made earlier, out of empty yoghurt pots . . .')

Throughout it all the editor sat in the press gallery, chewing gum vigorously, catching it, in the words of the song, on his tonsils and heaving it left and right. Not a good time to have just given up smoking.

He heard himself denounced variously as 'ethically flawed and downright criminal', 'mocking of decency and mocking of honesty', 'a knave' and 'completely unacceptable'.

But as the debate progressed it became clear that the issue was deflating before our eyes. Even the Attorney-General occupied his time by drawing a detailed portrait of Labour's Ann Taylor on the order paper.

The *Guardian*'s case was helped by those arrayed against it. Proposing the motion, David Wilshire (C. Spelthorne) made a thoughtful if at times bizarre speech ('that route lurks the jackboot and the lynch mob'), all in a boyishly naive tone.

When he announced that he knew he was setting himself up 'for abuse and criticism – but that is the lot of politicians,' Labour MPs sighed in feigned sympathy.

Mr Gale himself was called a 'demented hyena' by Brian Sedgemore (Lab. Hackney S), a remark he withdrew as soon as he was sure we had all written it down.

But the mood of the House can change completely in 24 hours. Labour MPs, silent on Tuesday, now sent waves of attacks on to the Tory benches, concentrating chiefly on the fact that the Government knew all about the forged fax in May, almost six months before it dialled 999 for the snatch squad from the ethics police.

One after another, Labour MPs demanded to know the reason for this delay. The one they suspect – that Downing Street thought it had screwed the lid back on the Ritz can of worms and was holding the fake fax back for use another day – was the one they couldn't say.

Tony Banks (Lab. Newham NW) even read out a letter from Mr Aitken, written last May when he knew about the fax. (Where could Mr Banks have acquired this missive?) Mr Aitken had decided, he wrote, to 'stay cool'.

Other MPs raised the question of Sir Denis Thatcher's use of Downing Street notepaper for his own purposes, and of course the use of the same Commons logo on the cover of Edwina Currie's dirty novel.

Mrs Currie (C. Derbyshire S) sweetly pointed out that the paperback was now available at only £8.99. 'Orders, orders!' someone shouted.

As so often in Parliament, the lynching had turned into a TV chat show. •

5 November 1994

Peter Preston
Looking beyond the week that was

Tiny Rowland told the *Daily Mail* yesterday where he'd gone wrong. 'My big mistake was after a lunch with Denis and Margaret Thatcher. My colleague said to me he thought we would get it [the House of Fraser] if we were to give £150,000 to the Conservative Party. Instead, I said we should give £150,000 to charities in Africa.'

Mr Rowland, confirming those quotes to the *Guardian*, adds that his 1984 Sunday at Chequers stretched from 11 in the morning until towards five in the afternoon. One senior hand at Lonrho at the time was Colonel the Right Honorable Sir Edward Du Cann MP – also Chairman of the Conservative 1922 Committee. Mr Rowland, of course, may have put two and two together and made 93. His colleague may have been a callow youth, innocent in the ways of the world and over-eager to jump to conclusions. The fact that the House of Fraser bid was contemporaneously going through an official grilling could be coincidental going on irrelevant. No one mentioned it over lunch at all. No one remembers whether the 'unacceptable faces of capitalism' ate beef or chicken.

The difficulty *always* with anonymous donations to the Conservative and Unionist Party – and probably any party anywhere in the world – is that an unstated bargain is an arrangement packed with potential for disappointment. If Tiny had lobbed in the £150,000 and still not got Harrods, he might have swung to the incandescent side of cheesed off. But if things had moved his way, he might equally have thought the spot cash cheap at the price. Nobody can ever say or know for sure.

Mohamed Al-Fayed, as the world indeed now knows, did give the Conservatives an anonymous £250,000 towards their 1987 election campaign. The world knows, it may be added, because Mr Al-Fayed is telling it so at the top of his voice. The fabled DTI inquiry, about which so much bitterness still lingers, was launched on 9 April 1987. The general election followed in June. That old unstated non-bargain problem again. Can Mr Al-Fayed possibly have been led to think that this generous donation to Central Office funds might somehow secure more than a smile from on high at a fund-raising cocktail evening? Was he really led to think anything? The scope for misunderstanding, of course, was panoramic. And so, over subsequent years, it has proved. Mr Al-Fayed got done over by the DTI inspectors, but kept the House of Fraser. Call it a score draw on the pools sheet. The Conservative need for big money was even then provoking hapless problems; and so it continued.

Such Tory backbench vituperation this Wednesday as missed the *Guardian* headed straight for Mr Al-Fayed. We were, said Ian Bruce MP, 'working with a blackmailer in an attempt to bring down the Government'. The fear and loathing is manifest and considerable – with that DTI report, delivered in 1988, as a core text. Surely, after its publication, the Conservative Party could never come rattling its cash tin again?

But now we are almost up to date, in the early spring of 1992, and who should climb the stairs to the fifth floor of Harrods than Tim Smith, MP for Beaconsfield, a deputy chairman and treasurer of the Conservative Party? Mr Smith isn't coming for an amiable natter and cup of cocoa with his old friend Mohamed Al-Fayed, on whose lavishly paid but undeclared behalf he once asked a string of parliamentary questions.

Mr Fayed remembers that meeting. 'He even had the cheek to come and see me with his begging bowl. He said the party was short of money and looking defeat in the face. He wanted me to introduce him to some of my Saudi friends. I showed him the door.'

Remember, this is 1992 – four years *after* the DTI report. The time of John rather than the time of Margaret. The supposed scales about Mr Al-Fayed have long since dropped from Conservative eyes. And yet the begging bowl is still rattling, private funds from a private company. Alms for the sake of re-election.

I find all of this pretty jolting. Big money, not small money. Big rages, not small rages. Big, big ambivalencies. Lord Nolan's committee has made a prompt and public start. Good, independent members; a strong open brief. But it must set the funding of political parties at the heart of its journey. While that remains off limits, while the money MPs earn on the side has to be registered but the money the party takes 'in privacy' is not, there will always be a stable door swinging wide open and a black horse heading off down the lane.

It has been, of course, a bruising old week here at the *Guardian*. The invective has hit screeching pitch. The refusal to understand what actually happened to the cod fax – rather than to recite a litany of evils – has been a touch frustrating. But readers, almost by the thousand now, have written or called in support: a real sustenance. And, in a while, perspective will surely return.

One final time: the use of the House of Commons logo a year ago, on a fax deceiving nowhere and buried straight in a private file, was clearly an error. The House feels its dignity affronted. It demands and seeks an apology. It will surely, on those grounds, be offered it.

But meanwhile there are no thanks for the story that preceded Tim Smith's ministerial resignation – and no two-and-a-half-hour emergency debate on Mr Smith's conduct either. Mr Roger Gale and friends have nothing to say about him or his resignation. Reactions to the charges of dishonesty or cheating or rule evasion involve much shooting at messengers and the silence of the club.

Well, of course. That is merely confirmation of the way things are. Mr Al-Fayed, his money once blessed in secret, is now some demon from outer space, able on the unpublished evidence of one unnamed informant to be called a 'blackmailer' and worse under rules of parliamentary privilege in advance of any investigation – or, still, any sign of a meaningful investigation. The Prime Minister, meanwhile, is protecting his source – whilst the hounds are unleashed in Farringdon Road on precisely the same issue. Even the Dreaded Rees-Mogg, the ultimate deterrent, is dropped from a great height.

It is a silly and rather desperate time, and it needs, as Mr Aitken said in May, to be taken 'coolly'. The press, of course, is not above the law; and we, on solemn advice, are told that we have not in any case broken it. Ministers and MPs, equally, have their responsibilities and their need to command public confidence.

The tide, on many beaches, is going out for the Government. But standards, in their complexity, are the toughest issues of all. It will not be tackled, nor assuaged, until angry defensiveness can be turned into an open acknowledgement that clean government is the legitimate aspiration of all involved.

Nolan is a good start here. A start that the events of the past fortnight have precipitated. A committee not volunteered, but dragged forth under pressure. Never mind, though, how it was born. The baby is already alive and kicking. It has the capacity to make things better. But once it starts it must be allowed to finish. That will never really happen until party finances – all party finances – are on a clear and open basis. Who knows? Mr Rowland, with a little more time on his hands, may even write a letter to the editor saying so. ●

- -

9 December 1994

Richard Gott
I was a mellow traveller

Dear Peter,

Reading this week's *Spectator*, with its allegations that I used to be a paid agent of the KGB, has caused me – as you might imagine – some considerable anxiety and anguish, if only because of the potential damage such allegations might cause to the newspaper for which I have worked, off and on, for more than 30 years.

So I thought it would be sensible to try to set down as clearly as possible the contacts that I – like many other journalists – have had over the decades with officials from the former Soviet embassy. But first I should state quite clearly and unequivocally that I did not receive money from the Russians that I met, a point that I shall return to in a moment.

I should also explain, at this early stage, that I was called in to discuss these matters with an official of MI6 in the late 1980s and he accepted my word then that this particular accusation was baseless.

But I *have* talked to the Russians (and the Cubans and the North Vietnamese) over the years and, if only to clear my mind and to shed light on the strange world that we have all lived through during the cold war years, I thought it would be useful if I were to lay out in some detail the experience of one sentient individual in his relations with people who were considered in those days to be 'the enemy'.

Before I joined the *Guardian* in 1964, I worked as a researcher at the Royal Institute of International Affairs, and I was approached at that time by someone from the Soviet embassy who obviously thought that Chatham House was rather closer to government and the Foreign Office than in fact it was. We lunched from time to time, and I used to find my contact rather more interesting to talk to than most of the people at my institute. We would meet in distant suburbs, and I rather enjoyed the cloak and dagger atmosphere which will be familiar to anyone who has read the spy stories of the cold war. I told one senior colleague at the institute about these meetings and asked him what on earth he thought the Russians would get out of chatting to me. He said that he thought that they would probably try and talk to lots of different people and then form an opinion about what was going on. He saw no harm in the meetings.

At one stage, though not through the Russians, I was invited to the East German equivalent of Chatham House in Berlin, and I asked Kenneth Younger, the institute's director, if it would be all right to accept the invitation. He said it would be fine as long as I went as an individual and did not make any public speeches. (I was known at that time, and indeed later, as a left-wing activist, being deeply involved with the Campaign for Nuclear Disarmament and the various teach-ins against the Vietnam war that were characteristic of that period.)

I also visited Havana in the early 1960s, and I was rather delighted to be able to finance the trip with the royalties from the American edition of a book I had written.

In 1966, after resigning as a *Guardian* leader writer to fight a by-election in Hull North in the interests of the anti-Vietnam war campaign, I went to work in South America at a new institute of international affairs in Chile, and I worked on a book about the guerrilla movements that had sprung up in Latin America in the aftermath of the Cuban revolution.

When I had finished that, I secured a visa to go to North Vietnam in 1970 – the first British journalist to do so since James Cameron had gone there in 1965 – and I enjoyed the hospitality of the North Vietnamese, a fact which was of course known to Alastair Hetherington, the editor of the *Guardian* at that time, for whom I wrote a series of well-received articles.

Subsequently I went to work in Tanzania as the foreign editor of the state newspaper there, and I had many contacts with both Soviet and Eastern Bloc diplomats and, of course, with the leaders of the revolutionary movements of the time, all based in Dar es Salaam. I was in those years notably anti-Soviet, taking the side of the Guevarists in Latin America and the Maoists in Africa.

When I returned to Britain in the early 1970s, the Russian embassy in London again made contact, and I resumed rather irregular lunches. As before, I rather enjoyed them; but as I was well-known for my ultra-leftist and anti-Soviet views, it did not seem to me likely that they would succeed in recruiting me as an agent – though I sensed that that is what they would have liked to have done.

In addition, since everyone has read all the spy novels and knows that all intelligence services are in bed with each other, there wouldn't have been much mileage in signing up a journalist already known as a Third World subversive. Indeed, I assumed, through my absolutely transparent presentation of myself as an incorrigible leftist, no harm could come from lunching with these folk. And as I say, I enjoyed it.

In the 1980s, the period about which the *Spectator* appears to be informed because of the defection of Oleg Gordievsky, the lunches continued, and I did sense that there was some new pressure for results. The contact, again meeting in obscure suburban restaurants, kept on pressing me to tell him things. But as the *Guardian*'s features editor, essentially bound to my desk, what on earth could I tell him? So we chatted about foreign affairs and anything else that seemed interesting.

Then he suggested that I should go on a trip to Vienna to meet his boss. That sounded fun. Classic neutral territory, reminiscent of *The Third Man*. So

I went. I met a man who I think I'd probably met before in London. He was a very genial Kazakh, and I've often wondered what happened to him since. We met again in Athens, Nicosia and Moscow. I could never quite understand what he wanted. I just assumed that somehow I appeared on some bureaucratic list somewhere, and the fellow was justifying his own existence in a manner typical of the Soviet bureaucracy.

In the course of the 1980s, Gordievsky defected, and the two men I had got to know in London went home. One was expelled, the other 'left hurriedly'. I have never heard from them again, which is a pity, as they might have turned out to be interesting contacts in the new era.

Some years after Gordievsky's revelations, I was summoned to talk to MI6, who were tidying up the details of the case, and the man in charge was the first to tell me of the allegation that I had accepted money as well as lunch. I told him that I had been pressed to take money, but I had refused to take it. I had no need of it, and I was enjoying myself, not seeking to make money on the side. The MI6 man said that he knew of cases where a Russian agent would say that he had handed over money and then keep it himself. So I left it at that.

I confess that I now bitterly regret not having come to tell you, my editor, about this encounter with MI6. It would have been sensible for you to have known about this long and essentially harmless saga – since it was bound to leak out eventually.

And there is an additional matter, which makes the *Spectator* allegation verge on the truth. The Russians did pay my fare and my hotel to go to Vienna, Athens and Nicosia, to meet their man. So I have to admit that I took red gold, even if it was only in the form of expenses. This, in the circumstances, was culpable stupidity, though at the time it just seemed more like an enjoyable joke. But on the occasions when I went to East Germany and to North Vietnam, I had told my boss. On these more recent occasions I failed to do so. I should have done so, and it was reprehensible of me not to. So I have absolutely no alternative except to offer my resignation. The cold war was a very bizarre period, and perhaps none of us always acted the way we should have done.

I have not been left in a darkened room with a bottle of whisky and a revolver. I am taking the decision of my own free will, because I perceive that to be the best way forward for the paper for which I have so enjoyed working for most of my adult life.

Yours sincerely,

Richard Gott. ●

18 May 1995

Leader
Mudwrestling:
A doctor writes . . .

The current issue of the *Spectator* carries an article by Germaine Greer in which she laments the fact that 'senior' feminists (such as herself) are shown insufficient respect by feminists of the more junior variety. She observes how their sex is left vulnerable by the tendency of females to quarrel amongst themselves. Since a version of this article was originally intended for publication in the *Guardian* a small explanation is perhaps due as to why it did not appear in these columns, and why Dr Greer has apparently decided that she will not henceforth write for this paper.

The origins of the dispute lie in a remark about Dr Greer's work reportedly made to a diary column by another *Guardian* columnist, Suzanne Moore. Ms Moore claims she was misquoted. No matter. Dr Greer chose to respond with a vituperative attack on Ms Moore, which encompassed her choice of lipstick, her taste in footwear, her cleavage, her manner of speech, her weight, her smoking habits and her hairstyle. We thought it fair that Ms Moore should be shown this attack before even considering whether it should be printed. Dr Greer, who candidly described her piece as 'mudwrestling', later sent an amended version, omitting some of the more vitriolic abuse. Ms Moore could not, in the event, be contacted until edition time on Sunday and it seemed sensible to allow a period of reflection. Dr Greer duly said that she would never write for us again, announcing yesterday that the *Guardian* was 'a nightmare to work for'. That is perhaps not something on which we should comment. Nor can we reasonably remark on how sisterly it is for one feminist to tear into another on the grounds of her appearance. We merely note how the extensive coverage devoted to the affair elsewhere proves the wisdom of Dr Greer's own observation in her column: 'Men who have known since birth how to run together as a pack . . . can easily pull down the straggling, bickering females.' ●

20 May 1995

Leader

Mudwrestling (part two)

Childcare experts are divided as to whether the best way to treat tantrums in small children is to engage with the child or to ignore it. We tend to the latter view and had not intended to return to the subject that has this week given so much innocent amusement to fellow newspaper columnists and broadcasters – Germaine Greer's new hobby of mudwrestling. But Dr Greer's extraordinary appearance on *The Frost Programme* on Thursday night requires a brief response, if only because her version of events is so wildly at variance with the truth that we fear she may be suffering unnecessarily.

Dr Greer set the scene for Mr Frost's viewers by explaining that Suzanne Moore 'thinks I understand contraception so poorly that in order to exercise my child-free option I had to have my womb cut out'. All Dr Greer's fury has been unleashed on account of a single disputed quote from Ms Moore in a newspaper diary column. Since Dr Greer herself is intending to contest the accuracy of the same diary item in the courts, it is surprising that she should attach such credence to the words attributed to Ms Moore. But nothing Ms Moore said or was quoted as saying bore the slightest resemblance to the Greer/Frost version. If Dr Greer can grasp this simple truth she may start to feel better.

Next Dr Greer told viewers that she was sacked by the *Guardian* halfway through last Sunday afternoon. That she also knows to be untrue. She resigned on Sunday night. But Dr Greer's most extraordinary claim is that she never intended the original version of her column (the one with repeated personal attacks on Suzanne Moore's appearance rather than the milder version served up for the *Spectator*) to be printed. It was, she says, a negotiating position. The first column, she now says, was 'unprintable . . . full of bad taste'. It was 'never meant to be printed anywhere'.

The unprintable column is certainly a novel concept in journalism. Future editors handling Dr Greer's work will at least have the advantage of knowing that the pieces she faxes to them are intended merely as texts for boisterous discussion rather than for actual printing. Dr Greer managed to conceal her intentions from anyone on the *Guardian*. She told the features editor she was out to get Ms Moore, and that he would be well advised not to get in her way. It was, as she memorably added, 'mudwrestling'. If the *Guardian* didn't print it, someone else would. So much for her claim that it was 'never meant to be printed anywhere'.

Dr Greer's *Frost Programme* version of events included other fantasies, as well as a bizarre libel upon the editor she dealt with, whom she accused of being 'the third man in the Craig Charles affair'. Follow the logic of that, if you can – he is a man. He objects to my column. Therefore he is a rapist. (Or, more baroque still, an acquitted rapist.)

Dr Greer was last night engaged in further tantrums, which may or may not be as detached from reality as her clever impression of Violet Elizabeth Bott on *Frost*. We hope she feels better soon. ●

Gerry Adams at the Palace of Westminster

Peace & war

3 September 1994

John Mullin

Guilty only of being a Belfast Catholic

The reference books will record him as murder victim 3,170 of the Troubles. But he was not a number. He was a real man. He was John O'Hanlon. He was, said the Ulster Freedom Fighters, a leading Republican. Everybody knew it to be nonsense. He was, though, a Catholic.

Mr O'Hanlon had just been talking about the cease-fire, said Feargal O'Connor, a friend for 10 years. He had prophesied that Northern Ireland's violence was far from over.

'John was standing beside me. I had just asked him to put a wheel on for me. The next thing I see is flashes, and then bullets hitting the ground.

'I just took off across the neighbours' hedges, nearly strangling myself on a washing line. I could hear them fire more and I could hear him shouting: "Fergie! Fergie!" and that was it.'

Mr O'Hanlon lived at No 1 Cedar Avenue. He was 33 and unemployed, and had to struggle by on £25 a week. He was paying off a huge electricity debt.

So he preferred to stay in. Maybe have a couple of pals around, sometimes stretching to a modest carry-out of beer with a few friends.

It wasn't much of a flat. A dingy bedsit in a run-down red-brick house. But it was home.

Never mind the cigarette marks on the cheap brown settee or the badly stained carpet. He always kept it clean.

He loved music. He had little in the way of possessions, but there were three players: an old music centre, a more modern mini-hi-fi and a ghetto-blaster.

His favourite was Belinda Carlisle. He would smile sheepishly when friends pulled his leg about his fascination for the former Go-Go. But he never liked to play too loud in case it disturbed his neighbours.

Some called him the Quiet Man. They thought it was because he enjoyed John Wayne movies.

Others used that most pathetic of tributes to so many of Northern Ireland's victims. 'He was a quiet, inoffensive, kind-hearted, happy-go-lucky fellow,' said one neighbour, aged 29, his eyes red.

There were few mementoes in the top-floor flat, but there was one which took pride of place: a framed photograph of him with his young son.

John Junior, aged three, was due to visit yesterday. His mum would bring him up the Antrim Road to Cedar Avenue every Friday. She had split from the lad's father a couple of years ago after two years together. But relations were on a good footing, and she would arrive as regular as clockwork.

One neighbour, also unemployed, said: 'He doted on the boy. He didn't do anything special. But he would take him to the park over there and buy him sweets. He loved him to bits.'

The boy's father had moved through a succession of foster homes as a child, according to friends. But he was reluctant to talk about his upbringing. 'He always played his cards very close on that one.'

He had never worked for long. He was, in the cold language of policespeak, an unemployed labourer. His eyesight was the problem. It was dreadful. It sometimes made him the butt of jokes, which he accepted with embarrassed good humour.

His disability marked him out. His walking was uncertain. One resident said: 'His eyesight was so bad he could barely see in front of himself.'

He was hardly mechanically minded. But he would help his friend Feargal O'Connor repair old cars to sell.

They were just about to finish work on a blue Mondeo. They had worked most of the day on it in the driveway of Mr O'Connor's house in Skegoneill Avenue, round the corner from Cedar Avenue.

This is north Belfast, a patchwork of Catholic and Protestant districts. Murders in the area account for one-fifth of all the Troubles' victims. But Skegoneill Avenue was thought to be different.

That was hardly how the gunmen from the Ulster Freedom Fighters saw it. They executed the man as he was putting a wheel back on to the car.

Another day; another statistic. Except this time Northern Ireland had hoped it would be different. ●

....

19 November 1994

Kevin Toolis
Peace and the Provo

Martin McGuiness is sitting in a ramshackle office in the Bogside in Derry, underneath posters of Bobby Sands and Malcolm X, charting out the future of Ireland. 'If the British Government does not engage in discussion with us, if the Unionists don't engage in discussions, then the peace process will run into sand very, very quickly. Our people will deduce the British Government and the Unionists do not want peace. The history of Ireland has shown that if the causes of the conflict are not resolved then the conflict will continue.' And then after a slight pause he added: 'That is not a threat.'

From anyone else these words might be construed as an observation on Irish history. But from Martin McGuiness, the man everyone in Northern Ireland believes to be leader of the Provisional IRA, his comments are a threatening and ominous reminder that Ireland's Troubles are still far from being resolved.

To his British enemies McGuiness is a terrorist mastermind, the man behind a thousand car bombs. But to his admirers and followers sandy-haired McGuiness has a heroic, exalted status that is unique within the Republican movement. 'Martin personifies the armed struggle. Martin is the armed struggle. Martin is a man who has come to epitomise the indomitable spirit of armed struggle Republicanism and does so with great charm and amicability,' says Eamonn McCann, the chronicler of Derry's Troubles, the story of McGuiness's hometown.

'Martin is a too-good-to-be true IRA man,' says a former IRA volunteer, who fought under McGuiness during the 1970s. 'If you thought about the idealised IRA man that you would like to have, doesn't drink, doesn't smoke, completely principled, man of integrity, respected by Republicans and non-Republicans, a good Catholic, you are in fact thinking about Martin. A lot of people would disagree with Martin 100 per cent but as a person they will say Martin lives by his words.' McGuiness's Unionist opponents, understandably, describe the Republican leader in different terms. 'He is a cold-blooded ruthless terrorist and a liar. He will weigh up the consequences of his actions only in terms of benefit to the IRA regardless of the cost in human lives. The effects on wives or children would only come into the equation if he thought that operation would backfire on the Provo public relations machine,' says Gregory Campbell, the Derry Democratic Unionist Party councillor.

Despite the current IRA ceasefire, McGuiness, 44, remains a difficult person to write about for any British publication. For his entire adult life, he has been and is engaged in a violent political struggle to deny the British Government's right to rule in what is constitutionally still a part of the United Kingdom. Our singular Irish province, as British as Finchley, Ulster.

McGuiness and the IRA do not accept what Conservative backbenchers, the editorial board of *The Times* and the British public hold to be self-evidently true, that the British Crown is the legitimate authority in Northern Ireland. 'The British Government has no right to rule in Ireland. The IRA will deny them the right to rule us and it will do everything in its power to make sure they do not rule us easily,' says McGuiness, simply stating the fundamental Republican position. McGuiness is a passionate and active enemy of the British state, and proud to be so. As the commanding officer of the IRA's Derry Brigade in the early 1970s, he personally fought countless gun battles with British soldiers and organised the destruction of the commercial centre of his native city. As director of operations of the IRA's Northern Command in the 1970s, he had a pivotal role in reorganising and strengthening the IRA's structures and capabilities. He was, security sources insist, the IRA's chief of staff in the late 1970s, when the IRA Army Council authorised the killing of Lord Mountbatten and a host of other major IRA operations.

Twice the IRA have come within feet of decapitating the Conservative Government, at Brighton in 1984, and with the mortar attack on Downing Street in 1991. IRA bombers have twice devastated large areas of the City of London, causing hundreds of millions of pounds' worth of damage in each attack. In that Irish province, the Troubles have spluttered and flared across a generation of lives, killing, maiming and scarring.

To look back is to remember only the highlights of an irredeemable catalogue of brutality, grief and human suffering: Bloody Sunday, Bloody Friday, the Abercorn, Birmingham, La Mon, the Harrods Christmas bomb, Enniskillen, Warrington and on and on. As a Republican leader, McGuiness bears moral culpability for the long list of killings and atrocities carried out by the IRA. But Republicans, of course, were not the only protagonists.

At Bloody Sunday it was British Army paratroopers who murdered 13 people in Derry in 1972. Just as Republicans have inflicted pain and suffering, so in turn have they had pain and suffering inflicted upon them. McGuiness is not beholden to the rules and constituencies of British politics. He doesn't care who is in power in Downing Street or Stormont. He doesn't read British newspaper editorials. He doesn't want to win friends within the British establishment. He wants them to go. His antagonism towards the British Crown is like a rock.

In his home town, the man once named by *Esquire* as the second most powerful individual in the United Kingdom after Rupert Murdoch lives an ordinary working-class life in a modest terrace house in the drab Bogside district with his wife and five children. He is thoretically unemployed and entitled to British tax-payer welfare benefits. He waits in line in the queue at the doctor's surgery, he loves his children and sends them to a local school, his wife, Bernie, works behind a counter in a neighbourhood store, and he drives around the streets of Derry, alone, in a four-year-old car. He dresses casually, polo-neck jumpers, tweed jackets, occasionally a shirt and tie, but I have never seen him in a suit. And, on the surface, Martin McGuiness is nothing other than what he purports to be: an intelligent working-class man from the Bogside.

He is remarkably self-contained, seemingly invulnerable to the thousand setbacks, defeats, or even the victories, of 25 years of militant Irish Republicanism. His equanimity is all the more surprising when you consider his position. For a generation he has been one of the top daily targets of the intelligence services. Every aspect of his life must have been minutely spied upon, in the search for a chink that would allow the Crown to trap, imprison or kill him; the files at RUC Special Branch headquarters must run into volumes. Every drive to the shops must have carried the threat of assassination, every encounter the prospect of betrayal. McGuiness once gave me a lift in his car but even within the safety of the Bogside I started sweating, silently praying that the inevitable loyalist hit would not happen during my few minutes as front passenger.

The constancy of the threat does not seem unduly to worry McGuiness.

When being interviewed he is blank-faced and it is impossible to anticipate his response. His mannerisms give the appearance of cold-bloodedness and his answers are often formulaic. He sticks close to a predetermined brief but he is not a devious or slippery conversationalist and comes across as being sincere in his beliefs. He has been known to make the journalists who interview him tea and bread-and-butter sandwiches in his mother's kitchen. On his days off from planning the destruction of British rule in Ireland he goes fly-fishing in the lakes of Donegal.

The dilemma of finding the right words to describe McGuiness's combination of obdurate sincerity and ruthless determination to prosecute the Provisionals' cause is not confined to British journalists. 'In many ways Martin McGuiness is an exemplary man. He is a good father, a good husband, a strong church-goer. I believe him to be honest and upright in his personal conduct,' comments the former Catholic Bishop of Derry, Dr Edward Daly, who clashed with McGuiness countless times over the issue of IRA violence. 'I fundamentally disagree with him on the issue of violence. I believe it to be immoral and wrong; he believes it to be morally justified.' Officially, Martin McGuiness is just a member of Sinn Fein's National Executive, the Ard Chomhairle, and if asked he will as a matter of policy deny membership of the IRA – a sensible device, given that IRA membership carries a six-month jail term. But few within Northern Ireland, and certainly no one with what McGuiness would describe as a 'titter of wit' within Derry's nationalist population, would believe his denials. 'No one should underestimate Martin McGuiness. He is a man of great capabilities, very able, and of considerable political ability,' says Bishop Daly. 'No other living person is a greater threat to the British state.'

Martin McGuiness was born in 1950 in the Bogside district of Derry into a society condemned by its minority Unionist rulers to failure. Catholics were ruthlessly excluded from positions of power and Catholic families corralled into the slums of the Bogside in order to prevent a shift in the narrow electoral balance and a subsequent threat to Unionist domination. In general, the Catholic population, conditioned by its church and its own political leaders, resentfully but apathetically accepted their inferior status. McGuiness came from a typical working-class Bogside family. His mother, Peggy, was a housewife, his father, Tom, worked in a foundry, Martin was the second-oldest boy out of a family of six. Like their neighbours, life for them held little promise of economic betterment, nor was any expected. The family voted for the local nationalist MP, Eddie McAteer, John Hume's predecessor, and had no contact with the 'communistic' agitators like Eamonn McCann, who had from March 1968 onwards begun a series of protests against the local council over housing.

Nineteen sixty-eight was the year of student revolution, Vietnam War protests and the Paris uprising. In Northern Ireland streams of middle-class students took to the streets, singing 'We Shall Overcome' and protesting against the Unionist monopoly of power.

A major showdown took place on 5 October 1968, in the Protestant Waterside district of Derry, after 400 demonstrators defied a ban on a civil rights march. Pointedly, McGuiness, like the vast majority of the Bogside, was uninterested and did not attend.

The marchers, in hostile territory, found themselves trapped between two police cordons with no exit route. The Royal Ulster Constabulary, the Protestant police arm of a Protestant state, began batoning their way into the panicking crowd and everyone, including the then West Belfast MP Gerry Fitt, received a severe beating. The film images of Fitt's bloodied head signalled the start of Northern Ireland's Troubles.

At the time McGuiness was employed as a butcher's assistant in a shop in the city centre, after having left school at 15. 'Word spread back to the Bogside that Fitt had been assaulted by the RUC and other people had been beaten,' says McGuiness. 'It was an absolutely shocking experience. The RUC had attacked the nationalist people of this city, who were the majority. I found it incredible that the RUC denied their right to march and then they beat them. I was 18 at the time and like 95 per cent of my acquaintances was very angry and distraught.'

Prior to the Waterside march, McGuiness had had only one encounter with the Unionist state. 'I had left school and there was a local garage advertising for a mechanic. I went for the interview and the first question was – what school did I go to?

'When I answered Christian Brothers [a local Catholic school] the interview immediately ended. I walked almost shell-shocked from the building. I thought they did not like the look of me.

'I went home and told my parents but there was no big discussion about it.' Three years later the mood of resigned acceptance was over.

There was an explosion of rage and an escalating series of confrontations as the city's youth began to hurl stones, bricks and petrol bombs at the now detested RUC. McGuiness kept his day job but devoted the rest of his energies to rioting. 'I would be rioting in my lunch hour, going home, changing my clothes and walking back through the same RUC men in full battle-rig, some of whom were lying exhausted on the floor, because of what the likes of me and other people were doing in their spare time.

'After work I would go home, get my dinner, and go back down and throw stones and whatever else was to hand until twelve o'clock at night. It was unreal.'

Northern Ireland spiralled out of control as sporadic street riots escalated into a full-blooded civil insurrection and a generation of young Catholics took to the streets. 'Suddenly people were not prepared to turn the other cheek any

more. The RUC became the enemy, the Unionist Government was the enemy,'
says McGuiness.

The final confrontation came on 12 August 1969, when Orangemen from
all over Northern Ireland descended on Derry to commemorate the lifting of
the siege of Derry in 1689. As the marchers skirted the edge of the Bogside
they were stoned; the police and the Orangemen charged the rioters; the now
infamous Battle of the Bogside began. The rioters threw up makeshift
barricades, established a petrol-bomb factory and fought the police to a
standstill. After 48 hours the police conceded defeat and the then Home
Secretary James Callaghan ordered British troops in to restore order. The
British Army has been in Ulster ever since.

In December 1969 a moribund IRA, based in Dublin, split into two
factions, the Officials and the Provisionals, primarily over the issue of
recognising the Dublin and Westminster parliaments but more importantly
over tactics on the erupting civil disorder in 'the occupied area'. The Officials,
influenced by Marxism, wanted to build a cross-community, class-based
workers' revolution and were reluctant to supply any weapons for fear of
alienating the Protestant working class. The Provisionals' aims were more
direct – get guns into the hands of Catholics so they could shoot dead the
Protestant mobs attacking nationalist homes.

McGuiness, like many of the enthusiastic rioters, joined the more
numerous Officials but soon left in disgust, bored by the tedious lectures on
class warfare, and the pitiful state of an organisation that aimed to blow up
electricity pylons with four ounces of gelignite.

'My own feelings were that the only way that this force that was being used
against the community could be repelled was through resistance. The only
people who were capable of doing that were Republicans, who were prepared
to resist, whilst others were prepared to sit back and hope for change.' It was
not long before the shooting war started and Derry was engulfed by daily gun
battles, car bombs and killing. The Army had quickly become the target of
the rioters' stones. In reply rubber bullets were fired, snatch squads deployed,
local youths beaten and harassed. The first lead bullets were fired in July 1971,
killing two local youths, whom the Army claimed were armed with a rifle and
a nail bomb.

'I was there the day Desmond Beattie was killed; his body was brought
round the corner near my home. It was obvious the fella was dead or close to
death. At that stage there was blood everywhere. I found it shocking. I was
very scared and couldn't understand it. It was the first time I had seen anybody
killed by a bullet,' says McGuiness. A few days later the Provisionals made
their first determined bid to kill British soldiers.

McGuiness's power base within the IRA rests on his reputation as O/C of
the Derry Brigade from 1971 to 1973. McGuiness emerged as a natural
leader from within those who flocked to the Provisionals' cause to channel

their anger down the barrel of a gun. In August 1971 the Stormont Government introduced internment, the traditional weapon for suppressing the IRA. The wave of arrests removed the top, older echelon of the Provisional leadership but left the street fighters like McGuiness untouched. 'The day before internment I was a nobody, the day after internment I still regarded myself as a nobody. I did not know what to do. People credit you with this great military mind but it was a débâcle, a mish-mash. A large number of young people who had joined the movement wanted to be organised. I wanted to be as organised as they did. Unfortunately for me, many of them felt I could do a good job. So that is what I did.'

The job 21-year-old McGuiness set about organising was the systematic destruction of what was then considered to be the alien Protestant-dominated city centre. In a devastating onslaught McGuiness's volunteers blasted and reblasted their own city until it looked, in Eamonn McCann's words, 'as if it had been bombed from the air'. Of the city's 150 shops only 20 were left trading. In interviews at the time McGuiness justified the campaign as a means of putting pressure on the British Government and the then Northern Ireland Secretary Willie Whitelaw. He was careful to instruct IRA volunteers to avoid civilian casualties.

There was no shortage of recruits but the risks of arrest or getting shot were high. The Provisionals might have viewed themselves as freedom fighters but in reality they were just a bunch of local kids with a few old rifles up against one of the world's most professional armies. The first volunteer to die was Eamonn Lafferty, an 18-year-old killed in a gun battle. In Republican eyes, Lafferty is remembered as a hero. 'Lafferty, who was very poorly equipped, stood his ground along with two or three other volunteers against the might of the British Army and lost his life.' As McGuiness is speaking, the words fall from his mouth with a weary precision. His face remains blank but it is impossible not to wonder if he had been one of the other 'two or three' IRA men.

On 30 January 1972, British Army paratroopers shot dead 13 civil rights protesters at a peaceful march on the fringes of the Bogside. A fourteenth later died of his wounds. Bloody Sunday hurled Northern Ireland to the edge of civil war and in Dublin a mob burned down the British Embassy. But on the day of the march McGuiness, like the rest of the Provisionals, was unarmed. 'I was absolutely raging. The decision had been taken to attend the march but there would be no aggro whatsoever. We ended up with paratroopers shooting people dead. I was helpless, there was nothing I could do.'

McGuiness was a natural leader with an unassuming air of authority. He was a rebel not a revolutionary and his social conservatism, respect for priests, the church and the social mores of Catholic Ireland bolstered his position within the community. He was a true son of the Bogside. 'Martin was a celibate priest of Irish Republicanism, a virtuous guy,' says Shane Paul

O'Doherty. 'Whereas other people would go out for a jar with a girl, Martin was not into that. He had one girlfriend prior to his wife.' Despite his lack of formal education McGuiness was soon considered to be an astute strategist. 'Martin was a relatively rare phenomenon in the IRA, he was a thinker at a time when there was a lot of blind faith. A common response to criticism was: "We know we are right and if you don't lay off we'll shoot ye." But Martin was articulate and could explain publicly where we were at. That was also unusual in the IRA and it secured his place very early on, and kept him there, because he is still able to think,' adds the ex-volunteer.

After internment the Bogside and Creggan areas were sealed off to the Army by barricades and the mini-Republican statelet of Free Derry was established. McGuiness, with his handsome looks and coy, boyish charm, came into his own as an IRA propagandist, giving tours behind the barricades to the world's media and holding daily press conferences where on one occcasion he introduced journalists to the sniper who had just shot and killed a British soldier on the city's walls. In later years he found the semi-glamorous image of the 'Boy General' hard to shake off and to his acute embarrassment in 1976 endured a visit from Hollywood film star Jane Fonda.

Martin's elevated status did not find favour with his mother, Peggy. In an interview with the *Irish Times* in April 1972, she was recorded as being worried about her son's future job prospects.

'His trade's been interrupted. His father is a welder, his brothers are at the bricklaying and carpentering, but what will become of Martin? That's why they'll have to get an amnesty, so's he can get back to work, and not always be on the run.'

But amongst the new 17-year-old recruits flooding into the Provisionals after Bloody Sunday there was no question about his pre-eminence. McGuiness's rapid promotion to command of the nascent Derry Brigade and the bloody events of the early 1970s have been the shaping forces of his life. One third of the 320 people killed in Derry because of the Troubles died in the street clashes and gun battles of 1971–3, 54 of them members of the British security forces. Over the last 25 years, 40 IRA volunteers have been killed. Derry city is a small close-knit community and McGuiness would have known all of the dead IRA men and been a personal friend to many. Inevitably that bloodshed must have inured McGuiness, and those like him, to violent death and the taking of human life.

'Obviously it does have an effect on you. Many of my friends have lost their lives. And on many occasions, through luck or whatever, I could have lost my life as well.'

As we sit in the shabby Bogside office beneath the posters of Bobby Sands, I ask him what is his strongest personal memory. 'I was with Eugene McGillan [an 18-year-old IRA volunteer who, the Army claimed, had fired on troops] the night he was shot by the British Army, 50 yards from here. I lifted him into the ambulance. There was only he and I in that ambulance. He looked at me, his eyes were wide open, and I looked at him. He had just been shot but he knew he was going to die and I knew he was going to die. It was deathly quiet and then when I left the ambulance Colm Keenan [who, the British Army said, was also involved in the gun battle] was lying down the street, shot in the head. They were two unarmed Republicans who had been murdered by the British Army and both of them were exceptionally close friends of mine.' Regardless of the exact circumstances of the men's deaths, it was clearly not an experience that induced empathy for the anguish of his enemies within the British political and military establishments when the IRA killed soldiers or politicians.

After Bloody Sunday, the British state in Northern Ireland was under siege. Bombing and shooting incidents soared to record levels. In 1972 nearly 500 people were killed, 150 of them members of the security forces. In defiance of his public rhetoric, Willie Whitelaw invited the Provisional leadership for peace talks in London on the future of Ireland in the splendour of Guinness family millionaire Paul Channon's house in Cheyne Walk.

Although only 22, McGuiness, as leader of the Provos in the North's second largest city, was included in the seven-man delegation along with Gerry Adams. The former butcher's assistant, who once worked in the pre-packaged meats section, had come a long way in eight months.

'The house was a mansion. I came from a working-class area of the Bogside. But it wasn't just the house, it was the way the whole thing was done. An RAF helicopter descended and we took off and were flown to the military part of Belfast's airport, where a private RAF plane was waiting to fly us to England. An officer was waiting for us at the bottom of the steps and as we walked past he saluted us. It was incredible,' recalls McGuiness.

The Provisionals listed their demands, calling for the British Government to recognise the right of Irish self-determination, a declaration of intent to withdraw by 1 January 1975 and an amnesty for prisoners. Whitelaw prevaricated. The gap between the two sides was too great but the venue afforded McGuiness the opportunity to put pressure on Whitelaw personally over the Bloody Sunday killings. 'I said it was disgraceful that he could sit there and say that British soldiers were not killing Irish civilians in Ireland. But like everything else it was just glossed over, moved on to the next item.'

The talks were a failure but the episode bolstered and sustained the Provisionals in their belief that sufficient pressure will bring the British Government to the conference table and that ministers' protestations about never 'talking to terrorists' are just lies. The Provisionals' fundamental negotiating position remains unchanged to this day. In January 1973, McGuiness was arrested in Donegal, across the border from Derry, close to a car filled with 250lb of explosives and 5,000 rounds of ammunition. He was tried in Dublin but refused to recognise the court and was convicted of IRA membership and sentenced to six months. In court he struck a defiant note. 'I am a member of the Derry Brigade of Oglaigh na hEireann [the Gaelic name for the IRA] and am very, very proud of it.'

A year later McGuiness was again jailed in the Republic on membership charges and spent most of 1974 in prison. He has never been convicted of a terrorist offence in Northern Ireland though he did spend several months in Belfast's Crumlin Road jail in 1976 before membership charges against him were dropped. McGuiness's imprisonment in 1974 absolved him from bitter internal recriminations within the IRA leadership over the handling of the last 1975 truce with the British Government. In February 1975 the then Sinn Fein President, Ruairi O'Bradaigh, backed by Daithi O'Connaill, both veterans of the IRA's abortive 1950s campaign and senior IRA Army Council members, declared an open-ended cessation of 'hostilities against Crown forces'. The IRA leaders mistakenly believed they had induced the British Government to leave Ireland and the protracted negotiations, at arm's length, between themselves and British officials were the preamble to a public declaration of intent to withdraw. In fact the British Army was digging in for a long war. By the time the truce collapsed in late 1975 the Provos were falling apart.

In the aftermath, O'Bradaigh's and O'Connaill's leadership was overthrown and replaced by McGuiness and Adams. A new IRA structure, the Northern Command, a mini-Army Council to oversee all offensive operations in the North, was created. Its first director of operations was Martin McGuiness. But the rancour over the truce and the feeling that the older leaders allowed themselves to be duped still persists within the top echelons of the Republican leadership today. 'This generation of Republicans is not going to be fooled by their fancy diplomatic language,' states McGuiness.

From 1976 onwards McGuiness kept a low public profile, his energies devoted to his roles within the IRA leadership, first as director of operations, then as the organisation's chief of staff from 1978 to 1982. On paper the IRA's structure has remained unchanged from the 1920s. The supreme authority is the Army Convention, which acts as a delegate IRA parliament with representatives from each active IRA unit. In theory it elects a 13-person Army Executive, which then elects from within its members a seven-man Army Council, who in turn appoint a chief of staff. But the Army Convention has only met twice in the last 25 years and only at times of great revolutionary change in IRA doctrine. In reality changes within the IRA leadership occur infrequently and the current members of the Army Council are drawn from the same small group of prominent figures who have been active within the Provisionals since the early 1970s.

It is not a coincidence that the two youngest members of the 1972 IRA delegation to London, Adams and McGuiness, are the two most prominent Republican leaders today. The IRA Army Council operates a collective leadership that seeks consensus rather than dangerous division within its ranks.

The command structure within the IRA is fragmented along geographic and personal lines. The potential for a split between factions is ever present. It was the Irish writer Brendan Behan, a one-time IRA activist, who perfectly satirised the incestuous, sometimes murderous, factionalism within Republican ranks in a mocking joke. 'What's the first thing on the agenda when three IRA men enter a room?' 'The split.' Both Adams and McGuiness have always moved extremely cautiously before challenging any contentious issue of Republican doctrine. In 1986 Sinn Fein at its annual conference dropped the traditional Republican abstentionist policy of refusing to recognise or to take seats in the Dublin Parliament. The decision was the result of years of careful lobbying, back-room alliances, and consensus-building between the leadership and the different factions and IRA units. The most important element in the whole process had been the calling of an Army Convention, a couple of months prior to the Sinn Fein conference, to endorse the leadership's position. Once that Convention had done so it was axiomatic that Sinn Fein would concur with the views of the IRA – in Irish Republicanism the IRA fire and call the shots.

The current IRA cease-fire was not preceded by an Army Convention but by an intensive lobbying effort by the leadership within every significant Republican grouping and IRA unit to secure unanimous support. Certain IRA units, including the hardline South Armagh and East Tyrone Brigades, were said to be lukewarm but reluctantly agreed to the Army Council's plan. But if the cease-fire is to be made permanent the Republican leadership will have to call an Army Convention and it is here that McGuiness's stature becomes crucial. 'You know with Martin that he would never ask you to do something that he has not done himself. If it was just Adams behind the cease-fire and the peace process, then you could see it as just another political move, a sell-out. But if Martin endorses it, then there must be something in it. Martin is the one who can carry the army. They trust him,' commented a Republican source.

In operational terms, the Army Council has much tighter control over IRA operations in England. The mainland active service units that bombed British cities were organised by its general headquarters staff, who reported directly to the chief of staff.

During McGuiness's tenure there were a number of IRA spectaculars, including the Chelsea Barracks, Hyde Park and Harrods Christmas bombs. The intention as always was to 'bring the war home to England'. Inevitably there were civilian casualties: Christmas shoppers killed, members of an Irish emigrant family blown up waiting at a bus stop near Chelsea Barracks.

I ask McGuiness how he could justify IRA actions like the March 1993 Warrington bomb, which was placed in a litter bin in a regional shopping centre and exploded killing two children and injuring dozens. 'I felt badly about the Warrington bomb, badly about those children. It was wrong and should not have happened. We would under no circumstances condone the killing of any civilian in England. There is no doubt there is regret within the Republican psyche.' It is impossible to read the emotions, assess the depth of his spoken regret, on his blank face. But far from being contrite, McGuiness is stridently robust in defence of the Republican position. 'There is an attempt by the media and the British Government to blame Republicans for the violence of the last 25 years. To make out that I am responsible, and I totally refute that allegation. Here in this city the state shot 14 people to death.

'The world and his mother accepts that every one of them was innocent. Yet the men responsible were marched up to Buckingham Palace and they were decorated by the British Queen. How do people think we feel about that? I do not think that the Brits have any comprehension whatsoever. Instances like that have enraged Irish people who are locked into this state.'

His enemies believe his stated regret at civilian deaths is naked hypocrisy. 'You cannot regret something that you have sanctioned. It's as if I got someone to put a gun to your head, or got someone else to do so, and blew your brains out and then said I regretted it. He is lying through his teeth,' comments Gregory Campbell. On another level, it is pointless to individualise the IRA's war. The killings in Warrington, the litany of the IRA's atrocities, are the collective result of the violent disaffection of thousands of individuals within the Irish Republican community. Martin McGuiness is a focus not the controller of that disaffection. There would be no shortage of like-minded substitutes to replace him in the Republican leadership. No single or multiple IRA act of terrorism, no matter how bloody, will shake their faith in the IRA's cause or its methods. 'For Martin and other Republicans this is war and in a war people suffer. As a supporter of the Republican movement he is surrounded by people who have inflicted grief. But I have no doubt that Martin McGuiness would be distressed, at least as distressed by the deaths of civilians as would British Army officers at the death of civilians killed by their troops,' says Eamonn McCann.

From 1982 onwards, McGuiness ceased to be chief of staff and adopted a more political role. He stood and was elected to a reformed Stormont Assembly, before it too was wound up and consigned to the political dustbin as another failed British initiative. He stands against SDLP leader John Hume at parliamentary elections and consistently garners 17 per cent of the poll, or around 9,000 votes in the Foyle constituency.

Although he, it is believed, is no longer involved in the IRA's administration on a day-to-day basis and holds no formal title on the Army Council, he remains the most important Republican leader and most influential figure.

Since the late 1980s, the Republican leadership has been involved in a complex political process to align the Dublin Government and their electoral rivals, the SDLP, in a pan-nationalist front to negotiate a British withdrawal. By politically dissolving the border so that the mass of nationalists in Ireland can be consolidated into one powerful negotiating bloc, Republicans hope to reorder the political stalemate that has marooned them as a minority within the Catholic minority inside the boundaries of a hostile Protestant-majority-dominated state. Such an all-Ireland political forum would be anathema to the current generation of Unionist leaders but a guaranteed victory from the Republican perspective. If the Provisionals can immerse the blatant desire of the Protestants of Ulster to remain separate from a United Ireland within the greater Catholic majority of Ireland's desire to be united, then the IRA will have dissolved partition. To create space for such a political reordering of present boundaries the IRA leadership will trade a cease-fire for negotiations with the Crown. And in return for such a prolonged IRA cease-fire and the prospect of peace, the IRA hopes, the Crown will, however discreetly, signal its intention to leave its Irish province and gradually force a historic accommodation with the people of Ireland on the Unionists. 'Our position has not changed. We would like to see a unitary state, we would like to see a 32-county republic, but we recognise that we are only a small percentage of the total people of this island. The people of this island might decide on some other type of structure. I am not going to oppose it. I might oppose it politically but there is no way I would defend anybody's right to use armed force to go against the democratic wish of the people of this island,' says McGuiness.

The aim of the current Republican leadership's pan-nationalist strategy is to achieve a 'historic handshake' with the Crown, like that between South African President De Klerk and Nelson Mandela before his release from prison in 1989, which indicated an intention to negotiate political change. The ANC did not overthrow the apartheid regime overnight or map out an exact plan for the transfer of authority, but from that moment on power flowed steadily from De Klerk to the future President Mandela.

Similarly in Ireland, power would at first trickle, then flow, from the Crown into nationalist Ireland until the balance of power was so weighted in the nationalist/Republican's favour that a section of the Unionist community would break away and strike a political deal with the ancient enemy. Many parts of the Republican plan are as yet unproven and after 25 years of conflict such a peace is likely to be gained slowly, only in piecemeal stages, and at the cost of some further bloodshed. The IRA Army Council and McGuiness are prepared to be patient with the Crown, but it is a patience that only stretches to the date, the period of transition, and the nature of interim political structures before the Union Jack flag is finally removed from Irish soil. The ultimate uncompromising aim of a united Ireland is never far from the surface. 'Republicans like Martin,' says Eamonn McCann, 'are fixated on the idea of a United Ireland. The Republican movement exists to get the

British out of Ireland. They move to the left and they move to the right, whatever seems tactically and strategically proper at a particular time. But all these things are dedicated to the one object – to get the British out.' Sometime the answer to McGuiness's ominous observations on Irish history will emerge in the aftermath of the proposed round table talks between all the political parties to the conflict. If the Republican leadership and Martin McGuiness become convinced that the causes of the conflict, British rule in Ireland, as they see it, are being addressed and British ministers and the Unionists are prepared to negotiate fundamental changes, then the IRA will call an Army Convention to make their peace permanent. Delegates from every IRA unit will gather in a remote corner of rural Ireland to vote on such a cease-fire motion and the handing over to the Irish authorities, at some future date, of some of the IRA's stockpile of arms and explosives. If McGuiness was convinced the peace process was genuine his voice *primus inter pares* within the Republican leadership would appeal to delegates for a permanent end to the IRA's war. But if the IRA leadership believes Republicans are being duped, and that the rhetoric of the Crown's ministers is lies, then there will be no such Army Convention, no more peace plan, and it is likely that the IRA's answer will be heard, loudly, on the streets of the City of London. ●

....

26 January 1995

David Sharrock
Where justice lies bleeding for decades

Congratulations to the *Daily Mail* for exposing the inadequacies of Northern Ireland's non-jury Diplock court system to Middle England in a searing leader column this week. Missed the deadline by a mere 23 years, but better late than never.

Private Lee Clegg was sentenced to life for the murder of 18-year-old Karen Reilly as she joy-rode around west Belfast in a stolen Vauxhall Astra. Law lords rejected his appeal last week. 'Yet no jury has ever been asked to weigh the evidence for or against him; no jury has convicted him,' said the *Mail*, its lower lip quivering with indignation.

At the *Mail*'s offices in Kensington High Street they can almost hear the cheers from the Maze Prison. Justice on trial – they can all relate to that in Northern Ireland.

Sorry, the *Mail*'s point is somewhat different. 'Paratrooper Clegg is an *Englishman* denied the most basic right known to *English* justice: trial by 12 men and women ... What many will find hard to accept is why this *British* soldier could not have been given the opportunity to face trial on so grave a criminal charge before jury and judge in mainland Britain.'

To paraphrase; the quality of justice in Northern Ireland is so unreliable that it is only fit for the natives. An English jury could never have returned a guilty verdict on one of its highly trained paratroopers, who was only doing his job. Well, that much at least seems to be true, if the *Sun*'s 'you the jury' campaign is to be believed. Thirty-six thousand *Sun* readers think Clegg should be released immediately, against 1,204 who disagree. The *Mail* has collected 60,000 pledges of support for Clegg from its readers.

The *Telegraph* continues to devote its letter column to readers commenting on their Clegg campaign and kindly carries an address at the bottom for donations to 'Friends of Private Clegg'. It interviewed the paratrooper in prison three times in barely more than a week, its main front-page headline declaring 'I am a scapegoat' on the day five law lords rejected his appeal.

And tabloid newspaper editors scratch their baffled heads when they hear that Amanda Clegg, the estranged wife of the object of their campaign, keeps turning down offers of three days, all-expenses paid, in a luxury hotel close to Wakefield jail. No doubt her refusal to co-operate – and thus make her contribution to maintaining the momentum of the campaign – will be interpreted by some as unpatriotic. She is, after all, from east Belfast and therefore not English, nor really British to the vast majority of Middle Englanders.

The gap which divides Northern Ireland's Protestant and Catholic communities is as nothing compared with the gulf of incomprehension separating 'the province' from 'the mainland'. While the majority of the *Telegraph*'s letter-writers send Clegg sympathetic quotes from Kipling and suggest we wear ribbons as we did for the Beirut hostage John McCarthy, the Ulster Unionist MP David Trimble is left to remind Middle England of an uncomfortable reality: 'If special treatment is given . . . then there will be no answer to the claims by convicted terrorists that they too be released because they too were convicted in a Diplock court,' pleads Trimble. The system cannot be at fault; another reason for this miscarriage of justice must be found and, of course, he supplies one: 'If Pte Clegg had presented a defence in terms of a belief that the car contained terrorists and that he was trying to stop the car in order to arrest them, then, provided he satisfied the court of the honesty of that belief, he would have been acquitted.'

Never mind that Karen Reilly and Martin Peake were joy-riders, racing a stolen car for laughs in an area infamous for the activity. Or that the car had been reported stolen for that purpose for several hours. Or that witnesses, including a police officer, threw the soldiers' version of events into serious doubt. The assumption lying behind Trimble's alternative defence, that a professional soldier would seek to arrest somebody by firing a high-velocity rifle at them, is not that important in itself. What is remarkable is the sudden and enormous effort to right a perceived wrong when the opportunity to do likewise in other, arguably more serious examples of injustice has been there for so many years.

Some 300 people have been killed by on-duty soldiers in the past 25 years but only two soldiers have been found guilty and manslaughter convictions are just as rare. Twenty-three years ago, the same year that the *Daily Mail*'s now discredited Diplock system was introduced, members of Clegg's regiment opened fire on a demonstration in Londonderry. Thirteen people died on Bloody Sunday, a 14th later of his wounds. Yet nobody has ever been tried for their killings.

Ignored by the media, the Bloody Sunday Justice Campaign is still trying to win the right of access to important papers used at the Widgery Tribunal. Hundreds will turn out this weekend to march to the Bogside and remember. Others will think of Derryman Pat McLaughlin, now in his 10th year in prison for the INLA's attempted bombing of Chelsea barracks, whose claims of innocence are supported by persuasive new evidence.

The campaign to free Clegg has brought the goal of seeking redress for all the past injustices in post-violence Northern Ireland into sharp focus. Why has there been so little interest in Bloody Sunday? Why did it take so long to overturn the convictions of the Birmingham Six and the Guildford Four? Who now, for instance, remembers Mary Doherty, shot through the head by a single bullet at the Strabane army border checkpoint as she returned from her 25th wedding anniversary party, and whose killer received a 12-month suspended sentence? •

10 May 1995

James Meek

Wartime memories are relived in fresh ruins

L ieutenant Dima Gorobets is a Moscow policeman, a scene-of-the-crime forensic man. He is at the scene now but he is overwhelmed. They are bringing in 10 to 15 corpses a day from the rubble of the Chechen capital.

Lieut Gorobets, aged 27, walks away from the stinking fly-blown remains on stretchers. He has been carrying out a rough post-mortem and gets someone to fish a cigarette out of his breast pocket.

He does not want to take off his stained heavy-duty gloves; there will be more work along in a minute.

'We don't have any holidays here,' he said.

VE day was celebrated in Grozny yesterday with the streets largely empty of civilians, who feared a Chechen rebel stunt that never happened, and a military parade behind a security cordon at the armed forces' airport fortress.

Wreaths were laid at a makeshift Russian memorial of blocks painted in camouflage colours. But Grozny's most poignant memorial is the bombed, crushed and mangled skyline of the city itself, where the dead of Russia's new war still lie.

There are almost 500 bodies in trenches at the graveyard, marked by a wooden stake and a number written on a square of hardboard, and an estimated 200 in a neighbouring grave. The victims were mostly civilians recovered from the rubble.

'Five thousand is the absolute minimum. There are a lot of bodies that will never be found,' said Lieut Gorobets.

Maria Yushko was at the cemetery with her mother-in-law, Marina, seeking her husband, Alexander, not seen since he set off home from work during the Russian assault on Grozny in January. They are both ethnic Russians.

'I want to send a message to [the defence minister] Pavel Grachev,' Marina Yushko said. 'I want him to be punished for bombarding his own citizens. The Chechens all left the city; only Russians remained. They are all Russians buried here.'

There was the atrocity at Samashki, and air raids on civilian districts, but most of Grozny's victims have died from artillery shelling, fired miles away by gunners who never saw their targets.

Not since the Second World War has a European city been subjected to such bombardment. Even Nazi shelling paled by comparison, a veteran said.

'I lived out this last five months in my third-floor flat and watched every shell fall,' said Sayeed Madalov, aged 78, an ethnic Chechen veteran of the Second World War. 'In Leningrad during the siege I'd count 20 minutes and hear the impact of a single shell. Here, I counted 42 explosives in one 15-minute period.'

Mr Madalov was one of a group of Grozny veterans, Russian and Chechen, invited to the airport celebration.

'We are here to help re-establish peace and order but it's not only dependent on us,' the Russian military commander in Chechenia, General Mikhail Yegorov, said in an address to troops and veterans.

'There have been a lot of victims, even during the moratorium declared by the president of Russia. But we are ready for negotiations to end the war.'

The Chechen rebel leader, General Dzhokhar Dudayev, ordered his soldiers not to attack Russian positions yesterday, and was pictured in his old Soviet air force uniform in the rebel newspaper *Ichkeriya*, alongside a congratulatory message to war veterans.

None the less, Russian forces were jumpy. Some roads to Grozny were closed, the city rang with gunfire overnight and there was sporadic shooting during the day.

The car I was travelling in came under long-range cannon fire, presumably from Russian troops, and was damaged by shrapnel on an otherwise empty road.

The ruins through which the veterans wandered yesterday resemble Stalingrad more than Leningrad. The centre of the city is virtually obliterated. There is no electricity or mains water. With the corpses still buried under the debris and up to 270,000 people living in the city, there is fear of epidemics.

Though they share the glory of past victory and a common hatred of Boris Yeltsin, Russian and Chechen veterans living in Grozny are divided over the present war.

The Russians emphasise how harsh life was under General Dudayev and are aware that the Soviet Grozny that was destroyed is a city that, like the Soviet Union itself, neither the Chechens nor the new Russians are interested in re-creating. ●

....

1 May 1995

John Ezard
The harsh toll of joybells

This is the war of the unknown warriors. The fronts are everywhere. The trenches are dug in the towns and streets. The workmen are soldiers with different weapons but the same courage. **Churchill, 1940**

I was a child, on a visit to Johannesburg in 1951, when a young English South African played my parents two records: Vaughan Williams's arrangement of 'Greensleeves' and Laurence Olivier declaiming 'Once More unto the Breach, Dear Friends', from *Henry V*. Then he said raptly, 'That was how you felt during the war, wasn't it?'

The frank answer would have been yes and no. My parents thought we had got into the war through a bugger's muddle of appeasement and that our early conduct of hostilities had been little better. They listened to all Churchill's broadcasts, but remained convinced until the end of their lives that he would have decamped to Canada with the royal family at the first whiff of Nazi invasion.

They did not benefit from the black market, but knew how furtively all-pervasive it had been. As the subversive Allan M Laing put it in the first *New Statesman* competition of 1945, in a hymn parody entitled 'A Grace for Black Market Turkey':

Let us with a knowing wink
Praise the Lord for food and drink,
Who his choicest gifts doth send
Unto them with cash to spend . . .

Yet my parents loved the Britain represented by 'Greensleeves' and, like millions of unremarkable people, had suffered for it. My father refused to watch 'Dad's Army', regarding it as a mockery of brave men. He had seen Captain Mainwarings and Private Pikes blown up on bomb-disposal squads during the Exeter blitz. One of the official duties of air-raid wardens when working on bombed houses was to collect a basket of 'unidentified flesh' to be approximately assembled, as decorously as possible, into bodies for coffins by volunteers trained in anatomy. One house in every seven was damaged by German bombing. War routinely took average citizens closer to the heart of darkness than the novelist Joseph Conrad ever conceived.

While my father worked nights on his squad, my mother was left to shelter two children under the staircase of a house, chosen for its rural seclusion, which turned out to be directly beneath the flight path of Luftwaffe bombers dumping their spare ironmongery on the way back from Exeter to the sea.

Not a remotely heroic story; typical of the quieter side of the average experience of the home front during the Second World War. I tell it partly because I know it, and because my parents' mixed reactions are reflected neither in the hagiography which dominated the public record immediately after the war nor in most of the nostalgic accounts which have surfaced for its 50th anniversary.

Yet almost any home-front veteran has such mixed attitudes, if you talk to them in some depth. And in this they have an unrecognised kinship with soldiers returned from war. They give casual listeners a simplified, censored version of events. They tell half-truths. Only on his deathbed in 1983 did George Chapman Potts, senior chaplain to the Second Army in 1945, say to his family, 'Dying can't be as bad as having a baby at Belsen.' He meant that the bodies of the babies of mothers who died in labour, as Belsen mothers usually did, were sometimes taken from the womb and eaten by fellow prisoners. What you sometimes saw at home, as well as overseas, fell short of that, though it stayed with you for life. But it was still virtually unmentionable. So, in the struggle to carry on, as well as in the *élan* of final victory and long afterwards, were your mental doubts and reservations the stains on your memory.

Yet the half-truths – Churchill's truths ('I felt encompassed by an exaltation of spirit among the people') – were also true. This was the generation which remained, at least publicly, solid at home and stood alone in the battlefield against Hitler long enough for his mistakes and his allies' mistakes to begin his downfall. For that, it deserves the 'joybells' (Churchill's word) to ring out over Europe one last time in its honour next weekend. Arguably, no generation in history has deserved more. The spiritual as well as financial costs were, however, terrible. Our South African friend in 1951 also played my parents a reading of Paul Gallico's best-selling semi-mystical Dunkirk novella, *The Snow Goose*. This came nearer the mark than the first two records. You knew every day from 1940 to 1945 that hundreds, normally thousands, of people were dying abroad and at home. It was not unduly fanciful to imagine, as Gallico did, the sound of their passing spirits as the wingbeat of geese in the sky. That sense during the conflict that a portal to another world had opened is communicated not in official records but through popular art, especially films: *A Matter of Life and Death, Outward Bound, Blithe Spirit, The Glass Mountain*, and many more.

Government statistics give a background to this. In 1940, only 3,400 people were receiving Second World War pensions; by 1945, some 650,000 families were on pension because their breadwinners had been killed or disabled. However, they were still outnumbered by 714,000 pensioners left by the greater bloodshed of the First World War; the earlier war's survivors were then middle-aged and the dominant generation in society, especially in politics and industry. Their forebodings, especially about the risk of a civilian Somme through aerial bombardment, hung over the scene in a way now hard to imagine after 50 years of peace.

The year 1945 was the cusp of the modern world, but it is easy to forget what a partly Edwardian and even Victorian world it still was, with its continuities less broken than ours. It was, in many ways, another country. In 1938, prices were only 40 per cent higher than in 1914. Almost everybody had a maiden aunt because of the slaughter of young males in the First World War (it was financially and socially unthinkable for them to become single parents). An old lady in my parents' village used to say she had not seen a good prime minister since Mr Gladstone died (in 1898). From her talk, children – without television – heard of Gladstone and Disraeli before they heard of Churchill and Attlee.

People then were an inch and a half shorter and two inches smaller round the waist than us. We know this from private Marks & Spencer surveys conducted each decade. We are bigger thanks to three generations of better nutrition inaugurated during the war. The war generation, however, was healthier than its parents, despite the 1930s slump: seven men out of 10 passed as Grade 1 in Army fitness tests, compared with only 30 per cent in the First War.

Free wartime vaccination cut deaths from diphtheria and typhoid by half. When my generation was growing up, only a few years later, diphtheria was close to being eliminated. Pay for a 47-hour week rose much faster than inflation, from £2 13s (£2.65) in 1938 to £4 16s (£4.80) by VE Day. Income tax doubled from 25 to 50 per cent. Smoking quadrupled and drinking of alcohol doubled, despite shortages.

The UK's economic growth, at 25 per cent, was second only to the United States. The growth leader must have been the sheet music industry. The hundreds of songs which will be resung at events all over the country next weekend are breathtaking in the unbowed directness of their hope. I do not see how anybody of any generation can hear a song like 'When the Lights Go on Again All Over the World' without understanding their joy and without sadness at the fading of that hope.

Collectivism was the spirit of the period. The Conservative, Labour and Liberal coalition did not contest by-elections, but Labour – out of power for 14 years – was far ahead in most opinion polls. Conservatives like Quintin Hogg, the present Lord Hailsham's father, thought it urgent to 're-establish a social conscience in the party'.

But the true clue to the long-term future may have come in a survey by the group Mass Observation. Above all, above housing, social fairness or a national health service, people most longed for personal possessions after the war – cars, records, radios, watches. It was this hunger, long pent up by the post-war Labour government's continued rationing and austerity, which the Tories successfully offered to gratify in 1951. Now the 1945 generation, having borne all the costs of its war and tried to make a new world, is deep into pensionable age. It finds trouble, as the Age Concern chairman Sir Michael Drury has said, 'coping with a world of computers, plastic money, the loss of local shops, and a public transport system designed for gymnasts'. In its youth it elected Attlee and in its heyday Harold Wilson – but it long ago lost dominance. No politician appeals to its Dunkirk or blitz spirit, as Wilson used to, and the verities on which it was bred are scattered to the winds.

Attlee, as Churchill's deputy in the coalition government, retorted to his left-wing critic Harold Laski by saying, 'I have witnessed now the acceptance by all the leading politicians in this country, and all the economists of any account, of the conception of the utilisation of abundance. From 1931 onwards in the [Commons] I and others pressed this. It was rejected with scorn. It now colours all our discussions on home economic policy. There follows from this the doctrine of full employment in this country. The acceptance of this again colours our whole conception of the postwar set-up in this country . . .' Both Paul Addison, in *The Road to 1945*, and Angus Calder, in *The People's War*, were convinced into the 1970s that the Attlee doctrine, plus nationalisation, were immovable pillars of policy for any government.

Addison recanted three years ago, in a new epilogue to his book: 'I did not imagine that any government had the power to repeal the postwar settlement. I was wrong; society had changed . . . The brave new world of Attlee, Beveridge and Keynes was never the enduring structure it appeared to be. It was more like a Ministry of Works prefab, intended for some deserving couple at the end of the war. Mr and Mrs Tebbit (let us say) were extremely grateful at the time, and later on it was used by the council to provide emergency accommodation for the homeless. But finally it was bulldozed away, in spite of many pleas to preserve it as a memorial to a more civilised era; and with it there departed the essential wartime vision of a society in which the state maintained a framework of social justice and citizenship for all.' But time adds its own epilogues. If social change gives pain to social historians, it does likewise to politicians. Since Addison last wrote, opinion polls have indicated that the present government is the teeniest bit unpopular for aspects of its reversal of the postwar settlement. Last month, a Gallup survey for the Women's Royal Voluntary Service found that what people most miss about the war years is 'community spirit, people working together' (61 per cent); 'a time when people cared about each other' (52 per cent); and 'national pride' (47 per cent).

Anyway, the spirit of '45 was in many ways less pretentious, with more of a touch of bathos than Calder and Addison allow. Jim Hovell, an army officer-poet, wrote:

> *Those of us who are about to return home now,*
> *With our wedding tackle still in good condition . . .*
> *Must obviously be grateful*
> *That we've got through it, got off lightly*
> *Compared with some of the other poor sods.*

It also ran deeper. On 25 April 1945, the Rev George Chapman Watts wrote home from Belsen to his wife Dorothy: 'One remembers the British Tommy standing guard at the heart of that hell and working like a Trojan among the dying, the dead, the sick, the living. How can one ever forget him? If one speaks to him, he replies softly. He cannot quite trust himself to speak. He is quiet, but in his heart is a burning white flame which will never go out . . .

'You will be proud that you are of the English who stood alone and held the gate until the strength of all decent men could be gathered to crush this satanic power. You will be glad and proud that you sent me to help as far as I could in it all.

'You will know that forever those of us who had a part in it will oppose all tyranny, all brutality, all strength that crushes defenceless things, all absolute power . . . So put your hand in mine now and keep it there till I can come home.'

Even as we sit over television, fretting about whether we should be doing something in Rwanda or Bosnia, whether we could do anything without dropping our standards of living and losing more blood, 1945 is a lucky inheritance to have. ●

14 February 1995

Jonathan Steele

'Your wounds betray the torment of the nameless ones'

t was one of those unfortunate coincidences. As the Duke of Kent stepped forward to bow his head before the memorial to the thousands of German civilians killed by the Royal Air Force raids on this city 50 years ago, the drone of an approaching aircraft wafted over the trees.

It grew in volume, lingered for a moment above the crowd around the monument, and then mercifully faded away. Unintentionally, the plane taking off from Dresden's airport served as a reminder for a particular horror of the 20th century – murder from the air.

The Duke walked to the memorial down a long avenue marked by concrete plinths, which left no doubt about Germany's wartime atrocities. On one side stood the names of Auschwitz, Theresienstadt, Buchenwald and four other notorious death camps. On the opposite side, places where Germans killed hundreds of other innocents – Coventry, Leningrad, Lidice, Oradour, Rotterdam, Warsaw.

Three red tulips and a single candle marked the Coventry plinth.

The dignitaries did not stop until they reached the main memorial stone. On it was etched: 'How many died? Who knows the number? Your wounds betray the torment of the nameless ones, burnt here in a hell-fire lit by human hands.'

Charles Redman, the American ambassador, was the first foreigner to lay a wreath. The two British raids on Dresden had been followed within hours by an attack from US planes. Then the Duke took his turn. No words were spoken, although at an evening church service he came close to an apology with carefully chosen sentences: 'We deeply regret the suffering on all sides in the war. Today we remember especially that of the people of Dresden.'

Several hundred Dresden citizens, most old enough to be survivors of the raids, stood under the trees around the memorial, some in tears. Five elderly men and one woman shuffled forward with their own ring of flowers. 'We represent the association of those who were persecuted by the Nazi regime,' Gerhard Grabs, his cheeks sunken with age, and wearing a blue beret, explained as the crowd filtered away at the end of the brief ceremony.

'There are still 500 of us left in Dresden,' he said, with the justified pride of a minority. 'I was a social democrat, arrested in 1933. We distributed leaflets, helped people escape into exile in Czechoslovakia, and acted as couriers between here and there.'

The British raid on Dresden killed thousands of civilians. But it was a salvation for one small group. The RAF and American attack on Dresden hit the Gestapo building in the railway station where the last group of Jews was being held. They had German spouses, and had been spared until last.

On 14 February 1945, they were due to be deported to Auschwitz. The air raids blew out the doors of their prison and they were able to hide until May 1945, when the Nazi nightmare ended.

Some Britons in Dresden remained adamant yesterday. 'I have no doubts about it,' said Derek Jackson, who as a 19-year-old flight sergeant flew in the armada of Lancasters which destroyed Dresden. 'Dresden was a legitimate target, although obviously for the Dresdeners it was a very tragic thing.'

Mr Jackson, who chairs the Manchester branch of the Air Gunners' Association, conceded that he had been apprehensive about returning to Germany for the first time. 'But it's been marvellous. Three ladies took us to their flat and gave us tea. They blame Hitler for it all.'

Roman Herzog, the German president, took a cautious line at a ceremony in the Palace of Culture. There was no way to balance the books of guilt, and exonerate Nazi Germany because of Dresden. 'No one in this room intends to indict anyone or expects anyone to show remorse or indulge in self-accusation,' he said. 'Grief, remembrance and commemoration, but no accusation, no settling of accounts.'

Erna Schirme, an elderly woman in the crowd outside, was more eloquent. 'The raid was a scandal, but the bigger scandal was the choice of Hitler in 1933 which began it all.'

At an ecumenical service the Right Rev Simon Barrington Ward, the Bishop of Coventry, said: 'When the British and American air forces destroyed Dresden we had suppressed our moral principles.' •

* * *

29 July 1995
Edward Pilkington
Bomb casts shadow over three generations

Kensuke Ueki carries the Hiroshima bomb around with him like a birthmark. It's not just that he lost his left eye in the blast 50 years ago, aged 11 months, nor that he swallows an alarming number of pills every day to shore up his fragile constitution. The bomb and its aftermath are also deeply embedded in his character. They have turned him into a stubborn free thinker. The emperor, Kensuke says, should have been held responsible for starting the war, and hanged. He rues the traditional emphasis on obedience and respect for authority.

'The Japanese are very afraid of being controversial. I think my views are unique – maybe because my brain was damaged in the A-bomb.' Kensuke has an encyclopaedic knowledge of Dickens, which he teaches as English professor at Hiroshima University.

The Uekis' house was built on a hill overlooking the centre of Hiroshima in 1967. The main breadwinner then was Matsutaro Ueki, Kensuke's father, born in Hiroshima in 1911. Matsutaro still sleeps on a futon laid on a grass mat, rising at 6am. Dressed in a loincloth, he bows before a Buddhist shrine and prays for the soul of his wife, Mieko, who died last year. The rest of the day he spends reading and watering his cherished garden. He never has enough time, he laments, to prune the bonsai trees.

Matsutaro was brought up to think of the emperor almost as a deity. He no longer holds such beliefs, but has an enduring affection for the royals. He is sprightly for an 85-year-old, but since his wife's death he has grown increasingly anxious about the future of Japan. For 30 years he was head-teacher in a Hiroshima school, and had the reputation of being very 'disciplined', which in Japanese implies both strict and patriotic.

'One of my misgivings is that young people today seem to have so little respect for authority,' he says, blaming the US system of education introduced during the post-war occupation. 'They put all the emphasis on democracy and equal rights, nothing on respect.'

Matsutaro fought in the Japanese army during the war and spent more than a year in China. He accepts atrocities were committed but thinks the country has apologised enough. 'During the war the fundamental principle of our country was pride, and that's not such a bad thing. Many people have lost pride entirely and feel too guilty about what Japan did.' That kind of unreconstructed talk irritates his son, Kensuke. He believes Japan is still too preoccupied with rank and obedience and not sufficiently concerned with democratic debate.

The bomb dropped when Kensuke was a baby, lying in a basket at home. A shard of glass from a shattered window pane left him blind in one eye. He was teased about his disability at school and when he applied for university, he was told he would never make a scientist because of his partial sight. 'I refused to be browbeaten,' he says, 'and resigned myself to having to fight for what I wanted.'

Since his mother's death, he has taken over her informal family role as mediator between the generations. At meal times he struggles to handle the pace. For if there is a divergence of opinions between Kensuke and his father, there is a gulf between Matsutaro and his three grandchildren. The youngest member of the Ueki family is Kousuke, aged 21.

Kousuke gets up late, wears jeans and an earring, and spends hours watching baseball. He is studying to retake his university entrance exam next February. He has little idea what to do: maybe he will become a guide for English-speaking tourists, though he doesn't want to have to work too hard. He thinks the national obsession with careers, and working long hours to please the boss, is stupid.

His grandfather was shocked when Kousuke bleached his hair a shade of ox-blood. In turn, Kousuke is angered by his grandfather's old-fashioned table manners. 'That's not an international way to behave,' he complains when Matsutaro plies me with saki.

Konsuke admits Japan may be losing some of its culture by imitating the West. But he thinks European ways are on the whole preferable. 'I would rather risk losing our tradition than staying as we are.'

It would be foolish to portray the Ueki family as typically Japanese. But in their household, the tensions and contradictions in contemporary Japanese society are plain to see.

And yet there are points of harmony between the three generations. They are bound by ties of love and common history stronger than the centrifugal forces of modernity. On 6 August the Uekis will come together to mourn Hiroshima's dead. They will remember Kensuke's uncle, killed by the blast, aged 13. •

• •

5 June 1995

Julian Borger
Expert in maths and mortars

This diary is being written in a Sarajevo psychiatric clinic. Not, however, by a permanent inmate. I just came to plug in my computer.

Working as a visiting journalist in a city almost entirely without electricity demands the skills of a moth. It involves wandering the streets at night, tracking down sources of light, and being able to distinguish the lustre of a 40-watt bulb from a handful of candles.

Two lamps glowed weakly in the clinic's windows on Saturday evening, so I turned up yesterday morning and the doctor on duty gave me the use of the tiny room where she sleeps at night. It has a bed, a desk, a chair and a plug socket.

In exchange, I brought fruit and biscuits. The clinic has no money. The patients eat bread and soup brought from a nearby hospital, and the staff have only recently received their wages for last November: £40.

The Bosnian Serb leader, Radovan Karadzic, cut Sarajevo's power supply the weekend before last, just after the Nato airstrikes. But a small amount still trickles into the city. The government says this is provided by diesel generators, but it is one of Sarajevo's open secrets that there is a power-line running through a tunnel under the airport and up Mount Igman, beyond the west end of town.

The meagre power coming in over Igman is distributed according to priorities which say a lot about how wartime Sarajevo functions. The hospitals are still first in line. But the brightest beacon in the neighbourhood is the police station.

The power of the police has grown with every month of the war. It is not necessarily a bad thing: the wave of crime and lawlessness which afflicted the capital in 1992 and 1993 is now under control. But much of what the police do seems officious, irrelevant and even dangerous. I have been in a car which was stopped for speeding after tearing down Sarajevo's Sniper Alley. The policeman on duty was not prepared to accept bullet-avoidance as an excuse.

The other ways of securing electricity in Sarajevo are paying a bribe, or siphoning power from overhead cables. But the electricity corporation has a full-time team of power-busters who – like the journalists – are on the look-out for bright windows. It pays to have good connections (in every sense) and thick curtains.

I share my workroom with Sasa, the doctor's 13-year-old son, who is doing his maths homework on the other half of the desk. He is as sharp as a razor and had a rapid-fire series of questions about my computer. He is disappointed that my cheap machine cannot do graphics.

His father, a Serb, works in a psychiatric hospital in Sokolac, 30 miles to the east, having decided to escape Sarajevo and live with the rebels. Sasa stayed with his Muslim mother when war broke out and has not seen his father for three years.

He wants to know if I could take a letter, as the present crisis has interrupted a Red Cross service delivering letters across the lines. It is hard to be encouraging. The front line is about a mile away, but to get to the other side under present conditions, I would have to travel to the Adriatic coast, then up to the Croatian capital, Zagreb, then to Budapest for a Serbian visa, which would get me a day or two later to Belgrade, where I would have to wait for a Bosnian Serb permit to enter their territory.

The clinic we are in used to be a primary school and there are still pictures of happy, healthy, optimistic children painted on the windows.

There are few staff and nothing for the patients to do. They spend most of the day lying on their beds, huddled in blankets or staring at the ceiling. For their own safety, they are locked indoors. Shells regularly land in the district, and the clinic abuts a rat-infested rubbish dump, bloated by three years of siege.

After a couple of days' respite, the shelling began again yesterday morning, and at about 11am one landed close enough to make the windows rattle. Sasa ducked, the way the local schools teach their pupils. He was up in a second though, and gave his appraisal: a 120mm mortar falling about 100 or 200 metres away.

As it turned out, he was spot on. The mortar landed on an old meteorological station just around the corner. The war has blessed Sasa with some unusual but essential skills. His father would be proud. •

....

27 July 1995

Martin Woollacott
'No Allah, no UN, no Nato can save you. Only me.'

There is something worse than the death of individuals; the death of a community. This is the tragedy enacted so many times in Bosnia, and it is happening again today as the human debris of Zepa, where generation had followed generation in the fields, the mosque and the town, reaches refuge in government territory.

The sick and wounded, the women, children and elderly of the former United Nations 'safe area' in the east were sent on their way, they say, by General Ratko Mladic himself. The Bosnian Serb commander boarded some buses as the evacuation began.

'No Allah, no Un, no Nato can save you. Only me,' they say he told them. After Gen Mladic had demonstrated his power, and as Serb soldiers gave their three-fingered victory salute, they were driven away from the houses and farms they and their forebears had occupied for centuries.

Many hours later, some filed into a room at the Kosevo Hospital in Sarajevo – men and women with the lined, strong faces of those who have worked hard physically all their lives. The men, all aged over 60, were in shirt sleeves, or wore rough jackets and sometimes berets. Their forearms were knotted with muscle and dark from the sun. The women, including some in their thirties, wore long print skirts, blouses and headscarves. They were there to tell their stories to a couple of Bosnian policemen. A few reporters were present.

These people were among 160 refugees from Zepa who early yesterday reached Sarajevo in Serb buses with UN co-drivers, the first of thousands arriving in government-held territory. Others, squeezed aboard buses and cattle trucks, were dumped several miles from Kladanj, a frontline town in central Bosnia. They were headed for Zenica, where the UN has prepared facilities for 7,000 people.

By nightfall yesterday, more than 2,500 people of Zepa's population of 15,000 had been 'ethnically clensed' – the second mass expulsion by Bosnian Serbs in two weeks.

Of those who came to Sarajevo, some were wounded, a number with missing limbs, and are being treated in the hospital. Among them were children and grandchildren, in track-suit bottoms and trainers. They have the fair skins, blue eyes and good looks of Bosnians, but are subdued and perplexed. They do not smile when given bars of chocolate by our Sarajevo taxi driver, who had bought, with his own money, a large carton to bring to the hospital.

The formidable old men of Zepa had no atrocities to report during the evacuation. The move out of Zepa, in contrast with that from Srebrenica, seems so far to have been relatively orderly. No atrocities, that is, except the total destruction of their small and isolated society. They had a message for the world which they were determined to deliver. 'I want to put a claim against the UN, against the Security Council,' began Ejub Batric, aged 65, 'and against [the UN secretary-general] Boutros-Ghali, because a tremendous injustice has been done against us, and to speak to the British, Spanish and American public.'

The shaming litany of Bosnian complaint continued. 'We can read in Zepa,' one said. 'We are not stupid and we know about England and France, and we wish you democrats could go to Zepa now.' There was something moving in the spectacle of these men, some in their eighties, speaking up for a place that, even as they lectured in their deep, stern voices, was ceasing to exist.

Bicir Imamovic, aged 75, spoke of a Zepa lost. 'It was the most beautiful part of the season. The potatoes are big, all kinds of good vegetables are coming up . . . and we saw the Serbs come and walk over it.' They also saw Serbs burning houses and crops. 'I would have preferred they kept it for themselves, rather than to destroy it,' Mr Imamovic said. His friend mourned '100 kilos of the best tobacco' left behind.

The men spoke of a mosque more than 500 years old, and of the famous bridge and tower of Zepa – all still undamaged. 'But I am sure they won't last long,' Mr Batric said.

Everyone in the room had left relatives behind: the young men in the army and home guard, whose surrender Gen Mladic demands; and the families that may still be in the forest. Mustaf Mehmeddovic, who lost his tobacco, decided his frail and nearly blind wife could not survive much longer out in the open. 'Since we have been married nearly 50 years, I had to do this,' he said. Leaving the rest of his family, he carried his wife down to the Ukrainian UN positions, hoping to find some protection there. But the Ukrainians refused to let them, along with about 100 others, into the camp. Some were later taken on to the buses, including Mr Mehmeddovic, and his wife Sejda. When they married in 1946, he said, 'we never thought war would come again.'

'I have only him,' said Ziba, touching the shoulder of her son Muhiddin, aged 14, who lay awkwardly on the bed by her side. Her bold-featured face crumpled into tears. 'Look at this,' she cried. 'This is what I have *now*, when before we had our own house and land, I had my husband. *This* is where I am now.' This was a bare hospital cubicle, with its bed and chair, on which lay a packet of Malaysian combat rations, meant for Somalia.

Since May, Ziba's life has been smashed. Her husband was killed by a Serb sniper three months ago, when he was on home guard near his house. Then

Srebrenica, where Ziba's sister lived, fell. She has heard no news of her sister since.

After Srebrenica, the war, which had already ravaged Zepa in early 1993, returned with a vengeance, finally bursting through the narrow gorge which protects the town and its outlying villages. Shells fell in the fields, tracer shells set houses on fire, including Ziba's house set in three acres of land. They fled to relatives, but soon the fire reached there, and with her husband's rucksack on her back, one loaf and a bottle of water, Ziba and Muhiddin moved, like thousands of others, into the wooded, stony country above Zepa town.

For several days – Ziba does not remember how many – they slept under the trees. Then on Tuesday, looking down into the town, they saw buses, and the shell fire stopped.

At that point, Mujsira Elix, a neighbour of Ziba's, said: 'We knew something had changed.' Tentatively, the women and children moved down the hill. Mrs Elic's husband, Mustafa, came with her, determined to see her off. She does not know if she will ever see him again.

The women removed their rings and earrings, fearing that the Serbs would chop off ears and fingers to take their valuables. They left their Korans behind, lest the sight of the Holy Book enrage some soldier. With a change of clothes, and a pocketful of family photographs – a father sitting beside his conscript son in the days when Yugoslavia was one country; a family smiling around a laden table at some feast – they climbed on the buses.

The people of Zepa come from a race that has almost disappeared in northern Europe. They are peasants, who define themselves by land and place, farmers and foresters. Ziba has never been to Sarajevo, or further than Rogatica, a small town 25 miles from Zepa. As well as their lost and missing, they mourn the unmilked cows left in the stall, the crops left in the fields, the woodpiles cut last winter, the soil itself.

A week ago, in spite of the war, the people of Zepa belonged to something, something that had endured for centuries and which framed their lives. Now, although they are still Bosnians, they have joined the sad tribe of the dispossessed. ●

12 July 1995

Julian Borger

Lonely death in a crowded cornfield

In a crowd of more than 10,000 refugees sprawled across Tuzla's cornfields, a young woman hanged herself yesterday. No one knew her name. No one wept for her when her body was cut down from a tree, and only a single, bored policeman kept vigil over the corpse as it lay abandoned by the gate of the heaving, sweating camp.

She died in bare feet which protruded, white and muddy, from a thin blue blanket someone had draped over her. She had taken a black cloth belt from her dress and plaited it with a brown shawl into a makeshift noose. Its lethal loop was still fastened around her neck, and its brown-black tail snaked across her shroud.

She had been one of the scatterlings of Europe, torn away more than once from friends, relatives and familiar places. First, when the Serbs went on a killing spree in 1992. Now it had happened a second time, in Srebrenica, a place the United Nations had said was safe.

Most of the men had been imprisoned, girls dragged off refugee buses to be raped, and children lost in the panic. The crowd surged back and forth past the forgotten corpse. In its midst, a young woman was weeping and kneading her hands as she walked, an older one following a few paces behind.

'I told you to keep an eye on the children, I told you not to let them out of your sight,' the older one said.

The younger woman nearly buckled in misery. 'I know you did, but I can't do everything,' she cried.

A few hundred tents had been set up overnight, and the UN High Commissioner for Refugees (UNHCR) was sending a few thousand more, but most people in the camp had spent the night outdoors. They propped up improvised shelters by stretching blankets on leafy branches torn from trees. A few red fire trucks appeared and the crowd rushed to taps on either side to fill their water containers.

But apart from the cisterns and police, there was little sign of Bosnian government help. UN officials – much criticised for their apparent lack of preparedness for the flood of refugees – said the Bosnian government had not only failed to contribute to the relief effort, but had even hindered it.

They said that earlier in the week the UNHCR had earmarked a number of schools and warehouses to be used as temporary shelter if Srebrenica fell, but they had been refused permission to use them by the regional government acting on orders from Sarajevo.

Crowds of women and teenagers brought on trucks from Tuzla by Bosnian government officials blockaded UN bases in and around the town for much of this week, UN sources said.

'I think they were trying to make it impossible for the refugees to be brought from Srebrenica because that would mean the end of the enclave,' a senior UN military officer in Tuzla said.

'When it was clear people were going to be forced out, the government saw a symbolic value in heaping them all on the UN's lap.

'They could all have been easily dispersed to different shelters. This has created a problem,' he said.

No government official was available for comment yesterday, but it appeared the local authorities had relented in the face of the enormity of the problem. After negotiations between Bosnian officials, the UN and the UNHCR, by late afternoon six busloads of refugees could be seen moving from the UN camp at Tuzla's airfield towards the town.

But for those who remained, conditions were still desperate. Sefika Becirovic had spent the night with her two daughters on the edge of a maize field. Since being bussed out of Srebrenica early on Thursday morning they had had nothing to eat but a tin of beans handed out yesterday at dawn.

'Better to finish us off now than leave us like this,' Mrs Becirovic said. Her husband Abdullah was 60 and blind and deaf, but the Serbs had taken him anyway.

'I shouted at them to stop, but they told me to shut up or they would find some use for me as well. I said nothing and they took him,' she said.

Someone had told her he had been seen on one of the later buses. She had positioned herself directly opposite the airfield's main gate, in the hope that would give her the best chance of seeing him. She and her daughters, Sabaheta, aged 23, and Sadeta, aged 20, were put on a bus with other women and children to the frontline. They said Serb soldiers boarded the bus at a checkpoint, took their pick of women and dragged them off.

Sabaheta was saved by her luggage: 'They pulled me by my wrist but my bag wedged between the seats and I was blocked. So they took two other women, a girl of about 19 and a woman with a child who was crying for help.' That pattern was confirmed by many other eyewitness accounts.

Women and girls appear to have been pulled off buses by rebel soldiers as they crossed frontline checkpoints. Aid workers who talked to refugees said a pattern of systematic rape was emerging.

The Red Cross yesterday began trying to trace the missing people. By yesterday morning the flow of refugees across the frontline had stopped, leaving thousands of residents of Srebrenica unaccounted for. In the village of Ravne, 30 miles south of Tuzla, aid workers and Bosnian army soldiers waited in vain at the mouth of a narrow ravine for fresh waves of refugees to cross.

Alvin Gonzaga, a UNHCR worker manning a Land Rover at the scene said:

'Twelve thousand have crossed so far and there were thought to be between 30,000 and 40,000 people in Srebrenica before, so that's a lot of people missing.'

Thousands of men and boys from Srebrenica have been held in the Serb-held town of Bratunac, together with 60 Dutch UN peacekeepers. The 400 UN soldiers still in Srebrenica have refused to leave without the refugees.

The last report sent from the enclave by UN military observers late on Thursday night said the rebels had taken the UN outpost's armoured vehicles and equipment. It said that Bosnian Serb soldiers were systematically looting the town. The report, clearly written under strain, departed from the usual clipped military vocabulary to describe conditions at the outpost. 'The place really looks like a pigsty. The shit is even on the walls. The smell is unbearable and really an inhuman situation to live in for more days,' the reporter said.

'Tears were in our eyes when seeing the desperate displaced persons with no secure future looking at us and seeking help we cannot give them. We really lost this enclave and our heads. We feel very sad that we were not able to do more,' it said.

Srebrenica'a new Serb rulers were crowing over their victory. Bosnian Serb radio announced: 'Normality has been restored to "Free Srebrenica",' and broadcast a song which the presenter said was being sung throughout the enclave. It was a peasants' song, a wailing melody without discernible words chanted in men's voices.

A few minutes later, another song was played. Sounding like a football chant, its words were: 'Die you scum, the Serbs are the champions. Come out on to your balconies and hail the white Serb race.' •

Bodies
politic

23 June 1995
Simon Hoggart
Stalking horse becomes front runner

A t last we have the name of the stalking horse, and it's John Major. He arrived in the Downing Street garden, late, having had the pleasure of leaving the hacks to broil in the sun for half an hour. Over in the lobbies the news was already spreading like an oil slick in the North Sea.

'I have good news and bad news,' said a Labour MP. 'John Major has resigned. Cheers! The bad news is, he's still Prime Minister. Booo!'

He arrived in the blue spotted tie he wears for historic occasions. As he opened his mouth to speak, the bell at Horse Guards Parade began to toll, very slowly. He started with dignity, but as so often, became peevish by the end. 'It is time to put up or shut up. I have nothing more to say,' he added, aligning himself firmly with the 'shut up' camp, and turning on his heel.

We should have guessed. Earlier, at Prime Minister's Questions, he had been poised and confident, like someone who has had the weight of a difficult decision taken from him. He even offered one – perhaps final – Majorism. Terrorism, he ringingly declared, 'is *unpleasant* and should be resisted.'

He spoke elegiacally about Sir Patrick Mayhew, the Northern Ireland Secretary, who had taken the extraordinary step of writing to the newspapers in his support. 'My right honourable friend is an honourable friend in every sense of the word,' he said. 'Few men have been blessed with better friends . . .' It was sounding like a funeral oration, but we'd got the wrong funeral.

Finally a rare sighting of a John Major joke, about nepotism in Monklands council: 'Their personnel department was more like a family planning department!' He drove back to Downing Street to polish up – not so much a suicide note, as his cry-for-help memo.

In the Chamber, Labour was covering itself with rage, like plastic veneer. You know the lads are making it up when they go on about the royal family. John Austin Walker (Woolwich) demanded: 'This is an important constitutional matter. Has Her Majesty the Queen been informed?' – as if he cared. Stephen Dorrell answered for the Government; he just happened to be there. He slipped easily into the pompous march-of-history mode.

The Chamber was full of survivors of scandals: Jonathan Aitken, Graham Riddick, Steve Norris, Alan Duncan – suddenly looking like figures from the distant past, as if on the page of yellowing newspapers.

Someone tried to keep the mood of excitement by crying 'I Spy Strangers!', the traditional way of obliging the House to sit *in camera*.

It made little difference. MPs poured out to the real centres of power. On College Green, the scrap of lawn opposite the House, I counted 108 people milling about, conducting or granting interviews.

Back in the corridors of impotence, one of the grandest of the Grandees admitted: 'I wouldn't be surprised if nobody ran against him.' Twenty yards away, on the Terrace, Norman Lamont was drinking wine, alone but not unaccompanied. Plotters hovered around him like plump dragonflies. Others were lurking in the corridors and crannies. 'Lurk before you leap' has always been the motto of serious Tory conspirators. •

23 June 1995

Hugo Young
The only thrilling thing he has ever done

In the circumstances, it is a brilliant coup. The circumstances are bad, and one's standards may be low, but this is a weak Prime Minister not a strong one, and in his weakness he has shown a boldness that may be the only way to give him strength.

He hasn't invented a contest, merely accelerated one that was bound to happen anyway. He is doing it on what might be called his own terms, not other people's, and by so doing has deprived the Tory Party of another five months' luxuriating in indecision. They must decide here and now whether they are friend or enemy. It is the only thrilling thing this leader has ever done, and it may save him.

The first people his *coup de théâtre* wrong-foots are those closest to him, the Cabinet. Their feelings will be mixed. For Michael Heseltine, anything that keeps Mr Major in place is a problem; for Michael Portillo a relief. The one must move now or never; the other must wildly prefer not to move at all until the people have spoken one more time.

By acting now, with managers swiftly in place and the whole 1922 executive, which includes some strong Euro-sceptics, apparently pledged in support, Major compels a show of unambiguous Cabinet unity. There are no hidden sub-texts. They did the same first time round for Mrs Thatcher, of course, and much good it did her. But now there's no sense that any of them, except perhaps one, has a secret agenda he's waiting to unfurl. Such enemies as the leader has around him need him rather badly to win.

To lose, he needs first to be challenged. There will surely be a challenge. How could Norman Lamont or any other hardline Euro-phobe look himself in the face if he let this chance pass by?

One thing the gambit means is that there will not be another. For a politician who believes Conservatism is betraying the nation, it is now or never. Believing with such un-Conservative passion in their cause, the phobes know that if Major, declining to bow to their extreme demands, is given a free run now, nobody will need to take them seriously again.

We come swiftly to the middle-minded masses. Not all the head-counts and all the polls of the last few months have told us what they will do now. Time has run out sooner than many of them wanted. Flirting with scepticism, toying with hypotheses, musing about dream-tickets: these playful pastimes must abruptly resolve themselves into the counting of majorities.

For the backbench masses, Europe is not the issue, but survival. They call themselves the most sophisticated electorate in the world. In a farmyard of headless chickens, this is an ambitious claim. But assuming intelligence hasn't entirely vanished, which way will it take them?

Logic must support the leader's offer to continue. It is an old logic, impatiently contemplated as the polls have collapsed, but never overturned. It says that Major is the best Prime Minister we've got because anybody else would come with hands dripping blood: maybe not Major's blood, but the product of internecine savagery that will certainly attend any second-round contest.

By acting now, Major has reinforced this logic. Compared with 1990, there is now no Major where Major was: no convenient middle-way resort between the Heseltine/Clarke option and the Portillo. Gillian Shephard is a joke. Ian Lang will lose his seat. There is no escape from the left/right, Euro/anti-Euro choice, no bolt-hole from which an abstaining MP, hoping to wound but not openly to strike the leader, can hope to extract a sudden saviour. Choosing to ditch Major now is opting for another choice many would hate to have to make.

By presenting now, moreover, he's wiped away one of the more insidious cases against him, which says that he is chronically indecisive. No Tory leader before him has done what he did yesterday, unless we count Ted Heath's unwilling frogmarch to the scaffold in 1975. Major may be cautious, he may be a balancer, he may lack charisma and machismo, but no-one can say again he hasn't got balls.

I think, in the end, that logic will prevail. But it cannot be certainly relied on. At 35 points behind, any MP needs to be pretty sure there's no better alternative before casting his vote for the status quo.

The Heseltine life buoy, if it could be launched, will be seductive to the school that says any gamble is worth taking in such a crisis. The Portillo raft, however, would sink at first contact with the water. One thing this contest, if there is one, will disclose is the severe limit of support enjoyed, at this stage, by a man whose main attraction is disengagement from Europe. Perhaps the greatest gain Major sees is that one. His enemies, the ultra Euro-sceptics, have acted as though both his fate and the party's depends on his Europe policy. By showing that he remains some kind of master, he spikes their personal venom and their policy obsession at the same time.

If he survives, this will hardly produce a united Tory Party. The division of opinion about a serious matter will not go away. Europe is not something that can be smoothed into obscurity, although the intensity with which it is fought over at this moment, many months before the issue needs to be put to a decisive question, betrays how this party has abandoned the last particles of commonsense.

Victory for Major would be only a temporary truce. But it would get a massive distraction out of the way. It would clear the air of poison if not argument. What the man says is true. With the sniping and the incessant speculation, government has become an impossibility. In 30 years it has never been more chaotic. By acting in this way, part weary part enraged, he has done his party a favour. And so he has the country. ●

11 November 1994

Joanna Coles
Smart guide to surviving in the sleaze spotlight

Barely a week goes by now without another sultan of sleaze being caught in the cross-hairs of tabloid sharpshooters. Honourable members look more vulnerable than sitting ducks at a fairground shooting gallery. The spectre of David Mellor conducting a panic-stricken round robin on the nation's breakfast shows raises the question of what *does* one do when the lurid spotlight of tabloid attention sweeps on to one's latest misdemeanour. Do you confess or not? Should you make a statement or shut up? Should you parade your family, or face the press alone?

In order to answer these bewildering questions, I have compiled a Cut Out and Keep Survivor's Guide to Sleaze. I have canvassed advice from the nation's leading practitioners of the art, both of damage infliction and damage limitation.

Our experts are: David Banks, a former editor of the *Daily Mirror* and now editorial director of the Mirror Group; Quentin Bell, chairman of the Public Relations Consultants' Association and head of the Quentin Bell Organisation, whose clients include British Telecom, BP and Norwich Union; Mark Borkowski, a showbusiness PR whose clients include Robbie Coltrane, Gary Glitter and the Australian Rugby League team; and Max Clifford, the celebrity PR whose clients have included Derek Hatton, Pat Cash and Antonia de Sancha.

Martin Argles

William Waldegrave

Each expert was asked for his professional advice if confronted with the following dilemmas:

You are a backbench MP. You are having an illicit love affair and you suspect the tabloids are about to expose it. What should you do?

Banks: Say absolutely nothing. Ever. Explain yourself only to your family. Rule One: It will always blow over.

Bell: Admit it. Issue an immediate statement to the Press Association saying you're sorry. The basic rule is always to be open and honest. Take the press by surprise and include an extra nugget that they didn't know about. Then refuse to talk about it again. Paddy Ashdown got it right. Speak up, then shut up and sod off on holiday.

Borkowski: Use the media as a confessional. Hold a press conference, then select one broadsheet and give them the only interview. Then disappear.

Clifford: Cover your tracks. Justify any time you spent together by saying the two of you were involved in charity work. Try to get the wife to confirm she was there too, that will stop the paper from printing anything. And never try to blame others like the media.

Despite your best efforts, your paramour decides to sell her story. What should you do?

Banks: Stay silent and maintain a dignified but wounded countenance. The story will run for a maximum of three days if it's a daily paper, or two weekends if you fall foul of a Sunday. Rule Two: Always choose your friends carefully.

Bell: Get an injunction. Threaten to sue. Robert Maxwell was brilliant at it.

Borkowski: Find out how much she's being paid and double it. Whatever it costs, bite the bullet and buy her silence.

Clifford: Hire me. You need a specialist to handle this. Then talk to a sympathetic journalist like Jonathan Dimbleby, who will put your side of the story. Say you were overstressed as an MP and it just happened, and now you desperately want to make things up with the wife and be left alone.

To make matters worse, you were in a similar position two years ago and now history looks about to repeat itself.

Banks: Assuming you were contrite last time and apologised for 'letting down my wife, family and constituents', you have no option but to resign. A silly mistake has become serial adultery. If last time you insisted that everyone could get stuffed, that it was nobody's business but your own, and you want to let the voters decide, then fine. That's democracy. Rule Three: Be consistent.

Bell: State it as it is. Don't lie because they'll find you out. Never use your family as props in the drama, it will rebound. Don't be seen to court the media either. Be open, but you must control the situation. Don't give an exclusive, all the others will misquote it. Give one statement, to everybody, then get out of town.

Borkowski: Get the wife photographed on the arm of an attractive man to suggest she is not the downtrodden, betrayed victim she may appear to be. Embark on a serious amount of community service in your constituency. Hire a ghost writer for your political memoirs and start looking for another job.

Clifford: Cover your tracks. Always bring in charity and the wife and suggest you were all working together on a charitable project. Then do an exclusive interview, preferably with the three of you. Never give a press conference because it's so easy for your comments to be taken out of context.

You are a politician and have agreed to ask a question in the House for a fat fee. You discover a broadsheet is out to expose you. What should you do?

Banks: Resign. You are a crook and should not hold office. Rule Four: Political life and the respect of the community ought, unfortunately, to be its own modest reward – and £1,000 is a paltry price for your political virtue.

Bell: Resign.

Borkowski: Contact a charity, ask them to confirm publicly that they received the money on your behalf and then send them a cheque for three times the amount. Use the media as confessional and charity for absolution.

Clifford: Insist any payment went to charity then set about proving it.

Finally, it was an oversight on your part, of course, but you forgot to disclose a company directorship and now a fellow director is threatening to mention this indiscretion to a tabloid.

Banks: Resign. Years spent in the House denouncing those taking money from the state while secretly moonlighting and defrauding the public by contributing to the black economy should tell you that you cannot do the same thing yourself.

Bell: Admit it. Say you're sorry and you won't do it again.

Borkowski: Ask him to reflect on the damage it will do the company. Insist you will declare it at the next opportunity.

Clifford: Threaten to blackmail him. Find a skeleton in his closet and threaten to exaggerate it. It happens all the time. Always fight fire with fire.

Embargo-breaking copies of the Guide have already been sighted in the Tory whips' office, ready for distribution as part of their new Safe Sleaze campaign. But the contradictory advice contained goes to show that for sleaze, there is neither a safe prophylactic, nor an effective stain remover. ●

23 May 1995

Simon Hoggart

Wiggin's apology for an apology

Dennis Skinner was the first MP to recover. As the Speaker finished, he shouted into the silent House: 'Is that it? Has he got away with it?'

And he had. With one bounder, he was free. Sir Alf 'Jerry' Wiggin had escaped. He can now walk through summer meadows, drink the heady wine of liberty, and table amendments in whatever name he pleases. It was sad to see Ms Boothroyd join the ranks of those who just don't get it, who don't realise the degree of contempt, disgust and despair so many ordinary electors now feel about Parliament.

We are told that Mr Wiggin had apologised to her in person (she must have been wearing her silver-buckled 'lick-me shoes'), and had later suffered the humiliation of having to apologise to the whole of the House. But there is no humiliation in grovelling before this lot. Who could possibly have any sense of self-abasement or chagrin at having to apologise in front of such people. As well expect Vinnie Jones to feel contrite for kicking an opponent's shin.

This was, we were supposed to accept a professional foul, something which would be understood by everyone else in the game. Of course he had taken money to promote a private interest. Of course he had hidden it by tabling an amendment in the name of another MP, whose permission he hadn't troubled to seek. But, hey, who doesn't?

Before his 'apology' Mr Wiggin had to sit through a lacklustre statement on competitiveness from Michael Heseltine. Once again, The President was saved by his opposite number, Jack Cunningham, who at one point in his rant appeared to be blaming the Government for the improvement in the Chinese economy.

If Mr Blair gets his way, and, instead of having them voted in, is able to appoint his own shadow cabinet – consisting, for the most part, of Mr Peter Mandelson – will Mr Cunningham last more than five minutes? I do not know; I merely ask the question.

Mr Wiggin waited. He knotted his fingers together. He embraced his sides with his arms crossed over, as if wearing an invisible strait-jacket. He glowered glumly up at the press gallery. You'd have thought he was in some kind of trouble.

Finally the moment came. The statement was a classic of its kind. What he had done, he confessed, was 'at odds with the proper expectations of the House'. If Mr Wiggin was leaving someone's house, and a cascade of silver fell out of his coat, he would say that this was 'at odds with the proper expectations of my hostess'.

Suspicions had been voiced, he said, ('Oh, surely not, Heaven forfend!' nobody was heard to cry) that he had done this to avoid declaring a financial interest. 'There was no intention to deceive. But I accept that my actions were open to other interpretations . . .'

It sank gently in that Sir Alf was not apologising for what he had done, but for something which might have been misinterpreted as being wrong. He had, you might say, merely been borrowing the silver for a dinner in aid of paraplegic Romanian orphans.

Personal statements are traditionally heard in silence, which made it easier for us to hear the murmurs of disbelief from the Labour benches.

The Speaker said she trusted this was the 'last distasteful occasion' on which she would have to inquire into the conduct of a member. I doubt it. If she cannot set their moral compass, who else is likely to try? ●

• •

21 January 1995

Will Hutton
The State We're In: Wrench this place apart

Britain's national affairs are reaching explosive levels of stress. The individualist, *laissez-faire* values which imbue the economic and political élite have been found wanting – but with the decline of socialism, there seems to be no coherent alternative.

The Conservative response is to intensify the policies sending the economy and society towards the ultimate free market. The New Right lobby in the party, the press and the business establishment hold up some combination of Hong Kong and the United States as the ideal economic model – and urges that a minimal welfare state, low taxation and little business regulation would allow the economy to take off into a virtuous circle of capitalist dynamism.

However, for a European country of 60 million people, this is a chimera. Capitalism requires the profit motive and a go-getting individualism if it is to function, but it also takes place within inherited social and political boundaries. It is not just that capitalism needs rules to function effectively; the firms that are its life-blood are social as well as economic organisations. They are formed by human beings with human as well as contractual claims upon each other, and behind this social world lies the moral domain. Unless this is recognised, economic performance is likely to be unsatisfactory.

For what binds together the disorders of the British system is a fundamental amorality. It is amoral to run a society founded on the exclusion of so many people from decent living standards and opportunities; it is amoral to run an economy in which the only admissible objective is the maximisation of shareholder value; it is amoral to run a political system in which power is held exclusively and exercised in such a discretionary, authoritarian fashion. These exclusions, while beneficial in the short-term to those inside the circle of privilege, are in the long run inefficient and ultimately undermine the wealth-generating process.

Like a Russian doll, the task of reform has many layers. We need employment, which requires more capital stock and higher investment, which will be the most effective instrument for the social objective of bringing the marginalised back into the fold. And that in turn will involve the redistribution of income, perhaps even of work. Yet all these measures depend upon a recognition that rights – to consume now, to pay as little to the commonweal as possible, to satisfy desires instantaneously – must be accompanied by responsibilities. Without lower consumption there can be no investment for the future; without taxation there can be no infrastructure of public support from which all benefit.

Corrective economic and social policies and institutions that embody them presuppose a system of values; and that demands a political constitution in which public values and common interests can be defined.

This implies nothing less than the root and branch overhaul of the Westminster version of democracy. If markets require boundaries and rules of the game, they must be set by public agency – but if such intervention is disqualified by the belief that any public action necessarily fails, then the initiative cannot even reach first base. The state must act to assert common purpose; but unless the state enjoys legitimacy and expresses the democratic will, it can make no such claim.

The constitution of the state is vital not only for its capacity to express the common good but also as the exemplar of the relationship between the individual and the wider society. The extent to which the state embodies trust, participation and inclusion is the extent to which those values are diffused through society at large.

What is needed is the development of a new conception of citizenship. If a well-functioning market economy requires skilled workforces, strong social institutions like schools and training centres, and a vigorous public infrastructure, these cannot be achieved if the governing class cannot understand the values implicit in such bodies. And if creative companies orchestrate the voices of all stakeholders into a common enterprise, embodying such a conception in company law is impossible if the state is genetically programmed to view the business of governance as the exercise of sovereignty, and the duty of the governed to obey.

To break out of this cycle of decline and to build co-operative institutions, Britain must complete the unfinished business of the 17th century and equip itself with a constitution that permits a new form of economic, social and political citizenship. Economic citizenship will open the way to the reform of our financial and corporate structures; social citizenship will give us the chance of constructing an intelligent welfare state based on active solidarity; and political citizenship opens the way to political pluralism and genuine co-operation. This idea of citizenship could subsume differences of gender and race, and instil a sense of obligation to our natural environment.

Yet no state in the 20th century has ever been able to recast its economy, political structures and society to the extent that Britain must do, without suffering defeat in war, economic collapse or revolution. Only traumatic events on that scale delegitimise the existing order to such an extent that a country concedes the case for dramatic change.

In this respect Britain's prospects must be viewed with great caution. The royal state is deeply embedded. The network of City institutions, public schools, regiments, landed estates and boardrooms that forms the Conservative base is no less entrenched. Opting out and the excuse of choice have become almost unchallengeable ideological pieties. The market-based financial system, unregulated labour market and minimalist welfare state now form an interlinked whole. The culture of the *rentier* governing class has the confidence that comes from being developed over generations.

The Conservative Party, the defender of this order, has become accustomed to power and has constructed an effectively hegemonic political position. Its supporters control most of the press and have a growing influence on television. The public schools turn out cohorts of Conservative supporters who staff the upper echelons of business and finance and are educated to believe in the superiority of the private, the self-regulated and the voluntary. They have little sense of the commonweal or responsibility to their fellow citizens and they can be relied on to echo the general party line to the letter. The sense that civil society needs to be protected from 'bureaucratic' intervention and regulation is strong. Any constructive suggestion involving public action is dismissed as 'socialist'.

But there is the ground for a guarded optimism. It may be that Britain, the first country to establish parliamentary democracy and modern industry, could become the first country to transform itself peacefully without the spur of some national disaster. The Conservative establishment may be hegemonic but its spectacular failure to create the good society may finally leave it defenceless against the forces of change. In any case, the looming economic and social difficulties – ranging from the growing army of marginalised adult men without work to the chronically underfunded public infrastructure – while not as catastrophic as defeat in war, are going to be traumatic enough. If this is the best 20 years of Conservative government can do, then perhaps even Middle England by the next election will concede that there is a case for change.

Indeed the crisis of Conservatism is more deep-seated and threatening to its internal cohesion than is commonly recognised. Part of the reason for its extraordinary political dominance is that it has been extraordinarily successful. Until the 1990s the party managed to avoid the blame for the great devaluations of the century, and rode both the booms of the 1950s and the 1980s. Yet in the 1990s it too at last was stuck with the humiliation of devaluation when the pound dropped out of the ERM. It is obvious that the subsequent recovery has come despite, rather than because of, the policies of the Conservative Party. Suddenly it is no longer the party of economic competence.

The totems that lend it non-political appeal as the guardian of Middle England – the royal family, Britain as Great Power, the aristocracy, the Church of England – are all themselves disintegrating. The party has even considered abolishing counties and county towns – an important source of its own social power – in its quest to centralise the state. It is becoming self-destructive.

The coalition that the party represents is under enormous pressure. The pro-European Christian Democratic wing is uncomfortable with the grudging approach to Europe and the zeal to privatise everything, while many working-class supporters, plunged into poverty and distress, are recognising that the party of land and high finance is no friend of the working class. With the collapse of scientific socialism as an animating ideology, and of the Soviet Empire, the excuses for the party's cynicism and lack of public morality are greatly reduced. The implosion of the Back to Basics campaign revealed a deeper malaise.

At the same time the evidence that change is necessary becomes ever more compelling. The multiplying abuses of the political system – patronage, politicisation of the Civil Service, secrecy, poor scrutiny of legislation, centralisation – are all becoming actively dysfunctional. The patronage state has diminishing legitimacy and the centralised state is overloaded.

Nor is the crown, which sanctifies the semi-feudal state, any longer wholly secure. Already this century, in the abdication crisis of Edward VIII, the system has come close to failure as an individual monarch fails to match the impossible moral standards of the institution. That episode may prove to have been the forerunner of greater change. Without a set of written constitutional obligations or democratic legitimacy, the royal family has to rely on its unimpeachable behaviour for its continuing legitimacy – and this is beyond the capacity of any family to guarantee. The enchantment radiated by the institution has been shattered by the all too human failings of Elizabeth II's children and their spouses, and it seems unlikely that the monarchy can survive unchanged. It is difficult to see how renewed legitimacy for the dynasty can be achieved without a new constitutional settlement.

Social cohesion is deteriorating year by year. The combination of repression, poorly paid work and moral sermons offered by the right as a solution is no answer to reasonable demands for decent working and living conditions, whose erosion is indissolubly linked with the rise of crime, drugs and violence. There comes a point, as with the collapse of apartheid, where even the theorists of a bankrupt ideology are compelled to recognise its non-correspondence with reality.

In this respect the country is at a turning point like those of the 1630s, 1680s, 1830s, 1900s and 1940s. In each of these periods there was a conflation of economic, social and political crises which forced the decaying network of institutions to admit new demands for inclusion and participation. Indeed, after the great exception of the Civil War, the hallmark of English life has been the capacity to organise such transformations peacefully – forming an historical memory of reformist change.

For the opposition parties, especially Labour, this is both an opportunity and a fearful responsibility. They must continue the progressive tradition in British life. But the demands of the present situation are very great, and require unusual imagination and subtlety. The limited constitutional reforms of the Liberal government at the turn of the century, and the economic and social reshaping of British capitalism by the 1945–51 Labour government, have to be reprised, but this time simultaneously and in contemporary guise, for the two are interdependent necessities.

With sufficient political creativity the coalition to sustain such a momentous political initiative could be constructed. In industry and commerce there is growing support for a focus on the values of production rather than finance. At the time of writing, one or two major companies are considering donations to Labour – unheard of for a generation. Every English region outside the Home Counties, together with Scotland and Wales, wants more power to govern its own affairs. Within the 30/30/40 society (see panel), there is a comfortable majority that would benefit from a less unfair, less insecure and more equitable society who might be prepared to enter a new social compact. Within the ranks of the marginalised and insecure, the majority for change is overwhelming, and it is extending into the privileged 40 per cent, alarmed by the society they see around them. Women are being radicalised by the struggle to reconcile the responsibilities of work and family with little support – and younger women especially are recognising that Conservatism is no ally in meeting their needs.

The 30/30/40 Society

Society is dividing before our eyes, opening up new social fissures in the working population. The first 30 per cent are the *disadvantaged*. These include the more than four million who are out of work, including those who do not receive benefit or have not looked for work – within official definitions – and so do not count as officially unemployed. It also includes unemployed women, and women who cannot work because the loss of their husband's income support would more than offset their wage. This 30 per cent, under stress and with their children poorly fed, are the absolutely disadvantaged.

The second 30 per cent are made up of the *marginalised* and the *insecure*, a category defined not so much by income as by its relation to the labour market. People in this category have insecure working conditions and have been at the receiving end of the changes blowing through Britain's offices and factories. There are now more than five million people working part-time, 80 per cent of them women. Then there are those with insecure but full-time work, unprotected through the growth of casual employment and fixed-term contracts.

The last category is that of the *privileged* – the just over 40 per cent whose market power has increased since 1979. These are the full-time employees and the self-employed who have held their jobs for over two years, and the part-timers who have held theirs for more than five years. The 31 per cent of the workforce still represented by trade unions generally fall into this category.

It is this segmentation of the labour market that is sculpting the new and ugly shape of British society. The fact that more than half the people in Britain who are eligible to work are either living on poverty incomes or are in insecure work has had dreadful effects on the wider society. Britain has the highest divorce rate and the most de-regulated labour market in Europe, and these two facts are closely related. The impact of inequality is pervasive, affecting everything from the vitality of the housing market to the growth of social security spending.

This groundswell of dissent is diffuse and so far has no clear political voice. Yet the Labour Party cannot hope to articulate it merely by inviting each element of the dissident coalition to sink its differences and sign up to be members of Labour's still tribal identity. Instead each component of a new coalition needs to be respected for its own integrity. This is the politics of pluralism.

Reconstructing the state and economy cannot be the preserve of one political party with a simple majority in the House of Commons; it needs many allies in Parliament and in society at large. Already the Labour Party, in signalling its willingness to change its own constitution and rewrite Clause 4, has made an important step towards widening its appeal. A party that cannot rewrite and modernise its own constitution can hardly pretend to do the same for the state. But beyond that there is an urgent need to broaden its political base and seek allies wherever it can.

For the task is nothing less than the country's renewal, which requires a full-hearted mandate. A written constitution; the democratisation of civil society; the republicanisation of finance; the recognition that the market economy has to be managed; the upholding of a welfare state that incorporates social citizenship; the construction of a stable international financial order beyond the nation state. These achievable reforms must be accomplished if the dynamism of capitalism is to be harnessed to the common good. ●

The State We're In by Will Hutton (Jonathan Cape, £16.99).

....

3 April 1995

Patrick Wright
Can the centre hold?

I arrived in Lichfield on Friday evening, in time to hear the Staffordshire County Choir and Orchestra, made up of peripatetic music teachers, deliver a much-appreciated performance of Vaughan Williams's Sea Symphony in the cathedral. Earlier that day, Jeremy Hanley had tried to brace the ailing Tory Party with a Blair-proof vision of Middle England. And now here was John Wilson, a Labour man who had invited me to this fine provincial event as chairman of Lichfield's Samuel Johnson Society, suggesting that this small Midlands city had been recognised as Middle England long ago by its most famous 18th-century scion. Johnson described the inhabitants as 'the most sober, decent people in England', who spoke 'the purest English' and were 'the genteelest in proportion to their wealth'. He brought Boswell here to show him 'genuine civilised life in an English provincial town'.

At the reception afterwards, Staffordshire's chief education officer talked of how pleased he was to have preserved 'the core of the county music service', leaving one of his Labour committee members to emphasise just how furious the school governors and parents had been in its defence. It was estimated that Staffordshire's education service would be £34 million better off if it were funded on the 'financially gerrymandered' basis that the Government applies in Surrey and the South-east.

The mayor of Lichfield, Terry Finn, had been in the front row with his gold chain, leading the applause as a mayor should. As a Tory, however, he revealed himself to be none too confident about the approaching local elections. He talked about the need to 'defend the historic centre' against inappropriate development, and was inclined to stand at a distance from government policy. This is 'a Conservative town,' he said, 'but we are having a difficult time. We work for the local population.' But the national Tory Party doesn't always help: 'There are times when we throw our hands up in horror.'

It is a disappointing truth about Middle England that a terrible transformation overcomes its centres on Friday and Saturday night. By 11pm, the youths are out putting traffic cones on the statues, leaving piles of regurgitated vindaloo outside the heritage shops, and then perhaps going on to ram-raid the Co-op. A lot of shops in Lichfield have been burgled recently, but this prosperous rural city also suffered something resembling a riot a few months ago. So the police were strongly in evidence, patrolling the parks, or sitting in strategically placed cars as they surveyed the shrieking, drunken crowds spilling out of the pubs.

These people, be they the disaffiliated young or soldiers from the nearby barracks, had hardly even got a familiar expletive to spare for John Major. Those I approached snorted at the very idea of Middle England, even as it looked back at them aghast from the lounge bar of the more sedate hotels.

Early on Saturday morning the traders were setting up their stalls in the market square. Over the years these small-scale entrepreneurs have provided both Thatcher and Major with many of their more homely economic metaphors; but here, too, Lichfield proved remarkably resistant to Jeremy Hanley's call. The garment trader Mohinder Singh Chohan quite liked Middle England, but thought the Tories were another matter. 'They've got no ideas,' he said, and 'it would be good for the country for them to go.' Business was bad and 'if you can't put things right in 15 years, there is a problem,' he said, quickly adding the disclaimer: 'I'm not a socialist.' He had come to Britain from the Punjab in 1962, convinced that England 'was the best country in the world'. But the Tories nowadays 'only look after multi-millionaires, and are the party of political corruption . . . I hate them,' he said in conclusion.

The man at the bread stall agreed, John Major was out of touch. 'I don't think they've got a prayer.' As for the market trade, that was going down the pan. 'It's all out-of-town shopping centres, and Americanisation and wine bars; everything trendied up with "have a nice day" and all that cobblers.' He wasn't a socialist either, but he would like to see a Labour government – adding that, 'They've got to get rid of the Red Robbo syndrome.' It galled him to think that he would be better off on the dole – like Mr Singh, he had no time for people with 'no intention of graft'.

After talking to a furrier and a second-hand book dealer, both of whom had definitely known better times, I moved on to Beacon Park, which certainly resembled a bastion of the old municipal values John Major seeks to revive: well-stocked flowerbeds, and an imposing bronze statue of a naval hero. Commander Edward John Smith looks out over a bowling green and a cast-iron fountain dedicated to 'the citizens of Lichfield' by a public-spirited benefactor in 1871.

The inscription on Commander Smith's monument commemorates his 'brave life' and 'heroic death', and urges the onlooker to 'Be British'. All this would surely serve to lift the hearts of Jeremy Hanley and John Major – except that Commander Smith turns out to have been the captain of the *Titanic*, and his statue is said only to be here because other towns, with which Smith was more truly associated, refused to have it.

The two elderly ladies resting on a nearby bench turned out to be cousins, just visiting from Walsall. Middle England had been important enough during the war, when many munitions factories were here. But what about John Major? Well, 'I'm disappointed in him, very disappointed.'

The yardstick, according to Mrs Sutton, was the vandalism. Arriving in the park, she had been horrified to find that one of the four stone lions around the fountain had been tipped up from its plinth and pushed into the pool. Dismayed, she observes that her doormat had also been stolen recently, saying: 'I'd have given it to them if they really wanted it.' Like Thatcher, Major goes on about law and order, but time had long since proved him to be capable of nothing but talk.

Major may have proposed compulsory identification cards, but both Mrs Sutton and Miss Ware pressed for stronger remedies: 'They ought to bring back the birch . . . and hanging.' And yet if these elderly cousins no longer went out in the evenings, it was not just vandalism and violence that had 'spoilt our little bit of pleasure'. The buses have been curtailed too, and the service on which they relied was now over by 6pm. So they turned to the thought of Tony Blair, whom they reckoned to be 'a decent man – just like John Smith was'.

By this time, a couple of men have come up from the bowling green. Having removed the hurled cider bottles of the night before and trod down the malevolently gouged turf, they too yearned for stricter discipline: 'They don't come back to the birch twice,' said one, adding that 'there are too many do-gooders in the world'. But they too drew up a long way short of modern conservatism. Asked about John Major, they deplored the firms which have squandered the pension funds of their employees. They were adamant that even the big supermarkets would rather provide two half-time contracts than a proper job with national insurance and benefits paid. The Tories are trying to mend their ways 10 years too late. 'They've already closed everything down,' said Bill Allsop, 'and kicked the working man in the teeth.' Meanwhile, the staff at Nearfield House, a residential centre for the elderly, were running their first car boot sale. 'We're fund-raising for the comforts fund,' a woman explained as she glanced out over tables covered with time-expired kitchen gadgets and redundant 1980s manuals on self-improvement.

Seriously searching for a Majorite by this time, I approached a farmer trading from a Land Rover. He was wearing confederate stripes and a peaked baseball cap, while his wife explained the attractions of the curious flower baskets he had made with a welding torch and a collection of spare horseshoes.

This fellow was a little cautious about talking politics, and certainly didn't want anyone to print his name. Of John Major he said, 'He's with me as a farmer, but not when I go home . . . We are country people,' he explained, working a 180-acre family farm, but the escalation of the housing market has meant that he and his wife can no longer afford to live near their farm. 'I married the neighbour's daughter and moved into town,' he explained, leaving his wife to explain that home was now a terraced house in Rugeley – OK, but not at all what she wanted.

Michael Fabricant, who has been the Conservative MP for Lichfield since 1992, was watering the plants on his doorstep as John Major stood up in Birmingham to talk about 'Duty' and 'Responsibility' and to warn his enemies – inside the Conservative Party as well as out – that a robust man like himself 'doesn't just drift into Downing Street'.

Fabricant is one of those who really did get rich quick during the Thatcher years. Having built up a radio company that was bought at a good price by an American competitor, he is, as he says, 'independent' – his own man financially and perhaps in the party too. Sitting in his flat near the cathedral, he says: 'I don't believe in Middle England for a start.' It is, he says from under a rustling mop of blond hair, 'shorthand for decent hard-working people who ought, naturally, to be Conservative voters'.

Despite the fact that he had to win it back from Sylvia Heal, who had won it dramatically for Labour in a 1990 by-election, he observes that this city has twice the number of ABs as the national average, 'so if Lichfield isn't safe, where is?' And yet 'only the most cotton-wool-encased MP would claim that all is right with the nation's perceptions of Conservative government'. As an MP who likes to carry out 'informal surgeries in Safeway', he admits to having been approached that very morning by 'quite a bad-tempered bloke', who wanted to know 'why we can't get the message across'.

Whatever Samuel Johnson may once have said, Middle England is no longer a stable and virtuous place on the map. Even in prosperous Lichfield it is more like a seething confusion of beleaguered moaning, insecurity and puzzlement

– a frantic reaching out for the birch with one hand and trying to defend public services with the other. The political parties may well try to appeal to this volatile mood, or trim their mission to it in accordance with the principles of public relations, but the real political challenge is to transform it into more coherent aspiration.

Speaking for the Labour Party as well as Lichfield's Johnson Society, John Wilson is feeling pretty confident about the forthcoming local elections. As for Michael Fabricant, he starts pacing the room when asked what will be the Conservative Party's message to the electors of Lichfield in the next general election. He will try to remind them of the distant horrors of the 1970s and he will stress the achievements of Thatcher and Major in cutting back the Civil Service and 'tackling' coal-mining. He will be stressing the values of market testing, the charter mark and rail privatisation too – although he is nervously determined to ensure that through ticketing will be available for Lichfield's commuters.

Chairman Hanley has tried to dismiss Blair as a Trojan Horse packed with 'luvvies and lefties'. And Fabricant looks forward to a bit of negative campaigning too – in the hope that, whatever the polls may say now, people will think again when faced with the real prospect of a Labour government. He can't see what's wrong with 'luvvies', but he claims to know about the 'lefties' from sitting opposite the Labour Party in the House of Commons. When Blair says his reasonable, trimmed-down things, two dozen of his 'brightest' Labour colleagues nod in sincere agreement, but that leaves 200 unreconstructed socialists, who scowl and glower and are only biding their time until after the election victory. Vote for Labour, he will say, and you will get 'a pig in a poke' and Maastrich-like splits in the party every other week.

So, after showing me the KGB uniform he keeps in the hall (a gift from a Russian business client), Fabricant led me out through the cathedral close and along Dam Street in search of a plaque marking the spot where a parliamentary soldier in the English civil war was shot by a Royalist sniping from the Cathedral spire. We couldn't find the place, so Mr Fabricant, who was recognised by smiling admirers and scowling enemies alike, quickly whisked me off, past the Lichfield Arts Centre – closed due to a fatal and surely not symbolic crack in its foundations – to meet a young man who was opening a French restaurant near the Samuel Johnson's Birthplace museum.

This new hostelry will have a garden and a rear entrance to spare the prosperous clientele any unpleasant encounters with drunken vandals on a Saturday night. I had already asked Fabricant what he planned to do if he lost the next election.

After pausing, he said he might try to get back into broadcasting. But he has recently bought a house in Maine, and he wouldn't feel too bad about spending more time in the US. •

22 February 1995

Henry Porter
Churchill's children

Looking down from the wall of the historian Andrew Roberts's sitting room is a very large portrait of the historian Andrew Roberts. To the right of the fireplace are two smaller framed photographs of Lady Thatcher and Ronald and Nancy Reagan, signed and inscribed with their good wishes to Andrew Roberts. Elsewhere in the flat there is a Christmas card personally signed by General De Gaulle when he was leader of the Free French. This was not dedicated to the 32-year-old Mr Roberts since it was written 21 years before he was born, but if he had been alive one suspects that it would have been.

Clearly Andrew Roberts is much more than a young historian with two successful books behind him and contacts and a self-possession spectacularly beyond his age. By common consent he has become a kind of nexus for a new young group on the right of British politics. Its members may not attend the dinner parties held in his flat just off Sloane Street but, if asked about the key figures, he is always the first to be mentioned.

The group does not have a name, no library of revered texts, nor premises, it being a moveable salon of chatty kindred spirits. But it is an important influence and will become more so with the lack of any sort of argument from young Tories on the left. In America, a similar formation of 20-something opinion-makers has been called the Counter Counterculture, but the name is far too clunky and it will not work here because there was never, in any real sense, a counterculture. It has been suggested, perhaps wickedly, that Roberts's group be called the Third Right, the idea being that it succeeds first the paternalistic conservatism of the 1950s and then Thatcherism. This is awkward too and may also be slightly libellous in the pun. So for the moment we will simply call them The Group.

From the outside it is not always easy to see the novelty in the various mutations of conservative thinking that well-up out of the party's troubles. Successive generations of young Tory thinkers appear much the same – well-spoken Oxbridge graduates, astir with the decline of Britain and the conservative establishment. Is there anything really so new about Roberts, or indeed Matthew D'Ancona (*Times* and Fellow of All Souls), Niall Ferguson (*Telegraph* and Don at Jesus College, Oxford), Michael Gove (BBC and former president of the Oxford Union), Anne Applebaum (Yale and deputy editor of the *Spectator*), Paul Goodman (*Telegraph* and former chairman of the Federation of Conservative Students) and Dean Godson (*Telegraph*)?

Well, yes, they are different from previous fusions on the right, especially the tweedy agitators that were drawn to each other at the end of the 1970s. The first obvious distinction is that its members come from widely different backgrounds and that most of them were literally children of the 1960s. Gove and D'Ancona were products of standard middle-class families and although Roberts has the whiff of the grand Tory about him, he picks his friends, according to one of The Group, 'to find the same mindset and congenial companions, rather than attempt to create a young England clique'. Most of them have links with, or were at, Oxford – unlike their predecessors in the 1970s who had strong connections with Peterhouse College, Cambridge. Quite a number are Jewish – Goodman, Godson, Applebaum and Danny Finkelstein, who was originally a member of the SDP but is now regarded by his friends as veering rapidly to the right. 'One thing you can say about us,' said Roberts, 'is that we are extremely philo-semitic.'

There are other members – banker Oliver Letwin, Steve Hilton who used to work for Saatchi & Saatchi and is now a prospective Tory candidate, Sheila Lawlor, an historian and education expert for the Centre for Policy Studies and Martin Ivens of *The Times*. The important thing is that most of them met after university and have come to know each other because of the congruity of their views. In this sense, The Group is a network which is spread through history departments, journalism, advertising and, in one instance, radio. As you would expect its main outlets are *The Times* and, more important, the *Telegraph* group, which also includes the *Spectator*.

In terms of thought, their views are different to the Peterhouse and Conservative philosophy axis of the late 1970s. For a start they are not absorbed by the confrontation between East and West. Moreover they have none of the free-market agenda of the early 1980s; they do not think deeply about social issues (unlike their American counterparts); and they are not in the least interested in the managerial side of politics, the nitty gritty of fiscal policy.

Matthew D'Ancona explained that theirs is a movement of 'first principles' – Britain's sovereignty, the union with Northern Ireland, the preservation of the crown, the protection of the BBC from pc tendencies, the Atlantic alliance and so forth. It is not, therefore, an ideologues' bunfight, and nor is it a coalition of excitable policy nerds. Rather, D'Ancona and his friends seek to stiffen conservative thinking on these 'first principles'. They do not expect to have any impact on the current government but are waiting for the next Conservative administration, which they assume will follow a period of Labour rule. One suspects that they hope for Conservative defeat just to hasten the departure of John Major, and in some sense regard themselves as presently being in the wilderness.

This is important because there is something Churchillian in The Group's view of itself. Like Churchill in the late 1930s, they believe they are the only ones to see the dangers of a superstate with Germany at its centre. The movement towards federalism is seen as Hunnish domination by other means, and not at all as a brave new union of friendly nation states. You find there are a number of passionate Atlanticists in The Group, although Roberts, who you would expect to be the most pro-American, is stricken with intellectual doubts. 'We argue against a single currency, but the pound has been very much tied to the dollar for the last 50 years.'

As D'Ancona says, The Group is 'jackdawish' in the ideas and policies that it embraces. They all admire Enoch Powell for his support of parliamentary democracy and the union and many still swoon at the memory of Mrs Thatcher's resilience and toughness. They admire Charles Moore, editor of the *Sunday Telegraph*, and like him use the writings of Edmund Burke, the 18th-century Whig and political theorist, and the late Michael Oakeshott, to think about today's issues.

Sitting directly below the Reagans, Andrew Roberts clasped his hands together and talked animatedly about the differences between the 1970s backlash and the 1990s vanguard. He is perhaps the most conventional Conservative of the lot and is stamped with the dry certitude of the mid-1980s. 'Back in the time of the Cold War it was easy,' he said. 'But now nobody is threatening Western values. The main thing is that federal Europe is a threat to the British way of life.

'Most of us believe that the nation state is not played out as a political force. In Europe their memory of nationalism is different. It led to ultra-nationalism, which led to fascism, which led to war. But our experience of the nation state this century has been good. It has led us to form the opposite conclusions.'

I mentioned social issues and Roberts exhaled impatiently: 'No, none of us gets hot under the collar about homosexuality, sexual mores, abortion or the death penalty. In the US and amongst people older than us in Britain these are terribly important, but not to us. When we are having dinner together we don't ask "What about pensions?" We talk about Europe all the time; that, and American politics. And of course there's a lot of speculation about whether Aitken is better than Portillo ... What was it that Balfour said? Very few things matter and lots of things don't matter at all.'

The things that don't matter to Roberts include everything from CrossRail to the conditions of the underclass. D'Ancona is a different creature, surprising for his liberal stance on many issues. He talks passionately about community, the need for improvement in state education and even about the *fatwa* against Salman Rushdie. But his liberalism does not extend to Northern Ireland. Two weeks ago he was revealed as being associated with a group called the Friends Of The Union. Through one of the group's members, David Burnside, a hardline Unionist who is well connected in Whitehall, he obtained a document that, after publication in *The Times*, nearly blew up the peace process in Northern Ireland. He was roundly criticised by the press and by Number 10 for irresponsibility, although it has to be said the implication of the criticism was that journalists should suppress stories if they are inconvenient to their own views and the Government's aims – not a sound argument at any time.

A jaunty and confident 25-year-old, D'Ancona is undaunted by the publicity, especially by the accusation that he published only a sketch of the discussions between Dublin and London and in doing so misrepresented them. 'It's plainly ridiculous for a government simply to be motivated by the desire not to blow up children, rather than all the many factors involved in a settlement. You still have to look beyond the immediate promise to the prospects of long-term peace.'

This sort of statement leaves one slightly surprised, just as Roberts's views on the poor do ('I don't believe in giving them money, but I do believe in helping them by creating jobs'). Perhaps it's their youth, or the excessive application of logic.

D'Ancona, who once worked at *Index on Censorship*, oscillates between a familiar liberalism and a hard, no nonsense Toryism. 'This country experienced a sort of moral panic between the case of Jamie Bulger and the death of John Smith, which was seemingly alleviated by the arrival of Tony Blair. You see, Blair has a linguistic project which is to construct a language that his party can win with. The fact of the matter is that Blair comes from organised Labour, but he is attempting to appeal to the bourgeois, professional classes with this reassuring language of his.' On education he said: 'The egalitarian education policy laid down by Labour in the 1960s was a real disaster because it meant that only the well-off got well educated.'

One of the fascinating things about The Group is its lack of political homogeneity, which is clearly the result of the post-ideological character of modern politics. Whereas it used to be relatively easy to predict a person's position on a whole range of issues once you knew where they stood on the political divide, today it is much more difficult, which is why you find in someone like Applebaum, Hilton or Gove strong elements of liberalism. The same is true of the left, which is in the business of reinventing itself by appropriating some thinking from conservative and liberal traditions.

When the dust has settled we may expect an emergence of 'first principle' politics on both sides – not quite a return to the century-old ideological stand off, but a more starkly drawn confrontation than today, based on elemental disagreement about such things as sovereignty. Europe is already the battleground and if you want one defining belief of The Group, it is that the single currency represents an unacceptable transfer of sovereignty away from these islands.

In the US, the Counter Counterculture 'elite' has no equivalent animus, although there are other overlapping areas of concern, the first being the spread of political correctness and its association with postmodernist teaching in the American academy. Anne Applebaum, the researcher for the *Spectator* story that revealed Richard Gott's links with the KGB, is in a good position to compare the young neo-con' thinking on either side of the Atlantic. 'I think of myself as a British journalist and an American citizen. I have opinions about the single currency and would certainly feel sceptical about it but I don't wake up in the middle of the night sweating. I have a rational view that it has huge political implications and it's ridiculous to pretend otherwise.

Applebaum came to Britain after Yale – where she had attended Jacques Derrida's seminars – to do post-graduate work in Britain, then she moved to Poland where she began writing for the British press. She sees the key mistake of the last few years as being the conservative failure to address itself to the Welfare State. 'It will happen in the US and a refining, or reforming, or a rolling back of the Welfare State must now be the issue here. It was the obvious thing to do after privatisation. But Major simply hasn't addressed it.

'One of the things I like about the British right is that it is not obsessed with social issues as the American right is. It doesn't seem to be interested in the private lives of people and it is interesting that Major got this so wrong when he started talking about personal morality. It didn't interest the general public, nor the right either.'

The genesis of the young rightwing groups here and in the US is utterly different. The Counter Counterculture 'elite' in America is as much a response to the liberal hegemony in the American press (the *New York Times*, *Washington Post*, *LA Times* are all liberal), as it is to the reforms proposed, but barely executed, by the Clinton administration. Here the new young right have emerged as a reaction to current Conservative policy. They pay almost no attention to the thinking in the Labour Party and do not feel the need to address the flow of pamphlets produced from left groups like Demos and the Institute for Public Policy Research. But if Labour wins the next general election The Group's range of interests will certainly expand and it will gain a greater sense of political mission.

'Except,' said Roberts, 'we will have to put up with all those ex-Conservative MPs writing in the papers, trying to set the agenda for the next Conservative government.'

There are big 'Balfour' issues, and a few small ones too. If you ask any member of The Group what he thinks of the BBC's latest plans to widen its appeal away from a southern, middle-class audience to include more minorities and a younger generation, they become quite angry. D'Ancona simply said of the plans: 'It's the bastard child of political correctness and the market place.' Roberts said: 'We don't see elitism as a bad thing. It is part of the BBC's job to better people, not to pander to what people want.'

Another obvious target is the postmodernist thinking which is deemed to have taken root here. Last year Gertrude Himmelfarb, a New York academic and the mother of William Kristol, a neo-conservative propagandist, published a short book in the US called On Looking Into The Abyss. For her, the abyss is the disorder that has resulted from the work of the French philosophers,

Jacques Derrida and Michel Foucault, who have won a vast following in American universities. Derrida pioneered his technique of deconstruction in the 1960s and showed that by taking the unspoken propositions of any text literally, and by pointing out its subtle contradictions, you could show that it had many different meanings. Indeed it might say exactly the opposite to that which its author intended. Thus no literature, philosophy or history can have a single agreed meaning.

'It has a terrible effect at Yale where it surfaces every time there is a new appointment. There are two exclusive views: either you believe there is a canon of work which should be taught or you don't. It really is pernicious, but it is fashion and it will go,' said Applebaum.

Himmelfarb objects to the way more and more academics have reflexively accepted deconstruction while rejecting the old tools of chronology and causality. Though she concedes, as Macaulay did, that history is 'debatable land', she objects to the way in which the postmodernist craze, with all its emphasis on discord, ambiguity and free interpretation, has placed history at the disposal of anyone who wants to abuse it. A key example in her argument is the postmodernist treatment of the Holocaust as just another 'text' which may be deconstructed to the point that its unique horror is dissolved away.

History is important to all political thinkers, particularly those that see themselves in the tradition of John Stuart Mill, who believed that without knowledge of what has happened in the past a society cannot have a moral or social setting, no reference outside the chaos of the present and no deep sense of cause and effect.

This debate naturally engages The Group and when Himmelfarb's book is published here she may expect some warm reviews, for a number of them are professional historians and all believe that the postmodernist techniques attack an essential quality of civilisation. What is ironic in all this is that both sides claim Mill as some form of intellectual ancestor. They both regard their approaches as being quintessentially liberal, the one by preserving a record, and the other by throwing it open to wider interpretation.

'It's so important to have a structure in a history book,' Roberts insists, lifting from his chair to emphasise the point. 'Chronology is a gift. The modern thematic approach has spoilt history for an awful lot of children. You have to have dates – they are the only context.'

This is crucial to all of them because history is endlessly deployed by The Group to argue its case over Europe. A fortnight ago, Roberts wrote in the *Spectator* about the attitudes to recent British history in support of his anti-federalist stance. At the same time, Niall Ferguson was preparing to give a paper in Oxford which drew an analogy between the evolution of the German Reich and the evolution of the European Union. The Group believes that the study of history and the way it is represented is an important, though generally unrecognised, battleground; if everything can be explained away by deconstruction, they say, a society may lose its sense of prudence and ultimately its self-determination.

I asked Roberts what would be the real effect of Britain losing its currency. He looked grave and a lot less genial for a moment. 'Well . . . yes, then we will be in a federal superstate. The only answer to that will be terrorism. I think there will be violence, especially if Britain enters a federal superstate without a referendum or one of the major parties opposing it at a general election.' •

5 October 1994

Simon Hoggart
Too beautiful a love to remain secret

Tony Blair scooped the Labour Party in his strong arms yesterday, gazed long into eyes like amber pools of light, and told it how deeply he cared. Then almost before the party knew what was happening, he led it, softly yet insistently, towards the bedroom door.

The speech was as artful a seduction as I've seen. He left the party quivering with anticipation, helpless in the face of his throbbing desire for office. Which leaves the question of whether, like James Hewitt, Mr Blair will turn out to be a Love Rat.

This is, of course, the view of the left, and specifically Arthur Scargill, who sat scowling during what was probably the longest standing ovation a Labour leader has received.

But he was virtually alone. Around him people cheered and bayed their support. In the plangent words of Anna Pasternak, 'it was too beautiful a love to remain a secret'. (Her book is full of resonant but unspecific euphemisms. At last they were 'properly united'; 'she lost her intolerable sense of isolation'. The trolloping captain sounds more like Tony Blair all the time, bringing joy to those who have suffered too long the anguish of rejection.)

The speech included some dazzling sleight of hand. The ending of Clause Four was never even mentioned, being murmured in the party's ear as 'it is time we had a clear, up-to-date statement of the object and objectives of our party', and cunningly linked to the name of John Prescott who has in this business the same role as the princess's detective – aware of what is going on, but powerless to prevent it. It took the delegates quite some time to realise what Mr Blair meant. We journalists, however, were luckier, since we had the benefit of Mr Blair's spin-doctors.

This profession, which was once thought unnecessary (Gaitskell's 'fight, fight and fight again' required no spinning), has now become a massive youth employment scheme, as Mr Blair's myrmidons fan out to explain precisely the significance of the text, like flying rabbis interpreting the Talmud.

Many of these physicians are unnervingly young, having just left Balliol with starred firsts in osculatory medicine. They line the aisle in the press room, which has become a Gyratory Gynaecologists' Gulch.

This is necessary, since quite a lot of Mr Blair's speech did require at least a gentle twirl. For instance, a boilerplate attack on the Home Secretary ended with a passage which could have come from a *Daily Express* leader: 'Michael Howard said he was building six tough new prisons. Butlins wouldn't win the contract, he said. He was right. The Savoy got it.'

His style, like all the most cunning seducers, is to pass swiftly over the reality and get on to the dream. The passage which said that the free market alone could not rescue the economy began: 'It won't be done by state control . . .'

After that he was free to rouse the party's fantasies. And the special achievement of the spin doctor is to furnish innumerable explanations of each passage, so that a single oration becomes a blend of several different speeches, the underlying pattern emerging, as in those Magic Eye books, only after you squint at it for hours.

Yesterday morning, to prepare for the speech, I rode on Blackpool's new roller-coaster. The Big One. It is terrifying. After an unnervingly long climb, you suddenly dip into the longest and fastest drop anywhere in the world. What makes it even more gut-wrenching is that the train is turning round 90 degrees on its own axis, so that you resume at right-angles to where you began the vertiginous descent.

But that's enough Labour Party metaphors for one day. It now remains to be seen whether they still respect Tony Blair in the morning. They certainly adored him last night. ●

14 March 1995

Roy Greenslade
Clause for the people?

'We are the people's party. We should speak the people's language,' said Tony Blair yesterday at the press conference to launch the new model Labour Party constitution. To find out if the drafters have achieved his aim, we put the text to Roy Greenslade, former Fleet Street tabloid editor and now media commentator, to see if sub-editing could make improvements. This is what he did: ⌐ *indicates where words have been inserted.*

Clause 4. Subbed version 1

The Labour Party is a democratic socialist party. It believes that ~~by the strength of our common endeavour, we achieve more than we achieve alone so as to create for each of us the means to realise our true potential and for all of us a community in which~~ power, wealth and opportunity ~~are~~ should be in the hands of the many not the few. ~~where the rights we enjoy reflect the duties we owe and where we live together, freely, in a spirit of solidarity, tolerance and respect~~. To these ends we it works for:

a dynamic economy, ~~serving the public interest~~, in which the enterprise of the market ~~and the rigour of competition are~~ is joined with the forces of partnership and cooperation to produce the ~~wealth the nation needs and the~~ opportunity for all to work and prosper; ~~with a thriving private sector and high quality public services, where those undertakings essential to the common good are either owned by the public or accountable to them~~;

a just society, which ~~judges its strength by the condition of the weak as much as the strong; provides security against fear, and justice at work; which nurtures families; promotes equality of opportunity and~~ delivers people from the tyranny of poverty, prejudice and the abuse of power;

an open democracy, in which government is held to account by the people: ~~decisions are taken as far as practicable by the communities they affect; and where fundamental human rights are guaranteed~~;

a healthy environment, ~~which we protect, enhance and hold in trust for future generations~~;.

Labour is committed to the defence and security of the British people, and to cooperating ~~in European institutions; the United Nations; the Commonwealth~~

~~and other~~ with international bodies to secure world peace, ~~freedom, democracy,~~ ~~economic security and environmental protection for all;~~

Labour will work with anyone in pursuit of these aims ~~with trade unions; co-operative societies and other affiliated organisations, and also with voluntary organisations, consumer groups and other representative bodies~~. On the basis of these principles, Labour seeks ~~the trust of the people to govern~~ power.

Note to author: The clause – or should it be clauses – is rather verbose, attempting to cover every worthy eventuality. There is no substitute for concise clarity. In that sense, at least, the Webbs knew the virtue of light sub-editing. ●

....

14 March 1995

Bernard Crick
Differing audiences dull the rhetoric

We do not live in an age of great political rhetoric. The sound-bite links the tongue to the politic brain, perorations are rare, the arts of the platform have withered away – basically, I think, because the majority of the population does not listen to sermons any more.

So good rhetoric no longer comes easily. So not to hope for too much.

Mr Blair (I use this name rhetorically to stand for any and all who had a hand in it) certainly knows what he wants to say (and has said it well, *vide* the first, powerful and sensible paragraph, and has a pretty good knowledge of his subject. But the difficulty in drafting rhetoric lies in the audience, or to be precise in having three audiences: party, public and press.

The first clause is aimed at the party and will be stamped on our cards. No flinching, great reassurance: 'The Labour Party is a democratic socialist party.' A good plain, Orwell-like sentence and without his provocative pedantry of always writing 'democratic Socialist'. The stress must now be the other way. Certain things have happened in the outside world. But the next sentence is far too long and ambiguously overcrowded. Oddly the old Communist or anarchist 'solidarity' is resurrected because 'fraternity' is frowned on by feminists (perhaps rightly, but it leaves a gap).

Couldn't we have had 'live together, exercising freedom' (not just 'freely') 'with tolerance and equal respect as if brothers or sisters'. That is my socialist morality, anyway; and 'respect' is too weak; 'equal respect' is what Jesus, Kant and moral philosophers have taught. There is no imperative to praise everyone equally, but we must respect everyone equally.

Roger Bamber

Quibbling probably, but details of the language worry me. Good it contains 'equality of opportunity', which God knows will take a long time to achieve, but 'and delivers people from the tyranny of poverty' simply does not follow. The more individualistic note needed sounding; but as it stands that is the Thatcherite illusion.

I am sure he meant to say that we aspire to a democratic, egalitarian and classless society. But somehow he doesn't. Is that offensive to Middle England? Mr Major got 'classless' across his lips (even if probably meaning only that if we ignore it, it will go away). The canard of socialism wanting literal equality is met by 'egalitarian' which is a way of acting towards people as well as a sociological description fitting some societies better than others (oddly the US better than the UK).

I used the word 'aspire'. The aims have got rather lost in the confusion, perhaps forced on by the need for such a public revision, between a constitution and a manifesto. I want no part of a party that does not aspire to full employment and an egalitarian society; but equally I want no part of a party foolish enough (as in 1982) to pledge that in an election manifesto for the next Parliament.

And I find in the language only a muted reference to devolution, when I had thought that pluralism had replaced sovereignty theory as a philosophy of the state. Yes, the state cannot directly and effectively manage industry. But the excessive centralism and confusion of an English state with a multi-national society is still unexorcised, in the halting language at least. And internationally we only aspire to environmental protection, not to ending poverty – ever. ●

3 October 1994

Seumas Milne
New kids on the blocks

In the parliamentary gossip shop, they are known as 'the creche'. Less generous Commons regulars deride them as 'Arkansas-style yuppie careerists'. They are well-scrubbed, ambitious and – like Diana Spencer when she married Prince Charles – free of any embarrassing past. They come with barely a briefcase-full of political baggage, but like to describe each other as 'bright and able'. These are the twenty- and occasionally thirtysomethings who staff the Labour leadership's Westminster headquarters: the 15-hour-a-day spear-carriers of Tony Blair's new Labour Party and his modernising reformation. Huddled together with the party's up-and-coming parliamentarians, they are the cocoon around the new regime, loyal to the point of hero-worship. And if all goes according to plan, in a couple of years they will be calling the shots in Whitehall at the heart of the first Labour government for a generation.

The emerging kitchen cabinet around Blair and Gordon Brown – John Prescott's likely role has yet to be put to the test – epitomises the political rupture Labour's new leadership team has made even with the late Kinnock years, let alone with the John Smith interregnum. While Neil Kinnock seemed to be groping towards continental-style social democracy and a revival of Tony Crosland's 1950s 'revisionism' that was still rooted in the Labour movement, Blair and his supporters are setting out an entirely different post-social democratic stall. As Frank Field, a true believer, enthuses: 'We are leap-frogging over the old social democracy.' And while Kinnock surrounded himself with former student politicians, battle-hardened in a thousand factional spats – former NUS presidents like Charles Clarke, Neil Stewart and Phil Woolas – the young fixers and researchers around Blair and Brown are from another world altogether.

They are more likely to have cut what political teeth they do have in television or the cluster of newish centre-left think tanks, like the Institute of Public Policy Research (IPPR), than in the trade unions or locked in mortal combat with Trotskyist entrists. As Geoff Mulgan, director of the think tank Demos and former Gordon Brown researcher, puts it: 'These people didn't go through the angst of being believers in a religion and then becoming revisionist, which is an uncomfortable psychological and political experience.' Most are unfamiliar with Labour movement culture and language, and even where they have a background of student activism it has been one of administration rather than protest. For the modernisers, this is a great advantage. As one of the pivotal figures in the Blair camp remarks: 'They don't see themselves as little politicians. They are there to produce ideas, research and strategies for politicians.'

Doyen of the Blair backroom boys – and boys they mostly are – is David Miliband, the 29-year-old head of policy, who will play a key role in drawing up Labour's manifesto. For an arch-moderniser, Miliband has an unusual background. His father Ralph, who died earlier this year, was an eminent Marxist intellectual and his best-known book, *Parliamentary Socialism*, was a sustained exposition of the argument that reformist socialism cannot work. Tested against such a foil, David Miliband – whose brother Ed works for Labour's Treasury spokesperson, Harriet Harman – is by far the most accomplished theorist of Labour's modernisation 'project', as the initiated call it. Like his father, Miliband regards the old social democratic formulas as dead and is hostile to the British tradition of 'Labourism'. Labour should be in the business of shaping an entirely new economic and social model, he thinks, based on communitarian principles and a redistribution of work in place of welfare dependency. As secretary of the Social Justice Commission – the controversial arms-length outfit due to publish proposals for reform of the welfare state later this month – he has already been at the heart of unofficial policy-making.

Miliband is influenced by American liberal thinkers, such as John Rawls and Amitai Etzioni – as are Blair and Brown – and the Clinton administration theorists he came across while studying for a master's degree at the Massachusetts Institute of Technology. Ed Balls, Gordon Brown's 27-year-old chief economist and former *Financial Times* leader writer, has even stronger transatlantic links. Balls studied at Harvard under a string of academics who have walked into jobs under Clinton's patronage: notably Larry Summers, now at the US Treasury; Larry Katz, at the Labour Department; and Robert Reich, Clinton's Labour Secretary. Before he switched to Brown's offce, Balls had been planning to join Summers at the World Bank, where the East Coast professor championed its infamous 'structural adjustment programmes' for slashing Third World government budgets and subsidies.

The Clinton connection does not augur well. The first US Democratic President for 12 years came to office, after all, with a retinue of famously clever and youthful campaign supporters. Several have since been elbowed aside by harder-nosed Washington insiders: notably George Stephanopoulos, king of the White House thirtysomethings and one-time Clinton communications director, who was last month demoted to be policy assistant to the new chief of staff, Leon Panetta.

Concern that the spectacularly inexperienced 'Blair babes' could similarly wilt under political pressure is privately expressed by some supporters. Unlike Kinnock, Blair has not seen fit to appoint a chief of staff to do the political dirty work. 'There is no strong political fixer and organiser to spot the internal party problems,' frets a backroom Labour veteran, who sees the quarrel about all-women parliamentary shortlists as an early failure of party management.

Instead, the leader's private office is staffed by people like Peter Hyman – a 26-year-old former BBC television researcher and protégé of Labour's resurgent spin-doctor-in-chief, Peter Mandelson – and Tim Allan, aged 24, a Cambridge graduate who worked for Channel 4's *A Week in Politics*. The pair have signed up for press and speechwriting duties, though it was Allan who did much of the spade work for Blair's abstentionist line on the Criminal Justice Bill. Liz Lloyd, also a Cambridge graduate, aged 23, is a key member of the Miliband research team. Another youthful member of the Blair office, James Purnell, has been put to work on an IPPR media research project, part-sponsored by Rupert Murdoch's News International.

To some in the Labour Party, these upwardly mobile new courtiers – and the offices of several other frontbench Labour MPs are staffed with similar characters – confirm their worst fears about the direction in which Blair is taking them. Mike Marqusee, writer on the leftwing Labour Briefing and coauthor of an acerbic book on Kinnock's leadership, remarks: 'They may be young, but they are socially conservative, they exist in a selfenclosed world and they are utterly unrepresentative of young people. What have they got to say, for example, about the huge grass-roots campaign against the Criminal Justice Bill?' A prominent soft-left MP takes a similar line: 'Most of the advisers are either well to the right of the party or entirely without any politics.' To those who are 'engaged with the project', as the modernisers like to describe themselves, this is no criticism at all. 'It's a sign of success,' says one, 'that we can attract people who aren't ideological, but who are bright and just want to get on.'

Not that all the older hands have been dispensed with, of course. Pat McFadden, a 29-year-old Scot brought in to the leader's office by John Smith, and Geoff Norris, who is transferring from Robin Cook's office to work with Miliband, both have a background in the campus factionalism of the 1980s. Murray Elder, Smith's 44-year-old head man, survives. Some continuity with the Kinnock ascendancy will be provided by Philip Gould, the marketing and electoral strategist with close ties to the US Democrats; Mandelson, Labour's ex-communications director who hustled and cajoled for Blair's leadership campaign behind the alias 'Bobby' to protect the candidate from Mandelson's many enemies; and Alastair Campbell, who as political editor of Maxwell's *Daily Mirror* was the Fleet Street journalist regarded as closest to Neil Kinnock and will now be Blair's press secretary. Campbell can be expected to deploy some of the rougher political skills and experience so palpably lacking in the younger members of Blair's office – as can Charlie Whelan, the former engineering union press officer who now works for Gordon Brown. Anji Hunter, Blair's teenage pal and longtime office manager, will be a powerful 'gate-keeper', controlling access to the leader.

Waiting in the wings for Blair's crucial autumn reshuffle are the lesser known modernising MPs, the parliamentary equivalent of the Blair babes. Among those widely tipped for advancement by insiders are people like Tessa Jowell, the new member for Dulwich; Stephen Byers, former lecturer in law; Geoff Hoon, barrister and ex-MEP; John Denham, MP for Southampton Itchen; Tony Wright, former university lecturer; Peter Kilfoyle, the former Kinnock hatchet-man on Merseyside now campaigning to be chief whip – not to mention the better known Margaret Hodge, ex-leader of Islington council. As Brian Wilson, Labour's transport spokesman, puts it: 'We've got to break the logjam. There are good people who came in in 1992, never mind 1987, who should be available for selection. There needs to be more fluidity.'

Fluidity there surely will be as the culture represented by the creche and the modernisers in Parliament and local government feeds into Labour's policies and power structure. Mark Seddon, editor of the leftwing Labour weekly *Tribune*, is alarmed at a potential gap he sees opening up between the leadership and the grass roots: 'It's not the party most councillors, party and union activists in the country recognise as their own,' he says. For the meanwhile, however, it is certainly the one they've got. ●

....

5 October 1994

Gary Younge
Talkin' 'bout my generation

L istening to some commentators pontificate on the political habits of the young, you'd think that anyone who qualified for a bona-fide InterRail ticket descended from another planet. When the spaceship landed, a group of professors cordoned it off and whisked away those on board to a laboratory for their psephological delectation. There they conducted surveys, examined values and finally produced reports which confirmed what they thought they already knew.

Most of their findings revived old clichés or coined new ones. These were then dispatched to columnists and pundits throughout the land as prima-facie evidence that there is a lower form of life on Planet Youth. A planet where people, with no interest in what is happening on Earth, lead a lifestyle which is as dull and insignificant as it is self-obsessed.

And so the word went out that Thatcher's orphans were 'politically illiterate' (Economic and Social Research Council funded report: 1992); 'apathetic because they feel they have no voice' (HK McCann advertising agency: 1993); 'loyal and trustworthy' not 'wild and unpredictable' (Mintel: 1993).

This must come as a bit of a surprise to the mostly young gay activists who threatened to storm Parliament after the debate on the age of consent. Not to mention the thousands of students on last year's anti-fascist demonstration who clashed with police in their attempt to shut down the British National Party's headquarters in south-east London last year. More insightful reports might have concluded that young people are not so much politically illiterate but use a different political language to the one pollsters are used to.

But at the root of much of this talk about apathy is not a concern for the political well-being of the young but a deep-seated sense of superiority among a core of 1960s veterans who believe their decade was a golden one – a time when you could demonstrate against the Vietnam war, occupy your college refectory, travel around India to find yourself and still have change out of a fiver.

The latest study, No Turning Back, published last week by the think tank Demos, claims the young suffer from widespread alienation but are living in a 'genderquake' in which the issue of sexual equality has come to the fore, producing 'a shift in power and values [which] is unravelling many of the assumptions not only of 200 years of industrial society but also millennia of traditions and beliefs'.

Hiding behind the report's prophetic jargon lies a more sophisticated appreciation than usual. Demos at least recognises that there is a lot more to politics than the mainstream parties and their election manifestos. It also acknowledges that the young are not a homogenous lump but a mixture of races, genders and classes, all of which can have as much, or more, influence on their political outlook as their age.

But most of the comment that has followed the release of the report bears little relation to the world that I live in, the young people I know or the experiences I have had. I was 10 when Margaret Thatcher moved into Downing Street. I knew that my mum was not best pleased by the result but I was more preoccupied by odd socks and eczema than the economic and social revolution that the new premier had in store for my adolescence and beyond. Three elections later, I am 25. The lady in blue has been replaced by the man in grey and thanks to their policies most of my friends are working hard to pay off graduate loans.

I have vague recollections of the IRA hunger strikes and the Falklands war but my political initiation came at the age of 15, during the miners' strike, when I was involved in a support group. My side lost and, with the exception of the climbdown over the poll tax and the advent of majority rule in South Africa, my side has kept on losing just about every major battle ever since.

None of this has stopped me joining political organisations, going on demonstrations or signing petitions. But it has made me aware that doing so nowadays is more about voicing protest than effecting real change. 'Politics,' said Bismarck, 'is the art of the possible.' Spending your formative years in a democratically elected one-party state, under a government that does not seem to listen to anyone – including, on occasions, its own supporters – certainly alters your expectations of what is possible. Especially when opposition parties have spent their time either bickering internally or so paralysed by electoralism that they have not dared to make a stand in what they consider to be controversial territory.

But this is not just true for the young. Trade union membership is at its lowest since 1946. There are fewer Conservative Party members than ever before and, despite a recent swelling of the ranks, the Labour Party is a shadow of its former self. With wranglings over the Maastricht Treaty and mudslinging over tax bands, domestic party politics is simply not as interesting as I am told it used to be.

The days of supposedly clear-cut foreign *causes célèbres* are also gone, replaced with a mixture of fudge and farce. Once, the young could always look abroad for their political kicks but since the collapse of the Soviet Union, and the breaching of the Berlin Wall, there has been only a handful of international issues that you could actually take to the streets over.

Most of the world's former pariahs – like South Africa, Chile and the Soviet Union, whose human rights violations mobilised thousands of young people – have opted for relatively peaceful transitions to democracy. And the days of revolutions and imperialist invasions in far-flung corners have made way for negotiated settlements and UN-sanctioned 'interventions'.

If you were ever in need of a radical icon to hang on your wall during the 1960s and 1970s, you could choose between Angela Davis, Che Guevara and Rudi Dutschke. Now there is only Nelson Mandela. And we must share him with our parents. Little wonder that the young are less idealistic, since there are fewer places, people or ideologies to invest their idealism in. But the effect this has on their political views is far more complex than some would have us believe. Young people are still more likely to vote Labour than their elders. At the last election, Labour won 39 per cent of the under-24 vote, compared with 35 per cent for the Conservatives and 19 per cent for the Liberals.

Their views are also more in tune with what the Labour Party stands for. In his thesis 'Patterns Of First Time Voting', Dr Andrew Brown reveals that the young are more sympathetic to the redistribution of wealth, preserving the National Health Service and welfare benefits. The only issue in which there was no gap between them and older voters, Dr Brown discovered, was on trade union reform.

Young people, however, are far less likely to use their vote. That is nothing new. What is new is the level that non-voting has reached. Whereas turnout among the young used to lag behind the rest of the electorate by just over 10 per cent, the gap has now jumped considerably. According to the Demos report, only between 55 and 57 per cent of the under 34s went to the polls in 1992, compared with an overall turnout of 77 per cent. A survey published by the British Youth Council last year revealed that one in five of the under-24s did not even register.

The survey went on to point out that Major's 21-seat majority in 1992 was achieved by majorities in the 11 most marginal seats totalling only 2,478 votes. By contrast, a total of 2.5 million young people did not vote.

'Young people could have radically altered the face of British politics,' the Youth Council said. So why didn't they? Poll tax evasion, cynicism and general disillusionment provide some of the answers but not all. The rest is guesswork and it is my guess that, since they started dumping their ideological baggage and travelling light, the main parties have become virtually indistinguishable in their blandness to many first-time voters. If we had proportional representation, these people might have followed the example of their European peers and dumped the traditional parties in favour of the Greens, the hard left or the far right. As it is, some simply turn their back on the process altogether.

'Young people think politics and politicians are sanitised and grey. If the parties don't wake up there could be a lost generation of young people who have no history of involvement in participatory democracy,' warned Graham Hitchen of the Youth Council.

It is true that some young people have lost interest in politics; others were never interested; and yet more are so busy flipping burgers and waiting on tables in order to supplement meagre grants that they have little time to think about it. But the one thing on which all the surveys agree is that a large number are motivated by issues like racism, the environment, homelessness, gender equality, human rights and Third World poverty.

This is reflected in support for such organisations as the youth wing of Amnesty International, which has grown by about 3 per cent every year since it was set up in the late 1980s. There has been similar growth in environmental groups like Friends of the Earth and the Trotskyist Socialist Workers' Party. A considerable proportion of its new recruits are young blacks and Asians who joined through their work in the Anti-Nazi League.

And the list goes on, with the campaign against the Criminal Justice Bill, the gay rights group ACT-UP, Band Aid and the Mandela concerts, all involving huge numbers of young people who would rather get involved in single-issue campaigns in which they can play an active role than the eternal compromise of party politics. All this from a generation which pollsters tell us is voiceless and apathetic.

Unfortunately, few of the issues these single-issue organisations embrace rank highly on the agendas of the mainstream parties, which might explain why so few young people join them. The average age of a Conservative Party activist is 62 and almost half its constituency members are 66 or older. Senior Tories are now planning to close down the Young Conservatives. A survey in 1992 revealed the average age of a Labour Party member is about 48. Labour has closed its youth section down no fewer than five times because of infiltration from Communists and Trotskyists and is now left with a shell of an organisation, Young Labour, with only about 65 regional branches nationwide and few signs of any campaigning activity. Last year, the Liberals merged their youth and student movements after their combined membership had sunk to just 1,000.

Both Labour and Liberal youth leaders conveniently blame the low profile of young people in their respective organisations not on apathy but on the effect of 15 years of Tory government, which has both punished the young financially – principally through benefit cuts and student loans – and alienated them politically. The YC national vice-chairman, Jason Holland, is wedded to a different dogma altogether: 'Young people are more apathetic these days and I think that's a good thing. They are just getting on and doing things themselves and not relying on the state. And now that socialism has died there's a lot less interest in political parties anyway.'

The knee-jerk response of the party leaders to their ageing membership has often been to resort to patronising stunts. The first I remember was when Neil Kinnock appeared in a pop video with Tracy Ullman in 1984. In 1991, John Major recorded a nine-minute cassette which mixed politics with pop and sent it to 150,000 unsuspecting 18-year-olds. In July this year, Tony Blair confessed his penchant for Guns 'N' Roses and talked about his times in a student rock band during a 45-minute interview with Nicky Campbell on Radio 1.

These attempts to 'get down' to 'their' level would be funny if they were not so pathetic. They betray a belief that capturing the youth vote can be bought on the cheap when, in fact, their price for political allegiance is the same as anybody else's. They support parties which stand for issues, principles and policies that will improve their lot and provide relevant answers to the questions they are asking. The trouble is that few of the parties do this.

The most recent example of what happens when they don't was at this year's Liberal Party conference, where the Young Liberals proposed motions on the legalisation of soft drugs and the abolition of the monarchy: two issues in which young people have a keen interest. Within minutes of the cannabis motion being passed, the Liberal leadership was insisting that it would have no effect on party policy.

Whenever party leaders dismiss the concerns of their youth wings in this way, they show that while they are keen to draw young people back into the political process they are prepared to make few concessions in return.

Every time the parties do that, they cut off one more line of communication with Planet Youth. That leaves them hopelessly out of touch and sends the inhabitants of Planet Youth seeking vehicles for change in other orbits. •

Zenica refugees driven from Zepa, Bosnia

Sean Smith

World views

....

3 December 1994

Chris McGreal
Blood on their hands

Rwanda's former minister of information, Eliezer Niyitegeka, looks more comic than intimidating. He wears a dazzling white suit, Afro-hairstyle and has an AK-47 slung across his shoulder. He last set foot in Rwanda in mid-July. He and the other ministers of the ousted Rwanda government have taken refuge over the border in Bukava, Zaïre. Not for them the miseries of Goma's refugee camps. Many have settled into the Hotel Riviera, where comforts include pornographic movies after midnight. The exiled regime's offices are furnished with computers and a satellite phone. Here they are attempting to rewrite the history of the Rwandan genocide.

Perhaps as many as a million people died in three months of anti-Tutsi pogroms. Hutus who opposed the slaughter were exterminated as well. The ministers in exile who presided over the killings are now the targets of UN investigators piecing together evidence to put them on trial for genocide – they are also at the top of the list of people the new Rwandan government wants to execute if it can lay hands on them first.

Foremost among them is the ousted president, Theodore Sindikubwabo, a paediatrician who set in motion the slaughter of Butare's Tutsis. His prime minister, Jean Kambanda, travelled Rwanda using the language of murder understood by all. The commerce minister, once imprisoned for murdering his wife; the justice minister, herself married to a Tutsi; the youth minister, who openly encouraged children to kill – all of them are preparing a common defence, intent on obscuring the world's already confused view of Rwanda's calamity.

The time may come when the former ministers run for cover, along with the army chiefs settled into a Protestant evangelical mission in Goma, and the other alleged Rwandan war criminals scattered, as yet unfettered, across Africa and Europe. But for now they are on the offensive.

'Why do you want to talk about these dead Tutsis? What about my human rights? I can't even go home. Do you know there are people in my house in Kigali who are not even paying rent?' Niyitegeka challenged me.

'Neither of the two groups, the RPF and us, is saints. We know that massacres have been on both sides. I don't see any difference,' deposed Prime Minister Kambanda argued. But the main purpose of the defence is to ensure that one of the swiftest and most organised mass murders of modern times is seen, not as a political act, but as an African tribal bloodletting that nobody could predict and nobody could prevent. Among those keen to obscure reality is Eliezer Niyitegeka.

Niyitegeka comes from Kibuye province in the far west of Rwanda, bordering Lake Kivu's placid expanse. Like most of once-crowded Rwanda, its terraced hills are shorn of trees so every scrap of available land can be made use of. It was once home to one of the highest concentrations of Tutsis in the country. Although Niyitegeka lived in Kidashya village, in the province's south-western corner, his influence ranged across the territory. As Kibuye leader of the Democratic Republican Movement (MDR), he was well known if not universally popular.

Josue Kayijaho, a Tutsi doctor prominent in a leading human rights group, was at school with Eliezer Niyitegeka. 'He's not a good man, he was never a good man. We were both Seventh Day Adventists. Almost everybody was in our village. Eiliezer used to lead the singing in church. In 1973, I was in school with him when the Habyarimana coup happened and thousands of Tutsis were massacred. I remember him promoting the massacres, urging people on. I fled to Burundi because it was bad,' he said.

Niyitegeka went on to study journalism in Romania. By his own account, he left disillusioned with communism. More accurately he was forced home after stabbing a fellow Rwandan. He thought the man dead. Then, in the early 1980s, by which time he had worked his way into parliament through the one-party system, the 'dead' man popped up and began court proceedings. Eliezer Niyitegeka proved too much of an embarrassment and was thrown out of parliament.

With the reintroduction of multi-party politics in 1991, Niyitegeka helped revive the MDR, which was previously known as an aggressively Hutu nationalist outfit. Niyitegeka's modern-day faction was to prove much the same, embroiling itself in anti-Tutsi attacks which followed the Rwandan Patriotic Front (RPF) invasion four years ago. This had been led by Tutsis whose families had been forced from Rwanda three decades earlier.

As the murders spread to Niyitegeka's home province in August 1992 and hundreds died, Dr Kayijaho contacted his old school colleague. 'I called him to ask what we could do to stop these massacres. I said leaders in Kibuye asked me to phone him as MDR leader. There was silence. I asked the question again. He didn't say anything and then I knew he was involved in these massacres,' he said.

The RPF's military success forced the government to negotiate, and concede. The MDR, like other political parties, split. Niyitegeka was among party leaders who were opposed to compromise with the rebels. He led a faction that joined with hard-line elements in President Habyarimana's MRND, and another extremist offshoot, CDR. They called themselves Hutu-Power, and came to control the Interahamwe militias that were to lead the slaughter. At the time they were portrayed as Hutu cultural organisations. Niyitegeka toured Kibuye province whipping up sentiment against peace accords.

President Habyarimana's death on 6 April opened the floodgates of violent mayhem.

When news came in that the president's plane had been shot down, the extremists were quick to blame the RPF. In Kigali, Hutus who favoured the peace accord were murdered. Within days, Niyitegeka was installed as part of the new government which seized power. It is one of the questions former ministers, now framing their defence, find most difficult to answer. Why, if you were opposed to the unfolding slaughter, were you not only spared but permitted to take control of the government?

'When they called to swear me in as minister of information, I had not left my house because there were those who wanted to kill me. Someone said there were about six soldiers who wanted to kill me and my children and my wife. I suppose I was lucky. I only accepted to be minister of information to save the country, to save the situation. I did my best and I don't regret it,' Niyitegeka said limply.

As the killing machine cranked into gear across Rwanda, the wheels started turning in Kibuye. Slowly at first, individual opponents of Hutu extremism, both Tutsi and Hutu, were picked off. The province's Tutsis knew it was wise to keep a low profile. But many thought they had nothing to fear personally. Then Niyitegeka descended on his home province.

'I went there to stabilise the situation. The problem was that the RPF had given the Tutsis weapons and there were infiltrators everywhere. Nobody prepared a massacre of the Tutsis, but we had to kill the infiltrators. If there were prepared massacres they were the massacres by the opposition, the RPF, not us,' he now claims.

In fact, the speeches he gave in towns and villages, broadcast by Radio Rwanda and the notoriously extremist RTLM radio, had a far from settling effect. 'I have trust in our armed forces. They will defeat all our enemies. And you, the population, should join the armed forces to eliminate every kind of enemy, wherever they may hide,' he said in a speech broadcast on RTLM. For those such as the Tutu mayor of Kibuye town, Augustin Karara, the message was clear.

'When Eliezer was moving around he was encouraging the people to kill. He couldn't say it openly. He would say they were doing very good "work" or they should "get to work"; Such a message meant killing Tutsis. He was on very good terms with some mayors where a lot of people were killed. He praised them openly for their "work",' Karara said. 'In some communes there were MDR party leaders who were not on his side. He told people they had to be "dealt with, dealt with the same way they deal with sympathisers". Some were killed.'

There were other euphemisms popular with political leaders and those leading the killing. Peasants were urged to 'clear the bush', which was understood as an instruction to kill Tutsis, 'the bush' in which the RPF might hide. At other times people were told to 'clean around their houses', which was meant to spur them into slaughtering their neighbours.

Kibuye town was about as far from the front line as you could get, yet the Interahamwe claimed to find those they called 'inyenzi' or cockroaches – the RPF and its supporters – at every turn. The militia delighted in prolonging the suffering of their victims, sometimes leaving them squirming in the road next to their severed limbs, not quite dead, futilely fighting for life. Bullets were not to be wasted. The victims were not limited to those who might prove able to fight. Small children, old women, the crippled, anyone could be selected. Those who were not party to the slaughter usually walked by. It was the safest thing to do.

Escape from Kibuye was nearly impossible. Interahamwe roadblocks were scattered along the only overland route out of town. Tutsis were sitting targets scurrying across the bare hills. And where would they escape to? Some looked longingly across Lake Kivu to Zaïre just a few miles away, but there were few boats to hand.

The hunted were encouraged by the provincial governor, Clement Kayishema, to flee for the traditional sanctuary of the church. The message was passed by word of mouth, by police knocking on doors, on the radio. Go to the church, or the football stadium. There will be safety in numbers. We will protect you. Thousands of Tutsis crammed into both sites. Everyone knew the church would be safe because even at the most dangerous times of the past 35 years, its sanctity had been respected. This year was different.

On Sunday, 17 April, Karara, the town's Hutu mayor, noticed new faces on the streets. 'Groups of men were discussing something. Some came from outside town. They went around collecting men. Some came willingly, they were enthusiastic to kill. Others were forced to go. Then the army passed out guns and the church was surrounded. The governor went up there but he didn't try to stop it. A lot of people think he was behind it. The militia and the army and police took part. Not all, but those that didn't stood by. Those who escaped the bullets and grenades were cut up with machetes,' he said.

'They wanted me to buy beer for the killers to make the killing easier. Afterwards there were some people who were still alive and wounded. I took some people to the hospital. The militia asked me what I was doing with those "inyenzi" but let me take them. Then they went there and killed them,' Karara said.

The next day the scene was repeated at the stadium. Probably 10,000 people were killed. But still it was not the end of Kibuye's Tutsi population. Fresh corpses continued to litter the town, but significant numbers of Tutsis survived by sheltering in the hospital, private homes and seeking out the few hiding places in the bare hills. A dozen Tutsi nuns were holed up in their convent, sheltering a small group of orphans but unable to leave.

Then two weeks later, Niyitegeka returned to the town, this time in the company of Prime Minister Jean Kambanda. The prime minister summoned the province's mayors and other notables for what was billed as a meeting to 'stabilise the situation'. Augustin Karara went along. 'The prime minister thanked everybody for their work. He said the enemy is the RPF but then he said "inyenzi" are everywhere and they must be treated in the same way. The mayor of Gishyita stood up. He complained he had too many "inyenzi" in his area and he had only been able to kill three or four hundred people. He asked for help. The prime minister told him to make a report. At that time there were bodies everywhere. People were being murdered but the prime minister didn't once say "stop the killings",' Karara said. Troops and militia were later dispatched to Gishyita to help the mayor with his 'problem'.

'Eliezer spoke after the prime minister. He said we had a revolution in '59 and it failed because it wasn't properly done. This time he said we must do it properly, we must finish the war against the RPF and its supporters,' Karara said. 'They didn't say the words "kill the Tutsis" but in Rwanda people understood what was meant.' The call to finish the 1959 revolution was a popular one with extremists. The Hutu rebellion at that time had overturned traditional Tutsi powers, abused in the run-up to independence, and had led to hundreds of thousands of Tutsis fleeing as refugees. Their sons and daughters had come back 30 years later as the RPF. The message of the new Hutu revolution was not to permit such a thing to happen again. In essence, it was a call to kill every Tutsi, no matter how young. It was an instruction that was to be swiftly followed after the meeting.

There had been one brave voice there, Karara recalled. It belonged to a Dr Hitimana: 'At that time there was a doctor who asked for some food to feed the Tutsi children in the hospital. He was insulted in public. Eliezer Niyitegeka told the doctor he should not be worrying about those children, about "inyenzi",' Karara said. 'There were about 20 children at the hospital. They were all killed that day. The doctor fled to Kigali.' It was the start of another rampage against the remaining Tutsis. This time very few were to survive.

Relaxing in Bukavu, Eliezer Niyitegeka has a different recollection. 'When I went to Kibuye I met the mayors. I saw one who was giving people beer so they would kill people. I asked, how is it possible to give people beer and then encourage them to kill? I also got a report that the mayor in my home commune was stealing things from people after he killed them. I wrote to him and I made a report to the government, to the prime minister copying to the president, asking him to remove the mayor. Unfortunately, they didn't. I am not an angel but I did my best in that situation,' he said.

'In my native hill in Kibuye, in my house, some Tutsis hid so they wouldn't be killed. Unfortunately, people found out and killed them. But it shows they believed in me,' Niyitegeka argued.

He is not alone amongst those implicated in the genocide in claiming to have protected Tutsis. Kambanda says he did the same. The former governor of Kigali province, Francois Karera, even produces a 13-year-old boy called Ntukanyagwe he says is a Tutsi he saved from certain death. Karera effectively runs the largest Hutu refugee camp in Goma through his control of the Interahamwe who fled there.

There are many other instances of Tutsis placing their faith in those with authority who, in some cases at least, appear to have used the Tutsis as a shield against the RPF or as a defence against the charges they now face.

Among the first victims in April was Niyitegeka's predecessor as information minister, Faustin Rucogoza. He was a Hutu, but that cut no ice with the fanatics. Rucogoza had threatened to shut down the extremist RTLM radio, which from the start pressed the case for the killing. As information minister, Niyitegeka had the authority to at least try to silence RTLM and to use Radio Rwanda to oppose the slaughter. Instead, while Tutsis were murdered in their hundreds of thousands, as children were slaughtered or encouraged to kill, as women were raped, as churches and hospitals were transformed into extermination centres, Niyitegeka says he could not interfere with press freedom.

'RTLM was an independent radio station. Anyway, nobody complained about RTLM except the UN commander, General Delaire, who didn't like what was said about him. I asked RTLM to offer him airtime for his views and they did. If others had complained, they could have had time to put their view.'

If a Tutsi had come out of hiding to demand a right of reply to the calls for his murder, he would have been granted it?

'Why not? I called the chief of broadcasting of RTLM. I told him he has to try to moderate the broadcasts. But it was independent. What could I do?' he asked.

Shut it down?

'What about press freedom? Can you, as a journalist, say we should breach that?' Niyitegeka responded.

As UN investigators, the new Rwandan government and human rights groups compile their cases, members of the ousted regime have been shaping a multi-faceted defence. It begins with a general denial of responsibility.

Former Prime Minister Jean Kambanda argues that his government did not seize power until three days after President Habyarimana's plane was shot down, by which time the worst of the massacres were over. Reminded that when the interim government was installed most Tutsis in Kibuye, for instance, were alive and when it collapsed they were not, Kambanda changes tack.

'I admit the killings went on but that is the RPF's fault. If the RPF had agreed to a cease-fire, we could have used the army to stop the killing. To say the government did nothing is a lie. On 10 April, my foreign minister asked the French ambassador to send troops to contain the situation,' Kambanda said.

It is a dubious claim. The appeal to France – which did dispatch forces at the start of the civil war – amounted to a cry for help in repelling the RPF, not in saving the Tutsis.

But the foundation of the defence is that the massacres were a spontaneous reaction, an unpredictable and uncontrollable tribal killing in response to the murder of President Habyarimana. It is an explanation favoured by Kambanda and Niyitegeka, perhaps in the expectation it will fit the international court's perception of Africa.

The truth, as brave Hutus such as Kibuye's former mayor can testify, is something quite different. The politicians, army leaders and others with a vested interest in blocking change, exploited ethnic rivalries to inflate real Hutu fears of revived Tutsi domination. It was designed to preserve political power they knew was sure to be lost under the terms of the peace accord.

'These were poor people. They believed what their leaders told them. There was no danger in Kibuye at that time but their leaders made out the "inyenzi" were everywhere and were going to kill them or steal their property. I did my best to discourage the killings. With some good policemen we smuggled Tutsis away. If I had had help from the government, if it had said stop the killing, people would have listened. It never did that. Never,' he said. 'It was difficult to understand that the government was supporting it. It took a long time for me to realise.'

Niyitegeka bemoans life in exile. There are rare expressions of remorse, for having lost the war. There are bellicose threats to start it again. And there is plenty of self-pity over life in a country with no law and order. In September, Zaïrean troops stole his Mercedes at gunpoint, and he has discovered RPF soldiers have occupied his home in Rwanda. He says he would not mind but they are not paying rent.

'I came with two cars. They have been taken. Life is very difficult. I would like to go to Europe or somewhere else but I have no money. When we arrived in Goma they took the money we had and put it in the bank in Zaïre. Now we can't get it out. They say we have to pay for all the damage done by the refugees,' he said. The Rwandan currency, gold and foreign exchange confiscated by the Zaïreans had been looted from Rwanda's central bank.

In Kibuye, plants are thriving now on top of a mass grave sloping behind the church. But they cannot stifle the stench that still permeates the building. The church walls are scrubbed clean but the outbuildings remain as they were on the day of the massacre. Bloody handprints and footprints speckle the walls like a child's painting. Recent rains washed away the topsoil from another mass grave near the stadium, exposing the rotting corpses. The UN used bulldozers to cover them over again.

Augustin Karara was replaced as mayor by the RPF. After a long interrogation it cleared him of any role in the massacres. He was one of many brave Hutus who did what they could to protect Tutsis at considerable risk to themselves, disproving the extremists' claim that the killing was nothing more than tribal warfare.

Those in Kibuye town who did not flee still shy away from discussing the genocide, and more particularly what occurred at their church. But Karara says that quietly and slowly they are beginning to face up to it.

'Now they feel ashamed. They are very ashamed. It is very shameful,' he said. ●

....

8 April 1995

Nicholas Ingram
Statement

In a sworn affidavit to the federal district court in Atlanta yesterday by Nicholas Ingram's lawyer, Clive Stafford Smith, Ingram made the following statement:

At around 5.30pm last night I was taken from my cell in the hospital section to H-5, the cell by the chair. I had to walk by the chair which was covered by a sheet. I was sweating it, because walking by really brought it home.

Apparently, at 5.55pm my case was stayed, but nobody told me. Indeed, at 6.20pm – the time I know because the guards told me – they began seriously to prepare me for execution. It was devoid of humanity, a bunch of sick people who apparently volunteered for the job, acting like I was an animal, a sheep being prepared for slaughter.

They shaved my head with electric shears. That was not short enough so they used a Norelco-type triple razor to cut it short, and to shave my right shin. I knew Lieutenant Stewart, an officer who used to work on death row, and Officer Kelly, a transport officer, who were doing it. They seemed like they had done it before. They treated me like an animal, and said that it was just a job. They had me put on some pants with a cut up the leg for where they would attach the electrode.

They asked me what I wanted for a last meal. I said I did not want food, but I did want some cigarettes. They said the new policies forbid smoking. The chaplains were there most of the time – even before, when they put a finger up my anus in the strip naked 'physical' exam. They would not do anything about all this, but were trying to get me to accept their beliefs. I have my own strong religious feelings and did not want a philosophical debate with them.

They have told me it all starts again at 4pm today with the 'physical' once more, and that I am to die tonight. ●

13 April 1995

Clive Stafford Smith
My private view of a ritual death

I watched my friend Nicky Ingram die in the electric chair at 9pm last Friday. One way or another, we spent a lot of our lives together, Nicky and me. We were three and a half years apart from meeting in the maternity ward in Cambridge, but our lives finally crossed when I was 26 and he was 22. I was fresh out of law school, and he was on his way to becoming a veteran of Death Row. By the time he died, we had been attorney and client, and then friends, for almost a third of our lives.

But what do you talk about to someone who is about to be killed? When I talked to Nicky for the last time at 8.32, the Supreme Court had not ruled on his case and Nicky still held out hope. I knew different. The court clerk had asked us whether we had anything else to file – shorthand for death.

It was still the same old Nicky, worried about what effect this would have on me. 'Give 'em hell, Clive, for all those other people,' he said. Should I give his Mum a message? 'Just tell her I love her.' Still present tense; soon to be past. At 8.46, they made me leave. All I could say was 'Bye'. Still no formal word from the Supreme Court, but I told my colleagues in Atlanta, who were still on the line, not to tell him until the last minute. False hope is better than none at all.

When I was waiting around, one of the guards spoke to me. Going on stereotype, he might have been one of the large-bellied rednecks driving the pick-up trucks outside. 'I knew Nick five years ago, when I worked his tier,' he said. 'Never gave us a moment's trouble. You could take half of those guys back there' – he pointed to Death Row – 'and let them out tonight, and you'd never hear from them again. Don't get me wrong. There are some real psychos back there, but Nick's not one of 'em.' All I could do was smile at him. If I had spoken I would have cried.

Most of the British journalists were our friends, but they had never met him, and even they fell for the prison's 'electrocutioneering', the public relations of death. At the court house two days earlier, they had seen Nicky staring at them, cold and unsmiling. What was that stare? they asked me later, after he died. If they had asked me then, I could have told them. They were sitting on the prosecution's side of the aisle, and did not know the etiquette. Nicky was wondering at all the assistant prosecutors wishing his death. He made his assumptions, and was wrong: they made theirs, and were wrong also.

That seems an age ago. Then we had hope. Now we only had minutes. Travelling to the back of the prison, at least I was allowed to be in a van by myself, away from all the witnesses who actually wanted to be there. I passed through a gate with a posted sign: 'Buckle Up for Safety's Sake'. In the chamber, the media craned forward in their seats as Nicky was brought in – a small, bald man surrounded by six massive guards, strapping him in, buckling him up for safety. He stared each person coldly in the eye, they said. He ignored a wave from his lawyer, they said. How sad. They did not even realise that the glass was a one-way mirror, and that all he could see was a reflection of himself. He and I had talked about it. We had heard he would not be able to see, and he said I would know for sure if he did not acknowledge my wave. He could not see either them or me. All he could do was stare into the future, and hope for better than the past.

He refused a final prayer, they said. Perhaps they should have asked the Pope what prayer he would want at his execution. Perhaps they should have remembered that the Pharisees mocked when he was being shaved, and Nicky did not need their bitter solace. Perhaps they should have remembered that Nicky was not Christian, and was denied Randy Loney, an ecumenical minister who understood his faith, to administer the last rites. There was a strange link between Nicky and the lone and level sands of the Outback; locked in his little cell, Nicky often told me that he felt a kinship with the Aboriginal people of Australia, and their faith in the spirituality of nature.

He spat on the warden, they said. It is true. He had told me he would do it. The warden had just asked him what final words he had. Perhaps Nicky should have asked Alistair Cooke what small speech he might give under the circumstances. But Nicky should not have had to announce his own death. He asked me to be his mouthpiece afterwards, if I could find the words. He had warned me that all he would be able to do would be to express his contempt for the rituals of death.

If truth must be known, unable to speak, Nicky wanted to spit on Thomas Charron, the District Attorney, but he could not see him through the one-way glass. After languishing in the polls of late, Charron had exploited the case for a few votes, tormenting Nicky as well as his family. It may be uncharitable, but I must agree with Nicky in his contempt for the man, albeit tinged with sadness that anyone could be so base. I was close by the prosecutor as he waited to watch Nicky die, but he could not look me in the eye.

Nicky died a painless death, they said. The guards buckled him up, two straps on each arm, one on the chest, one on the waist, one on each leg, and one around the head. Having leather straps cutting into your flesh makes it painless for the observers, you see. When Jimmy Gray died in Mississippi in 1983, his head thrashed around and graphically illustrated his pain. Witnesses vomited. We cannot have that, or nobody will believe the Great Lie any more. So before they killed my client Edward Johnson in 1987, they strapped his head tightly to a pole. That was so nobody could see the pain. Just the same old, same old . . . the public relations of death.

It astounds me that people can be so naive, and that good-hearted, intelligent journalists believed the nonsense that the prison fed them. If death is instantaneous, as the prison's glossy hand-out insisted, why send electricity through the poor man for two minutes? If he is dead in a second, why carry on cooking him? Try counting those extra 119 seconds. That's a long time when you are dying.

If he would not thrash about in agony, why tie him down so tightly? If he would not cry out in pain, why bind his mouth firmly shut? If his nose would not bleed, why block it off? If his face does not mirror his pain, why cover it with that large flap of beige leather? The witnesses who never knew Nicky in life even fell for the prison's electrocutioneering in death.

So they went ahead and killed him that Friday night. I watched it. I feel physically sick while I write this, but I am glad I was there. Perhaps I can help save Nicky from the ultimate indignity of dying as a number, not a human being, known to the world only by the state's accusation of murder.

He asked me to speak for him, and I will. Nicky was sorry for what happened to the Saywer family, and he was sorry that they believed he intended their agony. He hated to see them suffer as pawns in Tom Charron's political game. He wrote to tell them his feelings, a letter I am now charged to deliver. It is all over, so I am free to say that Nicky told me the same story consistently for 10 years: he had no recall of the crime at all. They said he did it, and he believed them. It was only when I was able to find the resources to look more closely that I convinced him that there was more to that day's tragic events than the prosecution pretended.

Nicky hated to see what happened to his own family, tortured by years of broken hopes. He refused to let me tell the courts all the details of his childhood – horrendous stories of his former stepmother bashing him over the head with a bottle, making him pile up rocks in the back garden to keep him out of sight and out of mind, or feeding him alcohol to the verge of a coma from age 13 onwards. He wanted to spare his family more pain, even though it might have saved his life.

He did not want me witnessing his execution for fear of what it would do to me. He wanted me to 'give 'em hell' for years to come on behalf of his remaining friends on Death Row.

But I went to his death. I owed it to him. I could not leave him there alone with all those numbers, those faceless prosecutors, guards and journalists. All we know about them is the sickening fact that they volunteered to watch him die. I wish someone would speak for them. I really want to hear something good about them. ●

14 March 1995

John Gittings
Leaps and binds

Ms Wang's entrepreneurial efforts in Guangan, hometown of Deng Xiaoping, would win the approval of the old man himself. Her Elegant Restaurant, just a few tables in the open ground floor of an old wooden building, is packed with customers eating chicken with red hot chillies. There is a queue for her Elegant Hair Salon across the road when it opens each morning. The tag is hard to resist: here in the provincial heartland of Deng's new revolution is the Good Businesswoman of Sichuan.

Wang dresses in eye-catching clothes for a small county town in the middle of China: high heels and a fur-lined outfit one night, a denim suit the next. But the elderly man in an old raincoat, helping out with the bills, is the real key to the operation. He is her father, and also the Communist Party Secretary (or boss) of a large factory, a crucial position from which to get the permits for opening a shop. Party officials are debarred from going into business but there is nothing to stop their family members from fronting the operation.

In Guangan's 'get rich first' atmosphere, Ms Wang has some serious competition. Outside the Elegant Salon last week, a leaflet was being distributed for International Women's Day. But the text was not so internationalist: 'To celebrate this important day, the Flying Geese Restaurant invites you to join a banquet on favourable terms. 237 Renminbi for six starters, seven main dishes, soup and fruit (drinks not included). See you tonight!'

Guangan is a traditional market town of the kind which has driven the Chinese rural economy since the development of urban commerce a thousand years ago. On the pavements are mounds of vegetables, the intense colours attributed to the fertile Sichuan earth, hanks of suspended meat dripping into the dust, piles of beans and pyramids of sugar cane. The shops sell tools, twine, spare parts, all the peasants need. But Guangan has also embarked on a new Leap Forward which transcends the traditional economy. There are stores stocked with electronic goods, 80 new private taxis hooting through the streets and two new Economic Development Zones.

The economic reforms of the past 15 years mainly benefited coastal China and the big cities. But Deng's strategy since 1992 has been to inspire a fresh wave of entrepreneurial activity across the country by extending the tax and other concessions the coast had. What better place than his hometown to study this phenomenon of economic boom and its uncertain effects on society.

Guangan still has a sense of civic responsibility which has been weakened in other towns where the economic revolution has gone further. Army officers sweep the road in support of a new health campaign – even if some look unused to handling a broom. The Women's League of the Guangan Electrical Company hands out essential information on 'What the Peasant Should Know about Electricity'. Don't explode fireworks near cables or dig ditches next to pylons. Don't confuse washing lines with electric lines. Don't divert power for private use to deter thieves, stun fish or kill rats.

The start in Beijing last week of the National People's Congress – China's mainly advisory parliament – did not cause much of a stir on the streets of Guangan. I found only one friendly policeman who had heard the opening speech by Premier Li Peng. But Sichuan's delegation to Beijing boasted of Guangan's connection with Deng and claimed that the lives of the peasants in his home village of Xie Xing, five kilometres away, had been transformed.

That was not the view of one angry farmer in the Guangan marketplace who displayed his heavily worn hands to me as credentials. 'Deng Xiaoping's birthplace is all for show. You don't know what we peasants really live like: not enough food, poor housing, while the officials get rich. I know what I'm talking about. I fought for Deng in Vietnam. The problem is: he's a good man but we are cheated by the people beneath him.' A couple of young men in cheap suits, come from the big city to check out business opportunities in Guangan, told me to ignore him. 'He's an old fool.'

Conflicts of evidence between official statistics and popular perceptions are frequent; so is the mutual contempt between many city-dwellers and peasants. In 1993, serious peasant riots broke out over excessive taxation in Renshou, an impoverished county only 60 kilometres from the provincial capital of Chengdu. Yet people in Chengdu today barely know what happened and insist that peasants everywhere are doing well.

A 400-mile journey across the Red Basin of Sichuan – from Chengdu via Guangan to Chongqing (the wartime capital known to Westerners as Chungking) – suggests that this is far from being the case. At an average speed of 20 kilometres an hour, long-distance bus travel offers a close-up view of the parts of China other methods rarely reach. Sometimes these journeys pass through areas technically 'closed' to foreigners. That is no problem if one has a convincing destination. (The real disincentive is the bone-bruising ride and knowledge that most road fatalities in China are caused by overloaded buses.)

Cutting across country proves the obvious but overlooked point. Even if the gross statistics are correct (and China's own Statistical Bureau has warned they are often boosted by local officials eager to claim success), the effects of the economic boom away from the coast and big cities are localised and patchy.

I travelled across eight counties with a population of as many millions. Away from Chengdu and Chongqing, the only sign of economic take-off was in Deng's home county – a remarkable coincidence, or is it more than that? Elsewhere life seemed much the same as 10 years ago after the first post-Mao Zedong reforms had restored peasant markets and led to some new building of peasant homes. The broad-bladed hoe is still the most common tool. Farmers work barefoot in the paddy with red mud stains up to their knees. There are no roadside advertisements, only one or two cars, and the main form of transport is still the bicycle or a bamboo shoulder-basket. The county towns are dusty and bare: one or two karaoke bars with tattered curtains give a whiff of modern life. Hairdressing is much less elegant than in Guangan. I saw one customer having her hair hosed down on a pavement stool.

Here the pressure of population growth has swelled the flow of peasant migrants to the south with special force. Slogans put up by the local governments stress the point: 'Warning to all citizens: the Chinese population has reached 1.2 billion.'

Other slogans hint at a rural life-style which has been lowered, not raised, in recent years and appeal in dated language for a return to socialist values. In one short stretch of road I noted down the following: 'Everyone get organised and smash down the criminals.' 'Politics in command is the key to the socialist road.' 'Those who refuse to pay taxes will be punished according to law.' 'Unite to abolish all illegal religious activity' (probably a reference to the Protestant 'house churches' which flourish in parts of Sichuan and other deprived provinces).

What on earth was going on here? These glimpses through bus windows more often black than grey with dust can only lift a tiny corner of a rural reality even harder to gauge further away from what counts for the main road.

Guangan's building boom is all the more startling by contrast. Hilltops have been tipped into valleys to form two new 'Economic Development Zones' to the north and south of the city. Clusters of shacks with matting for roofs have sprung up to provide shelter and food for the peasant contract workers. The red dust blows in everywhere.

Pursuing my historical research into Deng's early life, I was greeted with simple kindness. One encounter led gently to another. Some old folk chivvied a group of teenagers to practise their English on me. Two of the boldest invited me to their school.

I gave an impromptu lesson to a class of 100 − I had to count to believe my eyes (the average across the school is 70!). I was hijacked by an English teacher, struggling amazingly well with a language she had learnt only from fellow-Chinese and tapes. The headmaster told me, proudly, that here they were able to pay the teachers' salaries on time. Elsewhere educational funds are diverted for prestige development projects and teachers − like peasants − may get paid with IOUs.

Will the next generation of Guangan teenagers aspire instead to work for a joint venture or run a nightclub? My friends took me to see the new South Guangan Economic Zone. One of the roads, I was told with pride, is 40 metres wide. First to be finished are a set of 18 five-storey apartment blocks, nicely faced with tiles. Some are maisonettes of the kind built for foreigners on the outskirts of Chengu and Chongqing. Lavish substitute housing, perhaps, for the inhabitants of old Guangan's wooden houses, with their attractive balustrades but no sanitation? No, these are new apartments for the cadres of the Guangan Prefecture. Once again, the party connection. It begins to make better sense.

Guangan recently had a crucial promotion from the status of county (*xian*) to the much larger prefecture (*diqu*). This favoured and highly unusual treatment also explains a great deal. To do this it has sliced off a great chunk of the neighbouring prefecture to which it used to belong. With that territory, plus the immeasurable factor of Deng's connection, comes investment funds both from the three counties now absorbed into Guangan and from Beijing.

A special edition of the *Guangan News* offers tax incentives for foreign investors and a list of projects ranging from a paper factory to new classrooms at the local technical college. But Guangan has bigger plans than an assortment of light and medium industry. It aspires to build 'the biggest power station in south-western China' – a coal-fired plant generating nearly 2.5 million kilowatts at a price of $350 million – *if* it can get Beijing's go-ahead. The story is long and involved. Guangan's main backer in Beijing, a close friend of Deng, has died. New pledges are being sought. They will have to hurry up: the Deng connection may not outlive the man. Deng does not seem to have personally championed the cause.

Mao went back home twice in his later life, seeking inspiration at crisis moments of the Great Leap Forward (1959) and the Cultural Revolution (1966). Deng left home in 1920 to study in France, and has never returned to Guangan. The road to the Deng family farmhouse climbs high above the Qu River – one of many tributaries to the Yangzi – into a hilly but intensively cultivated terrain. The land is sculpted in man-made fields shaped to make the best use of water run-off. Rape seed and wheat are intermixed, with fruit trees on the margins and patches of vegetables sown between the other crops like embroidery.

Several dozen peasants were rehoused when the farmhouse was turned into a museum less than 10 years ago. It is a substantial tiled building with three wings – a landlord's home. One of Deng's brothers was an opium smoker whom Deng failed to save from being 'persecuted to death' during the Cultural Revolution. There are canopied wooden beds. A room of photographs disconcertingly includes Margaret Thatcher – twice. Monty is also there, being told by Mao that Deng (this was before the Cultural Revolution) is second in line for the succession. Outside, parties of schoolchildren and small groups of Chinese on vacation pose for the obligatory picture under the signboard saying: 'Deng Xiaoping's old home'. There are exactly two souvenir stalls selling postcards, notelets and medallions in praise of 'our great architect of reform'. Mao's birthplace in Hunan province has several hundred shops, hustling restaurant owners and its own railway access.

A 500-character poem, displayed on either side of the door to Deng's bedroom, celebrates in classical Chinese the modern concept of 'importing European capital and American technology'. Not far away, Deng's mother and grandmother are buried in an auspicious site overlooking the valley. Children play while their mothers hoe the vegetables. Mist floats up. There is a shimmer of fruit blossom. The loudest noise comes from above: a sandstone bluff, known as the Buddha's Hand, is losing its fingers to hammers and crowbars. The appetite for stone of an expanding Guangan must be satisfied.

What does Guangan tell us about the big 'After Deng' question? Poised for economic take-off, at first sight it seems to confirm the argument that there should be no big problem. The good businessmen and women of Sichuan and elsewhere will carry on regardless of whatever arcane struggles take place in Beijing. Yet there must be a limit to the number of Guangans that China can support, sucking investment from elsewhere. There is a limit, too, to the amount of land which can be swallowed up for construction. If the party is to survive, it must somehow also limit the appetite of officials aspiring to maisonettes and the profits of indirect commerce.

The biggest question remains in those villages off the road which itself is already off the beaten track. Migrant workers send back funds to keep their families alive, and provide cheap labour for the urban boom. No one really knows whether this will prove to be a satisfactory new social contract between town and countryside or the cause of more lethal friction when the boom subsides.

Guangan is still a place where one is woken by the cockcrow and there are fields through the back window. But not for long. In its headlong rush to modernise, it is like everywhere else in China which seizes the hour in a cloud of frenetic dust – even if it means smashing Buddha's fingers. •

··

31 January 1995

Jonathan Freedland
The right stuff

One of the best American cartoons of last year depicted Bill Clinton as a horse. It showed the President sweatily dragging a carriage whose sole passenger was a lordly elephant, togged up in tails.

The elephant, the mascot of the Republican party, represented Clinton's new masters, who had just won a landslide victory in November's mid-term elections. The caption had the elephant whipping the Clinton-beast while barking instructions. 'Turn right, my man! And right again, then right, right again, bear right . . .'

The cartoon is due for a reissue, with perhaps one alteration. Now the hectoring master should not be merely the Republican party but the American nation itself.

For America is turning right. Not just in politics, but in the workplace, on the airwaves, in the campuses, and on the street. Young and old, black and white, male and female, in the cities and in the sticks – throughout America there gusts a headwind, blowing rightward.

The election results were not the origin of this hurricane, only proof that it had come. Remember the scale of the storm: Republicans gained 51 seats in the House of Representatives, nine in the Senate and 10 governor's mansions, leaving both houses of Congress and 30 of the 50 states in Republican hands.

But evidence of the shift is everywhere, reaching beyond the ballot box and deep inside the culture. Ask the staff at KSFO Radio in San Francisco. All the on-air presenters lost their jobs this month after management decided the station's 'liberal-talk' format was a failure. Overnight, KSFO opted to ride the national talk-radio tidal wave and go conservative. Now its daily line up features Ronald Reagan's son Michael, as well as 1992 presidential candidate and self-styled 'cultural warrior' Pat Buchanan.

And that was in San Francisco, once the Islington of American liberalism.

Across the country, right-wing talk radio is entrenched. The king of the medium, Rush Limbaugh, is estimated to reach 20 million people a week on 660 stations, all tuning in to a daily monologue of Clinton-bashing and welfare-trashing, punctuated by Limbaugh's much-imitated riff, the angry cry of the put-upon white male.

There are now 1,000 talk stations in the US, five times the number on air 10 years ago. Most of them are conservative, plenty of them evangelical. Once the preserve of a fringe, who found medium wave a cosy and available hidey-hole, talk is now the nation's most wired medium. According to one poll, 44 per cent of Americans regard talk radio as their prime source of political information.

Republican Speaker Newt Gingrich has recognised its power: he now holds monthly briefings with the leading talk-show hosts and, hours after his election victory, pointedly refused a phone call from the president so he could do a talk-show interview instead.

Make no mistake, the radio ayatollahs are not just fiscally conservative. They are right wing in the old-fashioned, bruising sense of the term. Veteran talkmeister Bob Grant calls Martin Luther King a 'scumbag' and blacks 'savages', and his ratings go up. WABC in New York, where Grant and Limbaugh go back to back, claims to be the most successful radio station in America.

Polls indicate that the talkers are not garnering audiences because they shock. On the contrary, attitude surveys suggest that the firebreathers of AM radio are merely saying what everyone else already thinks. Put simply: compassion is out, harshness is in.

When, for example, Newt Gingrich suggested bringing back the orphanage for children of the indigent, the conventional wisdom said he had bungled. It was a gaffe, chorused the experts; Gingrich had evoked Dickensian images of the workhouse and cast himself as Scrooge. He would have to recant.

But no. The orphanage proposal may have been dismissed as 'unbelievable and absurd' by Hillary Clinton, but everywhere else it was taken quite seriously. Liberal columnists emerged to say Newt might actually have a point, that something did have to be done about the offspring of the (mainly black) underclass, who, raised by teen-moms, grow into gun-wielding, benefit-draining, drug-dealing hoodlums. It was as if Newt had tried to see how far he could go, and discovered the answer: further than you think.

Indeed, as the orphanage case proved, America's national conversation has shifted so far to the right that actions or statements which would inflame the liberal conscience anywhere else in the world now go without mention in the US.

A neat example comes from Texas, where two men were executed this month. One, Mario Marquez, was so retarded that when eating his last meal he put aside his dessert – a slice of apple pie – because he wanted to 'save it for later'. The other, Jesse Dewayne Jacobs, was put to death even after the Texas public prosecutor admitted he had not killed anyone, but had merely been an accomplice.

These cases did not prompt a liberal outcry. There were no bleeding heart demonstrations. The dead men's epitaphs were a few words in the news-in-brief column, tucked away on the inside pages.

America's attitude to the death penalty, and to crime in general, illustrates how far the pendulum has swung rightward. Capital punishment, once illegal under the constitution, is now so accepted it is political suicide even to question it.

Instead politicians scurry to keep up with a public that demands tougher and tougher action on crime. First came 'Three Strikes and You're Out', the baseball-rule-turned-crime-policy, which demands life imprisonment for any thrice-offending violent criminal. That wasn't hard enough, so California Governor Pete Wilson suggested a Two Strikes policy, and now some Republicans suggest throwing away the key after just one violent felony. To make room for all the new lifers the Republican Contract with America sets aside a colossal $10 billion to build prisons.

Driving this desire for iron justice are the 89 per cent of Americans who believe that crime is worsening – even though it's actually levelling off. They watch local TV news, with its nightly servings of rape, gang warfare and drive-by killings, and they hanker for a crackdown.

That urge translates into a nostalgic yearning for old-fashioned solutions. Newt Gingrich skilfully sold his orphanage idea by telling people to see Spencer Tracy and Mickey Rooney in *Boys Town*. Prisoners in Mississippi now wear 1930s style uniforms, complete with cartoon-style arrows and the word 'convict' stencilled on the back.

America, for so long the nation of forward-looking optimism, has begun looking enviously back at its past, to the days before the decay set in. That's why – besides special effects and Tom Hanks – *Forrest Gump* was the biggest cinema hit of the year. It struck this current nerve of deep conservatism dead on. Right-wingers lauded the film as an assault on the counter-culture and a homage to patriotism, capitalism and the family.

Think of the storyline: Forrest's sweetheart took drugs, hung out with anti-Vietnam types and was rewarded with Aids. Forrest, by contrast, wore his country's uniform, invested wisely and made a mint. When that's the ethos of the year's smash movie, you know something is going on.

Nowhere is the lurch to the right more obvious than on race. Witness the debate over *The Bell Curve*, published last autumn. A couple of scientists with a passion for numbers suggested that IQ is partly hereditary and that blacks have less of it than whites and Asians. The authors were not ridiculed as cranky eugenicists, but discussed instead in cover stories in America's leading periodicals. Charles Murray became a TV regular, and his book won the praise of respected thinkers.

Meanwhile another two white male academics have proposed the California Civil Rights Initiative, a state-wide referendum which, if passed, would outlaw positive discrimination. The plan is to roll back 'affirmative action' which currently allows employers to show favour to women and racial minorities at the expense of white men.

Underpinning this 'white-lash' movement is the widespread feeling that whites have done enough to compensate for previous generations' mistreatment of blacks. 'I didn't keep any slaves,' says Stuttering John, once the sidekick of shock-jock Howard Stern, now making a living as a professional Angry White Male. This month the state of Missouri began asking the Supreme Court to stop forcing it to desegregate schools saying that, after 40 years, enough is enough.

Popping up all over the nation are militias, armed groups, often influenced by white supremacists, readying themselves for battle in defence of their basic liberties. The religious right, written off as a spent force after Ronald Reagan, is back on the march, in the form of the mighty Christian Coalition.

Organised and committed, these Christian soldiers pulled off a turn-out spectacular in the mid-term elections, so that a staggering one in four voters described themselves to pollsters as evangelical Christians. Secular conservatism is on the rise, too: a recent survey classified 22 per cent of the American public as 'libertarian'.

'All the energy now is on the right,' says E J Dionne, author of *Why Americans Hate Politics*. He notes that the gun lobby, anti-immigration movement and even small-business sector are growing, while the civil rights and labour movements are splitting and shrinking.

The result is an American landscape dotted with slain liberal giants. Mario Cuomo – whose rhetoric once held the nation spellbound – is out of the governor's mansion in New York, and out of a job. Public Broadcasting, nominally America's BBC and a liberal bastion, is facing the axe of privatisation. Even the president himself has become a marginal figure, listened to and on TV less than Newt Gingrich. These days he skulks around the White House, remarked one commentator, like the ghost of Clinton Past.

Left-leaning notions of multiculturalism have become a punchbag. Baltimore's trendy WHFS music station revels in having a nightly Politically Incorrect show. Comedy Central uses the same title on cable TV.

Those on the left have become uncertain, apologetic and embarrassed about their politics. Pearl Jam topped the bill at an abortion rights benefit a fortnight ago, but instead of delivering a rousing attack on the recent spate of murderous attacks on abortion clinics, singer Eddie Vedder barely said a word. It was left to a half-hearted sentence from a support band: 'It's really sucky when people try and make you do things.'

Even the old, reliable constituencies of the left have deserted. In the 1940s the young were so pro-Democrat that Republicans tried to prevent GIs posted abroad casting absentee ballots. In the eight presidential elections since, the young voted Democratic six times.

In 1992 with Bill Clinton, the sax-playing Elvis-president who debated on MTV, the liberal lock on the youth vote looked safe. Yet now, by a ratio of 56 to 32 per cent, twenty-somethings say the Republicans better share their values than Democrats. Reagan's children, they seem to have inherited his brand of Me First conservatism and stuck with it.

Most alarmingly of all for the centre left, the ethnic coalition is beginning to come apart. Blacks still vote solidly Democratic, but their attitudes are changing. Black conservatives like controversial Supreme Court justice Clarence Thomas were once an exotic rarity. Now intellectuals like Thomas Sowell, and talk-show hosts Armstrong Williams and Ken Hamblin, are confounding the stereotype. Their message is that liberal, 'pro-black' measures like the welfare state or affirmative action have robbed American blacks of their dignity, making them dependent on a hand-out or a leg-up from the government.

Among Hispanics the trend is moving even faster: 40 per cent of them broke old loyalties and went Republican last November.

The common thread tugging all of these folks – the gun-owner, the angry white male, the Hispanic and the teenager – is distrust of government. Americans hold their government in lower esteem now than ever before. It's not mere dislike of politicians. It is a libertarian opposition to the very notion of the state. They want to pay lower taxes to a smaller bureaucracy with less power to intrude into their lives.

The Republicans have taken this potently simple message and made it their own. That forces Democrats like President Clinton to go back to first principles and spell out why America needs a government at all: to do the things individuals can't do alone, he says, to catch criminals and defend the Republic. The trouble is, the people are not listening.

In Britain, when things are bad, it is a reflex to say, 'the government ought to do something.' In America in 1995 the exact opposite is true. People complain that despite statistics showing the economy booming, their wages have stayed frozen – yet they don't demand government come up with a solution. They think government is the problem.

This put the forces of the centre left in a desperate hole. For one thing, Democrats are the party of active, interventionist government – an idea now seen as dangerously socialist. For another, they held the Congress for the last 40 years. 'People blame the government,' says E. J. Dionne, 'and the government has been the Democrats.'

Admittedly, much of this rightward tilt is aimed less at wholesale reaction than at restoring the middle ground: after all, in California they are asking not for a return to segregation, merely an end to positive discrimination. It's equally true that this march to the right has been on since 1968, with Jimmy Carter and Bill Clinton as mere detours on the way.

Nevertheless, the fact that this sharp right-turn is happening so soon after Clinton's election is striking. Those who predict a Tony Blair victory in Britain, and who plan in advance to see it as a national move to the left, should take note. America has no monopoly on fickleness. •

....

21 April 1995

Ian Katz
'It couldn't happen here'

J anice Hollis gaped at the floodlit carcass of the Alfred Murrah building in the early hours of yesterday morning and said what every Oklahoman has been thinking since a huge blast all but demolished the office block on Wednesday morning.

'Things like this do not happen here. Nothing happens here. Concerts don't even come to Oklahoma.'

Again and again, residents shook their heads in disbelief and bewilderment.

'You would never dream of something like this happening here,' said Mike Nash, a 36-year-old management consultant helping to comfort victims' relatives. 'I was at the airport when it went off and I was convinced a plane had crashed. Then I see this mushroom cloud over downtown and I'm thinking maybe it's a gas explosion.

'When I heard the first reports saying it was a car bomb, I thought how irresponsible of the radio to repeat it. This is Oklahoma City.'

No, such a thing couldn't happen in Oklahoma City, proud and cosy heartland of America.

Tornadoes are common here and, accustomed to the capricious extremes of nature, most Oklahomans thought 'earthquake' when they felt the blast. Reports said it could be felt 30 miles away but locals say it was more powerful than that.

At the city's emergency headquarters they received a call from a man 90 miles away who said he saw the water ripple on the lake where he was fishing.

Only the remains of the Murrah building can give you a sense of the true scale of Wednesday's blast, however. At first sight, it looks as though some giant creature has taken a ragged bite out of the north face of the building, swallowing a third or more of the structure.

Oddly, the building's two flanks remain almost intact, crisply framing the devastation between them. It seems that the block's entrails have been wrenched out and left hanging from the wound. There is no space between several of the floors, sandwiched down on each other.

By the early hours of yesterday, national guardsmen had staked out a six to eight block perimeter around the building. Their humvee combat vehicles did not look out of place amid the war-zone devastation.

Elsewhere emergency officials and investigators shuttled to and fro in commandeered white golf carts.

From a nearby street corner, Michael Smith watched as a crane hoisted a handful of firefighters to the higher floors. The 22-year-old paramedic had been called in to help treat the injured moments after the explosion.

But by 10am on Wednesday, they had run out of people to treat. 'Then we started with the bodies.'

All day, they tagged corpses so that rescuers would not waste time removing them from the building. 'I saw more than 40 bodies. People were impaled. People were crushed. There was a guy hanging out of one of the back windows with blood running down his head. A guy on the fourth floor had a filing cabinet embedded six inches into his head. I don't know if he was blown into it, or it was blown into him.'

The coming day was going to be worse, he feared. They had avoided counting the dead while there was a chance of finding the living. 'There has to be over 300 bodies in there.'

The last survivor to emerge from the building, a 15-year-old girl, was pulled out at 10pm on Wednesday night. Before that, a doctor had to amputate the leg of a woman as she lay under rubble in a foot and a half of water. He couldn't find a vein to administer an anaesthetic, so she had to do without.

By the morning, emergency authorities were appealing for sheets. They had run out of body bags.

At the First Christian Church, hundreds of relatives of men, women and children who had gone missing waited for news. 'We've had family members that are looking for three different people,' said Greg Dial, a 31-year-old database manager, helping to take information from worried relatives. 'We've had people who are looking for a mummy, a daddy and the kids.'

Mr Dial and his colleagues faxed each description to the medical examiners who were due to begin the task of matching them to bodies yesterday morning.

Oklahoma occupies an ambiguous geographical and cultural position in America. It lies a little south of the country's Midwestern core, but it is not really the South. It boasts the Cowboy Hall of Fame but it isn't really the West either.

Oklahomans are truly Middle Americans and they will weather this storm with their characteristic level-headedness. But few would disagree with yesterday's issue of the *Daily Oklahoman* which declared: 'Oklahoma City will never be the same.' •

....

3 September 1994

Maggie O'Kane
End games

Luis Alberto Benitus came back from the war in Angola with a Sanyo tape recorder, two pairs of jeans, two T-shirts, a tracksuit and Aids. Dania saw him for the first time on the last Wednesday of August 1989. He was standing at the bus stop in her home town of La Palma. She noticed a man with nice shoulders, brown eyes and a gold chain. They shared a taxi to the capital and about a mile outside town, their affair began in its back seat.

Benitus, 25, got to the Angolan war in 1989, just as things were winding down. He marked time in the brothels of the capital, Luanda, until the military sent him home early. After tests in the naval hospital in Havana, they moved him to Los Cocas, the luxury Aids compound outside Havana, where the first Cuban victims of the disease were sent to be confined and treated in 1989.

At the Pina de Rio provincial Aids sanatorium, 200 miles west of Havana, the white wooden cabins seem neat enough, but the grass has grown up around the legs of the park benches and the concrete puppet theatre has not been used for a long time. It is early afternoon and Dania is on a weekend pass home. Her husband, Benitus, whom she married in 1991, is in prison in Havana, serving 12 months for sneaking out of the sanatorium and having sex with a girl from town. 'There are 32 of us here now,' says Dania, four internationalists, infected in Angola, one homosexual, and the rest are Frikas.

In Britain, the Frikas of Dania's and Luis's generation are listening to rap music, taking ecstasy, heroin or crack and going to Acid House parties. Most of them just get older and move on. In Cuba, the Frikas are dying to the sounds of Guns N'Roses and Led Zeppelin.

In 1989, the Frikas rebelled against Castro, Cuba and life by directly infecting themselves with the Aids virus, passing blood from one to the other with a syringe. They formed part of a small exclusive club, The Sanatorium Frikas, injecting themselves to get access to the sanatorium, to what the former vice-minister for health, Dr Hector Terry, described as their own 'terrestrial paradise'.

In the pillared colonial elegance of the dining room at the Inglaterra Hotel in Havana, Papo is having trouble swallowing his lunch because his glands are swelling. His Adam's apple sticks out like a nose on his throat. He wants to sit beside one of the pillars – more discreet. Papo sees himself as a leader of the 'guerrilla rockers' – the Frikas. A boy from a small provincial town who liked rock music, earrings and bracelets, he spent his teenage years accumulating 20-peso fines for antisocial behaviour and 'upsetting the order of the community'. 'I felt bad. I wanted a world of rockers where the police wouldn't make trouble for us. In the sanatorium I thought we would find a way to freedom – a community of rockers – but it was a failure. Some are dead already and the others don't want to rock any more.'

Later, Papo stands in front of the tank – now a monument – that Fidel Castro drove in Havana on 8 January 1959, for the triumph of the Revolution, and strips off his T-shirt to pose for a photograph. He likes talking about the Frikas movement and showing off his tattoos. A faded tattoo reads: 'Rock, Sex and Aids'.

'Logical and complete,' says Papo. He took his needle in Los Cocas – Dr Terry's dream sanatorium, where $24,000 is spent taking care of each Aids patient in a country where the average worker earns less than $25 dollars a year. He took the blood of Juan Garcia, a fellow Frika, now dead.

The direct blood transfusion meant that the onset of the disease was rapid and the death sentence was passed quickly. Twelve Frikas have died in the Pina del Rio sanatorium since it opened in 1991. There are 14 provincial sanatoriums in Cuba. The Frikas dominated in Pina de Rio and in the central province of Villa Clara, where around 35 still live. '1989/90 was a bad year for us Frikas. It became sort of a fashionable thing to do, to inject the virus to make sure you could get into the sanatorium. Now we are dying. Mariela died when she was 21, Jasmine was 23 and Pedri was 26, or was it 27?' says Papo.

In a country where nobody eats meat and the ration books ask women to choose between one pair of knickers and one bra a year, the sanatorium offered an escape from the rules. Los Cocas sanatorium is, according to the blue and white road sign, 17 km from the Square of the Revolution in Havana. Elouisa Albertez, 34, has worked there for almost a year as a pharmacist.

She and her husband, Stalin, live at number 1003 Santiago de Las Vagas. On the veranda her two rocking chairs are painted in the same Mediterranean blue as Stalin's Cadillac, rusting in the driveway. They are pure Party people.

Elouisa comes out of her house, wiping her hands on her apron and eager to talk about the sanatorium: 'Everything is free for them. Of course they don't pay for anything. They get big capsules like bulbs that cost over $60 a time and must be paid for in dollars – but the Revolution doesn't mind how much it costs. We don't think of those things; the Revolution must look after them. They have *à la carte* menus for lunch: meat, chicken, different-flavoured yoghurts. Each couple has their own house and they have a special shop where they can get crackers, cheese, anything they want.'

Elouisa goes back inside to cook dinner from the family's monthly rations. 'No, I don't resent them. They are facing the death sentence and the Revolution must make their last years as comfortable and humane as possible.'

In 1989, the Frika movement was growing strong as the Revolution and Castro's socialist dream were beginning to fade. It was the time that Castro would call 'the special period', a period that is still going on, with soya substitute instead of meat, rationing, no spare parts, bus queues, medical shortages.

It was also the year in which Arnaldo Ochoa – a hero of the Cuban Republic, who led over a quarter of a million soldiers in internationalist battles in Angola, Nicaragua and Ethiopia – was executed in July for corruption, arms dealing and links with the Colombian drug baron Pablo Escobar. One of the most highly decorated soldiers in the Cuban army, he had betrayed the essence of the Revolution. The trial shattered Cuba. Dania was 19 then. She was looking for a Spaniard to marry 'who would take me out of Cuba'.

A few months after meeting her, Luis Benitus sent a message to Dania begging her to come to visit him in the sanatorium. He said that he was sorry he had not told her about the Aids, but that he was in love with her and, anyway, it was too late for her now. Dania, the beautiful country girl from the village of La Palma who dreamed of marrying a Spaniard, believed him. Luis told her it was better to be sure. He would give her his blood. A love pact. Then they could all live in Los Cocas.

On the evening of 4 June 1991, Dania climbed on to a wooden egg box and climbed over the 6ft-high concrete fence into the garden of Los Cocas sanatorium and her terrestrial paradise. It was a garden owned, says Elouisa proudly, 'by a rich family before the Revolution took it for the people'. Around the white walls and red roof of a Spanish villa, the gardens are planted with avocado, citrus and banana trees along pathways lined with tropical trees with white-painted bark. It is a silent Sunday evening; the air smells of freshly cut grass.

'I came that night to the fence. My cousin helped me to climb up on an egg box and I climbed over. Inside, it was like a hotel. Good food, air-conditioning, colour TV, and they took them on camping trips to Valadero. I spent a month with Luis hiding me there and bringing food. A month like a big party. We made love all the time – twice a day. He brought boxes of lemonade and big tubs of chocolate ice cream. We had smoked ham.'

After a week, he asked her to take the shot, to be sure she had the virus so she could stay with him in Los Cocos. He said they could get married and she thought about having a white dress. 'I said I didn't want to. He said it was because I didn't love him – that I was really a whore.

'There were six of us in the house and two his friends were saying, go on – you have it anyway – it would be great here. So one night before supper he said, do you want to or not? I started to cry and he got up and went to his friend and got a syringe. His friend drew out his blood and then one of his two friends gave it to me.

'I don't remember their names – they are both dead now. I felt weak afterwards and was shaking but he held me and said it would be fine, that he loved me and would take care of me.'

For a month they made love and ate chocolate ice cream and lived in an apartment the Revolution could never provide for girls like Dania, who liked rock music and wanted to marry Spanish men and leave Cuba.

The days of chocolate ice cream in Los Cocas made way for grimmer days in the provincial sanatorium at Pina de Rio. They married on 20 August 1991, and had their honeymoon night in the hotel downtown. A 'bittermoon' she called it. 'He's special, Luis, he has a temper,' Dania says. 'He beats her,' her mother says.

Most of the time in the sanatorium, where they watch TV, eat chicken and wait to die, the Frikas provide a fragile support group for each other. Sometimes the bitterness comes out. At the table in the Inglaterra, an Englishman on a diving holiday stops by the table. Dania turns to her friend and whispers in Spanish. 'He's so handsome.' Papo stretches his swollen scrawny neck across the table and hisses, 'Watch out, you'll give it to him.'

'I'm only admiring him,' Dania says.

The home of the man who created Los Cocas, Dr Hector Terry, vice-minister for health for 13 years, is not hard to find. On a shabby street near Revolution Square, the locals recognise the name immediately. Terry is well known in Cuba for his fight to stop Aids spreading on the island.

His method of confining sufferers to a sanatorium has been condemned by human rights groups, but Terry has had some success. He claims the proportion of infected people in the country is as low as 0.007 per cent. The country has carried out 14 million Aids tests since 1986. Cuba's population is around 11 million.

On a neighbouring Caribbean island, the number of infected in Haiti is estimated to be as high as 15 to 20 per cent. 'Yes,' he says, 'we have patients who admit to having voluntarily inoculated themselves with the Aids virus, but I believe many of them were taking drugs or were under the influence of alcohol at the time.'

In his study, surrounded by pictures of Castro and Che Guevara, Dr Hector Terry says: 'They were playing Russian roulette with their lives. Now they have seen death and the adventure is a failure. At least in the 1960s the hippies had an ideology, a philosophy. The problem with the Frikas is that they didn't have any.'

Dr Terry's Aids programme was conceived on the basis that Cuba, unlike her Caribbean neighbours, had a very small Aids problem in 1986. The economic embargo excluded Cuba from access to the hard currency that brought hard drugs. The country did not import US blood products which unknowingly helped spread the disease among haemophiliacs in France, Holland and Romania. The embargo also killed off the tourist trade and lessened the risk of infection from holidaymakers.

Dr Terry defends the setting up of sanatoriums in which anyone diagnosed with Aids was forced to stay for at least three months. 'We were at a crossroads in Cuba at the end of 1986. We discovered that we had 99 HIV-positive patients. We decided that they would all be sent to sanatoriums and kept apart from the rest of the population. Now, after three to six months, they are allowed to leave, but only after an education programme and when we are sure that they will not reinfect others. It is not a perfect solution, but in Cuba the disease was in the early stages and we decided that this was the only way to protect the rest of the community.'

Between 1986 and 1993, the entire Cuban population aged between 18 and 60 was tested for the virus. All airline workers, soldiers, Cubans travelling abroad, prostitutes, homosexuals and diplomats were tested at regular intervals.

'When our critics attack us for setting up the "concentration camps for Aids victims",' says Dr Terry, 'I ask how much are they spending taking care of *their* sick?'

Dania's mother is waiting at the bus stop. Every three weeks, when she has saved enough money to put chicken, meat and fresh vegetables on the table of her house in La Palma, Dania's mother comes to take her home. The houses along Dania's street were built in two phases. At the back are the wooden shacks where families first lived. At the front are the new bungalows, built on land donated by the Revolution. On 26 October 1991, the day they moved from the shack into their new house, a doctor called at Dania's mother's house to tell Marcellina that her daughter was HIV-positive.

Marcellina is dressed in a T-shirt and carries a worn black plastic handbag.

In Marcellina's street they call her The Taxi or Marcellina Arrive and Turn. She has devoted the three years since she found out about Dania to gathering money to bring her daughter home as often as possible before she dies. She gets up every morning at 4.30am and spends eight hours travelling to a town outside Havana, where she buys bulbs of garlic for three pesos. Then Marcellina Arrive and Turn goes back to La Palma, arriving between 10pm and midnight. She sells her garlic for six pesos. In a week she makes six dollars.

'It is all for her now,' she says. Dania will probably last longer than Papo. She is still healthy and beautiful and still has hope. Papo's swollen glands don't bode well for the rock concert he wants to play in January. For now, he relives his brief life as a rebel. 'Put that notebook away. People will guess. Let's go from here, I think we are being watched. Look at him over there – is he listening?'

The largest of the French tourists in the baroque dining room of the Inglaterra Hotel has no reason to pay any attention to the dying 'guerrilla rocker' in the yellow baseball cap who desperately wants to be noticed.

'Yes, I am sorry. We are all sorry now. It is too late, the satanic rite has been performed,' says Papo, and you wonder if he used the line in one of his songs. 'We didn't find freedom in the syringe,' he says.

'I'm sorry. I was young when I did it. Now I am 23 and it is very young to die,' says Dania. ●

. . . .

15 April 1995
David Hirst
The axe is sharpened for Arafat

Aweary-looking Yasser Arafat murmurs 'Welcome, welcome, welcome', as he greets the Russian foreign minister, Alexander Kozyrev. 'Thank you, thank you.'

There are some habits, like this favourite rhetorical device of repeating the same words three times, which the former guerrilla chieftain will never shake off. Once it was the fiery reiteration of the archetypal slogan 'Revolution Till Victory'; now, in his new incarnation as world statesman, Nobel prize-winner and 'president' of the Palestinian state-to-be, it is making himself triply nice to the foreign dignitaries who descend on al-Muntada, the converted sea-front 'club' where he holds court.

One glance at al-Muntada is confirmation that wherever his political fortunes carry him – from his bunker in the Ghor Valley, to the down-at-heel suburb of Fakhani, Beirut, to the leafy gentility of Jughurta Street, Tunis – another habit, or style, will always go with him.

Already, here in the fatherland itself, the colours of Palestine are chipping and fading on the concrete barricades; the vague patch of pink and yellow sunflowers fails to keep sand and litter at bay; the bored sentinels of the newly formed Presidential Security, the latest circle of smooth young 'presidential' aides, the inevitable posse of petitioners – all contribute to something ineffably Arafatian: activity without action, muddle, seediness, decay.

But he is acquiring new habits. The compulsively peripatetic PLO chairman used to joke about the passion for pomp and protocol he found in Third World dictators. Now he vies with them himself. Kozyrev first had to inspect a guard of honour; had he been a head of state, Arafat would have been out on the grubby red carpet with him. Mr Palestine is in love with such symbols of his coming sovereignty, with his flags and uniforms, his stamps which have no validity outside the Gaza Strip, his 'passports' for which few refugees will forsake their dog-eared *laisser-passers*. 'It is very important to him,' says Abdullah Hourani, Gaza-based PLO executive committee member, 'part of his make-believe. He just adored it when, for the first time, [Israeli foreign minister Shimon] Peres addressed him in Arabic as "Mr President". They know his vanity so well. He gets what he wants, and they get more and more of what they want – more and more of Palestine itself.'

Here lies the basic trade-off – ceremony for substance – by which Mr Palestine is turning himself into an ally of the historic 'Zionist enemy' – and into an enemy of the Palestinians. On Israel's behalf, he is ready to oppress those of them, the 'insiders', inhabitants of the occupied territories, whom he can, while he has simply abandoned those of them, the 'outsiders' of the diaspora, whom he cannot. He is systematically destroying that which he built, the PLO, in favour of the so-called National Authority, which is so far confined to about 6.5 per cent of original Palestine, and enjoys fewer powers, and less control over land, people and resources, than the most miserable South African Bantustan ever did.

Stated thus baldly, that might seem harsh, prejudiced, incredible; yet it is wholly uncontroversial among those who should know best, his own intimates, companions of 30 years, be it those who, in what is left of the PLO headquarters in Tunis, watch him, powerless, from afar, or even some of those who stick with him in an apostate odyssey which, they fear, can lead nowhere except to the next *intifada*, a violent and bloody one, against him and Israelis together.

He knows it himself. 'I am not the mayor of Gaza, or Antoine Lahd [the commander of the Israeli-created South Lebanese Army],' he sometimes shouts, with the exasperated air of a man who fears that a Lahd writ large is precisely what he is.

It would be exaggerating to say that it all came about because of the overweening egoism of one man, his determination, via the Oslo Agreement, to retain that central role in his people's struggle which he had been in danger of losing, and his autocrat's ability to impose this new order on his comrades, institutions and people. Objective conditions helped him: loyalists who, in their fraility or venality, tolerated lesser aberrations out of which his mighty one inevitably grew; a sterile and decadent PLO opposition, George Habash and the Damascus-based 'radicals', who offered no alternative; the greatly lowered expectations of a people exhausted by years of futile struggle and bloodshed, their natural reluctance to repudiate their only surviving icon, their desperate will to believe that perhaps he can, after all, pull off something worthwhile. And it has to be said that, even now, according to the opinion polls, he is still the leader whom some 40 per cent of the people would choose over any other.

His ratings actually tend to rise after the suicide spectaculars of his Hamas rivals. The emotional gratification which these arouse is offset by fear of Israeli reprisals, border closure, unemployment and further pauperisation. Thus is Mr Palestine still the only one to profit from something deeply confused, schizophrenic, even, in the Palestinian psyche.

Oslo could, perhaps, have worked. But its architect, the arch-moderate Abu Mazen, warned from the outset that it would lead 'either to a Palestine state or the liquidation of the Palestine cause'. Now he broods in Tunis, persuaded that it will be the latter. If so, there are two basic reasons for it.

The first is the Israelis' success in interpreting Oslo their way – in the Cairo Agreement of May 1994, which fleshed it out.

Historically, the Israelis have always looked for an Arab ally to subjugate the Palestinians with maximum efficiency. Their favourite was always King Hussein and his 'Jordanian option'. Yet who more ironically appropriate for the role than Mr Palestine himself? Israel's 'security' is the be-all and end-all of the Cairo Agreement. When Arafat signed it, an Israeli newspaper called it 'the agreement of abject surrender'.

One of Arafat's top lieutenants, Abbas Zaki, has no doubt about that either. 'In the past,' he laments, 'Arafat always tried to make an ally of the strongest power in the region. That, of course, was always Arab. Now it is Israeli. And it is far too big for him. Truly, he has put himself in the belly of the whale. He is a part of the state of Israel.'

The second reason is Arafat's failure to give the Palestinians anything in return for this surrender. For Abu Mazen's gamble had been that Oslo would, in the end, turn to the Palestinians' advantage if Arafat renounced his 'revolutionary' mentality in favour of a 'state-building' one, and set up a modern, democratic, honest, efficient administration that would command Palestinian goodwill, talent and investment. But Arafat cannot, because that alliance is just too crippling – or will not, because he just isn't made that way. His administration is quite disastrously incompetent and unpopular, with his old habits, especially the use and abuse of money, now reinforced by new ones, a resort to repression, and ultimately no doubt to despotism, that will become even more vital to his own security than Israel's.

It is a terrible irony. How often did Arafat, himself once an engineer in Kuwait, boast that the Palestinians, the most educated community in the Arab world, built the oil-rich, Bedouin states of the Gulf? How often did he contrast his 'Palestinian democracy' with the dictatorships of the Arabs?

How ironic that, in Palestine itself, he is rigorously excluding the educated, the honest, or even the well endowed. People of goodwill are plentiful in Gaza. Palestinians who want to build the country, foreigners, private or governmental, who want to help them do it. 'There are little points of light, little groups of bright people, throughout the National Authority,' says a UN official, 'but they can't do anything, and I think that if Arafat knew they were there, he would get rid of them.'

'Never,' says another UN official, 'have I seen someone so alone as Arafat, so determined to rule by dividing.' That well-entrenched habit of his starts with the instruments of repression, which are becoming the backbone of his new order. It seems that the Israelis now so trust their new-found ally that, in this domain, they give him a free rein. Under the Cairo Agreement there were supposed to be five security organisations; now there are at least eight. He was supposed to import 7,000 former guerrillas from 'outside' to become policemen 'inside', and to recruit 2,000 locally, making a total of 9,000, but already there are 17,000.

These competing organisations are headed mainly by 'outsiders', members of the Tunis-based bureaucracy, whom Arafat, with Israeli approval, has imported to dominate the 'insiders'. And most belong to Fatah, the main guerrilla organisation round whom he seeks to construct not a 'national' but a narrow factional, one-party regime in the manner of an Assad or a Saddam.

The unquestioning loyalty of these imported 'strongmen' stems from the fact that Arafat can destroy them as he made them. The most notorious is Jibril Rajoub, head of Preventive Security in the 'autonomous' West Bank enclave of Jericho. The most significant thing about him is that, a favourite of Israeli intelligence, he operates far beyond the confines of Jericho. His men roam the West Bank and East Jerusalem, suppressing anti-Arafat dissidence where they can. Most of these men are 'insiders', former Fatah hawks, often heroes of the *intifada*, who have given up fighting for a policing role. That is not as surprising as it might seem, a fruit of the extraordinary political and psychological turmoil which Arafat has produced.

'Fatah,' says one of its members, 'was always an organisation without any ideology or political training, and if Arafat himself becomes a collaborator, is it surprising that many of his followers do likewise?' Through these and other agencies, Arafat now swoops on Hamas activists, and, more ominously, closes down newspapers and arrests or intimidates journalists or human-rights activists who rose to prominence in defiance of the Israeli occupiers, only to find themselves in similar collision with their Palestinian 'liberators'.

As for finance, no wonder Arafat fights tooth and nail to preserve control of that time-honoured source of his power. Uncorrupt himself, he systematically exploits that weakness in others. 'I knew they were bad,' says a disgusted 17-year inmate of Israeli jails about the imported Tunis bureaucracy, 'but I didn't know they were that bad.'

It is wholly typical that Arafat should appoint, as attorney-general, a man whom Fatah once sentenced to death for stealing funds destined for the *intifada*. Not long ago, on Arafat's urgent instructions, 'strongman' Rajoub kidnapped one of the most discredited of his apparatchniks from the American Colony Hotel in East Jerusalem, where he was in bed with a mother of four, bore him off to Jericho, beat him up, and sent him to Gaza – where Arafat installed him as head of one his new departments.

In economics, as in security, Arafat is ready to lock himself into the fatal Israeli embrace. It is not simply that Oslo and Cairo would reduce the Palestinian economy to a neo-colonial appendage (they would); it is worse than that. He systematially subverts or bypasses his official institutions, notably the Palestine Economic Council for Development and Reconstruction (Pecdar), which was supposed to receive international funds and direct their disposal.

He places all business he can in the hands of 'brokers' and intermediaries, not necessarily Palestinians, whose primary task is not development or the welfare of the community but the raising of ready cash for his 'operating costs'. That is to say, for the unscrutinised patronage he requires to guarantee the loyalty of an apparatus which, in addition to the already bloated police, probably numbers some 15,000 people, including about 750 'director-generals' without known functions.

Most of the cash comes from governments, international donors or inter-national agencies. 'We're supposed to spend it on development,' says a UN official, 'but basically Arafat blackmails us: pay up, or see my whole government collapse. His weakness is his strength.'

Other business which the 'brokers' handle are the 'concessions' granted for the import of Israel cement or petrol. But their most scandalous and revealing transaction was for the development of the Palestinian telephone system. They got Arafat to award an exclusive contract for that to an obscure Cayman Islands-based company called ITI which was really a front for the Israelis. But Farouk Kaddoumi, Tunis-based PLO 'foreign minister' and official head of Pecdar, didn't know about it and awarded another contract to America's AT & T. Kaddoumi opposes Oslo but, in spite of that, US Secretary of Commerce Ron Brown at one point telephoned Arafat and urged him to give the contract to the American not the Israeli company.

The upshot is that, 18 months after Oslo, the existing telephone system creaks on, a symbol of chaos, corruption and incompetence, and of the way, as a result of that and Israel's economic reprisal for the Hamas exploits, most Gazans are materially far worse off since Arafat arrived in their midst than before.

The Ghor Valley, Lebanon, Tunis, Gaza – Arafat must at all costs continue to move on, achieve at least a semblance of progress towards the West Bank, and then Jerusalem. But of one thing his Israeli ally will make sure: the more firmly Mr Palestine manages to establish himself there, the less the Palestinians will like the means by which he does it.

'Some of us,' a leading citizen of Ramallah says, 'have seen Gaza and don't want Gaza here. People daren't say it openly but, among themselves, a growing number do say: if it is a choice between Arafat and occupation, then let's have occupation – or King Hussein.'

As for the inhabitants of Jerusalem, it is reported that up to 20,000 of them have suddenly started applying for the citizenship which Israeli always offered them.

There could hardly be a more damning indictment than that from the 'capital' of Arafat's improbable state-in-the-making. If 'insiders' feel this way about the blessings that their 'president' is about to bestow on them, they are only catching up, in their bitterness and disappointment, with the 'outsiders' whom, with Oslo, the PLO chairman abandoned altogether. ●

....

6 May 1995

Jonathan Fenby
Man out of time

The old man, terminally ill and about to relinquish the power he had sought all his life, sat stiffly in his chair. At times, he spoke with difficulty, hesitating before replying to the questions being put to him. Quite frequently, his right hand darted to the pocket of his jacket. Was he touching a talisman or reaching for a drug? Some said later that all he was seeking was a sugar lump. Nobody knew because the television cameras panned away from him at those moments.

At the end of the interview, the old man was asked what he expected God to say to him when he died. A confirmed agnostic, he showed a shaft of wit. 'Now you know,' God would say. 'And I hope that he would add – Welcome.'

François Mitterrand's 14 years in the most powerful elected post in a Western democracy ends in the coming week. His successor will be elected tomorrow. Mitterrand is 78 and has prostate cancer. Despite his achievements, the reforms and the great buildings he has caused to be put up in Paris, the president leaves office under a cloud.

On the surface, France is still one of the most enjoyable countries in the world – as the huge number of tourists it attracts shows. But alongside the beauties of its countryside, the food and wine, the TGV trains and the native wit, France has one of the highest unemployment rates among major Western nations. Its political class has been undermined by a wave of scandals.

Extremist parties of right and left got 25 per cent of the vote in the first round of the presidential election. Social tension is high. Everyday racism is common. Immigration worries the right, homelessness the left. The French have become great consumers of Valium and Prozac.

Not all of this is Mitterrand's fault, but if a man rules his country for 14 years, he must take much of the responsibility for what happens, particularly when he enjoys the executive monarchical powers of the French presidency. Mitterrand is not a man to refuse praise; neither can he escape blame. Louis XVI, after all, lost his head.

There could be no greater contrast than that between the uncertain, worried country Mitterrand bequeaths to his successor and the heady days of May 1981 when the new president's election was greeted with red roses, dancing in the streets and a triumphal procession up the rue Soufflot in Paris to the Panthéon, resting places of the great figures of France's past. Daniel Barenboim conducted Beethoven's 'Ode to Joy' in the open air, an all-star international political and artistic cast milled around as the new president climbed the steps of the great building and basked in the hopes for a new era (while hysterical right-wingers warned of political commissars and panicky businessmen smuggled suitcases stuffed with currency across the border into Switzerland).

François Mitterrand had been waiting for such a moment for more than half his life. The story of how he got to the summit of power in 1981 and held on until this spring is one of extraordinary perseverance, of a man who first entered government in 1944, who was a minister 11 times between 1946 and 1957, who spent years in the wilderness and ran twice unsuccessfully for the presidency before finally entering the Elysée Palace. His years in power have been touched with grandeur, but, in the end, they constitute a melancholy saga of a politician who could not rise above the habits and conditioning of a lifetime. Once in power, François Mitterrand, in the words of one long-time observer, had all the conditions for greatness except greatness itself.

Secretive and elusive, Mitterrand has been the object of rumours and legends for half a century. His decade and a half in power nurtured a fresh crop of stories, ranging from hagiography to hatred. Now, in the twilight months, something closer to the truth is finally emerging about the true character of this president who kept a mistress and their child in the Elysée, who maintained a range of unsuitable friendships even after he had become head of state, two of whose close associates committed suicide in 1993 and 1994 – at least in part because of him – and who, at the end of his life, looks back with deep emotion to the provincial childhood which formed him.

My childhood, which was happy, has illuminated my life. When one is a child, when one arrives on this planet of which one knows nothing, everything is to be learned, everything to be felt. The first sensations are so strong and dominate the rest of of one's life because they are the first ones. They make their mark on a virgin canvas.

I draw the largest part of my reserves of strength from my childhood. I have the impression that what I had at that moment and the little of it I have preserved (I have kept some of it) represents the purest and cleanest part of my personality.

Jarnac in the Charente department of western France is a thoroughly ordinary town surrounded by open countryside and rivers. François Mitterrand was born there on 26 October 1916, the son of a station master who later changed profession and became president of the National Federation of Vinegar Makers. With four sons and four daughters, the Mitterrands were a close-knit family into which, their second son said later, 'guests entered as if they were burglars'. They were devout Catholics, who distrusted money-making and rarely displayed emotion.

The boy who was sent to boarding school in the nearby big town of Angoulême was a withdrawn child. He had trouble communicating with others and made few friends. One lifelong character trait was established at an early age. 'I have never tended to confide in others,' the president said seven decades later. 'In a big family, one has to develop zones of solitude.'

Instead, the young Mitterrand went for long country walks, with a particular taste for strolls along rivers. He developed a habit of writing poems about them, starting with the Charente and the Gironde of his native region and later taking the Rhine, the Rhône, the Nile and the Niger as inspiration. Seventy years later, he remembers with pleasure the sound of the wind blowing at night through the riverside trees of his native region.

On his walks, the shy boy from the Catholic school spoke to imaginary crowds, haranguing them with speeches inspired by the revolutionaries of 1789 and 1848. To this day, Mitterrand remembers climbing up to the attic of the family home, littered with corn-on-the-cob husks, and launching historic appeals through the window overlooking the garden, 'changing the course of history according to my preferences'.

I think that there is only one role to play: to bring to the political groups to which it is necessary to belong and which are approved by the church the directives and principles of our faith. The National Volunteers want a clean and strong France.

If François Mitterrand has always looked back with happy nostalgia to his childhood in the Charente, he was less forthcoming for many years about his early life in Paris. Arriving by train from Angoulême just before his eighteenth birthday in October 1934, to study politics and law, he felt 'lost, small at the foot of a mountain that was to be climbed. I was without an identity.'

That was not strictly true. Product of a Catholic education, he naturally lodged in a religious pension on the rue de Vaugirard. He quickly gravitated into reactionary politics. In the fevered climate of the mid-1930s, that was not surprising for somebody of his background. But when one of last year's most notable books, *Une Jeunesse Française* by journalist and historian Pierre Péan, revealed the socialist leader's involvement in the world of extreme right-wing pre-war politics, there were two reactions – one of shock, the other of resignation as yet another contradictory element coming to light in Mitterrand's past.

The law student joined a group called the National Volunteers, the youth wing of a big extremist movement, the Croix-de-Feu. Mitterrand told Péan that he had been 'seduced' by the Croix-de-Feu's leader, Colonel de la Roque, who, he insisted, was neither a fascist nor an anti-Semite – an opinion not shared by many at the time. Above all, Mitterrand was influenced by his religion. He was put off the main extreme-right movement, the Action Française, not by its political stance but because the Pope had declared an anathema on it.

Within a month of arriving in Paris, Mitterrand took part in his first right-wing march. A photograph taken on 1 February 1935 shows him at a demonstration against foreign students: a banner beside him proclaims: 'Go on strike against the wogs.' The future leader of the left wrote for a far right-wing newspaper which admired Mussolini; he gave 500 francs to a campaign against the socialist Popular Front leader Léon Blum. He became president of a right-wing student group – and he fell in love.

One Saturday, I had the blues. I went back to my room. On the table, I came across an invitation I had forgotten about. It was to a dance at the teachers' training college. I went. I saw a blonde with her back to me. She turned towards me. My feet were riveted to the ground . . . Then I asked her to dance . . . I was mad about her.

Women had always been important to François Mitterrand. There have been as many rumours about his love life as about his real political beliefs. He has been said to have had a string of celebrated journalists as mistresses and to keep a love nest in Venice. Any attractive woman who rises to a high position in the socialist party is suspected of having slept with him on the way up. His first love was Marie-Louise Terrasse. At the student ball, she was not as struck by him as he was by her: 'I did not give him my name because my mother forbade me to do so,' she recalls. In his mind, Mitterrand dubbed her 'Béatrice' in a reference to Dante. He spoke incessantly about her to friends and watched her as she travelled between her home and her *lycée*. Finally, he accosted her. Defying her mother's order never to speak to a man in the street, she joined him at a café table and shared a pancake with him. In the spring of 1940, when Mitterrand had been called up to the army, they were engaged.

After France's defeat, he became a prisoner of war and, as the months dragged by in his Stalag, her letters became rarer and rarer. Friends said his frustration at not seeing her was a motive behind his three escape attempts, the last of which was successful. But she no longer fancied marriage and broke off the engagement early in 1942. Years later, as Catherine Langeais, she became more famous than her former fiancé for a time as an early television speakerine [announcer].

Some amateur psychologists believe that rejection hardened the young man's character and contributed to the cynicism which has run through his life. At the time, he spoke of the 'dryness of my feelings'. But he still sends Langeais flowers on her birthday.

Six years after falling for Marie-Louise, Mitterrand was in love again, this time with a photograph. In March 1944, when he headed a Resistance network, Mitterrand attended a party at the Paris flat of Roger-Patrice Pelat, a friend he had met in a prisoner of war camp and subsequently worked with in the underground – and who would remain a close friend up to his death in 1989 while at the centre of an insider-dealing scandal linked to the presidency.

On the piano in the flat was a photograph of the sister of Pelat's partner at the time. 'I want to know her, I will marry her,' Mitterrand said.

A meeting was arranged at a restaurant on the Boulevard Saint-Germain. Again, Mitterrand was not an immediate hit. Wearing an off-white raincoat and the large hat which became his in later years, he also sported a pencil moustache and looked like a caricature of a tango dancer.

The young woman, Danielle Gouze, who was in her last year at school, found his acid tone irritating; he only fell more deeply in love with her. His powers of persuasion and of seduction, which politicians as well as women bore witness to over the years, were deployed to the full. Within a couple of months, he had persuaded her to agree to get married. There then followed a series of adventures, including a train trip to her native Burgundy during which a friendly German soldier unknowingly ushered Mitterrand through a police control which had him on its wanted list. In October 1944, after the liberation of France, they were married.

It has not been the easiest of partnerships for Danielle Mitterrand. Her husband's philandering has never been much of a secret, even if many of the rumours can be discounted. Last year, *Paris Match* magazine printed photographs of the president stepping out to a 20th birthday lunch with his daughter, Mazarine, born to an archivist whom he met near his home by the south-western Atlantic coast. The mother and daughter had been housed for some time in the Elysée Palace.

There was more shocked comment on the intrusion into Mitterrand's private life than on the propriety of his domestic arrangements. The existence of Mazarine had been suggested in a *roman-à-clef* novel some years earlier. Working backwards, it became apparent that Mitterrand fathered her just before he embarked on his second presidential campaign in 1974.

Danielle Mitterrand has dedicated herself to good causes, particularly in the Third World. It was largely at her prompting that Fidel Castro was received as an honoured guest in Paris earlier this year. In that anyone has influenced

Mitterrand over the years, she has been good for her husband – though what she thinks of his decision to maintain close relations with some of Africa's worst dictators can be imagined.

She could have become an object of pity; instead, she has remained dignified, a woman who has never lost the courage and steadfastness she showed when she hid Resistance fighters as a girl, as serious today as when a friend of Mitterrand's warned her to flee Paris after her photograph had been seized by the Gestapo. The teenage Danielle replied: 'But what about my exams?'

I didn't think about the anti-Semitism at Vichy. I knew that, unfortunately, there were anti-Semites who filled senior positions round Marshall Pétain, but I didn't follow the laws of the time and the measures that were being taken.

François Mitterrand has a genius for putting out of his mind anything he does not want to know about. That trait may have begun when he got back to France from his German prison camp and worked for the Vichy collaborationist government. His job was to look after French prisoners of war. He did so well that he was awarded the Francisque, one of the regime's top decorations. It is not something he likes to be reminded of.

At the same time, under the pseudonyms 'Morland' or 'Capitaine Monnier' he organised a Resistance network of ex-servicemen, travelled to London for an unhappy meeting with General de Gaulle and risked his life.

Critics have made much of the Vichy decoration, and of his decision as president to continue the tradition of sending a wreath to Pétain's grave each Armistice Day. But there is no doubting his involvement in the Resistance. Cynics would say that, in a very Mitterrandish way, he was playing both sides of the street, hoping to come out well whichever side won the war.

That may be a shade too knowing – even Mitterrand's duplicity has limits, and his Resistance activities were far more dangerous than his involvement with Vichy. Had he been arrested on the train to Burgundy with Danielle Gouze, he would have been tortured and shot; when Vichy collapsed, all that remained from his work there was a shadow of suspicion that has dogged him ever since.

Mitterrand's own conduct has nurtured that suspicion far more than any of his denigrators were able to do. Most damaging has been the recent disclosure of his post-war links with René Bousquet, the Vichy police chief responsible for the deportation of Jews from France to concentration camps, including the most notorious round-up of women and children known by the name of the cycling stadium where they were held in Paris, the Vel d'Hiver.

Bousquet was murdered by an apparently unbalanced gunman in June 1933. Mitterrand says he found him to be a brilliant man with whom he had interesting conversations. He grows indignant at criticism levelled at him for going on meeting the former police chief until 1986 – four years into his presidency and after well-publicised moves were made to try to get Bousquet tried for crimes against humanity. The president, a man with access to the full panoply of official French records, insists that he did not know of Bousquet's wartime activities. In a new book recording his conversations with the Nobel Prize-winner Elie Wiesel, Mitterrand talks as if he is the wounded party when the subject of Bousquet comes up.

Paul Webster, the *Guardian*'s Paris correspondent who investigated the Mitterrand–Bousquet association in the course of research for his revealing new book *Mitterrand:L'Autre Histoire*, has established that the president's past connections with questionable wartime figures go a good deal further than is generally known in France.

Three weeks after Bousquet was shot, Mitterrand referred to the accusations against the former police chief and another Vichy official, Maurice Papon, who was later France's budget minister. 'I made it known on several occasions during cabinet meetings that I was not in favour of reopening this case,' he said. 'I take entire responsibility.' In television appearances, the president pointed out in his defence that, although Bousquet was sentenced to five years of national disgrace in 1949 for wartime activities, the punishment was immediately lifted because of unspecified associations with British intelligence. (Bousquet, presumably, was playing both sides of the street.)

Mitterrand's persistent refusal to condemn Bousquet – together with unanswered questions about his old compact with the far right – has become the most emotive issue of the last months of his presidency. Some would say that the president protests too much. Each time he has denied anything more than social links with Bousquet, new signs of deeper contacts have emerged, according to Webster's research.

There is no evidence that the two men actually met while serving Vichy. But Mitterrand's Resistance group, based on ex-prisoners of war, had contacts with the Vichy Ministry of the Interior and the police. In 1945, he got a job editing a magazine financed by a cosmetics group founded by a businessman of the far right who had funded pre-war terrorists.

Two years after the war, as a minister, Mitterrand employed a former Bousquet aide as his press officer and, in 1949, he introduced an amnesty bill which was said to have weighed on the judges' decision to give the former police chief a nominal sentence.

As Interior Minister in 1954, with access to all the files, Mitterrand appointed three members of Bousquet's wartime entourage to his staff. At that time, Bousquet was on the board of the Banque de I'Indochine, which later merged into the Indosuez Bank. This bank financed anti-Gaullist politicians after the General's return to power in 1958. In that year, Bousquet ran unsuccessfully for parliament, with the backing of a small political party headed by Mitterrand.

When Mitterrand made his first presidential bid in 1965, the Toulouse-based newspaper *La Dépêche du Midi* printed Mitterrand's electoral tracts for free and contributed half a million francs to his campaign funds. During the election, the paper ran an appeal by former Pétainists and extreme right-wingers to vote for the left-wing candidate. Bousquet was a director of the newspaper.

At the end of 1973, Mitterrand and Bousquet met at the funeral of a man called Pierre Saury, who had been Mitterrand's parliamentary aide since 1965. A friend of Mitterrand has identified Saury as the link man with former Pétainists. Paul Webster's research shows that Saury was with Bousquet in 1940 and was sent by him to Paris to work with the police during the deportation of Jews.

The two men met again during Mitterrand's second presidential campaign in 1974. A magazine photographer snapped an intimate lunch party at the candidate's country home in the south-west. Bousquet and his wife sat opposite Mitterrand; the caption did not mention them.

The president has not acknowledged these contacts. Given his fascination with history, it is difficult to swallow his professions of ignorance about Bousquet's wartime crimes. The police chief's role in demanding that the French should be in charge of deportations of Jews was outlined at Nuremburg in 1946 by the lawyer and politician Edgar Fauré, a close friend of Mitterrand.

France's leading Nazi and Vichy hunter, Serge Klarsfeld, published a book in 1983 including documents on Bousquet's offers to deport Jews, but Mitterrand did not break off contact with Bousquet for another three years – in the run-up to the 1988 presidential election, when the Jewish vote was considered important. The head of state was booed by young Jews at a commemoration of the 1942 round-up of Paris Jews. He promptly appointed his own lawyer, Georges Kiejman, whose father died in Auschwitz, as junior justice minister, but Kiejman blocked legal proceedings against Bousquet in the name of national unity.

Inevitably, Bousquet's murder in 1993 sparked conspiracy theories. How did the gunman, Didier Christian, slip through Bousquet's heavy security protection and get into his flat in the very week when a date was to be set for his trial? The mystery may be cleared up when Christian comes to court in September. By then, Mitterrand will have been out of the presidential palace for four months. He will, he says, be living life as usual, 'except that I won't be going to the Elysée'. And that, for him, will be far from usual.

I could have devoted my life to reflection, have lived in the country in the company of trees, animals and a few loved ones. Perhaps that is a bucolic dream, but I think I could have done it. But the stimulus of action was doubtless stronger than that of reflection, since in the end I launched myself into politics.

When Mitterrand first ran for election, Attlee was in Downing Street, Stalin in the Kremlin and Truman in the White House. In October 1946, after an unsuccessful attempt to get elected in the Paris region, he set off for the Nièvre department in central France which was to become his electoral base for the next 35 years.

The 30-year-old aspiring politician attracted big crowds and won enough of them over to be elected. He was also helped by a network of local notables, including several noblemen. He denounced the tripartite government of socialists, communists and moderate Catholics; in particular, he preached hardline anti-communism.

The Nièvre went on electing Mitterrand throughout the Fourth Republic as he moved smoothly between ministerial posts – from ex-servicemen's affairs to the information ministry, then on to superintend France's overseas territories before taking the powerful post of Interior Minister in 1954–5 and ending up as Justice Minister in 1956–7.

Serving in socialist-led governments, Mitterrand declared that Algeria must remain French. As Justice Minister, he preferred not to be informed of the use of torture on the other side of the Mediterranean. Heading a series of small parties and political combinations, he never had a strong popular following but was one of the most skilful exponents of the Fourth Republic game of ministerial musical chairs. He never got what he most wanted – the premiership.

The ever-shifting back-room politics of the Fourth Republic shaped Mitterrand's political style. When de Gaulle swept away the discredited system in 1958, the shock was terrible. Mitterrand voted against the General's investiture. In the first parliamentary elections of the new republic, he lost his seat. He was said to have broken down in tears as he contemplated defeat.

After losing, Mitterrand wrote an article in his tame local newspaper, forging his new image as a true republican standing up to de Gaulle's military coup. At the same time, however, he was realistic enough to dissociate him-self from the old republic which had served him so well. 'For a long time, I have said "no" to complicated party combinations, to immobility, to colonial wars,' he wrote. Mitterrand never has any trouble disowning yesterday's beliefs.

Such a man does not stay politically unemployed for long and in 1959 Mitterrand was elected to the Senate – a body whose members are picked by local dignitaries. He dramatically announced that he had been the target of an assassination attempt, which soon appeared to have been either a put-up job engineered by Mitterrand to win sympathy or an attempt to smear him by right-wing policemen. He stayed in the Senate for three years, writing anti-Gaullist tracts in fine, biting prose before winning back his seat in the more important National Assembly.

At the same time, the one-time provincial boy from the west strengthened the roots he had put down in the Nièvre by becoming mayor of the town of Château-Chinon in the hilly, wet Morvan area of the department. In recognition of its only connection with national fame, this town on the edge of Burgundy has turned its 18th-century convent into a Mitterrand museum, crammed with official gifts and mementoes. It has also destroyed the most enigmatic testament to this most engimatic of politicians, room 15 of the Hôtel du Vieux-Morvan.

The 1960s and 1970s were long, grinding years of hopes and disappointments when Mitterrand needed all his inner reserves to survive politically. He struggled back from the wilderness of the early Gaullist years and won a more-than-respectable 45 per cent of the vote against the General in the 1965 presidential election. But he consigned himself back to the political desert with an ill-judged offer to take over the government on behalf of the left during the 1968 riots and strikes. Bouncing back again, he was narrowly beaten in his second presidential run in 1974 by Valéry Giscard d'Estaing and then settled down to rebuild the socalist party into a major political force in the 1970s.

At successive elections, he went to the old-fashioned hotel in Château-Chinon on polling day and awaited the results there. He ate lunch with the hotel owners and always occupied the same first-floor room.

Lit by a single weak light bulb, room 15 was sparsely furnished with a lumpy bed, a simple chair and a plastic-topped table where Mitterrand wrote late into the night. There was a wash basin but the lavatory was on the landing. A window looked out on to the surrounding hills. If François Mitterrand had become a reflective man, it is just the kind of room he would have been expected to occupy – the latter-day equivalent of the attic window from which he had once imagined himself addressing the nation. For a famous politician, a minister and a presidential candidate, it was a superb anachronism, a symbol of a man from the provinces who had achieved the summit of self-sufficiency and who delighted in distancing himself from the metropolitan world he was out to conquer.

Question: Isn't it a bit frustrating for the politician and intellectual that you are that your name will be attached to walls rather than to laws?
Answer: Posterity will decide.

Mitterrand's greatest conquest may have been his programme of public buildings. The question from a television interviewer in mid-April, and the president's equivocal answer, were both right. Mitterrand will be remembered as the first left-wing president of the Fifth Republic: historians will argue over whether he was ever really a socialist, or simply a weird combination of a head-in-the-skies humanist and a dedicated political fixer. But what will interest the crowds for centuries to come will be the wonderfully restored Louvre museum with its I M Pei transparent pyramid. They will sit in the newly immaculate Tuileries gardens, will look up the perspective of the

Champs-Elysées to the new arch built behind the Arc de Triomphe and cross the Seine to the fine Musée d'Orsay devoted to the 19th century.

The huge new national library and the Finance Ministry building along the river are less generally appreciated and the new opera at the Bastille has come in for criticism – Mitterrand himself admits to doubts about the architecture. But the new natural history museum is superb, as is the science and culture complex on the northern edge of the city. An Arab World Institute has been built at the end of the Boulevard Saint-Germain, and the dome of the Invalides has been restored to golden glory.

A man of culture, with a deep knowledge of French literature, Mitterrand is a rare intellectual among world leaders. He has been seen reading poetry on his way to summit meetings. He enjoys the company of artists and writers. He is knowledgeable about architecture. His followers make fools of themselves when they pander to his whims – changing the seats at the new opera house because he raised his eyebrows at the original ones, or choosing an architect in the mistaken belief that he was a man the president approved of.

Mitterrand is deeply content reading alone or on solitary walks with his dog in the pine forests behind the Atlantic coast. He professes to be above material things – he never carries money and does not wear a watch. But concrete and glass will form his enduring monument. Typically, not one of his *grands travaux* bears his name.

There is nothing wrong with dreaming.

The year of 1981 was a time for dreams on the left and nightmares on the right. A dozen big companies were nationalised, the minimum wage and welfare payments were raised, the death penalty abolished. Mitterrand's lieutenants spoke like revolutionaries; the president began his ascent to the clouds, as solitary in power as he had been when seeking it.

The year of 1982 was more difficult. The franc was devalued. The finance minister, Jacques Delors, made his worries known about the way the implementation of Mitterrand's election programme was undermining the economy. The president, who cared little for economics, hardly listened; the social affairs minister said it was not her job to worry about where the money was to come from to pay for government spending.

In 1983 and 1984, Mitterrand had to face reality. To save the franc and keep France a part of Europe, he was forced to be ruled by his head against his heart. Friends and protégés argued for socialism in one country, for a France standing proudly on its own. Over a wrenching weekend, they lost out to a combination of reality, Delors and Helmut Kohl. For the left, Mitterrand had sold out to international capitalism. For the rest, he had taken the only possible path. After two years of dreaming, his presidency had woken up.

In 1981, François Mitterrand had finally been a free man, master of all he surveyed. After decades of compromise, collusion and struggle, he could finally become the man he had dream of being in his boyhood. He had achieved the revolutionary feat of showing that the Fifth Republic did not have to be the preserve of Gaullism and the centre right. By 1983, his freedom had vanished and he reverted to the old Mitterrand, a leader with few scruples for whom politics was an end in itself.

In his 14 years at the Elysée, he has got through five prime ministers of the left – and two from the right imposed on him by socialism's electoral defeats. He has reigned over a monarchical court, with favourites coming and going at the master's will. Nothing better illustrated the Mitterrand presidential style than his treatment of a one-time gas-fitter, Pierre Bérégovoy.

Bérégovoy was one of Mitterrand's main fixers in the party and then at the Elysée. He became finance minister and finally prime minister in 1992. He was the ultimate Mitterrand loyalist. Once, I called on him in his ministerial office. As I sat down, the telephone rang. It was the president. Bérégovoy said: 'May I allow myself to say that the speech you made today was the most brilliant address I have ever heard. It should be printed and distributed to every schoolchild in France.' As finance minister, he picked up the fine plate in front of him at lunch and marvelled aloud at how the son of poor Ukrainian immigrants could end up eating off antique porcelain.

After the socialists lost the 1993 legislative election, Bérégovoy went back to his city of Nevers in the Nièvre in deep depression. He telephoned the Elysée. Mitterrand would not take – or return – his calls. On 1 May 1993, beside a canal in Nevers, Bérégovoy shot himself. His suicide cast a huge shadow. Mitterrand blamed the press, which had been reporting an interest-free loan the former premier had taken from one of the president's oldest friends.

The old friend was Roger-Patrice Pelat, the Resistance colleague in whose flat Mitterrand had seen the photograph of Danielle Gouze which made him vow to marry her. Pelat had built up a motor parts business which was nationalised under Mitterrand, at an unusually high price. Then Pelat heard from the Mitterrand circle about a take-over planned by a state-owned firm in the USA. Pelat bought shares and made a killing.

But then, the American authorities discovered this transparent piece of insider dealing. Their evidence could not be ignored. Pelat was had up for trial in France, but died of a heart attack before his case could be heard – another timely death, like that of Bousquet.

The mortality count around Mitterrand rose on 7 April 1994, when a man of mystery called François de Grossouvre shot himself. De Grossouvre was a long-time Mitterrand associate who enjoyed contacts with the secret services and with African dictators. But he fell out of favour at court. In desperation, he gained entry to the Elysée and shot himself there with a hunting rifle. It was an appropriate weapon; his official job under Mitterrand had been master of the presidential hunting estates.

Mitterrand has always been a man who has professed great fidelity to his friends. Now, who was left? He had devotion in spades from the energetic culture minister Jack Lang and figures like Yves Saint-Laurent's partner, Pierre Bergé, who was put in charge of the new opera house at the Bastille and who has also been accused of insider dealing. But the socialist party was riven by feuds – Mitterrand had eliminated his long-time *bête noire*, the social democrat former premier Michel Rocard. Jacques Delors was cool about plunging into electoral politics on his return from the European Commission in Brussels.

Mitterrand had shown his own winning way with the voters by gaining easy re-election in 1988, but the succession became more and more of a poisoned chalice. The right was on the rise – one legacy of the Mitterrand years was the way in which the National Front had staged an electoral come-back to take up to 15 per cent of the vote. In what was either an old man's whim or a sign of how little he cared, Mitterrand advanced the career of a huckster businessman, football-club owner and latter-day alleged socialist, Bernard Tapie, who ended up facing a string of court cases for his financial tricks.

Other socialist politicians, including senior party figures, were had up over illicit funding schemes. As the Mitterrand reign ended, the protection of the Elysée counted for less and investigating magistrates slipped the leash which had protected the president's friends for so long. A final sign of how the president had become yesterday's man came early this year, after Delors formally ducked out of the 1995 presidential race. Mitterrand backed the socialist first secretary, Henri Emmanuelli, as the party's candidate to succeed him. It would have been a hopeless choice, prompted only by loyalty to the president. The party ignored Mitterrand and wisely chose Lionel Jospin, who headed the first-round presidential poll on 23 April.

Such a gesture of lese-majesty would have been unthinkable a few years ago. Michel Rocard's presidential ambitions have been thwarted by Mitterrand for more than a decade because he once had the temerity to put himself forward as a candidate for the Elysée. Now it is normal. In an ideal world, Jospin would have been revelling in the Mitterrand inheritance, promising to build on the last 14 years with a new version of *socialisme à la Française*. As it is, the left's candidate in the presidential run-off ballot tomorrow is fleeing from the Mitterrand heritage as fast as decency allows. The president's long march is almost over. Four decades of ambition have ended in a cul-de-sac. ●

The quotations at the head of each section are all from François Mitterrand. They are taken from his televised interview with Bernard Pivot on 14 April 1995, from his book of conversations with Elie Wiesel, *Mémoire à Deux Voix*, from *Mitterrand: L'Autre Histoire 1945–1995* by Paul Webster, and from *Une Jeunesse Français* by Pierre Péan.

Harold Wilson's cortège, Scilly Isles, 1995

Fond farewells

....

25 May 1995

Michael White

Harold Wilson

As both a connoisseur of political occasions and an unabashed man of the people, Harold Wilson would have thoroughly enjoyed the tributes which poured in to honour the memory of this century's most successful election-winner. They came from Westminster and the Wirral, from the Huddersfield of his childhood and the Isles of Scilly where the Wilsons maintained their holiday home – as much in defiance of fashionable opinion as the former prime minister's passion for HP Sauce. Like Harold Wilson himself, they veered on the generous side after the news broke that the former prime minister had died early yesterday at St Thomas's Hospital – within sight of Big Ben. He was 79 and had been ill for some years. Both Lords and Commons rose early in his honour. Had he watched the parliamentary rituals, as his devoted wife, Mary, plus Lady Falkender – his political secretary 'office wife' – and their families did, side by side in the public gallery, one thing in particular might have pleased the man who managed to lead Labour to victory in four out of five elections and occupy 10 Downing St for eight tumultuous years between 1964 and sudden retirement in 1976.

What Lord Wilson would have spotted was that every speaker from John Major onwards alighted on some feature, or several, of his many-sided personality and identified it with his own career and agenda. James Harold Wilson KG, OBE, FRS may frequently have been written off as a failure, but there are plenty for fellow-professionals to admire. What Mr Major detected was pure Major. Breaking class barriers from humble beginnings, an instinct for consensus, a complex, sensitive man 'who never wore the armadillo skin of the fictional politician', he also presided over England's 1966 World Cup win. MPs laughed, as friends should at a good wake. Though he noted Wilson's failures in those recurring crises – Europe, sterling and industrial unrest – Mr Major was generous, but then so was everyone else. Even Ian Smith, who defied him over Rhodesian independence in 1967, said he had always found him 'straightforward and honest' – not what he said at the time. But Jim Molyneaux detected a touch of the Ulster Unionist in Harold, Paddy Ashdown insisted that pragmatism did not mean lack of principle.

Tony Benn recalled his warning that technological change must be properly planned if mass unemployment were to be avoided and how he had kept a disparate cabinet united. Praising Wilson's great speeches, Mr Benn ('Tony immatures with age,' Harold had once joked) even managed a dig at the new Tony. No soundbites then, he said. The Tories spotted the dig. Even without the debilitating illness which ruined his memory in retirement, Lord Wilson would have had a job recognising many of the day's speakers. He was born in 1916, the son of a Yorkshire industrial chemist who lost his job in the Great Depression. Entering Parliament in the Attlee landside of 1945, two years later he became – as the prime minister's potted biography pointed out yesterday – the youngest cabinet minister since 1806. He was 31.

At that time Mr Major was four. As Tony Blair later admitted, Labour's fifth post-Wilson leader was only 11 when he won his first election in 1964, promising a social and economic revolution powered by the white heat of technology. That was the crucial point Mr Blair alighted upon in a crowded Commons yesterday, using the opportunity – as Lord Wilson would have done – to turn a tribute into something approaching a party political broadcast for Labour. He was at it again on radio and TV last night. 'It was a new era in which the British people were looking forward in a spirit of hope and optimism. Harold Wilson in a sense was to politics what the Beatles were to popular culture. He dominated the nation's political landscape and he personified the new era: not stuffy or hidebound, but classless, forward-looking modern,' Mr Blair told MPs. From Brussels Neil Kinnock said much the same. Lord Callaghan, who succeeded Mr Wilson as prime minister, declared: 'His purpose in politics was to remove the disfiguring evils of poverty and to create a caring society with equal opportunity, open to advancement and in tune with the changing needs of our time.'

Michael Foot, Wilson's arch-critic turned employment secretary, noted: 'He knew how to win political victories. That's one thing we will remember him for.' It was a talent that has eluded all successors – so far. ●

....

25 May 1995
Ian Aitken
Lord of the rings

One of the many sparkling one-liners tossed off by Harold Wilson in his long and witty career was uttered to some left-wing cronies shortly after he succeeded Hugh Gaitskell as leader of the Labour Party. 'I'm running a Bolshevik revolution with a Tsarist shadow cabinet,' he told them, between puffs on the famous pipe.

This was clever not because it was true (which it wasn't) but because it demonstrated how a man who had resigned from the Attlee cabinet with Aneurin Bevan succeeded in keeping the loyalty of the Labour left even as he led them up the garden path. He may have had a Tsarist shadow cabinet, but he certainly wasn't running a Bolshevik revolution.

For the paradox of Wilson's long stint as party leader and prime minister – during which he dominated British politics like a colossus – is that the people whose policies he pursued hated his guts, while the people he was hoodwinking continued to like him. Just why this should have been so is hard to grasp, unless you appreciate the deep personal hatreds that existed between the Bevanites and Gaitskellites during the 1950s.

On this personal level – though not in matters of policy – Wilson remained a Bevanite almost to the last. He couldn't stand the so-called 'Frognal set' of Gaitskell's rather snooty friends, a group which got its name from the upmarket Hampstead street where Gaitskell lived. Wilson had less posh quarters in Hampstead Garden Suburb, where some of the Gaitskellites claimed to believe he kept china ducks on his wall.

He didn't, as I can testify. But it is a fact that the Wilsons were distinctly grammar school, while the Gaitskellites were mainly public school. Moreover, Wilson never aspired to be anything else; there was, alas, just a smidgen of truth in *Private Eye*'s snobby 'Mrs Wilson's Diary', in which Harold's favourite drink was supposed to be Wincarnis.

As it happens, I can also testify that Wilson never touched Wincarnis. When I took him out in Soho sometime around 1962 the future prime minister rejected even good French wine. Instead, he insisted on an enormous jug of lager, which he drained to the very last drop. This man-of-the-people impression was only slightly tarnished when he asked for cognac and a cigar with the coffee.

His advice to me then – I had just become a lobby correspondent – was that I should give up the cigarettes I then smoked in favour of a pipe. This, he informed me, would convey the air of gravitas appropriate to my new status. I forbore to ask what sort of message was conveyed by a fat Havana cigar.

We first met almost 10 years earlier, when I was working in Scotland. Harold came to stay the weekend in my digs, in between two meetings. I took him to a football match on the Saturday afternoon, between Stirling Albion and (I think) Stenhousemuir. Neither was a star team, to put it mildly, but he remembered the event when we met again. He quoted the scoreline, and would probably have named the linesmen if I'd asked. He was proud of his memory, and loved to show it off.

Which is why it was more than usually unkind of God to inflict on him, of all people, the loss of memory which marked his last few years. I have always believed that it was an early intimation of this approaching misfortune, and not the dramatic nonsense advanced by some spooky ill-wishers, which persuaded him to astonish everyone by resigning in 1976.

But to get back to the paradox: the essential feature of Wilson's leadership of the Labour Party is now widely acknowledged to have been his success in holding it together through the turbulent period before and after Britain's entry into Europe. Somehow, he managed to convince both the pro-marketeers and the anti-marketeers that he was really, deep down, on their side. The anti-marketeers thought he was being forced into equivocation by the need to placate the pro-marketeers; the latter almost certainly knew better.

In fact, Wilson was persuaded quite early in his first term as premier that Britain's future lay in Europe. I know this because I asked him shortly before he made his own application whether he thought it would be a disaster if we stayed out. 'Yes,' he said, laconically – and turned to someone else before I could ask him to elaborate.

Yet he had fought the 1964 election on an anti-European platform, and his application was sold to his own party as no more than a ploy to discover what terms might be on offer. His old Bevanite friends, who were anti-European, swallowed this subterfuge whole. His old Gaitskellite enemies, who were predominantly pro-European, were happy to settle for the substance.

Yet such was the history of past hatred that it was the right which did most of the plotting against Wilson, while it was the left which invariably rallied to his defence. In fact, the left was being fractionally more rational than the right in its behaviour, since any conceivable alternative to Wilson would have been a lot worse for them.

But the conspiratorial behaviour of the right was wholly irrational. Had they succeeded in toppling Wilson, it is virtually certain that their hell-for-leather approach to European membership would have split the party from top to bottom and brought down the government. As it was, Wilson managed to keep the show on the road right up to, and after, the 1975 referendum.

It was, of course, the subtle Wilson who spotted the value of a referendum as a means of patching up his party after its massive split over Ted Heath's successful application. Even then, the Labour right didn't know what was good for it, for Roy Jenkins resigned as deputy leader when the party decided to take the issue to the people. Both John Major and Tony Blair might benefit by studying how Wilson finessed this episode, allowing even cabinet members to disagree publicly over the issue so long as they agreed to accept the result.

You can, if you feel sufficiently sour, describe all these machinations as devious, unprincipled, even dishonest. But it is equally possible to describe them as brilliant politics in the service of a firmly held conviction that Britain's future lay in Europe.

The real tragedy of Wilson's premiership is different. For he failed in his original purpose, which was to break out of the trap of Britain's post-war stop-go economic history. That failure was caused, at least in part, by his absolute refusal to contemplate a sterling devaluation when he took office in 1964. True to the paradox, it was the left which supported him in this, while the right vehemently disagreed.

But there it is: if an ability to ride two horses at once is the principal qualification for being in the circus, then Harold Wilson was abundantly qualified. His technique was wholly different from that of Lady Thatcher, who eventually overhauled him as the longest-serving post-war prime minister.

Her method was to shoot one of the horses. Harold kept lumps of sugar for both.

Even after the experience of the past 16 years, there still remain some crackpots at Westminster who claim to prefer the head-down, bull-in-a-china-shop politics of Lady T. For my part, I would welcome a spot of unprincipled, shabby, devious compromise – a little touch of Harold in the night. •

....

25 May 1995

Hugo Young
Architect of Labour's ruined inheritance

Harold Wilson was one of the men who ruined post-war Britain. He was a small, posturing, visionless politician, personally pleasant to his friends and even to his enemies, amusing and irreverent and apparently kind. But his public work was a long-strung-out disaster, overlaid at the time by the widespread impression that at least it was most dextrously accomplished.

That's what Wilson was about: the triumph of means over ends. It was the opposite of the reason why he was elected. In 1964, Labour came to power because the party seemed to embody, and none more eloquently than its leader, the values of the new Britain, finally shaking off the shadow of the war and, with particular gratitude, the Edwardian penumbra of Harold Macmillan. More than any post-war prime minister, Wilson was blessed with concerted goodwill and great expectations. Margaret Thatcher, by comparison, was a devisive ingenue, of whom half the country was apprehensive and the other half terrified.

Wilson seemed so promising. He was clever, fast, thoroughly modern. Talking about technology in what was then not known as a soundbite, he seemed in charge of the future. He did not need matchsticks to help him with economics, and he had the intelligentsia, as well as the working class, eating out of his hands. He appealed successfully to a nation thirsting for a new start.

Very quickly he showed the first of his true qualities, sentimental unrealism, by refusing to devalue the pound. This was the sign that Labour put past grandeur before future growth. Wilson wanted to prove that a Labour pound was a pound in anybody's money, and when he was forced to devalue, far too late, continued (in one of his memorable little phrases) to pretend that it was. This set the tone for much that happened in the four governments he led.

Perhaps it is unfair to call him visionless. Somewhere in there, long ago, was an idea about what he wanted Britain to be. But it was soon overtaken by his inability to achieve the economic reform he promised that vision quickly became the last quality anyone associated with his name. The 1960s, quintessentially his era, to which his 1970s administration was a diminuendo coda; are remembered not for anything associated with him, but for the raft of permissive social reforms masterminded by Roy Jenkins, to which Wilson's own Methodist conservatism was, if anything, unsympathetic.

What Wilson was about was not reform but the management of non-reform. At this he was a grandmaster of the board. The diaries of Crossman, Castle and Benn ensure that his is the most chronicled administration in British history. What they all revealed to a possibly startled world was the total ascendancy of method over content in all that time. Government, it turned out, could be run only by a prime minister whose preoccupation was with manoeuvre.

'Wilsonian' resounds as loudly as 'Thatcherite' in the political lexicon, but its connotations are ones to which history is unlikely to give much of an afterlife. At the time, we were enchanted. Every story that came out of Wilson's sublime duplicity, his brilliant feints, his cunning deflation of one minister by enhancing another, attracted mesmerised fascination. His friends will doubtless be looking back on it today with loving admiration. But it signalled not the solution but the profound problem of Labour politics, which Wilson did nothing to correct.

He did, under duress from Barbara Castle, authorise the making of one attempt, with a batch of trade-union reforms promulgated under the wishful title, 'In Place of Strife'. This was the Wilson era's sole attempt to rectify some of the imbalances that make faction and its handling the problem that dominated the leader's life to the exclusion of most other considerations. But instead of making a creative inroad on the status quo, it produced merely another occasion for Wilson to talk his way out of a fiasco, in which the present had exerted an iron veto on the future.

Similar nullity marked the contribution abroad. Behind defence cuts and a shrinking empire, Great Powerdom still beckoned and Wilson loved trotting around beside President Lyndon Johnson, even at one point sending a junior minister, endowed with plenipotentiary powers, to make peace with Hanoi. This farcical episode was only slightly more futile than the lengthy nego-tiations he himself carried on with Ian Smith to try and lure Rhodesia towards political change. But even with the aid of the sainted Arnold Goodman, he found yet another hard issue that would not yield to their sibilant ministra-tions, the combined manoeuvrings that we have now brought them, so fittingly, to die within a week of each other.

One exception can be sighted in the barrenness. At least Wilson was an important accomplice to Britain's entry into the European Community. This was almost entirely accidental. When Macmillan applied, Wilson opposed. When Macmillan failed, Wilson decided to try again and, with George Brown as his drunken companion, lurched from capital to capital, before being seen off by General de Gaulle. After Heath got in, Wilson again operated in a hostile spirit. But in the crucial middle moment, when Heath applied, he could say he was building on what Wilson had abortively attempted and thus was approaching the watershed with what could be represented as bipartisan support. It was one occasion when Wilsonian duplicity, culminating in the referendum that was the only way of accommodating Labour differences, worked in the national interest.

What is happening now in the Labour Party is an attempt to recover from the ruin Wilson bequeathed. Having been elected as the acme of modernity, he failed to take a single step towards modernising the instrument that was his curse and his delight. He took exquisite pleasure, and others with him, in his mastery of the party's antique machinery and historic quarrels.

But if it ever occurred to him that these might be better confronted and overriden, he never allowed the thought to cross even the uttermost horizon of his public mind. He therefore has no relevance, other than that of an alien spirit, to Blair's attempts to make Labour a party of government at the centre of British life.

This is curious. If Wilson did have a vision, it was precisely that: of a party of government whose time had come. In a retirement book, he prated about the art of what he called governance. But his legacy, after the Callaghan interlude, was a party that came within a hair's breadth of never governing again. And we let him loose for seven years in what he was pleased to call power! ●

· ·

17 May 1995

Francis Wheen
A legend in his lunchtime

So farewell then, Lord Goodman. 'A farrago of opprobrious falsehoods ... not a scintilla or tittle of truth ... scandalum magnatum ... beyond any peradventure' – these were your catchphrases.

Younger readers may wonder why the obituary pages should be filled with loud and lengthy tributes to a half-forgotten libel lawyer. The answer is that in the 1960s and 1970s, as the adviser to leaders of all the main parties (Wilson, Heath, Thorpe), he more or less ran the country. Every quango in the land was constitutionally obliged to have Arnold Goodman on its board, and whenever a government found itself in a pickle (over Rhodesia, say, or private patients in NHS hospitals) his lordship would be called in to 'mediate'. I asked him once about his negotiations with the doctors over pay-beds. 'The matter,' he murmured, 'was satisfactorily disposed of.' Jeeves himself couldn't have put it better.

But there were two other reasons for his fame, both of which have been played down in his obituaries: he was enormously litigious, and he was enormously fat.

Goodman disliked being known as the man who launched a thousand writs. Since his death last weekend, eulogists have therefore hastened to assure us that he always – or nearly always – turned the other cheek. According to Roy Hattersley, Goodman 'spent most of his time trying to persuade his famous friends not to sue for libel'. Lord Callaghan agreed: 'He was a great lawyer, yet rarely encouraged people to go to law.'

This will come as a surprise to those of us who were in Fleet Street when Goodman held the gorgeous East in fee. In those days, one could scarcely mention Lord G or his clients – even *en passant* – without receiving a fearsome thunderbolt from the offices of Messrs Goodman Derrick, solicitors to the high and mighty. It is true that few of his libel actions ever came to court, but the same could be said of Robert Maxwell, the other great writ-server of modern times; with Goodman, as with Maxwell, editors were so intimidated that they would capitulate at once.

A rare case which did go all the way was the one he brought in 1957 on behalf of three Labour politicians – Richard Crossman, Morgan Phillips and Nye Bevan – against the *Spectator*, over its allegation that they had been drunk at a conference in Venice. Although they won damages of £2,500 each, Crossman later admitted that the *Spectator* story was largely true. And yet, to the end of his life, Goodman still refused to believe that his clients could have perjured themselves.

When I wrote about the trial a few years ago, my editor was bombarded with furious telephone calls from Goodman, Bevan and Phillips. 'There ought to be a law of posthumous libel,' he spluttered. In his autobiography, published in 1993, Goodman insisted that complaints about the case had come 'entirely from the extreme right of the social, literary and political worlds . . . No one who was not on the extreme right wing has associated himself with any doubts about the justice of the verdict.'

As this suggests, he was sometimes careless with his facts. In 1981, for instance, his client Robert Murdoch was asked by the chairman and chief executive of the publishers Collins, Ian Chapman, to promise that he wouldn't launch an unwelcome take-over bid for the firm.

At a meeting in Lord Goodman's flat in Portland Place, Murdoch duly gave an 'unequivocal undertaking' – which he then broke, making a hostile (and successful) bid for the company. In his memoirs, however, Goodman described Murdoch as 'a man of absolute integrity and truthfulness'.

Still, I mustn't be too hard on the old boy. He had many redeeming virtues – including that magnificently healthy appetite. His obituarists have been rather coy about this, but Goodman himself wore his girth with pride.

On page five of his autobiography he records that his mother cooked 'ample' meals, 'and I may say that I tucked into them with extreme gusto'. When he was a young articled clerk at an office in Gray's Inn, 'not the least of the attractions was the close proximity of an excellent Italian restaurant called Manzoni's. There, for 1s 6d per day, it was possible to have a substantial luncheon, normally escalope of veal *napolitano*, implying a substantial addition of spaghetti. When some sauté potatoes and Brussels sprouts were added to the loaded dish, even my appetite was satisfied. For an additional 4d some kind of suet rolls would be supplied, heavily soaked in golden syrup . . .' A few years later, suffering from stomach pains, Goodman consulted a doctor who, after prodding the affected area, issued an unanswerable diagnosis. 'You are very fat.'

In the 1980s, Goodman managed to settle a case brought against one of his clients, Granada Television, by inviting the two sides to lunch. 'Food played a large factor in the matter,' he reports. 'The heavy lunch had certainly reduced the belligerence of both parties and I was at pains to supply a good tea over which the ultimate discussions took place.' At meetings of the board of the Royal Opera House, which he often found wearisome, he sought solace in 'the excellent smoked salmon sandwiches'.

Imprisoned in every fat man, Cyril Connolly wrote, a thin one is wildly signalling to be let out. Inside Lord Goodman, however, there was nothing but a bellyful of smoked salmon sandwiches, syrup-soaked suet rolls and all the other titbits he managed to cram in during his busy lifetime as a member of the Great and the Good. For those of us who eat too much and work too hard, he is an inspiring example. RIP. ●

. . . .

2 May 1995

Maggie O'Kane
Now is the time to say goodbye . . .

Everyone in the Three Horseshoes pub beforehand was drinking Diet Coke and the church service was for ticket-holders only. The Peter Cook memorial was the kind of service that he probably would never have dreamed of going to himself.

'He would have left for the bookmakers,' said Dave Allen as the names in comedy, drama and publishing filed out pew by pew from a one hour 20 minute memorial service in Hampstead, north London.

Spike Milligan, frail but feisty, agreed: 'He'd have gone off halfway through this if he were here.' Dudley Moore went further: 'He probably wouldn't have turned up.'

As the Rev Phillip Buckler delicately welcomed the congregation to the church that Peter Cook had 'lived in the sight of for 30 years', one pew wondered who had got an invite to the lunch afterwards. But when it came to the business of saying goodbye, the egos of the great and talents of the good displayed such genuine warmth and sadness that even Peter Cook might have been tempted to hang on for the final tune.

Playwright Alan Bennett went first, with the memories of a man he had met 35 years ago in Old Compton Street in white winkle-picker shoes and a tie with silk horizontal bars. A man whose sole shortcoming was that he could do only a passable imitation of Elvis and whose only regret was saving Sir David Frost from drowning in Fairfield, Connecticut, in 1973.

John Cleese, almost in tears, could barely whisper a final 'God bless you, Cookie' after recalling the life of a man that was 'extraordinarily free of ambition, envy and rancour'. Richard Ingrams, former editor of *Private Eye*, agreed on the envy bit but revealed that Peter Cook had pursued an 'irrational vendetta against the late, great Gracie Fields'.

Fellow football fan Dr Sidney Gottleib told of a passion for Tottenham Hotspur that led Cook to abandon Broadway one Saturday night to lose a front tooth at a fervent cup semifinal. Yet, despite his status at the club, he scoffed at the notion of blagging season passes and a parking space. He was also, according to the doctor, a bad loser at golf.

Around 1,000 people turned up to say goodbye to the man who showed up, in Cleese's words, 'men, particularly English men, so trapped by their culture they never knew how to live'. Richard Ingrams said that Peter Cook and Spike Milligan were the icons of their time in comedy and, well, 'he wasn't sure who would ever take their place'. Dudley Moore played 'Three Blond Mice' and a cheery 'I am the Lord of the Dance', and recalled a man who was 'the crème de la crème, an extraordinary wayward talent' who was 'addicted to life and to friends'.

In the end the send-off was from Cook himself. His voice flooded through the church, reading selected excerpts from his diary and saying 'I must do something with my life – something to be remembered for', concluding with his thoughts on the attributes of killer bees.

The five-boy choir from Cook's old school, Radley College, looked slightly unnerved when called to accompany Dudley Moore's rude rendition of 'Goodbye-eee'. They managed. Singing out the congregation who had come to pay tribute to a man Alan Bennett says 'proved that a life of self-indulgence, if led with a whole heart, may also bring a certain wisdom'. Outside in the May sunlight, Spike Milligan signed autographs and said everyone must buy the video but he was going home.

'How dare he clear off and leave us, what a terrible thing to do, to leave us all,' he said.

Then everyone wandered off up Church Row, Hampstead, looking just a little bit lost. ●

11 January 1995

Arnold Wesker
An entertainer's farewell

Arnold Wesker recollects his final meeting, at a summer dinner party at Buckingham Palace, with fellow playwright John Osborne.

Instructions commanded us to begin arriving between 8.45 and 9.15pm. Cars already queueing under the guidance of police outside the Palace gates, crowds peering to catch sight of celebrities. At 8.45, as last time, we were motioned through to take a place in the courtyard and requested to leave our keys in the car.

The routine gradually becomes familiar – drive through gates; man in uniform collecting tickets; vast hallway; ladies loitering in long, undistinguished dresses for partners to return from cloakroom; the wide staircase halfway up which two young women handed out a small concertina map of palace rooms: State Dining Room, Blue Drawing Room, Music Room, White Drawing Room, Picture Gallery, Green Drawing Room, Throne Room. In the last two – the buffet. Dusty [Wesker's wife] went to the loo, reported it was a splendid affair, urged me to go to the gents. At the top of the stairs greeted by a stately couple, man and woman, who shook hands with us (and 800 others) saying 'Hello, good evening.'

Drinks and canapés offered from trays. I stopped a young man with a card on his lapel and asked was he part of the household. He replied, pleasantly, yes he was and smiled a faint smile through thin lips. It struck me he looked like royalty – the Earl of Harewood in fact, who I'd known back in the early days of Centre Forty-two. I asked instead who had been the stately couple greeting us. 'Oh, that would be,' he said, 'the Master of the Queen's Household, Sir Simon Cooper. And the woman would probably be one of the ladies-in-waiting, a duchess, most likely the Duchess of Granston.'

Continued strolling, glass in hand, accepting the canapés from the trays as they passed by. In the Music Room the band – dressed in red and black uniforms – were being seriously conducted by a huge man, very tall and thick-set, incongruously wielding a tiny baton over his men incongruously playing melodies from musicals like *South Pacific*. 'Some Enchanted Evening', I think. Trying to move from the Music Room into the White Room, we were politely held at bay as though it were filled with more important guests. But it wasn't. After some minutes we could drift through. There seemed no reason for having held us back in the first place. Curious. I didn't understand until later when, standing at the end of the White Room, I noticed that the door to the Picture Gallery was now closed as though it were a forbidden area. At one moment it briefly opened. Dusty peered in.

'Pinter's here. I saw him in there. I'm sure it was him.' The doors finally opened, permitting us to enter after all. I think the system was to let rooms fill up gradually, avoiding a sudden rush into an area. A kind of crowd control. I saw Antonia [Fraser] first. If Antonia comes, can Pinter be far behind? There he was, talking with Penelope Wilton – with whom he's working – and Ian Holm, who'd been in *Moonlight*. They're married. Holm and Wilton, that is.

Suddenly saw John Osborne and moved to greet him. Helen sat nearby. He was so pleased to see us and already quite drunk. John is a compelling mixture of disarming docility and sharpness, of nonsense and common-sense. He talks slightly nasally with a drawl that carries a lethal concoction of self-pity, good nature and bilious contempt which, when he's drunk, becomes maudlin.

'You old cunt,' he greeted me. 'Oh, how wonderful to see you here, you commie cunt.' I'm at once comfortable with the crude heartiness of theatricals to which John is more prone even than Pinter. The sober Helen added something not so crude but just as nervous – about left-wing bolsheviks at the Palace. They're all so embarrassed to find themselves there, they have to send it up with a garrulous, loud foolishness, tongues running away with them like kids let out into the playground. Normally I'd run a mile from it.

John introduced me to a handsome blonde woman called Nightie, daughter of a Prussian general involved in the unsuccessful plot to kill Hitler. She's married to Lord Gowrie. We fell into instant conversation over *The Kitchen* which, she informed me, she'd been taken to see when a student in New York. Paul Johnson, sitting at the same table, called her his little Hun, or his favourite Hun, in that tone and manner the English employ to enable them to be both sneery and affectionate at the same time. Sets my teeth on edge. Asked her didn't she mind. No, no, Paul was a dear friend and she could take it.

Spent much of the evening talking with John O, who kept muttering: 'I *am* enjoying myself . . . Oh, what a good time I'm having . . . it's so good to see you, you old cocksucker you . . .' He took up the theme of one of his last letters to me, about becoming increasingly anti-Semitic, in that same tone of voice Johnson used for addressing his 'Hun'. 'I'm becoming more and more anti-Semitic as I grow older,' he said. 'I'd never met a Jew until I was 25, and then I was at a party in New York and I realised – I was the only fucking gentile in the room.' Helen seemed to shift uneasily over all this and tried to hush him up. I repeated what I'd last written to him in a card: 'Don't lose your anti-Semitism. We need it. It's what makes you endearingly quaint.'

We talked about Dexter and his posthumous autobiography. John asked me twice had I read it. *So* drunk! And these days a little hard of hearing, too. I had to shout. We agreed there had been no one quite like Dexter as a director, which I knew better than him because Dexter had directed more of my work. I could only recall a revival of *Look Back* in the early years. 'And then,' said John, 'he did that play I didn't really want done at the National, *A Bond*

Honoured.' But Osborne had met Dexter before I had. They'd shared early acting years together.

He told me he'd just reviewed Oscar Lewenstein's autobiography. 'Not well written, but my word, what a life. He'd been behind all the greats . . . did you know? Joan Littlewood, Brecht . . . What was *your* relationship with him?' None, actually. I pointed out: 'He was more involved with you and Tony Richardson and the Woodfall Film Company.' They'd made *Look Back, The Entertainer, The Charge of the Light Brigade* and others. John had been one of the directors. 'These days,' John complained, 'I'm barred from going into the Royal Court.' Could that be true?

I told him how pleased I was that things were looking up for him and asked what was it precisely that had changed. He mumbled something about how Jill Bennett, his last wife, had persistently told him everybody out there had hated him. 'And you know, if someone keeps telling you that, you begin to believe them. So suddenly I find that everyone is being kind to me . . .' But I never got to understand in which way and about what.

I asked did he mind me asking about his daughter – the one he'd had with Penelope Gilliat, his third wife. No, he didn't mind. Did he ever see her? No, she was an unpleasant young woman, they had nothing in common. Did that upset, hurt him? The tone of his reply said more than his words.

'Yes, well of course it hurts me.' The hurt was in the tone. I got the feeling that he'd have loved a child and would have been a loving father.

The biggest surprise was his reply to my question: had he ever been offered any of the honours? I was certain he had been but had turned them down. No, he told me, he hadn't. 'Never!' I was incredulous. How could Harold have been given the CBE and not John? He'll surely be offered a knighthood, something, sooner or later, especially now that he writes a regular column for the *Spectator*. We talked about other writers. He and Helen hated Tom Stoppard's plays. Loved the man, not the work. I told them I admired *Arcadia* and they were surprised at that. It's to do with Tom being intellectual. John and Helen, I suspect, share the old English mistrust of intellect. John couldn't resist saying: 'It's because he's Jewish.'

'It helps!' I couldn't resist replying. I asked did they like Hare's work. They didn't. The playwright he rates highly is Charles Wood.

After a few more of his outbursts of crude bonhomie of the 'cunt' and 'cocksucker' variety I felt I wanted to confide in him a few of our differences.

'You know,' I began, 'you're very much more a man of the theatre than I am. Both you and Harold. You were both actors, you were both in rep. I had none of that, except as an amateur. I came to the theatre very much as an outsider. Few of my circle of friends are or were theatre people . . .'

Some such words. Because John was drunk – he kept looking for more champagne – and I wasn't certain he was taking it all in, I was not as coherent as I might have been. There's something about drunk people that obfuscates one's own thoughts, disjoints one's sentences. He went off at a tangent to reveal that yes, he and Harold both had the good fortune to work with Wolfit and Devine.

'I can remember Ronnie Harwood, Harold and me, we all three went after acting jobs in the same play. They got the parts, I didn't.' Left it at that.

Another curiosity. Helen confessed to not using a PC. I tried to persuade her it would save her time. She couldn't understand how. I explained how. 'And you'll get so much more work done.'

'I don't want to do *more* work. And the more people talk about them the more I'm determined not to use one. I get very bolshie about it.' They also refuse to use the postcode. It ties up with John's dislike – or mistrust – of foreigners, vegetarians, non-smokers, minorities, gays . . . An odd but endearing couple.

I'm fond of John. I owe him my beginnings, and almost turned down the offer to write my autobiography because I'd thought his two volumes so beautifully written. But that hearty, theatrical crudeness makes me wince.

I think he was genuinely delighted to see me but I shuddered inwardly when he kept calling me either 'you old cunt' or 'you cocksucker', no matter in what endearing tones. And all on top of that banter about why are we all here. Helen said: 'I'm glad to see you're corrupt, that pleases me that you're corrupt also.' I replied: 'Being at the Palace has nothing to do with being corrupt. Being corrupt is when you stop writing what you want to write in order to gain favour. None of us have done that.' I don't understand why they talk such juvenilia when they're all so bright.

At one point Princess Margaret hovered in the doorway near us, waiting to be spoken to. We should have greeted her. John quite likes her, he said. But we didn't move.

'It's funny,' Dusty observed, 'all the women were up and wandering around looking for the royal family, the men just sat.' It was true. At the end I had to drag John away.

'Why should we go, I'm having such a wonderful time?' he wailed. I bent low and whispered in his ear. 'Because otherwise they'll throw us out and that will be very undignified.' He rose at that, put his arm around my shoulder and moved off. We'd offered to drive them to their hotel.

Hobbling away from the evening down the wide, palatial staircase with John leaning on me, his arm heavy on my shoulders, two of the unknighted, must have presented a funny sight to stragglers sitting out their last dregs. He told me he owed an astronomical sum.

'But how are you going to pay it?' I asked, stunned. 'Well, we can't,' he said pitifully. Helen confirmed to Dusty what a terrible financial state they were in. He asked, as we walked cautiously down those stairs, how much advance I'd received for my autobiography. When I told him £50,000 he was surprised. He thought that a huge sum. (The 18 months it took to write worked out at about £14 an hour.) I didn't ask and he didn't volunteer, but surely he'd received more for his two volumes?

Out in the courtyard a handsome young blond man moved in our direction towards his car. 'We know him,' I said. He smiled and introduced himself. 'Charles Anson, press secretary to the Queen.' We didn't know him. I introduced myself and John – though he must have recognised us, certainly he couldn't have mistaken John – and we chatted. He seemed to think it had been a splendid and relaxed evening. I asked, does the Queen enjoy these events?

'Well, she's still there and it's nearly midnight so that's a good sign. Margaret is the late bird but the Queen retires rather early.'

Helen and Dusty walked up. They'd been to the loo. I introduced them, they hovered a few seconds then made their way to the Volvo, uninterested in press men, royal or not. I too moved away to open car doors for them. From behind I heard something which amused me. The Queen's press secretary was saying in humble tones to John – who despite being desperately unsteady on his legs manages to maintain, especially with his grey old man's beard, an air of commanding distinction – 'We're terribly grateful you could come . . .'

I didn't catch John's reply. It could only have been a repeat of how much he'd enjoyed himself. I understand why. He, along with most, is delighted and relieved to be included, to be counted in. And with him were his colleagues. It was comforting.

We drove them to their hotel, the Cadogan, in Sloane Street. 'It was where Oscar Wilde was arrested,' John informed us, 'and where Lily Langtry lived. She bought the place.'

Helen told Dusty it costs them over £300 a night. If they're in the kind of debt they say they're in then paying such a figure is crazy. 'John refuses to give up his standards,' Helen explained. More of that stubbornness – like not using postcodes or computers.

Outside their hotel, John, in dinner suit and black bow tie, performed for us a little farewell hop-skip-and-tap-dance routine as we drove off. The Entertainer! •

....

8 July 1995

Frank Muir

A little foil to big Jimmy

The death at 85 of the actor Arthur Howard, best known as the dithering schoolmaster in the Jimmy Edwards television series *Whack-O!*, although coming after a long, full life, still leaves those of us who knew him well with a lingering sense of loss. Arthur was like that. He was not, perhaps, massively gifted as an actor – most of his work before *Whack-O!* was playing small parts in films and on stage – but he had a beautifully deep, modulated voice and was quite excellent in that narrow area of comedy for which nature had marked him.

But he was really gifted as a human being. Arthur was charming, gentle, funny, and also hopelessly ill-equipped to cope with life's complicated challenges, such as changing a 15-amp plug or riding a bike. He was one of those rare, kind friends one was always glad to see, at any time, anywhere.

I first met him during the war at RAF Warmwell, which was my first posting after an aerial photography course. I remember that Arthur's cousin George was the Wing Commander in charge and deeply keen on persuading the airmen under his command to spend their off-duty hours knocking each other senseless in the station's boxing ring, so I took pains not to come to his notice.

As a photography unit had yet to be built and I was spending my days sitting on a borrowed chair in the armoury watching armourers pouring kettles of boiling water down rifle barrels, I was delighted to find that there was a station concert party I could join. Flying-Officer Arthur Howard was Warmwell's entertainments officer and did not just encourage but bullied me into writing innumerable sketches for station revues, excellent experience, and made me go on stage and be a compere, work for which I developed a morbid liking.

Then I was posted to Iceland and Arthur was posted to Cairo. We met again some four years later at RAF Henlow, both waiting to be demobbed, and Arthur told me with glee that he had found a new protégé in Cairo, an excellent young actor and airman named Richard Gale. Richard was my cousin.

Some years later Denis Norden and I felt that it was time to finish writing *Take It from Here* for radio and move on to television, taking Jimmy Edwards with us. We set up a series based upon Jimmy's orginal comic persona as a boozy venal school headmaster, called it *Whack-O!*, and wrote in a character for him to bully unmercifully, his assistant master, the timid Mr Pettigrew. When it came to casting Mr Pettigrew I remembered Arthur and persuaded Denis that Arthur might well be exactly right. He was acting in the Pitlochry Drama Festival so we wrote, pointing out that it was not as yet much of a part; all we knew about Mr Pettigrew was that Jimmy had to have a foil to talk to and if it did not matter which of the masters he spoke to it would be Mr Pettigrew.

What we did not know was that Arthur desperately needed some well-paid work and a BBC Television comedy series starring Jimmy Edwards would certainly be that. Arthur's work had mainly consisted of cameo comedy parts playing fussy vicars and pompous civil servants. He also understudied Rex Harrison in *French without Tears* and had a spell as dialogue coach to Maurice Chevalier. But Arthur and his actress wife, Jean Compton-Mackenzie, were then going through the experience which most actors have to endure during their working lives – a sticky patch financially. One of Arthur's fellow actors told me that when *Whack-O!* began its long run (1956–60), Arthur was kipping down at a friend's flat and Jean was in a Soho hostel for actresses. When their young son Alan – now the widely admired actor – came home from school they hired a room so that the family could be together for the weekend.

Arthur was a huge success in *Whack-O!* and in a few weeks progressed from being just one of the masters at Chislebury School to being Jimmy Edwards's co-star. He was very funny as the dithery Mr Pettigrew and the perfect foil for Jimmy's bullying headmaster; they rapidly became a classic comedy partnership of the strong but not honest big man and the inept but thoroughly decent little man. In one scene you had an injured Mr Pettigrew, with his head swathed in bandages which the headmaster, packing to go to a conference, kept banging with his fist to emphasise what he was saying. Eventually Mr Pettigrew snapped and gave Jimmy an enormous kick on the behind. Jimmy lay speechless, spread-eagled face down on the bed while Mr Pettigrew trembled with the enormity of what he had done. The laughter from the audience went on and on until Mr Pettigrew finally whimpered: 'I wish I was dead!' and Jimmy rose up very slowly and said, 'That can be arranged!' It was the longest, loudest and most satisfactory laugh Denis and I ever won in many years of writing comedy.

A treasury of anecdotes illustrating Arthur's inability to cope with real life are much cherished by his friends. One weekend he brought Jean and the infant Alan down for Sunday lunch. He was buzzing along happily in his little Morris car when halfway up Egham Hill the steering-wheel came off in his hands. He turned round in panic to Jean in the back seat, waved the steering wheel at her and cried, 'Jean! Look, it's come off!'

'Well, put it back *on!*' said Jean.

Which Arthur promptly did. Afterwards he was told by an awed garage mechanic that on that particularly model of car the steering-wheel was not on a spline but, like an interchangeable camera lens, could only be fitted back in one position. He and his family had survived injury by a one-in-365 chance.

One evening Arthur was walking a little ahead of Jean along Jermyn Street when a Lady of the Night stepped from a doorway and murmured to Arthur, 'Hello, darling!'

Arthur, always the soul of good manners, whipped off his hat just in case it was a family friend he had not recognised and said with his warm smile and beautiful voice, 'Hel*lo*! How lovely to see you again . . .'

Jean grabbed his arm and hissed, 'Oh, come on you fool!'

Then Arthur's luck, such as it was, ran out. Jean, who had stopped him from tripping over so many of life's broken paving-stones, died. A little while later Arthur was arrested for 'cottaging', the slang word used to describe anonymous homosexual encounters in public lavatories.

Denis Norden and I agreed to stand surety for Arthur to be bailed out. Our magistrates' court appearance began in farce and then descended to drama. The farcical moment came when Denis and I moved into the witness box which was built for one person and became jammed in it.

The drama hit us when the clerk of the court asked us whether we could put up a hundred pounds each as surety. The court immediately rang with our sincere and ringing cries of 'Oh, yes!' 'Certainly!' 'No problem at all, your worships!' But then the clerk went on 'after all your debts are paid?'

An awkward pause hung in the air. Eventually we mumbled, without conviction, 'Er – yessir. Yes. We have the money. Er – it's invested.'

My wife and I invited Arthur to convalesce at home with us, which he did. What was so typical of him was that during his period on remand in Brixton prison his colleagues were mostly hardened drunk-and-disorderly regulars, and burglars, and his best friend had stabbed his girlfriend in the cheek with a pair of scissors, but to a man they protected Arthur and eased his way through the tough prison regime, for instance making sure that he had first shave with the morning's communal razor-blade.

While he was with us, Arthur scoured the newspapers daily for reports on how his new friends had fared when they came up in court. He was deeply concerned about them.

Arthur's great personal problem seems to have been that he was the least successful duckling of his family. His parents were Hungarian refugees, the family name was Steiner, later pronounced 'Stainer'. His brother Leslie was a big star, famously playing Ashley in *Gone With the Wind*. His sister Dorice Stainer had an Ascot dance school and his other sister, Irene Howard, was the powerful casting director of MGM in England. His son Alan and nephew Ronald were both leading actors. Jean also had highly successful relations: her aunt was the actress Fay Compton and her uncle was the novelist Monty Compton-Mackenzie.

So Arthur explained to my wife and me that at a smart party where everybody was more talented and had achieved more than he and Jean could ever have hoped to do, he would slip away and 'cottage', and when he returned to the party he was someone for a few hours. He had a secret. It was a case of 'I know something you don't know'. It does seem a pity that life could not have been just a little more kind to dear old Arthur Howard. He was kindness itself. ●

16 January 1995

David Beresford

Soweto mourners keep Joe Slovo's red socks flying

They buried the most popular white man in Africa yesterday. If the proceedings ended in pandemonium, it seemed just another tribute to Joe Slovo, the erstwhile Stalinist who — in the words of his wife, Helena Dolny, when she finally battled her way to his Soweto graveside — had so enjoyed wine, women, song and his red socks.

The red socks of Joe Slovo have long been an affectionate national joke — a symbol of a lifetime of loyalty to the South African Communist Party by its former chief. Their evocation was one way by which the country paid its fond farewell.

No moment was more poignant than when the plain pine coffin of the country's one-time 'public enemy No 1' was loaded on to its place of honour, on a Second World War gun carriage provided by the army that had spent years trying to kill him.

Mr Slovo had wanted the ceremony kept simple, and so it was, to the extent that the crowds would allow.

He was accompanied on his final journey through the streets of Soweto to the cemetery by tens of thousands of mourners. They eventually swamped marshals, creating chaotic scenes which apparently forced President Nelson Mandela to cancel a graveside appearance.

But the African National Congress leader had already said his last good-bye in the packed Orlando soccer stadium, telling the man who was probably his most influential adviser: 'If you see tears welling in our eyes, it is because we cannot bear saying, "Farewell, dear comrade, dear brother, dear friend."'

A full-scale state funeral was staged for Mr Slovo, who died in office as minister of housing after a four-year battle with cancer. Flags flew at half-mast on government buildings yesterday, and most of the cabinet was present at the Soweto stadium for the funeral service.

Mourners filed past the open coffin for more than two hours for a last sight of Mr Slovo, a familiar if emaciated figure in spectacles and red tie. On a platform behind the coffin sat the Slovo family. Alongside them the main stand was crowded with VIPs, including Kenneth Kaunda, Walter Sisulu — who is recovering from a heart attack — and two National Party cabinet ministers, one of whom, Pik Botha, represented the former president, F. W. de Klerk.

Mr Slovo, who was born a Lithuanian Jew and died a South African atheist, had told friends any religious presence at the funeral should be multi-denominational. Alongside South Africa's chief rabbi, Cyril Harris, was the Rev Barney Pityana of the Anglican Church, a key figure in the 1970s black consciousness movement.

'Today, as the nation bids you final farewell, we are at the same time celebrating a life lived to the full, the richness of which touched the hearts of millions and made an indelible mark on the history of our country,' Mr Mandela said.

'The irony that Joe so succinctly captured, that life is after all a terminal illness, is the tragedy of the natural order that we can do nothing to change. But like him, we can so live that, when we depart, we shall have made life that much more bearable for others.'

Police helicopters, which not long ago flew low over political funerals to try to disrupt them, clattered high in the sky. Far below, mobs of dancing teenagers in ragged clothes, black political and business leaders luxuriating in limousines, and youths riding on the roofs of police vans formed a funeral procession three miles long.

In the mud of Avalon cemetery – beside the grave of another white hero of the black liberation struggle, Helen Joseph – Mr Slovo's widow appealed for calm.

Her husband was an endearing man, Ms Dolny said. 'People related easily to the things he enjoyed in everyday life: the peanuts, the whisky, the red socks, wine, women and song.' •

....

30 March 1995
Duncan Campbell
The gang's all here to pay last respects to Ron

As Lee parked his van at the entrance to Chingford cemetery in east London yesterday afternoon, he was moved to observe: 'There's nothing like a gangland funeral for bringing people together.'

And certainly there had been nothing like the funeral of Ron Kray that Chingford, or indeed many other parts of Britain, had ever seen.

Lee was one of thousands who lined the streets to catch a glimpse of Ron's coffin as it was drawn by six black-plumed horses from the service in St Matthew's, Bethnal Green, to the burial plot next to those of his mother, Violet, and father, Charles, in Chingford cemetery.

The limousines, 25 in all, had started arriving at English's funeral parlour early in the morning. Enough police to mount a dozen dawn raids kept crowds of onlookers at bay as the cortège drove past Pellici's, the coffee bar where more than 30 years ago young East Enders learned not to blow the froth of their cappuccinos at the Twins.

And young men who would not have been born when Ron and Reg Kray were jailed for the murders of George Cornell and Jack 'The Hat' McVitie in 1969 hung from lamp-posts – by their arms, it should be said – to catch a few of the faces who had turned up to pay their last respects and of course to see in the flesh bother Reg himself, allowed out from Maidstone jail for the ceremony.

The pallbearers had been chosen to represent the four different corners of London, which were, literally, at each other's throats so often in the past.

'It is a symbol of peace that the four pallbearers will be Charlie (Kray), Freddie ("The Mean Machine") Foreman (out on parole from his 1983 Security Express robbery sentence), Johnny Nash (of the club-owning north London Nash family) and Teddy (Ginger) Dennis,' said the order of service.

It was a sign that, for some anyway, the hatchet was being buried as well as the Colonel.

There, too, were 'Mad' Frankie Fraser, flanked by identical twins Andrew and George Wadman, young boxers who visit Reg Kray in Maidstone jail; Tony Lambrianou, jailed for 15 years for his part in the murder of McVitie; Lenny 'The Guvnor' McLean, king of unlicensed boxing; and Charlie Smith, a double murderer wearing handcuffs and a grin, out from Broadmoor for the day.

There were others less happy to be recognised: one kilted and tattooed mourner identifed himself merely as 'Robert the Bruce'.

The doors of St Matthew's had barely closed when Frank Sinatra's 'My Way' starting drifting over the mourners, to be followed by 'Morning Has Broken' and the reading by a family friend, Sue McGibbon, of 'Invictus', the W E Henley poem.

> It matters not how strait the gate,
> How charged with punishments the scroll,
> I am the master of my fate.
> I am the captain of my soul.

Reg was reminded how little a master of his fate he currently is by the prison officer attached to his wrist. But the security was less obvious than when his mother was buried in 1982 and the twins were handcuffed to the two tallest officers in the prison service. This time a woman officer flanked him, brushing his hair down when it blew in the wind.

His own message was simple: 'My brother Ron is now free and at peace. Ron had great humour, a vicious temper, was kind and generous. He did it all his way but above all he was a man. That's how I will always remember my twin brother.'

Reg emerged from the church, blinking in the sunlight, as teenagers chanted, 'Let him go' and, 'We love you, Reg.'

Young heavies who were not sure whether they were auditioning for *Pulp Fiction* or *The Lavender Hill Mob* shouldered people aside to let the glass-covered hearse begin its journey.

Two hours later the coffin arrived at the cemetery, where more crowds had gathered, standing in the trees, clutching cameras and even opera glasses as the police helicopter fluttered above.

Reg paused to stroke three of the black horses – he had once given his mother a racehorse as a present – and kissed the gravestone of his wife Frances, who committed suicide in 1967 at the age of 23. Then, surrounded by his clan, he watched 'the other half of me', as his own floral tribute had it, laid to rest. While the mourners piled off to a wake in Stepney, Reg returned to his prison cell. He and his twin had heard many judges tell them that one day they would answer to a higher court. Ron will be hoping for a lenient sentence. ●

....

30 March 1995

Leader
Two funerals; two murderers

They came to say their farewells to two terrible murderers yesterday. The first was a furtive affair, far from home with few relatives present and singing strictly forbidden. The other was almost a festival, on home ground with the family in full attendance, and to the sound of songs ranging from 'Fight the Good Fight' to 'I Did It My Way'. The first murderer was cremated almost in secret because local people would not tolerate having such a killer buried in their midst and because of fear of invasion by a hostile media circus. The other was buried in the full and bizarre pomp of what was almost a dignified civic occasion, amid a vast and generally fascinated media circus.

Fred West and Ronnie Kray were two of the nation's most famous murderers. Yet the contrast between their funerals yesterday could not have been greater if one had been a national hero and the other a national traitor – which in a sick sense they almost were. Fred West hanged himself in a Birmingham prison cell on New Year's Day. Villagers in his local Gloucestershire village protested against plans to bury him in the churchyard next to his parents. So yesterday the village priest went without fuss and notice to a Coventry crematorium to conduct a simple ceremony. The family, many of whom did not attend, requested no hymns. The priest simply offered the bleak prayer that Fred West might have repented in the moments before his death. It was the shortest and grimmest of ceremonies, the cruel absolute minimum due to a dead man.

Ronnie Kray's crimes are not so vivid in the public mind of the 1990s as those of Fred West. Yet Kray lived a life of crime every bit as fully as the Gloucester builder. He was convicted for two dreadful murders which were among the most shocking crimes of the 1960s. And if Fred West indeed repented as he went before his God, there was not much sign in yesterday's festivities that Ronnie Kray had done so. Kray's funeral was an extraordinary exhibition. It reinvented a caricature version of East End gangsterdom, with the glass-sided hearse drawn by six black-plumed horses, the black top-hatted undertakers, the close-cropped, barrel-chested, iron-jawed bodyguards in their dark suits, the dapper ageing hoodlum mourners in their designer shades, the deep-lined streets and the kitsch floral tributes. It was memorable theatre but a pretty sick show. And in any case it was a parody of an East End which no longer existed. That East End of Lionel Bart, Jack Dash, Joan Littlewood, Alf Garnett and the Krays has gone with the docks and the markets or has moved out to Chingford and deep Essex. Time, England and East Enders have moved on. The Kray funeral was like the Beatles' latest single, a bad idea from a distant decade, best forgotten and not worthy of our continuing obsession. •

24 July 1995
Frank Keating
Ashes and sackcloth

The bodyline dramas of 1932–33, and Harold Larwood's part in them, will be stored at the front of historians' files for as long as the game of cricket is chronicled. The theory that Australia's batsmen – and especially Don Bradman – would funk a concerted attack of pace bowling aimed at their bodies was hatched by England's autocratic public school captain Douglas Jardine. He called it 'leg theory'. Larwood, who has died aged 90, led the pitiless assault, working in tandem with his Nottinghamshire colleague Bill Voce and the Yorkshireman Bill Bowes.

England won the series, which stirred colonial passions and hatreds, by 4–1, Larwood obeying orders with such fearsome and cruel panache as to finish with 33 wickets at only 19 apiece. (Bradman, career Test average 99.94, was confined to 396 runs at 56.57, and fell four times to Larwood.)

Back home, Larwood was ordered to apologise to the MCC for his bowling. He refused. He never played for England again. His last first-class match, for Nottinghamshire, was in 1938, after which he retired to keep a corner sweetshop in Blackpool, refusing always to talk about cricket, let alone Bodyline. He emigrated to Australia with his wife Lois and their five daughters on an assisted passage in 1950, where the former miner worked successively as a nightwatchman, storekeeper and packer in a soft-drinks factory. The gently shy, blind old man whose surname more than any other remained an eponym for virulent fast bowling – patron saint and forerunner to Lillee and Lindwall, Ambrose and Holding and Waqar – was awarded the OBE in 1993, 60 years after his last Test match.

In 21 Test matches he took 78 wickets at 28.35 apiece, and in 14 seasons for Nottinghamshire 1,427 at 17.51. He took five wickets in an innings 98 times, and ten in a match on 20 occasions. He made 234 catches and, a decent straight driver with the bat, he averaged 19, with three centuries and a top Test score, in his final match at Sydney, of 98.

The year before Gooch and Gough made their pilgrimage to the tiny wooden bungalow at Randwick, I had rung the doorbell and begged an audience. The eyes which greeted you might have been blind, but still managed a suspicious beady aggressiveness. I said I bore greetings from the *Guardian*, and dropped the names of Cardus and Arlott. That got me past the porch. 'But I'm not talking cricket,' he said, 'and certainly not Bodyline. Ask me one question about either, and you're out.'

But I did, and I wasn't. 'And don't "Sir" me,' he ordered, 'the name's Harold, one time coal miner and later professional cricketer.' The accent was still ripely recognisable as Nottingham. 'You can come in for a minute or two and look at my pictures if you must,' he said. In his dotage, he could not have been more than 5ft 6ins, but he was still straight-backed. In his prime, he was only 5ft 9ins. 'I got my pace from my back, didn't I? Well, I was a miner, wasn't I? And my arms were longer than most. I used to sometimes graze my knuckles on my follow-through, y'know.'

The walls of the spotless little sitting-room were dotted with framed photographs, some homemade in passe-partout or Sellotape. Team groups of blazered and sepia heroes stared down. He knew exactly where every one was, and who was in it. Photos fade faster than fame.

His first tour with England was to Australia in 1928–29. Percy Chapman was captain. It looked a happy bunch. Sixteen of the 17 were dead, he remarked. Now all 17 are. 'Mr Chapman' – still 'Mr' notice – 'was always cheerful, but always a gentleman. Had an awfully nice wife, too, a real lady; she visited me in hospital when I had a knee operation. Third from the left from me is Les [Ames]. Les was always my best pal in cricket. I'd stay with him when we played at Canterbury, and him with me when Kent played Trent Bridge. We were the babies of that team – along with Wally [Hammond]. Funny chap, Wally. Moods, y'know. Nice as pie one day, never even speak to you the next. Hell of a bat, mind, and ruthless with it too.'

And on the mantelpiece and various homemade shelving silvery-shining mementoes were lit by the bright southern sun which streamed through the window. I tapped my pipe out on an ashtray. The old man heard the clink. 'That's my most treasured possession,' he said, though without a trace of admonishment. 'Read out what the engraving says,' he ordered. – 'To Harold. For the Ashes. From a Grateful Skipper.'

Fond farewells

The unseeing eyes misted over and stared at the wall in a reverie of content. 'Mr Jardine gave me that when we came back. It has always meant the world to me. Always will. He was a real leader of men, a true commander. I'd bowl two or three overs on that tour for him and then he'd come up and say "Anything in this pitch for you, Harold?" and I'd probably answer "Yes, it's pretty lively, skipper."

'Sometimes he might say, "Let's wait for the little bastard [Bradman] to come in." Then he'd clap his hands and everyone would move over to the legside and all of a sudden my field would be Les, at wicket standing back, not even a slip just a short-gully for the batsman's sort of jump-and-jab; perhaps a mid-off close-ish in, and every single one of the rest in the legside ring. And I'd bowl real fast skimmers which rose up, very uncomfortable to play because I would "follow" them if they backed away. I never once actually aimed at the body of a batsmen, never. But I just used to watch Bradman's feet as I bowled. If he shuffled slightly to leg, I'd "follow" him; if he moved across his stumps I'd follow him there. No, the barrackers in the crowd never got at me. But they gave Mr Jardine hell. He didn't care that they detested him. He simply didn't like Australians I think. They called him "Sardine" and they loathed that coloured cap he sometimes wore.'

A framed, faded, official scroll on another wall of the tiny room was signed by the 'Union Officer' and marked a long-ago 'appreciation of your cricketing feats from fellow members' of the Miners' Union branch at Nuncargate, the Nottingham pit village in which he was born. 'I always feel honoured for knowing that's there,' he said. 'I left school at 13 and first worked in the grocery, humping bags of flour. But at 14 I was old enough to go down the pit. At first I helped with the ponies. I was only 4-foot high, but the tunnels were only 3ft 6ins, so I still had to bend. That's where I began to get the strength in my back. Then, about 15, I was on the coke carts. One day I cut a fellow's arm off. He was oiling the wheel-drum where the ropes went round and I called to him, silly sod, to put the brake on first, but he didn't. I knew what was going to happen when I put the carts on, but I couldn't stop it by myself – and then I heard his terrible squeal and, oh, my God, in a moment he was squirming around the floor with his arm cut off cleanly by the chains. I met him a few times after, one armed, and he always told me it was all his own fault, not mine.

'I was always one for the cricket when we had time off. Old Joe Hardstaff lived in the street next to ours. He was a Nottingham bat and a few games for England, too. He said I should go for a trial at Trent Bridge. I wasn't keen. I was quite happy mining. But my Dad took me down on the bus one day. I had to bowl in the nets to Art Staples and Ben Lilley [two stalwart county pros]. Our village pitch was all bumps and dents, but this was as flat as a pancake, so they hit me all over the shop. I went over to dad and said, 'I'm no good at this lark, let's go home.' So we started packing up when a message was sent over to say I was wanted in the committee room. Mr Dixon was the president. He owned half Notts didn't he? He didn't let my dad come in. He said to me, "Look here, Larwood, how much are you getting down the pit, boy?" I tell him "32 bob a week, sir." He says, "Right, that's settled, you can join the groundstaff at 32 shillings per week"

'Outside, dad was fair livid I hadn't asked for more, especially when the secretary followed me out with a list as long as your arm for stuff I'd need to bring with me, like a bat, flannels, new boots and all. It came to around £9, which dad said was near impossible to find. But dad said we'd try, and on the way home on the bus I said, "Dad, if I make the grade at cricket, I'll really make it all right with you and more. I did too.'

A couple of years later, in the midsummer of 1925, the 20-year-old groundstaff oik – net-bowling, scorecard-selling and picket-painting till then – received a telegram at home: 'Proceed to Sheffield. Be prepared to play – Carr.' The county's longtime squirearchical captain was A. W. Carr.

Dad and mum took him up on the train. When he bowled they say he made Herbert Sutcliffe 'hurry' a few of his shots. In no time he was blowing like a gale and in that last half-summer of 1925 he took an astonishing 73 wickets at 18 each and even celebrated giants were jumping . . .

'Jack Hobbs was the best by far I ever bowled at. But little Andy Sandham never flinched at all, he'd just jam his two great pads in front of the stumps and never give you a look at them. All you could do was go for lbw's . . .'

He shuffled a hand around a drawer and pulled out a parchmenty old newspaper cutting. 'Is this the right one?' he asked. The *Sunday Express* headline of August 21, 1926, proclaimed 'Larwood Too Young, Rhodes Too Old'. He said, 'That's it, my first Test at the Oval.' It was his first Ashes clincher. Larwood took six wickets in the match (all in the top order) and Rhodes the same. 'He was a genius was Mr Rhodes.'

Seven years later, in what (criminally) was to be his final Test, the last at Sydney of Jardine's infamous tour, Larwood twisted his foot as he ran in to bowl. 'I collapsed in agony. Mr Jardine picks me up and says I must finish the over at full pelt. "I can't, skipper, I'm finished," I say. He orders me. So I do, in terrible pain. "Can I go off now, skip?" I say. "No," he whispers, nodding towards Bradman, "not till the little bastard's gone. Let him think you can come back for another spell any time you want. So stand at short-cover and just stare at him with menace." So I do what I'm told, and Hedley [Verity] comes on at my end and that's where Mr Jardine was right, because Bradman loses his head at once, thinking to "cash in" while I'm resting.

'He dashes out at Hedley's second ball, head up, and it bowls him. At once, Mr Jardine signalled me off. He'd done the trick – and Bradman and me walk off together, me limping badly, and though we go off beside each other neither of us spoke one word. And little did I know that I'd never play for England again. Well, I wasn't about to apologise, was I? And I never will. Well, I didn't have anything to apologise about did I?'

One of those Australian batsmen he so demoralised in that series was Jack Fingleton, later a noted journalist. On the 1948 Australian tour of England, Fingleton looked up Larwood, anonymous and finding it difficult to make ends meet in his Blackpool corner shop. The two old adversaries readily chewed the fat.

Eighteen months later, at home in Australia and out of the blue, Fingleton received a cable which clean-bowled him more comprehensively than anything else he had received from England's demon bowler – Leaving Orantes London tomorrow stop Can you arrange accommodation for self wife five daughters eldest daughters fiancee stop Also jobs signed Larwood.

Fingleton telephoned the former Australian Prime Minister and cricket lover, J B Chifley. A plot on which to build a bungalow was fixed. So was the necessary loan. A choice of jobs was offered. The Larwood tribe took to Australia. It was mutual. The darling old miner, prophet without honour until John Major's OBE at 89, was serenely happy to live in Australia – and, I fancy, honoured to die there. ●

....

18 July 1995
Richard Williams
Best and bravest racer of them all

Decades after their prime, the immortals can still change the mood of a room simply by their presence: Bradman, Pele, Ali. In motor racing it was Juan Manuel Fangio, who has died aged 84. More than 30 years after he last acknowledged a chequered flag, fans who had never seen him in action would jostle to glimpse the unprepossessing little Argentine who, by most available yardsticks, had been the greatest racing driver of all time. During his occasional visits to Europe, to take part in anniversary celebrations, there were many who would rather watch Fangio in his eighties, the survivor of several heart attacks, tiptoe round a circuit in a restored museum piece than the present generation race at full throttle in their computer-designed super-machines.

For his admirers, the 'Old Man' symbolised the heroic age when racing drivers went about their business in cork helmets, polo shirts, string-backed gloves and suede loafers, forearms bare to the wind, their faces streaked with hot oil. It was an age in which chivalry still played a part, and when the physical danger was such that each race seemed to thin the ranks of the participants. Perhaps the two were not unconnected.

For all the affection lavished on him throughout his long retirement, Fangio was nevertheless a hard case, a professional in the postwar world of dashing amateurs. Although capable of kindness and consideration, he never allowed sentiment to obstruct his path. Sound judgement and mental toughness served him well throughout a career whose greatest triumphs – 23 grand prix wins in 51 starts, five world championships (still unmatched) in seven and a half seasons – were achieved in his fifth decade, and thousands of miles away from his homeland. But the bare statistics tell nothing of his extraordinary qualities – the combination of delicate virtuosity, carefully deployed aggression and mechanical sympathy that often allowed him to rise above unhelpful conditions, superior opposition, or faulty equipment. Sometimes, being Fangio, all three at once.

Fangio was born in Balcarce, a potato town in eastern Argentina, in 1911. Both his parents had their origins in the Abruzzo region of Italy. Juan's father, the accordion-playing Don Loreto, arrived in Argentina at the age of seven, becoming a stonemason and house-painter; his wife, Doña Herminia, a seamstress, produced six children, of whom Juan was the fourth. The young Juan was a good student, and loved boxing and football. An agile inside-right, he was nicknamed *Chueco* – Bandylegs – by his team-mates.

Argentina had held its first motor race in the year before Juan's birth. At the age of four he was enthralled by a neighbour's single-cylinder machine. At 10, he was hanging around the garage of a Señor Capettini, fetching and carrying tools for the mechanics, and driving a car – a chain-driven Panhard-Levassor – for the first time. At his father's wish Juan was apprenticed to a local blacksmith, but he soon talked himself into a transfer to Capettini's premises. There, and later at Miguel Viggiano's Studebaker garage, he learnt the intimate details of the internal combustion engine: how to profile a camshaft by hand, how to use a stone to grind a cylinder head. At night, after work, he began to modify machines himself. By his mid-teens he was also volunteering to deliver cars to customers, and ascribed his famous skill in slippery conditions to his early experience of driving on muddy tracks, which encouraged him to acquire a delicate touch.

At 16 he briefly ran away from home to Mar del Plata, 35 miles distant, but was recaptured by his father. Soon afterwards, without telling his parents, he took part in his first race, as the riding mechanic in a four-cylinder Plymouth driven by one of Viggiano's customers. He performed a similar role the following year, accompanying his brother-in-law in a Chevrolet during a closed-circuit race in Balcarce. In 1931, however, Juan contracted pleurisy, and needed a long convalescence with relatives in the countryside before, in 1932, he reported to the artillery barracks in Buenos Aires for a year's compulsory military service. When he was able to return home, he set up a garage with a friend, José Duffard – the first step in a long business career which ran in parallel with his life as a racing driver.

Fond farewells

Races on the open roads were the highlight of Argentinian motor sport, and Fangio's first really significant result came with seventh place in the 1938 Gran Premio Argentino de Carreteras, over 4,590 miles. His potential was now so obvious that the people of Balcarce clubbed together to buy him a decent car, a six-cylinder Chevrolet coupé. His first great win with the Chevrolet came in 1940, in the Gran Premio Internacional de Norte, which ran from Buenos Aires through Bolivia to Peru and back, a total of almost 6,000 miles in a fortnight, up mountain roads reaching 13,500 feet. Exhaustion and altitude sickness were enemies as formidable as the unmade roads. 'In the mountains of Peru,' he recalled, 'we chewed coca leaves' to counteract the symptoms. Victory in this, plus another in the Mil Millas Argentinas, made him the country's 1940 road-racing champion. He won the title again the following year, and was beginning to grow accustomed to street parades in Balcarce when, in 1942, the war halted racing.

He was 31. For another sportsman, these might have been the lost years of his prime, but Fangio was only just beginning. He concentrated on his garage business, and made solo drives from one end of Argentina to the other. With the resumption of racing in 1947, he was ready.

That year, the Argentine Automobile Club invited two great Italian stars, Achille Varzi and Luigi Villoresi, to take part in races at Buenos Aires and Rosario. The following year they returned, together with a third Italian, Nino Farina, and the French champion Jean-Pierre Wimille. Fangio began this series, known as the Temporada, in an old Maserati, but for the third race, in Rosario, he was offered one of a pair of Simca-Gordinis brought from France by their maker, Amédée Gordini. Fangio comfortably matched the performance of Wimille, a European grand prix star, in an identical car.

When Fangio arrived in Europe in 1948 with a delegation from the Argentine Automobile Club, Varzi and Wimille were among those who welcomed him. Fangio's only appearance during that trip was at Rheims, driving a Simca-Gordini at the French Grand Prix meeting. He failed to finish, but the party returned home in possession of a pair of new single-seater Maserati grand prix cars. For Fangio, though, the year also held sadness; he had been at the Bremgarten circuit in Berne when Varzi died under his capsized Alfa Romeo; and back in Argentina, while competing in the epic Gran Premio de la America del Sur, he rolled his old Chevrolet, killing his co-driver and friend, Daniel Urrutia. Only three months later, during practice for the Gran Premio Juan Domingo Perón at Buenos Aires, Wimille was also killed.

That race was the first of the 1949 Temporada series, in which Fangio was to make his real impact on the Europeans. At the Grand Prix of Mar de Plata, driving the fast little Maserati 4CLT in front of 300,000 ecstatic fans, he beat Farina, Villoresi and Alberto Ascari in a straight fight. Now he was ready to take on Europe. Within weeks he was leading the little Argentine team to

victory in a grand prix along the San Remo seafront. It was followed by wins
at Pau, Perpignan and Marseilles. So enthusiastic were his home fans that
Perón's government bought him a new two-litre Ferrari, and he repaid his
country's faith by winning his first race, the Monza Grand Prix, matched
against Ascari and Villoresi in similar cars on a circuit that he had never seen
before.

It was enough to attract the interest of the Alfa Romeo management, then
preparing a team for the first world championship, to be held over a seven-race
series in 1950. Fangio, Farina and Luigi Fagioli were their drivers, and between
them 'the three Fs' won all six European rounds in their crimson Alfettas, the
Argentine gaining victories at Monaco, Spa and Rheims to take second place
in the final championship table, just behind Farina. But the following season
three more wins – in Switzerland, Spain and France (the latter shared with
Fagioli) – plus two second places gave Fangio his first world championship.
He was 40 years old.

Alfa Romeo, though, decided to retire from racing, and during the winter
Fangio accepted two offers: the first from Maserati, for whom he would drive
in Formula Two races; the second from a new concern, known as British
Racing Motors. The first turned out to be the better deal, since the 1952 and
1953 world championships were run to the two-litre regulations of Formula
Two. As for the supercharged 16-cylinder Formula One BRM, it turned out
to be one of the great motor-racing fiascos, a costly disaster made the more
embarrassing by the fact that the project had been paid for by public
subscription. Fangio raced the ill-handling beast six times, and the two second
places which were all he had to show may, in the circumstances, be counted
among his most heroic feats.

But 1952 was, in any case, his worst season. It ended on the weekend of
June 7–8. On the Saturday he was due to race the BRM in the Ulster Trophy
race on the Dundrod circuit near Belfast, followed on the Sunday by his first
race in the Maserati, in the Grand Prix of Monza. After the BRM's customary
retirement he flew from Belfast to Paris, there to be told that bad weather had
ruled out all flights to Italy. Undeterred, Fangio drove non-stop through the
night to Monza, just north of Milan, arriving two hours before the race was
due to start. Although he had not practised, and was therefore not qualified to
race, his fellow drivers immediately voted to let him participate. 'You look a
bit tired,' Ascari told him. 'Oh, it's nothing,' Fangio replied. But, starting
from the back row of the grid in an unfamiliar car, he misjudged the Seraglio
curve on the second lap and woke up in hospital with broken vertebrae. It was
the only serious accident he was to suffer in the whole of his European career,
and it put him out for a year.

Three races into the 1954 season, Mercedes-Benz made their long-awaited
reappearance in Formula One. Alfred Neubauer, their peerless talent scout,
always hired the best – which meant Fangio. Together, they reduced their

Fond farewells

Italian, French and British competitors to the status of also-rans, Fangio winning six of the eight European grands prix (the first two in a Maserati), and taking the championship with a points total almost double that of the runner-up.

The arrival at Mercedes of the brilliant young English driver Stirling Moss, in 1955, at least gave Fangio some competition, although Moss was generally content to follow in the master's wheeltracks, learning the finer points of racecraft in a sequence of one-two finishes. Fangio took the maximum points in Argentina, Belgium, Holland and Italy.

By contrast, in the British Grand Prix, Moss 'won' by a tenth of a second after 90 laps of the Aintree circuit. For many years Fangio did not reveal that he had run the race to the orders of the team management — which was looking for a public-relations coup in Britain and had fitted Fangio's car with lower gear ratios, restricting his speed. In any case, the championship had already been decided in his favour.

Curiously, Fangio's finest drive of the season may have been among his least praised. In the Mille Miglia, the non-stop time-trial over public roads from Brescia to Rome and back, he finished second to Moss in a race that became recognised as the Englishman's greatest triumph. But whereas Moss had enjoyed the prompting of a well-prepared navigator in the passenger seat of his eight-cylinder Mercedes 300SLR, Fangio accomplished the drive single-handed. And, for more than half the distance, on seven cylinders.

At the Le Mans 24-hour race though, Fangio's Mercedes was peripherally involved in the crash which saw the machine of his team-mate Pierre Levegh flying over an earth bank into a public enclosure, killing 80 spectators. Fangio and Moss, sharing a car, were leading the race when, at two o'clock in the morning, orders came from Stuttgart to withdraw the entire team — a gesture of respect which also served as a partial safeguard against the consequent storm of bad publicity. The disaster bore heavily on Mercedes' subsequent decision to withdraw from racing.

Fangio, now 44, was contemplating retirement when a call from Enzo Ferrari changed his mind. Although they carried off the 1956 championship, the relationship ended with a bitternerss which was vented in their respective memoirs. Ferrari, typically acting the injured innocent, wrote that Fangio had portrayed that season 'as a sort of adventure story blending betrayal, sabotage, deceit and many kinds of intrigue, all perpetrated with the intent of making him eat the dust'. He summed the Argentine up as 'a truly great driver, but afflicted with a persecution complex. A strange man, that Fangio. A sort of mystery.'

For the following season Fangio moved back to Maserati, whose 250F model, introduced in 1954, was reaching the peak of its development. The loveliest of all front-engined single-seater racing cars, it now became the tool with which Fangio could demonstrate the most profound elements of his genius. Its superb chassis permitted the refinement of the high-speed cornering technique known as the 'four-wheel drift', in which the driver pushed the car just past the limit of its tyres' adhesion, setting the front wheels against the direction of travel and steering with small movements of the throttle pedal. It was a skill requiring enormous sensitivity, and its masters were Fangio and his pupil Moss.

Of Fangio's four grand prix victories in 1957, the greatest was undoubtedly the win at the Nürburgring, a 14-mile circuit around the Eifel mountains, whose innumerable corners provided a test that revealed the relationship between the world champion and his Maserati. After leading the race in its early stages, Fangio was delayed by a pit stop which put him almost a minute behind the more powerful but less agile Ferraris of Peter Collins and Mike Hawthorn, with 10 laps to go. Constantly pulverising the lap record, he drove with a rare combination of raw ferocity and technical brilliance, astonishing the two young Englishmen with the intensity of his assault. He caught and overtook them both with a lap to go, in that moment setting the seal on his legend.

He had won five world championships. But, at 46, he entered 1958 with misgivings about prolonging his career. They were only reinforced by the first grand prix of the season, on his home ground in Buenos Aires, where the revolutionary little rear-engined Cooper-Climax of Moss, its undersized four-cylinder engine adapted from a fire-pump motor, defeated the might of the classical front-engined Ferraris and Maseratis. Fangio missed the opening three races of the European grand prix season, but returned early in July for the French Grand Prix at Rheims. As he went through his old preparation routine in his hotel room, he suddenly realised that 'racing had become an obligation. And when racing begins to feel like work, well . . .' And after dragging the outclassed Maserati around in fourth place, Fangio discovered that Luigi Musso, his former team-mate, was dying in hospital after running off the track.

It was one accident, one race, too many. Quietly, without fanfare, Fangio returned to Argentina, where he settled into the life of a garage owner-cum-national hero. His Mercedes-Benz dealership expanded, a museum of racing cars was built in his honour by the people of Balcarce, and he was often flown across the ocean to be the chief VIP at Mercedes functions in Europe. At home, his door was open; abroad, crowds attended him wherever he went.

His personal life was always something of a mystery: in his ghosted autobiography, published soon after his retirement from racing, he offered his thanks to 'my wife, Andreina, for all she has done for me and our son Oscar'. They had married, he wrote, in 1941: 'She has not left my side since.'

In the early seventies, though, he described the relationship differently: 'We were not married, but we spent 20 years together. Then one day we had a discussion and she said, "If you don't like being with me, you may leave." So I left.'

Was he, then, the greatest racing driver of all? His record says so, but in motor racing, as in any sport, it is impossible to draw exact comparisons between different eras.

If we say, as some critics would, that he was merely the shrewdest (which is beyond dispute), and not as divinely gifted as Nuvolari, Rosemeyer, Moss, Clark or Senna, then how do we explain the incandescent virtuosity of his drive against the odds at the Nürburgring in 1957? All we can say for certain is that Fangio raced against the best of his time, and beat them. And became, in the process, the embodiment of his sport. ●

17 May 1995
Simon Hattenstone
The gentle art of perception

Fiona McCall, who committed suicide at the weekend, aged 32, had been the Guardian's arts page secretary for nearly five years. Born in Bristol, she went to Watford Grammar School for Girls and Goldsmith's College, and then worked for Penguin Books, Pluto Press and at the Institute of Contemporary Arts.

There are few pure people in the world. Fiona McCall was one of them. She was gentle and kind, funny and generous, a Marxist with a brilliant, non-dogmatic mind and a huge, quiet heart that caused her too much pain. She could have been a great critic – in film, theatre, art, opera, anything. In fact, she *was* a great critic, but instead of typing out her reviews, she would simply talk them.

Every night she would go and watch the preview of a new production and return the next day with a devastating and heartfelt deconstruction. Often at lunch, we used to go to the park next to the *Guardian*, sit on the grass, her with Diet Coke and newspaper in hand, dressed invariably in one-tone black with shades (she looked like Anna Karina in the early Godard films, but she would never believe it).

Fiona would tell me about last night's play or film, start diffidently as if there was nothing to say, then it would all pour out, softly and perceptively – why it failed politically, why it succeeded emotionally, the games the writer had played with language, the one moment that would stay with her for ever. I have never heard anyone speak with such eloquence, insight and love, and always wished I had a tape recorder with me so I could simply transcribe Fiona's mind into the paper.

She was also a wonderful (if unacknowledged) editor – writers discreetly handed Fiona their copy and, with a bit of judicious cutting here, an invaluable addition there, a decent piece was transformed into a very good one.

Everyone went to her for comfort. She was like the agony aunt in Alan

Rudolph's film *Choose Me* – desperate within herself, but giving herself totally to the needs and feelings of others. Writers would phone up, bitterly asking why their article had not been used. Fiona would talk them through it, highlight the best bits, make them up if necessary, and by the time she had finished they felt like God's gift to journalism. Sometimes, she would put the phone down and cry. People fell in love with Fiona on the phone, without having met her. Then they would come in to the office and fall in love with her in person. She was always convinced she looked a mess.

She left university in her first year – the work was easy, but coping with student life had become impossible – and lived at home with her parents, whom she loved dearly. Everyone was aware she had incredible talent, but it was never realised. A few weeks ago she was persuaded to write a theatre preview column. Fiona agonised over it, wrote and rewrote and rewrote, and every version was quite brilliant. She told me that she had forgotten how much she loved words, and for a brief second there was a glimmer. She had just agreed to write some fringe theatre reviews for the arts pages. Again agony, but she was working (and reworking) on her first review.

Fiona was passionate about everything, but nothing could override her despair or fear; not about anything in particular, she was just unfairly cursed with hopelessness.

Yesterday, the office was silent with regret and misery. ●

Alan Bennett

Sean Smith

Culture

....

30 December 1994

Jon Snow

Bylines, spy lines and a hidden agenda

T he manner of the British intelligence services' invitation to me to work for them persuades me that enlisting journalists was, and possibly still is, commonplace.

The letter and subsequent interview came as I was joining ITN. A Mr D Stilbury, writing from the old War Office Buildings, had done his stuff. He certainly knew a great deal about me – relationships, friends, politics and career prospects. He was also pretty certain that I would accept his tax-free offer to double my then salary and that for years to come he would be able to count on me to continue in the media, whilst at the same time keeping tabs on subversive or left-wing journalists on Fleet Street. My refusal, after two interviews, to have anything to do with him or SIS, for which he said he worked, angered him considerably. I left his office 18 years ago flattered and appalled in equal measure, recognising how easy it would have been to give in.

The commendable speed with which Richard Gott resigned from the *Guardian* following the disclosure of his contacts with the Soviets stirred a frisson of excitement in many of the nation's newsrooms. The supposed existence of a list of several dozen other names about to be 'outed' by the Soviet defector Oleg Gordievsky inspired plenty of speculation as colleagues tried to remember who had last taken a holiday on a Crimean beach. There was very little evidence of any matching introspective questioning as to how many of us operate for our own side.

Mr Stilbury's annoyance at my failure in this regard centred on a perceived lack of patriotism, less to my country, I suspected, than to my class and to the establishment I was fast joining. Yet the greatest defence of democracy, we have been taught, lies in a free press. I sometimes wonder what kind of compromise might have had to have been entered into for me to present a major television news programme at 7pm, a few hours after a dash from some clandestine salaried encounter to disclose or receive intelligence about some issue of interest to the security services. How often has the viewer, or reader, been denied the full facts as to precisely where the 'messenger' – be he or she a television news operative or a newspaper columnist – is coming from?

We fiercely protect our sources, not least because we depend on them. But that protection serves another purpose too – shielding our viewer or reader from the true nature of the relationship we enjoy with the authorities about whom we write. This is not a matter of spying, nor taking payment for information and services exchanged – at least not usually. This is about signing up to an unwritten clutch of rules, to join an undescribed club, in which both the journalist and the subject of interest enter into a pact to deny the 'information consumer' the full facts of what is going on. In its most vibrant form it is called the 'lobby'.

Although Downing Street is but the most controversial end of the lobby arrangement, it infects every aspect of government life, from fisheries to transport. Approved groups of journalists are ritually briefed on terms never properly discussed with the public. All too often, the correspondent so briefed almost becomes an extension of the department doing the briefing. The flattery of acceptance in the inner sancta of Whitehall, the occasional brush with a minister or a permanent secretary, combine to provide the striving journalist with a sense of importance and belonging. This sense of journalistic access frequently amounts to becoming sucked into the culture of 'what it's good for the public to know'.

A few months back, after a particularly serious overspend in the Ministry of Defence budget, a BBC defence correspondent came on air to discuss the matter and entered so spirited an account of the ministry's excuses that John Humphrys cried out in exasperation: 'It is *our* money, Mark.'

An aspect of Parliament that renders it still more remote from the electorate is that all exchanges with MPs or officials can be regarded as 'on lobby terms'. Despite the televising of Parliament, there remains an effective ban on the free access of TV cameras into the Palace of Westminster. Our elected representatives retain the absolute right to say nothing about anything. There is no facility for the media even to gather an on-the-record 'No comment', unless the MP wills it.

Given the information revolution, perhaps in the late 20th century the time has come to clean our media houses. What excuse can there be for not stating that at 11am and 4pm every weekday Mr Christopher Meyer briefs the press in Downing Street on behalf of the prime minister and his government? Why should his remarks not be 'On the record', televised, and recorded and relayed to the public, sourced to Mr Meyer? Named individuals should do the same for other departments; where any 'background' briefing follows, it should be made clear under what terms this information is collected.

The matter of journalists operating for and on behalf of the intelligence services takes media/governmental collusion to unacceptable lengths. This is not a time of war, in which the existence of the democratic state is under siege. After Watergate in America, Senator Frank Church was charged with investigating the CIA, which had regularly hired working journalists. Church found the practice seriously threatened freedom of information and described it as unconstitutional. In the late 1970s, Stansfield Turner, then CIA director, effectively banned the employment of any working journalist for the gathering of intelligence. We should do the same.

Some of my colleagues will take issue with any sense of linkage between working for the security services and working within the 'lobby system'. There is obviously a difference in degree. But the lack of transparency in the relationship is common to both. The connivance of editors, managers and owners is also common to both. For whilst cash may be the lubricant for one, preferment through the honours system, or other unclarified rewards, 'in kind', tend to cement the other.

A few weeks ago a senior minister spelt out to me how John Major could completely recast the image of his government and be seen to be preparing it for the 21st century. After listing a Bill of Rights and reform of the House of Lords, he suggested Major would have no difficulty in driving through a Freedom of Information Act. Labour is already committed to all this. But such changes would blow the current cosy media/government relationship out of the water. The media are singularly ill-prepared for any impending change, and aren't even pressing for it with any energy. Those who run the media know they could trigger change overnight instead of continuing to replenish the D-Notice Committee with new editors and continuing to dine the intelligence services. Editors could withdraw from such compromises and replace the lobby, security committees and covert contact with the intelligence services with published, open and democratic procedures for relating to the government of the day.

Some may argue that over the past year the Government has been living through the worst of times with the media. The reality is that the relationships on the ground remain as matey as ever. There's precious little evidence that such relationships have done national security, government, journalism, or indeed the voter, much good. ●

....

17 April 1995

Roy Greenslade
The nuts and bolts of the Screws

Here is a modern morality tale about the free market and the freedom of the press. Be warned. There is material likely to offend. And there isn't a happy ending.

Chapter one opens with the figure of Rupert Murdoch, imperialist media tycoon, walking along a Miami beach. Beside him, baby of face, sparkling of eye, skips a young man on the make. Piers Morgan, then gossip columnist on the *Sun*, having just been offered the editorship of the *News of the World*, is outlining his ideas for improving (sic) the editorial content.

His message, not surprisingly, pleases Murdoch. For Morgan, then 28, was an archetypical product of Murdoch's favourite decade, the 1980s. In Britain, it was a turning point for Murdoch, the culmination of a dream, a time when his political ally ruled in No 10, espousing a crude economic theory which she dared to put into practice.

The free market was god: organised labour was crushed; regulation was relaxed; profitability was the designer drug of choice. The establishment was a stifling anachronism, a closed shop of privilege which also required smashing. Society did not exist. And Britain was instead a nation of individual consumers, a ready market to be exploited by freely competing entrepreneurs.

All ills – economic, political and social – could be cured only through the market. What a blessed era it was to be Murdoch. He obtained *The Times* and the *Sunday Times*, and Wapping and *Today* and then Sky satellite television. And that was only in Britain. Competition rules were avoided. Cross-media regulations were evaded. And all was enthusiastically applauded by Murdoch's most important newspaper, the *Sun*, provider of enormous profit, promulgator of the ideology of Murdoch and Thatcher.

This was the journalistic university in which Piers Morgan studied. Rules and regulations were stumbling blocks to success. The establishment is the enemy. Ethics equal compromise. True democracy is allowing the people to decide. To buy or not to buy: that is the question and the answer.

Chapter two opens with Morgan in charge at the *News of the World*. He is the youngest national paper editor in 50 years. Nice, personable, middle-class, raised in true-blue Sussex, son of a small-time businessman. Morgan was early imbued with the values of business and Toryism.

Once he started work on a local newspaper he stood out from the other young reporters. He was intelligent, he worked hard, he always got his story and he showed he was going places. Yet he remained well mannered and well liked. Truly, this would be a formidable man if given power.

Indeed, Morgan has proved himself to be the most clear-sighted editor of the *News of the World* (with the possible exception of Wendy Henry) since Murdoch bought the paper in 1969. He knows that it is the sex which sells his paper and is aware that all the rest is dressing. But he stepped into the editor's chair just a couple of years after the creation of the industry's first code of practice administered by the self-regulatory body, the Press Complaints Comission (PCC).

So he also realised he had to temper every kiss-and-tell revelation with a justification that it would pass muster at the PCC. It must therefore be deemed to be in the public interest. That is defined in the code as detecting or exposing crime or serious misdemeanour; protecting public health and safety; or – wait for it – 'preventing the public from being misled by some statement or action of an individual or organisation'. In other words, it was fine for Morgan's *News of the World* to expose hypocrisy at just the moment Thatcher's successor, John Major, declared a back-to-basics policy, asserting the moral values of this government.

Morgan immediately jumped through that large loophole. As one of the staff told me within weeks of his arrival in January last year: 'I must say, Piers loves the old rumpy-pumpy. We can't get enough to please him.'

So it proved. Sex has always been the staple diet of the *News of the World*. But Morgan increased the content and raised the stakes. We read page after page about sex in high places, low places, any places, especially in palaces. Needless to say, the cheque book also loosened tongues about looseness on a scale never witnessed before.

Though Morgan will say in public that his paper is crusading against hypocrisy, he knows he is being economical with the truth: he is using the free market to determine ethical standards by pointing to the 4.8 million copies sold every Sunday, more than 2 million more than its closest rival.

But the public are now not the only audience praising the *News of the World*, for chapter three of our tale opens in February with Piers Morgan stepping up to collecting the Scoops of the Year award from *What the Papers Say*. Weeks later the *News of the World* is runner-up at Newspaper of the Year in the British Press Awards and Gary Jones wins Reporter of the Year. Once of Jones's exclusives was the revelation about Princess Diana's phone calls to a married man.

So the industry has also been happy with the principles and practices of Morgan's *News of the World*. But the three latest stories which intrude into privacy all appear to fall outside the PCC code's public interest defence. Surely posing for *Hello!* doesn't offer sufficient reason to splash Countess Spencer's admission to a clinic?

Surely three unmarried adults sleeping together is no justification for publishing a story about an MP 'in three-in-a-bed romp'? Nor indeed are the entrapment and secret bugging methods used to obtain it defensible.

As for yesterday's exposure of a judge's daughter running call-girls, where is the public interest? What point is there in having our much vaunted press freedom if it is used only for such tawdry nonsense?

Then again, so deep is the hypocrisy that we read in *The Times* Woodrow Wyatt, the *News of the World* columnist, lambasting his own newspaper for intruding into privacy. But he doesn't think about resigning on principle. He keeps quiet in his *NoW* column about his genuine feelings and goes on taking their money.

But the real prize for Pecksniffian of the Year goes to David Mellor MP. For he is the anti-hero of our final chapter. When he resigned as a minister he excoriated the tabloid press, referring to it as 'an alternative criminal justice system'. In November last year he was the subject of a *NoW* exclusive which revealed his relationship with Penelope Cobham and he once again rounded on newspapers. The man had the brass neck yesterday to write a column in the *NoW* under the slogan 'Tory MP gives it to you straight.'

Oh, yeah? Fat chance of Piers Morgan, loose cannon on the deck of Fleet Street, being hauled in when his paper is sanctified by the public, the newspaper industry and the politicians who affect to loathe it. The whole business stinks and debases us all. ●

24 April 1995

Jon Katz
Tomorrow's Word

For millions of Americans, especially young ones, newspapers have never played a significant role. That's why it's sometimes hard even to imagine that there's almost no media experience sweeter – at the right time, in the right place – than pouring over a good newspaper. In the quiet morning, with a cup of coffee – so long as you haven't yet turned on the TV, listened to the radio or checked in online – it's as comfortable and personal as information gets.

Newspapers are silent, highly portable, require neither power source nor arcane commands and don't crash or get infected. They can be stored for days at no cost and consumed over time in small, digestible quantities. They can also be used to line bins and train pets. They're recyclable. At their best, they have been fearless, informative and heroic. They can be deliciously quirky, useful, even provocative. And they're under siege.

Newspapers have been foundering for decades, their readers ageing, their revenues declining, their circulation sinking, their sense of mission fragmented. Television has stolen much of their news, magazines their advertisers and best writers, cable many of their younger readers. And the digital revolution has pushed them still closer to the wall, unleashing a vigorous flow of news, commentary and commerce to many millions of people. Computer online services and CNN ensure that newspapers are stale before they're tossed on the trucks. Almost everything a newspaper used to do, somebody else is doing more quickly, more attractively, more efficiently and in a more interesting and unfettered way.

Newspapers have never liked change, at heart because of an ingrained belief that they are the superior, serious, worthwhile medium, while things electronic are trivial or faddish. Over the past decade, newspapers have made almost every kind of radical move except transforming themselves. They are the biggest and saddest losers in the information revolution. With the possible exception of network-TV newscasts, papers are now our least hip medium, relentlessly one-way, non-interactive and smug. We all know the formula: plopped on the doorstep once a day; breaking news, stories broken up and jumping inside. Grainy photos. Culture, features, TV, listings, recipes and advice columns in the back. Stentorian voices on the editorial page. Take it or leave it, and if you don't like it write us a letter.

But the growing millions of people sending and receiving news and their opinions of it to one another via modem are another story. Digital news differs radically: no other medium has given individual people such an engaged role in the movement of information and opinion or such a proprietary interest in the medium itself. The computer news culture fosters a sense of kinship, ownership and participation that has never existed in commercial media.

When, in January 1994, a wireless modem was used to flash news of the LA earthquake to the Net well before CNN or the Associated Press could report it, a new news medium was born. Within minutes, subscribers had pinpointed the quake location, notified distant relatives and organised rescues. No information structure has ever been able to do anything remotely like it. Now, after years of papers ignoring computers or relegating them to corners of the business sections, you can't pick up a paper without reading the words e-mail, Internet or cyberspace. The media, burned so often by techno-hype, are belatedly realising that this time it's not all fantasy.

So-called electronic publishing is the hottest thing since cold type, and one of the last great hopes for a reeling industry trying to preserve a vital role for itself. About 500 weekly and daily US papers have now joined the panicky digital rush, including major and influential papers like the *New York Times* and *Washington Post*. By the end of 1995, an estimated 2,500 weekly and daily publications will be offering online services, from local news to supplemental real estate listings. But the 'techno-hype' has raised expectations about online publishing and confusions about the impact of new media on life in general and journalism and publishing in particular. Do newspapers have any viable future, and if so, in what form?

Although no one has surveyed all these new digital publications, media analysts believe that few, if any, are profitable in their own right and none is known to be attracting any significant numbers of additional subscribers or readers to their print mothers. Some have become vigorous and influential public forums and have taught their owners a lot about the new culture, but the vast majority are cumbersome, Frankenstein-ish hybrids of their masters — expensive hedges against onrushing techology with little rationale of their own. They take away what's best about reading a paper and don't offer what's best about being online.

The online culture is as different as it's possible to be from the print press tradition. Outspoken and informal, it is continuously available. It is so diverse as to be undefinable, a home to scientists, hackers, pet owners, quilters, swingers, teenagers and homemakers. Online there is the sense of perpetual conflict, discovery, sudden friendship, occasional hostility, great intensity, lots of business being transacted, the feeling of clacking through your own world while whole unseen galaxies rush above and below you. The experience bears no relationship to reading a newspaper. In fact, one of the major selling points of a paper is its organisational and informational predictability. The weather, sports and TV listings are always in the same place, or ought to be.

What does this tell us about the future role of conventional print media? Newspapers have missed the real lesson of the past half-century. Their mistake wasn't that they didn't invest in TV or put their stories on screens, it was that they refused to make any of the changes that the rise of television should have mandated.

TV meant that breaking news could be reported quickly, colourfully and – eventually – live. Live TV supplanted the historic function of the journalist. Cable TV meant a whole new medium with the time and room to present breaking and political news, entertainment news, live trial coverage. Computers meant that millions of people could flash the news to one another. All of these changes have given newspapers a diminished role in the presentation of news. But the explosion of new media needn't eliminate the traditional journalistic print function. Quite the opposite; it could make papers more vital, necessary and useful than ever.

The need for the traditional functions of print journalism is enormous. The more complicated the gadgets become and the more new media mushroom, the more we need what papers have always been – gatekeepers and wellheads, discussion leaders on politics and and public policy, distributors of horoscopes and sports listings. We need distinct voices offering detached versions of the best truth they can find in the most factual way. We need fair-minded, if less arrogant, fact-gatherers and opinion-makers to help us sort through the political, social and cultural issues. We need something very close to what a good newspaper is but with a different ideology and ethic: a medium that gives its consumers nearly as much power as its reporters and editors have, that isn't afraid of unfettered discussions, intense passions and unashamed opinion and recognises we've already heard the headlines a dozen times.

The problem is that newspapers continue to demonstrate the profound difficulty of bringing radical change to entrenched, formerly monopolistic institutions. Hierarchies and bureaucracies are inherently hostile to change and seem to exist as much to perpetuate themselves as to find creative ways to evolve. Even as they rush online, newspapers continue to make their reporters and editors largely inaccessible to readers and viewers. Even as tens of millions – especially the young – come to take interactivity for granted and learn to control, manipulate and find voice in new media, our most powerful news organisations cling to absolute editorial control, arrogant, out-of-touch and often elitist, reachable only through voice-mail and letters to the editor columns.

Most print media cling angrily to their eroding control over political and social agendas, expanding their unspoken but ferocious cultural civil war against new media. They focus relentlessly on real but narrow aspects of online culture, like online pornography, and sensationalise the dangers surrounding problems like computer hacking and theft. The screen, cable and digital culture are savagely assaulted as dangerous, destructive to the civic discourse of the country and responsible for mass apathy and indifference.

It's not the means of delivery that newspapers need to change, it is their content. No major newspaper in America has yet dramatically examined or changed the way it presents itself graphically, reconceived elemental notions about the kinds of news it can and should present, the way it hires staff and the kinds of staff it employs. In the face of the most sweeping change in information delivery in centuries, newspapers still come out once a day and look more or less as they did half a century ago.

Do newspapers have a future in the new information world? Why not? Lots of magazines have made the transition happily and profitably, by attracting good writers and designers and covering the new culture that now surrounds them. Newspapers haven't. For them, answers probably lie in their past more than in the future; in their fading traditions of idiosyncratic voice, ferocious point-of-view, adventuresome reporting and more access to non-journalists.

If they recognise that they can't compete with electronic media in the gathering and dissemination of breaking news. If they embrace notions of interactivity and convivial media and begin to give their users a real say in the editorial production of the paper or broadcast – putting e-mail addresses at the end of every story or editorial, for example. If they embrace proven and successful magazine techniques like attractive use of graphics and colour. If they accept the fact that their real challenges are creative, not technical. If they open their pages up to wider representations of political opinion and individual expression. If they expand and emphasise enterprise journalism such as investigative reporting, rich cultural coverage, innovative writing and public service projects extremely difficult for the online culture to duplicate.

In the US, this seems increasingly unlikely, not so much because newspapers have no role to play but rather because they seem unable or unwilling to change. Can a newspaper change and remain viable in the 21st century? What makes it so hard to say is that we have yet to see one try. ●

15 *July 1995*

Joanna Coles

Hanging on in there for dear life

The front door swings open. Hullo, cries a muffled voice. 'Come in . . . I'm just putting my shirt on.' In the hallway of her Hyde Park flat Marcelle D'Argy Smith is struggling with a reluctant Aertex sports shirt. On the table is a newly delivered bouquet. She fishes out the card. 'Thinking of You, Ken and Barbara Follett.' 'Oh how nice of them,' she says, disappearing into the kitchen and quickly re-emerging with a silver jug. 'Come through. I am a woman whose time has come, but whose cleaning lady hasn't!'

Once in the sitting room, she deposits the jug on the zebra-skin table. 'I sent Ken and Barbara flowers once. I've been to dinner there three times. Everyone's been great. I had 26 messages on my answerphone on Tuesday and 16 yesterday . . . really great.'

Everybody but the *Daily Mail* that is, which has just published a vitriolic profile of her, positively relishing her unexpected departure as editor of *Cosmopolitan*. 'They said I spend all my time going out with married men. It's not true. I've never been out with a married man, I can't abide them, no, no, NO! I *hate* married men.'

The scent of the Folletts' flowers drifts across the sunny room and the French windows open on to a thicket of lavender and roses. It is Friday morning and for the first time since she can remember, D'Argy Smith is not swinging her stilettos from the editor's chair. She is 48 and has had enough.

Or at least that's her side of the story. 'Look,' she says, nursing a pair of taut, tanned legs which end in a dramatic pair of crocodile sandals: 'I came back from holiday four weeks ago and I said to Terry [Mansfield, managing director of National Magazines which owns *Cosmopolitan*] I want a change. And he said: "Well do you want to run another magazine, or run our books for us, what *do* you want to do? . . ."'

She trails off in mid-sentence as, it turns out, she does a lot, this time briefly distracted by one of her cats.

'Do you know I noticed my cats were getting thinner, and a friend of mine said: "Do you know why your cats are so thin, it's because you're feeding them dog food." And I went to the cupboard and there were four tins of dog food!' Then the phone rings, as it will do several times during the morning.

Darling, how are you, oh Jamie, are you in bed? You sound awful. I do miss you, I need you . . . I might come to visit.

Well? What *does* she want to do? And — there is no kind way to ask this — was she fired? She shakes her head. 'It was a negotiation. I'm just desperate for a bit of my life . . . I am obsessed with freedom, though it took a shrink to tell me that!'

Indirectly it took a cardiac arrest on the dance floor of a New York club to get Marcelle D'Argy Smith to the pinnacle of British magazine journalism. 'I remember thinking as I was carried out to the ambulance, I've got 10 minutes left and I haven't got married, I haven't had children, been to China or Africa and I didn't have an affair with Helmut because I was scared he wouldn't call the next day . . .' She was 36.

Two months and a pacemaker later she was back in England and had dumped her previous career selling advertising for the post of contributing editor on *Cosmopolitan*. Deirdre McSharry, the then editor, told her she had six months to prove herself. Six years and hundreds of articles later, she was editing the magazine. Seven years later and minus the pacemaker — which a British doctor whipped out saying it was unnecessary — she's throwing it in.

'My mother said, "Oh good, you've been looking so tired."'

Yes, but what *is* she going to do . . .?

Brian! I'd love to talk. Can I call you back?

'I want to do a cookery course, I want to finish arranging the flat, not for ever of course, but for a bit. I need some time, maybe a three-month sabbatical. I used to think about friends on maternity leave and think, "Well, I know it's not all great, but at least you've got time at home."'

Let's be frank, this is not what you expect to hear from such a champion of have-it-all feminism. 'I never said I wanted it all,' she says quickly. 'But I've had a big chunk.'

But does she regret, say, not having been married? 'Marriage? When people used to ask me why I hadn't been married I used to say, "I've just been lucky." Now I say, "Hey, marriage is the first step to divorce!"'

What about children then? Does she regret not having them? 'No. I always assumed I'd have them, but I never wanted them.'

Did she never even think about it, or come close? 'I had a termination,' she says. 'He was an American musician and would have been as suitable a father as I would have been as a mass caterer. I had had a problem with the loop and my doctor refused to prescribe the Pill. I felt fine and I went to him and said, "I'm having a terrific affair, I need the Pill," and he refused.'

She became pregnant and sought an abortion which the doctor only agreed to because of what he called the 'exceptional circumstances' in which she'd been denied the Pill. 'As I sat there across from his desk in Harley Street listening to him saying it was "exceptional circumstances", I thought I could plunge the paper knife into his heart . . . But I wasn't traumatised by it, or any of that stuff.

'The boyfriend was very sweet to me that weekend but the week after, well, it was never the same. He started going out with Miss World shortly after.' She takes a sip of tea. 'I saw him not so long go, he's still frightfully good looking.'

Curled up on a cream sofa, D'Argy Smith looks as if a weight has been truly lifted from her shoulderpads. But to many women, not least her readers, her position must look not a little ironic. She's spent the last seven years telling them how to get a better life, a better man, a better job, and now look. She's got no child, no man and no job. Will she be lonely without the crutch of an office to lean on? 'No, I'm not lonely. I love being on my own. I used to have a monkey. A friend told me it was a child substitute. I said her child was probably a monkey substitute.'

'My boyfriend built it a sort of cage in my bedroom, otherwise sleeping arrangements might have been tricky. I used to tuck it in my shirt and take it out and about with me. I would tie him round my neck on a little chain. But in the end I put an advertisement for "an affectionate baby monkey for sale" in *The Times*. I cried buckets when he left. He went to a couple in Cheyne Walk. They were lovely.'

According to several of her ex-colleagues, D'Argy Smith is herself lovely to work for. She's a good motivator, full of energy, ideas and, of course, neurotic.

'Neurotic?' she looks astonished. 'I'm not neurotic! I would *never* go to a therapist or counsellor. I've only ever gone to top-class psychiatrists.' So why has she claimed she's terrified of bridges?

'Oh, *that*. Yes, I can't drive over the Chiswick flyover. I thought it was a metaphor for not being able to cross into marriage. Um, I noticed it first in Milan. I was staring at an escalator and I thought it reminded me of a bridge. So I took the stairs.'

On her return to England she sought help to conquer this phobia. 'I went to behavioural therapy and they gave me drugs and after three weeks told me to go out and negotiate the M25.'

What sort of drugs? 'Oh, I should be taking them, but I forget. I still can't drive over the Chiswick flyover, and I hate driving on the M25, but not being able to cook Sunday lunch is far more annoying.' She pauses. 'I'd adore to be able to cook Sunday lunch . . . Phobias are supposed to be about stress but I've always been terrified of heights.'

Yet she has not been scared to scale the heights at *Cosmopolitan*. She was voted best Magazine Editor of 1991, but shrugs. 'Awards are meaningless,' she says. 'You know if you're doing well. I never filled out my entry to Who's Who because I couldn't put "pottering" under interests. But Glenda Bailey [the editor of *Marie Claire*] has even got her Glenfiddich Award in there. I don't give a damn. I tell you it's meaningless. So is this fuss over me leaving. No other *Cosmo* editor has had this attention.'

No other British *Cosmo* editor has had to cope with such competition in the market place. Indeed, hers is arguably the hardest job at National Magazines given the growing threat from *Marie Claire*, with which MD Terry Mansfield is said to be obsessed. In spite of this threat, *Cosmo*'s circulation figures have held up well. Though the next figures, due later this month, are expected to show a fall. The last ones for June to December 1994 were up by 50,000 to 460,582.

Nevertheless, there is something distinctly unfashionable about *Cosmopolitan* now. It feels tarty when compared to *Marie Claire*. 'Cosmo grew up on sexual freedom, but real freedom is economic,' D'Argy Smith says, suddenly leaning forward. 'You can't put that on the front cover, it won't sell. But it's all there inside. We tell readers to pick the decent men and work hard, get trained and make sure he's supportive. I mobilise women to take control, tell me something more important than that.'

The cleaning lady arrives. One final try. What *is* she going to do next? 'The little island of Gozo just off Malta is perfect,' she says wistfully. 'But then South Africa looks interesting. This feeling of freedom might not last. I may come a cropper. I don't feel smug. I *know* how fragile everything is.'

Grey, hello darling! I wish I WERE in bed with someone! Can I get back to you? •

....

10 February 1995

Nancy Banks-Smith
Soap suds of life

As Dylan the Rabbit once said . . . twanging a lethargic chord on his guitar . . . too laid-back to keep his ears upright . . . 'We're trying to change the image.' The joke was, perhaps, a little over the heads of the tinies watching *The Magic Roundabout*. From the very start, *EastEnders* was hell-bent on changing the conventional image of chirpy cockneys. This came as a surprise to cockneys, who despite all discouragement actually *are* rather chirpy.

Our local lottery millionairess in Poplar got 15 cheerful proposals while walking through the market. Some of them even of marriage. The East End is not a place for keeping yourself to yourself. Nor, as another lottery winner discovered, is Lancashire. It happens that I used to live in a Lancashire pub and I now live in an East End square and not entirely by chance. They felt very similar, very familiar.

My mother, who, like Annie Walker, led a doomed crusade to raise the tone of the place, preferred to call it an hotel, whacking the unaccustomed aitch on the head like a hard-boiled egg. Everyone else called it t'new pub. It was, in fact, quite old, being built in 1901 as King Cotton and Queen Victoria were dying. Mill Chimneys surrounded it like guardsmen but they soon came down straight-backed and crumpling at the knees, like soldiers falling before some in visible, but withering, fire.

Just where the Queen Vic stands, like the precise location of Railway Cuttings, East Cheam, is a matter of conjecture. The opening titles to *EastEnders* show the Isle of Dogs hanging down like a cow's udder cooling in the river and, above it, the bony rump of London. Roy, the used-car tycoon, who has recently taken a shine to Big Pat, the barmaid at the Vic, took her on a sentimental tour of a cinder patch in Poplar, the derelict site of his first used-car lot. Pat, game girl, took it on the chin.

Roy says he's never seen anything like Pat. It was the same awed tone that Grant used once as he stared at the massive bulk of Canary Wharf tower on the Isle of Dogs: 'I don't care what they say, I think it's beautiful.' He was, admittedly, drunk at the time.

A glass tide of offices has flowed over the Isle of Dogs like an ice age but stopped just short of the last cockney village. Ther's a pub here with Ma Baker's Bar engraved on the door. It's in memory of a regular, Danny Baker's grandmother. Ma, and I'm sorry I missed her, was clearly a matriarch, a knees-up-Mother-Brown old girl if ever there was one. I see her as Danny in a hat. How many old girls so stamp their personality on the air that they have a boozer named after them? Only Queen Vic and Ma Baker.

Ena Sharples stamped her personality on the air the moment *Coronation Street* started. The corner shop was changing hands. 'They won't eat you, you know,' lied the old owner to Florrie, the new owner, and exited stage right sharpish as *Coronation Street*'s chief carnivore entered. Ena said: 'I'm Mrs Sharples . . . Where are you being buried?' 'I haven't given it much thought,' flinched Florrie. 'Well, you should.'

EastEnders opened with death, too, but with a difference. Three men from the square kicked down the door of old Reg Cox's flat to find him decomposing in his armchair. 'Cor!' said Den, landlord of The Vic, 'Stinks in 'ere, don't it?' A certain change of tone here, wouldn't you say, Professor?

What Reg's room really smelled of was *Z Cars*. *EastEnders* was conceived by Julia Smith and Tony Holland, who met while working on *Z Cars*. The documentary drive and life of that series was like a hotpot full in the face. The Chief Constable of Lancashire, under instructions from his wife, took the first train to London to complain that police officer's wives did not throw hotpots at their husbands' heads. *EastEnders* inherited that documentary smell, the kicked-down door, the old man lying dead for days. Reg had even been murdered.

Coronation Street started like a documentary too, gritty and grainy. Looking for inspiration for a new series, Tony Warren went up to the roof of Granada and saw a hundred little grimy streets radiating out like the spokes of a wheel. At that moment Elsie Tanner was born, full-blown and blowsy, as the sort of woman every commercial traveller hopes will open the door, and Ena Sharples as the sort of woman who always does. The script editor closed his eyes and smelled the burning sausages, the cheap hair-spray and the tang of bitter beer.

Thirty-five years on, *Coronation Street* feels more like snuggling down in the darkness of a theatre, watching the curtain go up on a succession of top-notch variety acts. Derek and Mavis and their performing budgerigar. Raquel, the dazzling blonde with the 40-watt brain. Percy and his patriotic monologues. Don Brennan, the one-legged taxi driver. (In this small but specialised field, Don is second only to the famous Peg Leg Bates, the wooden-legged tap-dancer, whose only hazard were the knotholes in the stage.) When her husband slithered off, Bet ran the Rovers on her own. How like Madame Zelfredo, who, when her snake snuffed it, went on and did her snake-charming act without it.

Comedy runs through *Coronation Street* like marrow through a bone, most in evidence after a serious fracture. Recently Raquel, the beautiful barmaid, broke her engagement to Curly, sobbing: 'I don't want to hear another word about marriage or engagements ever again! All I want is to be left alone.' 'Most women,' said Bet drily, 'don't feel like that until after they're married.'

EastEnders has had a funny-bone bypass. If humour was butter, it would be fat-free. Look, lads, life's not that serious. It's not football. Peter Cook said: 'I don't want to see plays about rape, sodomy and drug addiction . . . I can get all that at home.' It is tempting to add 'on TV'. It is a treat to see how, plucky to a fault, *EastEnders* stand up to the incessant battering of family life. When Arfer, husband of Poline, escaped from his customary doghouse into the warm arms of Mrs Hewitt, Poline hit him with a frying pan.

Running the Queen Vic is like wearing a lightning conductor in your hat. If you are not shot, stabbed, run down or run in, you will be blown up, beaten up or burned down. Christmas with loved ones is the worst. Den Watts and Grant Mitchell, both arsonists and certifiable psychos (shouldn't someone *mention* this to Luxford and Copley?) each served their weeping wives with divorce papers on Christmas Day. Sometimes little can be heard in the Queen Vic above the slamming doors, passionate sobbing and, in extreme cases, shotguns. How unlike the life of our own dear Queen. Oh, I don't know though.

Advertising auditions for East Enders only (hence the title), they tapped some raw, unrefined, risky acting talent. To mark the 10th anniversary, there will be a series of repeats called *The Unforgettable EastEnders*. Frankly, I had forgotten how tenderly effective the 16-year-old Susan Tully was in 1985, waiting by the sour canal to meet the man who had made her pregnant. The writing was teasing – every eligible, and ineligible, man in the square had had a mysterious phone call – until the pub poodle jumped out of a car, identifying the father as Den, landlord of the Queen Vic. Then it flowered into the first of those intense *EastEnder* two-handers, where everyone ceases to exist except the couple concerned.

Susan Tully was neither pretty nor hair-dressed, nor well-dressed, nor well-spoken. When Leslie Grantham asked her what she wanted to do about the baby, she waited for a beat of three seconds. The wind lifted her unset hair about her set face, then she said flatly: 'I wanna have it.' A better actress could not have done it as well. It could have been a scene from *Cathy Come Home*.

EastEnders is essentially one family, the Beales, with their interlocking intermarriages, biblical begettings and tribal feuds. You really could not be as *rude* as they are to anyone outside the family. Only a nuclear family could detonate such explosions.

Do you know any cause or just impediment why Vicki should not marry (a) Young Ricky (b) Tricky Dicky or (c) Little Willy? Vicki could legally marry Ricky, who is the stepson of her great uncle's ex-wife, Pat. But of course, Ricky, while still looking younger than Adrian Mole, has already been married to Sam, the sister of Grant, the husband of Sharon, the daughter of Vicki's father, Den, and is now living with his stepbrother's illegitimate daughter, Bianca, who is, clearly, his niece by marriage but he doesn't know that.

Tricky Dicky was involved, among many others, with Kaf of Kaf's Caf, who used to be married to Pete, the great uncle of Vicki. Kaf was going to marry Phil, the brother of Grant, the brother-in-law of Vicki. Until, of course, Phil slept with his brother's wife and spent some time in intensive care feeling as well as can be expected. Personally, I would recommend Little Willy as a lifelong companion. A dog, admittedly, and poorly endowed but faithful to a fault. (And his name is the answer to the Win A Visit To EastEnders Competition in next week's *Radio Times*.)

On Monday Arfer was urging Poline to watch a television programme. It sounded remarkably like *EastEnders*. 'Come on, love. It's good stuff,' he said. 'It'll help you unwind.' I think this more than doubtful, Professor. Arfer will shortly de-camp for good with Mrs Hewitt. ●

· ·

18 May 1995

Suzanne Moore
Look what's under the patio

For one reason or another I have been thinking a lot about female solidarity this week and in order to switch off, switched on the box. I thought I had stumbled into one of those BBC2 theme nights, the theme being 'All men are bastards', but in fact I was watching Channel 4. First there was The Verdict on the Mandy and Beth Jordache trial in *Brookside*, then a programme on Ike Turner and how he used to bash up Tina. To top it all came the first episode of *The Politician's Wife*, written by Paula Milne and focusing on a Tory sex scandal and the effect that it has on the wronged wife.

There may be those who feel that to engage with popular culture is a waste of time and we should be concentrating on more important matters. Clearly I do not belong to this precious gang. Nor does the wife of the next prime minister – Cherie Blair – who chose to have her photograph taken with Sandra Maitland, the actress who plays Mandy Jordache in the soap opera. The photograph, which appeared on the front of a national newspaper, was taken to help launch a campaign of cinema advertisements intended to increase awareness of domestic violence by the charity Refuge.

The plight of Mandy Jordache, the fictional character who has been sentenced to life imprisonment for the murder of her abusive husband, has touched a nerve in a way that the plight of Sara Thornton hasn't. *Brookside* has demonstrated just how the law continues to fail women and generated sympathetic publicity that will doubtless help those who are trying to change it. The issue of what constitutes provocation is precisely the one that *Brookside* has highlighted and that various groups have been campaigning around for some time.

What *Brookside* has so cleverly shown us is the background to the case, the brutality of Trevor Jordache, the desperation of his wife and daughters, the powerlessness that women feel in such dreadful situations. The magnificent acting of Sandra Maitland and Anna Friel, the melodrama of the last-minute wedding, the voyeurism as well as the kindness of neighbours, has pulled us into a plot which at first felt like a gimmick – a body under the patio – and has ended up reducing us to tears.

No one believes that it is legitimate for women to go around stabbing men, but without understanding the appalling circumstances in which these things happen, we cannot easily make a judgment.

A popular soap has contributed to that understanding in such a way that has reached all kinds of people. *The Politician's Wife*, on the other hand, is in its own glossy fashion as topical and gripping a deconstruction of patriarchy as you could wish for. Flora Matlock, played by Juliet Stevenson, is married to a Tory MP who wants his wife to stand by him after his affair has hit the tabloids. She is surrounded by men (including her husband, his aides and her own father) who put the requirements of 'the party' and political power over any consideration of her feelings.

To discuss feminism in the abstract in such a context, as though it belonged simply to a few strange women, misses the point entirely. There is little mileage to be had in arguing over which particular feminists are allowed to speak and which aren't, an old and trivial dispute which at the end of the day is of little concern to anyone except those who make a living flogging dead horses and even deader books.

What is much more interesting is the way that feminism has entered the culture to such a point that popular drama, from *Prime Suspect* to *EastEnders*, is increasingly full of feminist attitudes although no one actually mentions the horrible F-word itself. The place we are most likely to hear debate about sexual politics is in the pub after a night out at the movies. This is obviously unsettling to those who want to own certain ideas, whose very souls who while asking for wider debate actually feel threatened when 'ordinary people' manage to do it all by themselves.

It's not the case that there has been a concerted attempt to make feminism popular; it is rather that those who make the products that become popular culture are young women and men who have grown up with feminism. It matters not how they choose to describe themselves, it matters enormously that what they see as hooking in viewers, as intelligent drama, as relevant, doesn't come in a box marked 'women's issues' but is literally the stuff of everyday life.

I am happy to say it is becoming increasingly difficult to demarcate what is said to concern over half the population in this manner. One reaction is simply to ignore what is in front of our eyes and to revert to older certainties. The rise of the boorish lad at a time when traditional masculine identities are crumbling is but one example. Another is to focus on what we believe to be the truly important issues for women today – cellulite and make-up. What all this misses, however, is that at a time when fewer women want to actually define themselves as feminists, they are already defined by implicitly feminist attitudes.

It's too late to try to contain what's happened. The image of feminism has never been so far removed from the reality.

I understand perfectly why so many young women refuse this sort of labelling. Countless female stars, musicians and actresses give interviews where they say that they want to be judged on what they do and not merely as a representative of some outdated cause. When women are equally represented in all walks of life that burden of representation will be lifted. We will have what men take for granted – to have a set of political opinions that weave in and out of lives but do not act as a strait-jacket preventing all room to manoeuvre. Feminism is not about the power of faith but about understanding how power currently operates.

Here popular culture comes to our rescue. Mandy Jordache and Flora Matlock are not feminists, but it would be fair to say they have had a few problems with men. Their narratives are driven by their experiences rather than a few batty theories about the position of women in society. Just like real life, eh? Even David Crosby, the token fogey of the Close and hardly any sort of liberal, has had his view of British justice 'severely dented' and is helping organise the 'Free the Brookside Two' campaign.

Jimmy Corkhill is 'gutted'. Well, so am I and it's a rum do when prime time is where we find such progressive entertainment. Or maybe we shouldn't be shocked that while we are constantly told feminism no longer has a home to go to, something that bears a remarkable resemblance to it has found a way into all our homes. I wouldn't miss it for the world. And now that both Mandy and Flora have stopped shaking, the real stories will begin.

Revenge is always sweet; it's even sweeter when you don't have to leave the house to get it. •

....

15 December 1994

Catherine Bennett
Write 'em, cowboy

He used to be one of those men's things women could safely ignore. Indeed, when men first began to talk about Cormac McCarthy it seemed kinder just to change the subject. Clearly, this was one of those rarities that brought out the romantic in the poor things. You mentioned the words Cormac McCarthy to normally self-possessed Englishmen, and they would go all droopy and bashful and confiding. Reading Cormac made them feel they could let themselves go.

Adepts – McCarthyites – talked and wrote about Cormac as they had once spoken about Gazza, only worse. If Gazza had been a priapic monolith in the Mediterranean sun, Cormac was a whole heap of monoliths, mighty and big as you like, throbbing in the glow of a Mexican sunset. When *All the Pretty Horses* was published here in early 1993, the most jaded reviewers struggled to convey the full scale of their exaltation and delight. They used words liked 'muscular', and 'freighted', and 'biblical'. But somehow, words weren't enough. You had to *be* there.

'In truth,' Gordon Burn confessed in the *Independent on Sunday*, 'there is no easy way of explaining how McCarthy achieves his effects. The only thing clear is that, with this novel, he has finally found a way of talking to the reader that is direct as a horseman talking to his horse . . .'

Giddy up there, reader! It was clear, from the wholly favourable reviews of *ATPH*, that this is how male critics had always longed to be addressed, or, as it were, ridden. 'Uniquely brilliant,' swooned Stephen Amidon. 'Darkly shining,' breathed John Banville, 'at once intricate and direct, and intent with a kind of primordial simplicity.' At the time, this seemed a bit over the top. McCarthy had, after all, been writing for years without any British critics calling him a genius. Until *All the Pretty Horses* came out, few had gone to the trouble of reading him at all. So at first, Cormac fever looked like a craze, specific to a certain type of desk-bound, enfeebled urban man. In six months, I complacently assumed, they would all be talking about football again, and feeling a bit primordially simple.

How wrong can you be! In the past year, Cormac fever has only intensified and spread, advancing from books to feature pages, from *Spectator* readers to the audience of *Esquire* magazine, which gave away 125,000 copies of *All the*

Pretty Horses, stuck on the cover of its August issue. In September, Waterstone's made *The Crossing*, the sequel to *ATPH*, their book of the month, and reviews of the new novel indicated that McCarthy's male readers were still foaming at the bit, nostrils flaring. Writing in this newspaper, Geoff Dyer suggested that if anyone *did* find *The Crossing* somewhat less magical than its predecessor, the author was not to blame. 'It's our problem, not McCarthy's: his characters ride on and he writes on regardless, obsessive, following a trail only he can create.'

As a writer then, he could do no wrong. As a man, McCarthy again turned out too good to be true. Like Salinger, like Pynchon, like every cult author worth his salt, he is a conscientious recluse. The few available personal details are calculated to endear him to *Esquire* readers: tough, sexy, gifted in the dry-stone-walling department. Brainy – but not sissy – McCarthy reads *Moby-Dick* eight times a year, in between shooting pool and driving fast cars. When the journalist Mick Brown approached him in a restaurant in El Paso, McCarthy said, perfectly: 'I'm sorry, son, but you're asking me to do something I just can't do.'

Brown shook McCarthy by the hand and flew back to London, where his account of his quest touched many hearts. As the recent Books of the Year lists demonstrate, the worship of Cormac McCarthy flourishes among the most apparently hard-headed. Even in Jeremy Paxman. 'This was the year I discovered Cormac McCarthy,' he disclosed in the *Sunday Times*, with the air of one born again. 'I immediately read everything of his I could get my hands on . . . He's up there with Steinbeck and Faulkner.' So, when Paxman cross-examines cabinet ministers on television, in his mind's eye he's hunting down rogue cowboys across the great sierra. Useful to know that.

A book which provokes such a quantity of consensus, compulsion and identification among such a motley assortment of readers must offer valuable clues to male behaviour. Men do not listen to *The Locker Room* and say it makes them feel glad to be alive. They don't look up from Nick Hornby and say their lives have been turned inside out. But Cormac McCarthy makes them do both these things, then boast about it. Why? 'I suppose there's a male bonding thing in it,' says Peter Straus, McCarthy's British publisher. 'He's celebrationg the triumph of spirit in adversity, in one sense. And on the banal level you can talk about the outdoors, men in the outdoors.'

Most men, the kind of men we know, spend most of their lives indoors. They do not know how to break horses or set wolf-traps, to construct muzzles or cauterise their own wounds with the barrel of a smoking gun. But men in Cormac McCarthy novels do this kind of thing the whole time. Their lives are free, literally, of everything pedestrian: free of routine, of money, even of women, who intrude only rarely, as women should, offering platefuls of food, freshly laundered shirts, and occasionally, their bodies.

Simply, McCarthy is supplying quality wish-fulfilment, top-of-the-range fantasy to men who still dream of being cowboys. For such educated romantics there are not many places to go. Tom Clancy and Wilbur Smith are too crude, hardly respectable reading for a Paxman. But McCarthy's horsy escapism comes wrapped up in orotund sentences, adorned with archaic words and patches of obscure stuff which looks as if it might be wisdom. His cowboys are men of few words (and no apostrophes), but when moved to speak they say things like, 'A goodlookin horse is like a goodlookin woman ... They're always more trouble than what they're worth.' Actually, when McCarthy's heroes speak they do so without quotation marks, which has the effect of making the prose look yet more virile, stripped of frills and fancy punctuation.

Some of the philosophising is unyielding – 'All is telling. Do not doubt it' – but such opacities add enjoyably to the idea that the books are rather challenging. McCarthy's admirers like to assert how difficult to read his novels are, perhaps because they sense that this is all that really distinguishes their subject from the works of Louis L'Amour, or their ideas from the thoughts of Marco Pierre White. In fact most of the difficulty resides in the many long exchanges in Spanish. The absence of a glossary suggests that perhaps you are not meant to understand the prose anyway, so much as slap it on the back or buy it a drink.

It is a measure of McCarthy's skill that it is possible to read dialogue like 'You ever think about dyin?' or 'Some people don't have a price' without smirking. He has enough literary manner to master what William Empson defined as 'the essential trick of the old pastoral' – to make simple people express strong feelings in learned and fashionable language.

And what of his readers? Their lives must be melancholy indeed. Frustrated hunter-gatherers, they still yearn to be men's men, loners out on the range. Instead, their dreams are squashed between the covers of two smallish Picadors. The warmth of the response to McCarthy among successful middle-aged men shows how hungry they still are for the great simplifications of the past. For once, the Books of the Year lists have told us something worth knowing. A Cormac McCarthy makes the ideal Christmas present for the man who has done everything except grow up. Just remember to keep a straight face as you hand it over. ●

....

19 May 1995
Mark Lawson
Always connect

Funny things have been happening to Britain's comic novelists. A fortnight ago, David Lodge was to be found assuring several newspaper interviewers that he had never been unfaithful to his wife during their 36-year marriage. This week, Monday's *Daily Mail* carried a banner across the top of the front page which under the headline WOMEN, WHISKY AND WORDS, trailed the four-page story inside: KINGSLEY AMIS: MY FIRST BIG AFFAIR.

These stories may seem very different – the first about an uxorious novelist, the second about an adulterous one – but both are part of the same phenomenon: a significant change in the way in which works of art are now consumed.

Lodge, whose novel *Therapy* concerned the sex-life of a middle-aged writer, was faced with a literary equivalent of the politician who makes a speech about 'the family' and then finds cameras trained on his bedroom window. Interviewers felt they had the right to check that there was consistency between his life and his public pronouncements. Although, paradoxically, Lodge's 'hypocrisy' turned out to consist of speaking publicly (in novels) about promiscuity while himself being faithful, a perfect and rather touching reversal of the standard political tactic.

Kingsley Amis – and his life of 'women, whisky and words' – was brought to the attention of readers of the *Daily Mail* by the newspaper's decision to serialise the forthcoming biography of the writer by Eric Jacobs, which will be published in June. On Monday, four pages covered the beginning of the novelist's affair with Elizabeth Jane Howard, later his second wife, in 1962. 'They seemed perfectly matched,' the extract ominously concluded. 'In time the strains would start to show.' Tuesday's fillet of biography narrated these strains, under the five-deck headline: 'Give up drinking or Our Marriage is Over, Demanded Jane. Amis Chose the Whisky Bottle.' The Lodge interviews and the Amis serialisation are part of a significant – and, for many, worrying – development in modern culture: an overwhelming fascination with the lives of artists.

In 1968, the French literary critic Roland Barthes published a celebrated (at least on campuses) essay called 'The Death of the Author', in which he declared that a writer had no absolute parental connection with a book. It belonged not to them but rather to the individual reader, who created the work by reading it. According to Barthes: 'We now know that a text is not a line of words releasing a single "theological" meaning (the message of Author-God) but a multi-dimensional space in which a variety of meanings, none of them original, blend and clash.' But, although their obituary had just been posted on the noticeboards of universities, the conventional Author-Gods refused to lie down. The old-fashioned deities went on to receive, in the 1980s particularly, ever greater adulation in the newspapers, television arts programmes and bookshops. Profiles, interviews, signings, and readings proliferated. Huge colour posters or even cutouts of best-selling writers such as Jackie Collins, Frederick Forsyth and Jeffrey Archer would loom in high-street windows like a kind of cosmic rebuke to Barthes.

As recently as the last two years, literary novelists have moved up to a different level of celebrity: from being part of the cast list of the broadsheet papers, they have been admitted to the repertory company of the middle-market tabloids. The *Daily Mail* book-extract slot, in which the Amis biography has been appearing, is generally the province of the memoirs of movie stars, soap-opera actresses, Beirut hostages, miracle mums and tragic dads. Both Lodge and Sir Kingsley have been interviewed for the *Mail* in the last two weeks by Lynda Lee-Potter, traditional amanuensis to the heroes and heroines of Middle England.

The encounter between Sir Kingsley and Mrs Lee-Potter was probably the ultimate example of the rise of the Life of the Author. Where David Lodge was merely being interviewed about the points of connection between his fiction and his life, Sir Kingsley found himself being grilled on the similarities between his life and the account of it in the Eric Jacobs biography. For there to be a biography of a living writer is itself an intriguing and contentious development, but when we reach the point of the subject of that biography being quizzed about its contents, then the great publicity crusade has surely found its Holy Grail.

Some have argued that the obsession with the life of the author has led to the death of the novel. Martin Amis – whose recent book *The Information* was the subject of more pre-publication author publicity than any other novel – objects that the biography and the interview are a sort of Literature Lite for those too lazy to take the real thing: 'The truth is that we are more interested in writers than we are in writing. A writer is much easier to understand than a body of work . . .'

Amusingly, Amis voiced his lament on LWT's *South Bank Show*, a television programme which some would regard as an illustration of the difficulty he mentions. Around two million viewers may tune in to its profiles of literary authors; a tiny fraction of that number will go out and read the book which is the peg for the documentary. It is not that they have been put off the writing. Exposure to the writer was enough to satisfy them.

These may seem very fitting thoughts for today, the 200th anniversary of the death of James Boswell, the founder of the biography business. Yet the theory that readers would now rather have the writer than the book is really one for gloomy literary purists. Sales of serious literary fiction in the 1980s and 1990s have reached figures unthinkable in earlier decades. This is partly due to the push of the Booker and other literary prizes, but the market has also been spectacularly bucked by the profile, and by publicity culture.

As a result of the extra-literary fuss surrounding it, Martin Amis's *The Information* entered the *Sunday Times* best-seller list at number one, an Archer-like achievement. Following his confessional sessions with Mrs Lee-Potter and others, David Lodge's *Therapy* entered the same list at number three, the fastest-selling start of any of his novels. Neither of these books had yet won an award or been adapted for television, the traditional stepladders to success for a serious text. They reached readers quickly because their authors were willing

— and were invited — to come out of their studies and put themselves about in the public prints.

But, if concentration on a writer's biography does not necessarily distract attention from the work, it does raise a more subtle worry. Might the sheer weight of information now in the public domain about the creators of most works of art change the way in which the work is received? Have we become The Readers Who Know Too Much? Has the contemporary obsession with the artist's life actually changed the way in which art is consumed?

This first began to worry me while I was reading Martin Amis's *The Information*. I had become grumpy, in private and in print, with critics who kept nudge-nudging that the two novelists who are the book's central characters were 'obviously' Martin Amis and his then-friend Julian Barnes. The real Mart and Jules had played tennis, snooker and chess together, as did the fictional Richard and Gwyn. QED.

This seemed to me a bizarrely stupid reading. The career paths and literary output of Richard and Gwyn in the novel intersected at no point with those of Amis and Barnes. And fiction, surely, was more complicated than this. It seemed obvious that a novelist might take elements of his own writing life — competitive games against another author, for example — and exaggerate and twist them into comic fiction.

However, this smug conviction of my own sophistication as a reader soon began to disappear. Part of the plot of *The Information* is that the novelist Richard dislikes his wife, is unable to make love to her, is resentful of her past promiscuity with other novelists and poets, and eventually feels vindicated when he discovers that she has been betraying him with his friend Gwyn. Now, it had been well reported in newspapers — and in a gossipy article in *Vanity Fair* — that Martin Amis has left his wife for a younger woman, Isobel Fonseca. Although the mechanics of a marriage will always be unknowable to outsiders — and still more so to those who are only reading of it in the papers — the general consensus seemed to be that Amis was the guilty party in the separation, his wife the innocent.

Reading the passages in *The Information* dealing with Richard's marriage, I found myself becoming angry at what seemed an attempt by the writer to pin the breakdown of the marriage on his wife. Dangling the red herring of male impotence — when *Vanity Fair* and other sources had suggested that male priapism was more the problem — looked like an especially low trick. It was when the revelation that Richard had a cocaine problem led me to wonder whether Martin Amis was himself on drugs that I feared I was becoming ruined as a reader, cursed by the mind fever of bio-blight. Never was a book more aptly titled. My problem was the information.

Perhaps, I needed therapy. What a reader in this condition didn't need was *Therapy*, by David Lodge. Its hero, Tubby Passmore, was a writer, though one of situation comedy, in his late fifties (as was Lodge), but overweight and totally bald, whereas the author, as his jacket photographs and television interviews have established, is a flyweight with an enviably thick, dark mop of hair. This book seemed safe enough from bio-blight. But then Tubby mentioned his crocked knee. There had been a reference in a recent interview – in connection with the novelist's BBC adaptation of *Martin Chuzzlewit* – to Lodge having undergone unsuccessful arthoscopic surgery. By the end of the book, I was convinced that David Lodge had left his wife and embarked on a grotesque world tour in search of sexual redemption, as Tubby did. Subsequent interviews reassured me on this point, but this was a small consolation, as it was interviews that had started the problem.

Soon there was evidence that bio-blight was spreading; that even a work which is obviously removed from the surface circumstances of the writer's life will now merely be seen as an exercise in concealed autobiography. The critic simply has to dig deeper for the links.

Kazuo Ishiguro's contentious recent novel *The Unconsoled* is a good example of this. A 535-page novel about a concert pianist arriving in an unidentified European city, the book appeared immune from autobiographical interpreta-tion. Indeed, the Nagasaki-born Ishiguro seemed to have escaped the is-it-him critics when, after two novels set in Japan (*A Pale View of Hills* and *An Artist of the Floating World*), he produced a third, *The Remains of the Day*, set in a 1950s English country house, which led no reviewer to accuse him of having been, or having wanted to be, a butler. *The Unconsoled* seemed to have the same built-in defence against the memoir police.

Yet Pico Iyer, reviewing the novel for the *Times Literary Supplement*, saw its depiction of a disoriented stay in a strange hotel as resolutely rooted in the writer's own recent experience: 'Sometimes, indeed, the book reads like the harried, disoriented report of someone who has just been on a book-tour (Ishiguro spent 18 months touring with the *The Remains of the Day*).' Reviewing the book on BBC2's *Late Review*, Professor John Carey suggested that *The Unconsoled* was about being a successful novelist, about what had happened to Ishiguro since he won the Booker Prize.

Sometimes you feel that if Kafka's *The Trial* landed on the desk of a literary editor as a new novel, the features department would at once be set to finding out exactly what was this guy's gripe against the judicial system. Finally, a critic would triumphantly reveal that the story was clearly sourced in Mr Kafka's rough treatment in the small claims court over non-payment of a parking fine. There seems to be a bias against the mysterious and unknowable side of fiction-writing, a determination to demystify novelists by showing them as mere transcribers of their own lives.

Another recent victim of the belief that any work of art properly lock-picked will reveal the artist cowering inside is Woody Allen. Several reviewers of his new movie, *Bullets Over Broadway*, objected that the women in the film were treated cruelly. Yet *Bullets Over Broadway* is a broad comedy, in which a majority of characters, male and female, are jokey grotesques. It seemed likely that a public perception of Allen as an unpleasant man – a product of his lurid divorce and child custody hearings and accusations (unproved) of child abuse – had aroused critical suspicion about his artistic treatment of women. And, even if that aspect of the film did not trouble you, there was an equal risk of being distracted by how non-autobiographical it was. I spent more of the screening than was ideal trying to think of equivalent examples of an artist producing light work during a dark period in their life.

In another sense, though, Allen could be seen as a beneficiary of bio-blight. Many intelligent observers believed that his career could not survive the scandal in his private life. The same was said about the pop star Michael Jackson, another target for unproved allegations of paedophilia. Yet *Bullets Over Broadway*, the director's first film since his troubles, was his most commercially successful for years. Michael Jackson makes his comeback with a new album. *History*, next month. A record company executive talking to rock critics excitedly said that the album was 'autobiographical. It's about every-thing that's happened to him in the last two years.' In a world convinced that all art is autobiographical, scandal becomes survivable. The public is simply keen to see what use you make of material as raw as that.

Although this particular way of reading and seeing is a phenomenon of our culture, it would be wrong to believe that earlier audiences were entirely pure. An example of bio-blight reviewing can be found as early as the first part of the 19th century, when Tennyson's *In Memoriam* was published anonymously and a critic gushed that the lover's lament clearly came from 'the full heart of the widow of a military man'. Byron's main problem, and the reason for his flight from England, was rumours about his private life, but there was also a perception that his scandalous work was indiscreetly self-revealing.

In the last century, though, a writer was less likely to suffer from the assumption that their work was automatically autobiographical than from a very Victorian variant: that their biography was not fitting for an artist. It was common for literary critics – rather in the manner of political commentators now – to draw sardonic contrast between the books and their creator. George Eliot was accused of an unvirtuous private life, hypocritical in the author of moralistic novels. Oscar Wilde's difficulty was not that people thought his work came from his life, but that his life turned people off his work.

But the two main encouragements to a clue-to-you reading of art – biography and publicity – are purely 20th-century phenomena. The idea of interviewing writers was popularised by small American magazines, who saw a way of getting big literary names on the cover without paying the fees they would demand for an article or short story. The most famous series of author profiles – the 20- or 30-page encounters with poets and novelists in the American quarterly *Paris Review* – began in 1953. The first subject, the then 74-year-old E M Forster, found the idea of a long journalistic conversation interesting but peculiar, whereas an equivalent literary veteran of today would have breakfasted with reporters from the *Anchorage Times* to the *Zimbabwe Gazette*. And, although no newspaper would interview writers at the length of the *Paris Review*, the 4,000-word author profile is now a staple of the broadsheet supplements.

Similarly, literary biographies are almost as old as literature – Walton published lives of Donne and Herbert in the mid-17th century and Mrs Gaskell did Charlotte Brontë in the mid-19th – but literary biography as a genre equivalent to, or even dominant over, original literature is something which dates from the publication of Richard Ellmann's *James Joyce* in 1959, and has become an epidemic only in the last 10 years. And, even then, a Life meant a life; the subject was underground. The concept of a Life before death – such as the current Kingsley Amis biography, or Ian Hamilton's attempt on the life of J D Salinger – is a startling new development.

The first writers to be subject to such attention were generally alarmed by it. The elderly Henry James would often complain that people were becoming more interested in writers than books, and his story 'The Reverberator' was about the corrosive effects of tittle-tattle. W H Auden grumped that biography was 'always superfluous . . . usually in bad taste'.

Evelyn Waugh informed John Freeman in a *Face to Face* television interview that he was only appearing because of the size of the fee, and being interviewed for *Paris Review* in a London hotel room, got up, went to the bathroom, re-emerged in his pyjamas and got into bed. But, if they felt like that, James, Waugh and Auden were lucky to be dead by 1916, 1966 and 1973 respectively. They were the last generation of artists to, as it were, get away with their lives.

Why then, has bio-blight happened? First, we have to acknowledge that a great deal of modern fiction is autobiographical. In 1987, unaware perhaps of offering a hostage to fortune, Martin Amis wrote, in a profile of John Updike: 'For some reason (won't anyone tell us why?), modern fiction tends towards the autobiographical, and American fiction more than most.'

Clearly, this tendency invites identification, which may be misidentification. The central characters in the novels of Philip Roth tend to be Jewish-American novelists; sometimes, in recent extreme examples, called Philip Roth. The collapse of categories is happening at the supply end of the market as well as the demand one.

In the genre of best-selling adventure, romance and thriller fiction, the links between author and story are more or less institutionalised. Dick Francis was a jockey, John Le Carré was a spy, Barbara Taylor Bradford is a working-class girl who made it big, Jackie Collins a Beverly Hills socialite, John Grisham a lawyer. But one of the points of genre fiction is its authenticity of detail: a practitioner with no personal knowledge must be a diligent enough researcher to fake it.

If this expectation has also spread to literary fiction, then there are two possible explanations. One is that this has been a notably solipsistic century – from Sigmund Freud to Oprah Winfrey, confession has been the dominant mode of thought – and that autobiographical writing and reading are a reflection of this. The second is that fact has become a more fashionable narrative method than fiction. The huge growth in news outlets and other information sources has perhaps led reality to be prized over invention. Not for nothing has 'based on a true story' become one of the key publicity sales slogans.

David Lodge, reflecting on his recent experience, says: 'I find that most readers – even sophisticated ones – assume that everything in a novel that is convincing and memorable must be based on fact. It's a huge surprise to them to discover that it might have been made up . . .'

The main cause of this autobiographical assumption in critics and readers is surely the vast increase in publicity about artists. It is easy to explain why publishers now push so hard to promote literary novels. In the 1980s serious writers began to be paid larger advances, but were required in exchange to go out into the marketplace and sell their wares hard. Lodge comments: 'Writers are increasingly assumed to be in a business relationship with their publishers. The relationship between literary fiction and publicity has been called a Faustian pact . . .'

Essentially, there are two possible ways of publicising a book: subject and author. The former will usually depend on high sexual or violent content: Nicholson Baker's *The Fermata* and Bret Easton Ellis's *American Psycho* were hyped in this way. The second method focuses attention on the character or life of the author – the interviews connected with *The Information* were a good example of this – and are particularly likely to promote autobiographical readings.

But, if it's simple to see why publishers want publicity, the question of why the media should have become so keen to provide it is harder to answer. Maybe the Salman Rushdie affair raised the profile of novelists in general and the size of advances being paid (£500,000, famously, to Martin Amis) lifted authors to the ranks of big-salary entertainers – television stars, footballers – who have always been a central subject for the press. There is also a circular explanation. Interviews with artists encourage the assumption that all art is drawn from life. But the assumption that all art is drawn from life in turn encourages interviews with artists.

It's also the case that the present generation of consumers of the arts must have read more biographies than any audience before them. And the central proposition of biography is that work and life are systematically and significantly linked. What has happened in recent years is that a shortage of subjects – and a general hunger for the genre – has directed biographers for the first time towards artists still alive. These interim reports have, alongside the rise of the lengthy interview and profile, accelerated the process of making connections. Once, writer X died, and, five or 10 years later, a biographer explained that X's character Y was based on his relationship with Z. These days, readers have the information before they open the first edition.

Revealingly, there are now signs of writers resisting this process. John Le Carré refused to give any interviews to promote his new novel because, apparently, of some armchair biography produced last time he faced the press. David Hare, to the distress of the National Theatre press office, imposed a similar blackout on his new play.

David Lodge, fresh from answering questions about his sex life generally endured only by presidential candidates, says: 'I had to make a decision about *Therapy*, because certain aspects of it were very close to my own life. Either I refused to give interviews – leading people to assume that the book was heavily confessional – or I gave interviews, in which I tried to make points about the categories of fact and fiction. I chose to do the latter, but I do have concerns about it and I'm taking stock now of whether I would take the same approach again. There is a risk that the aesthetic status of the novel is diminished by all the gossip surrounding it . . .'

Meanwhile, as readers of the *Daily Mail* digest the life of Kingsley Amis with their breakfast – 'Amis seems to have thought of sex on the side as a child might think of a slice of cake,' they learnt yesterday – they may be interested to know that his forthcoming novel is called *The Biographer's Moustache*, and concerns a cantankerous novelist whose biography is being written. Now that should produce an interesting interview for someone. •

* * *

25 October 1994

James Wood
In defence of Kelman

Since winning the Booker Prize a fortnight ago for his novel *How Late It Was, How Late*, James Kelman has been attacked as 'unreadable' by lexical paupers who are themselves not worth reading. The *Sunday Telegraph* suggested that the use of expletives in literature was little more than a ruse to sell more books; the *Daily Express* demanded that the Booker Prize be closed down. A caricature has emerged of Kelman's novel as a literary experience no different in kind from being buttonholed by a Glaswegian drunk. This reached its loudest notes in a shocking peal of prejudice and snobbery by Simon Jenkins in *The Times*. Likening Kelman to 'an illiterate savage', Jenkins compared Kelman's novel to an encounter he once had 'in a no-smoking compartment of a corridor train to Glasgow. An ambassador of that city lurched into the compartment and crashed down opposite me . . . he requested money with menaces, swore and eventually relieved himself into the seat.' It was, apparently, a horrible experience – for the Glaswegian, one would think, who had to put up with Simon Jenkins relieving *himself*: 'For almost an hour I humoured him, chided him, remonstrated with him,' he writes.

Kelman does not need defending against such attacks. But it may be worth attempting a literary explanation of his work. First, reading *How Late It Was, How Late* is like being grabbed by an elaborately angry Glaswegian man. Kelman's authenticity seems to me to be intense – his stream of consciousness is less literary than Joyce's. 'Joyce's mistake consists in that he gives too much verbal body to thoughts,' said Nabokov: Kelman shrinks that verbal shroud and dulls its colours in ways that risk monotony, but that accommodate considerable authenticity. Many people over-use 'fuck' for instance, while most people are not porous scouts like Mr Bloom, continually smelling the urinous odours of kidneys or 'the flabby gush of porter' from a pub.

On the other hand, this is a stylised world, and Kelman is a self-conscious literary artist of great shaping power. (His latest novel is a lovely wrangle of unusual words, like 'blootered,' 'blagged', 'bampot,' 'skited'.) The critic David Sexton has brilliantly suggested that *How Late It Was* is a spoof of Milton's *Samson Agonistes*, for in it, an ex-convict called Sammy Samuels wrestles with strange forces, is blinded, and talks a lot about how he needs a shave.

This is suggestive, for Kelman writes a kind of prison literature. The principle of such writing – in some of Céline, in Camus' *La Peste*, in Solzhenitsyn, in Breytenbach's *Memoirs of an Albino Terrorist* – is a luxurious oppressiveness whereby the smallest things, like getting an extra gram of bread per day, or looking at timetables for trains out of the sealed city of Oran as Camus's narrator does, are subject to intense scrutiny. Eventually, these small things become the *only* things, and hence metaphyscially suspenseful. It is the biblical inversion of being rich in poverty. For Kelman's blinded ex-convict, the most trivial task becomes newly difficult: walking home from the police station, feeling about in the fridge for food. Beckett, from whom Kelman has learnt most, does a kind of ontological spoof of this genre, a comic concentration on nothing (Molloy's smooth stones are the equivalent of daily prison bread). Kelman, in turn, does a spoof of Beckett in his story 'Not Not While the Giro', whose narrator is waiting not for Godot but for his Giro: 'How in the name of christ can one possibly consider suicide when one's giro arrives in two days' time.'

Some of these writers describe real prisons; but all of them mean the prison of life, the sentence that cannot be commuted. 'However much you pray it doesn't shorten your stretch. You'll sit it out from beginning to end anyhow,' says Shukhov symbolically, at the end of *One Day in the Life of Ivan Denisovich*. 'Brutal between two fits of panic,' is Baradamu's characterisation of most people's lives in Céline's *Journey to the End of the Night*; Kelman has said of his latest novel, 'All you have to do is go round and look at someone's existence for 24 hours and it will just be horror.'

Some of these writers describe real criminals; but all of them gesture towards our universal taintedness. All of us are plague-ridden, as Camus would have it. The criminal or rebel is chosen because, as the socialist heroine of Christina Sead's novel *Cotter's England* puts it, 'All suffer, but the criminal suffers more; all his life is suffering.'

Kelman, like Céline, Beckett and the novel-writing Camus, is a nihilist-stoic. This vision finds its natural expression in a Swiftian coarseness, for language itself has become infected by the metaphysical raggedness of life. Both Céline and Solzhenitsyn use 'fuck'; Kelman, whose organising principle as a stylist is repetition, uses it a lot. 'What he had been hoping for – he had been hoping for something. What in the name of fuck had he been hoping for, he was hoping for something. Hope. What a strange fucking word. Hope. Here I am, hoping. I am hoping. Hope hope hope, little bunnies, hope hope hope.' (*The Busconductor Hines*.) Like the new novel, this goes on too long. But is quite as powerful as Shukhov in *One Day*: 'And now Sukhov complained about nothing: neither about the length of his stretch, nor about the length of the day, nor about their filching another Sunday. This was all he thought about now: we'll survive. We'll stick it out, God grant, till it's over.'

Yes, the new novel is too long, and not his very best (it is his eleventh book). Yes, Kelman is a limited artist, who, like Nabokov's ape, tends to draw again and again the bars of our cage. But Kelman most certainly deserved to win the Booker Prize. For this artist writes movingly and with passionate attention to language, and in his fiction his politics is the great decent socialism of imaginative sympathy with the neglected and previously unseen – the socialism that the imprisoned Wilde meant when he wrote in *De Profundis* that Christ was the supreme artist because He had 'the imaginative sympathy which is the sole secret of creation in Art'. It is the socialism of Dresier, whose poor Sister Carrie, working in a shoe factory, 'felt the drag of a lean and narrow life', and whose Hurstwood, forced to work as scab labour as a driver on the trams feels: 'This was a dog's life . . .' It is the socialism of Dickens; and in our own time of Raymond Carver. This tradition is Kelman's hospitable home; he belongs *there* just as much as with the 'Scottish literature', under whose smaller porch he shelters so noisily. •

Pass Notes

1 November 1994   Martin Chuzzlewit

Age: 152

Appearance: Dog-eared.

Former status: Classic novel by Charles Dickens.

Current status: Lavish BBC production and source of argy-bargy between director Pedr James and writer David Lodge over how it should end.

What's the problem? Lodge wants a happy-ever-after triple wedding; James prefers a stoical soliloquy by Tom Pinch on the vanity of human love.

A sample of the speech, if you would: 'People who read about heroes in books, and choose to make heroes of themselves out of books, consider it a very fine thing to be discontented and gloomy, and misanthropical, and perhaps a little blasphemous, because they cannot have everything ordered for their individual accommodation.'

Hardly Hamlet: No, but better than Lodge's 'soft soapy' ending, insists the director.

Which would Dickens have preferred? Difficult to say as his original bears no resemblance to either, dealing instead with the jilting of termagant Charity Pecksniff.

How confusing. Could you attempt a plot summary? I was rather hoping not to, but if you insist. Young Martin Chuzzlewit quarrels with his grandfather, old Martin Chuzzlewit, over old Martin's ward, Mary Graham. Martin the elder has his grandson, a pupil of the hypocritical architect Pecksniff, dismissed. Young Martin goes to America, loses his money, almost dies of fever, and, suitably chastened, returns to win the heart of old Martin and the hand of young Mary.

That's it? There's a complicated sub-plot concerning the evil Jonas Chuzzlewit, who tries to kill his father, beats his wife, murders the man who is blackmailing him, and commits suicide. Also includes the usual comic cavalcade of Dickensian grotesques, notably the hard-drinking nurse, Mrs Gamp.

Typical Gampism: 'Rich folks may ride on camels, but it ain't so easy for 'em to see out of a needle's eye.'

Is the book any good? Not one of Dickens's best. It's long (of course), rambling – the American section was introduced in a bid to boost flagging sales – and even more dependent on coincidence than usual.

And the series? Well, it cost £4 million to make, so it must be good.

When does it start? Find out yourself – Pass Notes is art, not a listings service.

Alternative name for the Lodge version: Three Weddings and a Funeral.

Do say: 'Marvellous deconstruction of the way selfishness poisons individual families and an entire society.'

Don't say: 'Who's playing Mr Micawber?' ●

....

29 March 1995

Jan Moir
A nice bloke called Nick

Nick Hornby is drinking tea and eating hot iced buns in the headmaster's study at William Ellis School, an all-boys comprehensive in north London. His crisp white shirt sparkles, his ankles are neatly crossed and he is behaving very nicely – we are all behaving very, very nicely – because there is something about the hush and quiet horror of a headmaster's study which still churns the stomach after all these years.

Hornby is here as part of the school's admirable Book Week, where authors are invited along to read extracts of their work and to talk to the pupils afterwards. First nice thing about Nick Hornby: he is nervous about doing this.

Beryl Bainbridge and Nick Rankin were guests earlier in the week, but you suspect that Hornby will prove the main attraction. He will be reading from *Fever Pitch* – his 1992 opus which was widely acclaimed as the best book about football ever written. In the assembly hall afterwards he will tell the pupils that – 'it is a book about what it is like to be a boy and later, what it is like to be a man' – but for the moment he is chatting to the teachers and making his own quiet doomed bid for football as a curriculum subject. Second thing about Nick Hornby: he is a man *obsessed*.

European cup ties are excellent for geography, he points out. History and politics come with the territory. Football can also improve your arithmetic. 'Goal averages are very complicated things to work out,' he pleads. The teachers munch on their iced buns, amused but unconvinced.

We move into the hall where about 100 pupils in royal blue blazers and various states of mandatory schoolboy dishevelment are waiting. You could, if you wanted, roughly divided them into two groups: the shy, little ones who ask intelligent questions after the reading ('Did you have to look up all the information that is in the book?' 'I'm afraid to say that it was all in my head.'/ 'What do you think of Arsenal's style of football?' 'If you go to watch them regularly, it is torture.') and the bigger show-offs who take the opportunity to remind Hornby of recent Arsenal drubbings. But he takes it all in good part and he goes down a storm. 'Did I do okay?' he asks afterwards. He did great.

We go for lunch and he very politely asks if it is all right if he does not have the cheaper, no-choice set menu because he does not like liver. 'Would you mind?' he says. At moments like this, it is not hard to imagine which kind of schoolboy Nick Hornby was; sometimes he is confident and funny – he is always articulate and wise – but there are moments, little moments, when he has the demeanour of someone who has been freshly whipped.

He began watching football when he was a shy, troubled 11-year-old who lived in the home counties and who travelled up to Arsenal regularly, tailoring his accent to match that of his contemporaries on the terraces and dreaming of owning a home nearby – which he now does. He was the only boy in his class whose parents had divorced and his football found him friends, devotion and a constant ballast throughout his life.

He went to Cambridge, he worked as a teacher, he went bald young, sometimes he felt old, he fell in and out of love. 'I think that men use women as crampons. You dig another one into the rock in order to climb up the next step.' He suffered, but in the end he did not mind. 'You have to hurt once to really, really understand most things. To understand music at the very least. It would be very difficult for anyone to know what Morrissey or Neil Young were going on about if they had not suffered.'

He ran a computer shop, he wrote book reviews, he bought records, he got a contract to write his first book. He furiously enjoyed his classic trinity of male obsessions – music, football, girls – but was never bothered much about work. 'I wish I had a really ambitious streak in me. There were times when it would have helped.'

He says that one of the greatest moments in his life was being recognised in the Kentucky Fried Chicken in Finsbury Park, shortly after *Fever Pitch* was published. 'This bloke in the queue turned around and said, "Fucking great book, Nick." That isn't going to happen to a lot of English writers and I am very proud of it.'

He is now 37, but for nearly two decades, before he settled down, got married and had a baby, the only constant in his life was Arsenal Football Club, who, he admits, have saved him in more ways than one. 'I suppose it was a substitute for life to a certain extent. If there is not much going on in your life, then you fill the void with music and football and books.'

If he had to compile a list of his top five authors, he says that Anne Tyler would be right up there in his pantheon of print heroes. 'She writes wonderful books which sell loads of copies *and* she gets the kind of reviews that most writers would die for.' There is a parallel here; for if this is Hornby's own game plan, then he is already in the penalty area, trotting nicely towards an open goal.

His debut novel was published this week to the kind of reviews that most writers, including Anne Tyler, would die for. 'Triumphant, moving, very funny, wonderfully authentic,' concluded the *Financial Times*. 'Funny, compulsive . . . bet your mortgage on this going to the top of the bestseller list,' said *GQ*. 'Charming, funny, an instant classic,' according to the *Guardian*.

Hornby modestly describes *High Fidelity* as a book about music, monogamy and football, but this is only a tiny scrap of the story. *High Fidelity* is about the nature of relationships, about being A Bloke, about being a bloke called Rob who knows what he doesn't want but doesn't know what he wants, but who thinks what he might really want is for it to be Christmas every day with a girl he hasn't yet met. Most importantly, it is a book about getting by and about *being okay*.

'Art isn't about being contented,' says Hornby. 'There aren't many books or records about being okay. Ha, imagine an opera about being okay. But I wanted to write about being okay because it is the most common experience of life.'

He writes with a funny, fresh voice which skewers male and female foibles with hilarious accuracy. This is how Nick thinks: he thinks, for example, that girls have got it easy when it comes to sex. Girls only have to worry about cellulite ('and men have fat bums, too, you know') while the poor chaps are a-boiling and a-toiling about everything from premature ejaculations to female orgasms on demand, to will-it-won't-it erections. 'And things that go wrong in the middle,' Hornby tells me, and I think I know what he means.

High Fidelity is also about getting it wrong in your rite of passage and about who wears the best knickers. 'I did some research. I asked some women if they wore their best knickers when they thought they were going to sleep with someone and they said, of course we do,' says Hornby, his eyes still wide with disbelief. 'I found that terribly depressing. I mean, I *did it* but it didn't occur to me that women did it, too. What a con.'

He also writes about how girlfriends wear lots of make-up in the beginning of relationships but by the time you both get around to arguing about splitting up, they don't wear any because they want to look tragic and distraught. Posh pants and pale faces? No wonder the boys at William Ellis School loved him so much, no wonder there is so much to admire in his sharp-eyed, soft-hearted prose style. Nick Hornby has drawn a bead on our deepest, girly secrets – and he is ready to spill the beans.

He believes – perhaps generously – that misunderstandings between the sexes are invariably rooted in male incomprehension. 'All the quirks and strangeness, all the sports stuff and the inability to communicate stuff, that is firmly in the male camp. Women are just more . . . sane than men.'

Are we? Just at this moment, something extraordinary happens, something that would not even dare happen in a Nick Hornby book. We are talking once more about obsession – he is obsessed with obsession – and how he once made 10 phone calls in one evening to a girl he was splitting up with. 'I think you get a bit more obsessive when you are upset,' he says. 'Yes,' I say, nodding wisely, 'that can happen.' At that very minute, that exact minute, the waitress hands me a portable phone. There is a call for me. It is from my boyfriend and we have one of those short, tragic, mutually misunderstood conversations before he slams the phone down. I burst into tears. Poor Nick Hornby looks stricken. 'Are you okay?' he asks. 'Just give me a minute,' I say. A long, silent moment passes while I smear mascara all over the nice, linen napkin. 'Shall I pop out and get us some more cigarettes?' he asks tactfully. 'That would be great,' I blub. Another thing about Nick Hornby he is a great man in a crisis.

When he comes back, he asks the right questions, he is kind and sensitive, for he is no stranger to heartbreak himself. We have a cigarette then we are both okay again, the awkward moment is forgotten.

The enduring crisis in Nick Hornby's life, the one that keeps him awake at night – and which has surfaced in both his books – is this: what would he do if his wife fainted during a vital moment of a cup tie? Would he help or would he, as he did with another friend many years ago, keep his eyes fixed on the pitch? He thinks about his answer very carefully.

'My relationship with my wife is the most important thing in my life,' he concludes finally. 'My life now could not be sustainable without my wife and our baby. If I had to, I could get by without football and music, but not without them.'

He thinks some more. 'But if she did keel over in the Cup Winners Cup Final, it would be very hard to break the habits of a lifetime. It would be hard to help.' And he nearly bursts into tears at the thought. ●

....

3 March 1995

Dan Glaister
Audience with the ex-Prince

A large and rather tedious chunk of the *Symbol* album by Prince (as he was then known) is taken up with a series of telephone calls between a reclusive pop star and a journalist trying, and failing, to secure an interview. It all ends in tears, mutual recrimination and a burst of pomp symphonic rock.

My interview with The Artist Formerly Known As Prince (TAFKAP – but let's call him the Artist) had been set for 5pm at Wembley Arena, during rehearsals for a five-night stint, the opening dates of a world tour. Two minutes to five and I was sitting in the back of a cab on the North Circular in a traffic jam, sweating.

There had been a week of indecision as the half-joking request for an interview – the man had not done a newspaper interview for 10 years – was passed on, pondered, resubmitted and finally, ludicrously, approved. The promoters could not be serious. 'But he doesn't give interviews,' I protested. 'Hmmm,' they said. 'But he will. Tuesday afternoon. You'll have 15 minutes, no tape recorder, no notebook.'

Monday night was spent in a state of minor anxiety, avoiding having to think about the possibility of meeting one of my musical heroes, a man who is anyway one of pop's more eccentric characters. I was, I admit, intimidated. Tuesday afternoon, the call came through. 'Wembley Arena, 5pm, be at the blue door.'

So there I was, at 5pm, stuck in the slowest cab in the world on the slowest road in the world, with a chirpy cabbie. 'The last time I went to Wembley,' he told me, 'I broke down.' I glance at my bag and wonder if I should take an anti-stress pill.

At 5.15 we arrive and I'm led down a complex of tunnels and passages beneath Wembley Arena. I pinch myself. Crossing the auditorium I catch a glimpse of the set for the new tour. 'That's the endorphin machine,' the press man tells me, pointing to a prop that dominates the stage, looking like a giant inflatable castle with a slow puncture. I nod.

And then I'm led to the regal presence. A search outside the dressing-room door and I'm shown in. And there he is, hovering behind the press man. I immediately stop myself thinking 'Gosh, isn't he little', because I know that was what I had been thinking I would think before I went in.

The door closes and we are alone in his dressing room, a standard stadium dressing room, its tacky furniture draped in turquoise, scarlet and purple crushed velvet. Off it is a smaller room with make-up arranged before a mirror, to the side a bathroom with the deepest shag-pile carpet imaginable.

Two scented candles burn in glass jars on a low table. The lighting is subdued. The Artist wears brown sunglasses. Underneath them is his personal Mark of Cain, the word Slave scrawled, rather tastefully, in black across one cheek. This he has pledged to bear until his record company, Warner Bros, release him from his contract.

The half-hour that follows is by turns relaxed and bizarre. Bizarre because I am in a dressing room talking to the man who for me has the greatest pop mind of his time. Mundane because, well, loathsome though it may be, he is really rather normal. Likeable even. So who cares if this is a charm offensive designed to offset the negative publicity 'the loony with a squiggle for a name' has received of late? I am just happy to play along.

The Artist's mood melts from defensiveness as he talks about his legal problems to an almost raucous joshing when we move on to music. Unexpectedly, he is an easy person to be with. There is none of the coquettishness, the eye-rolling and the puckered lips of his public persona. He listens and engages me in conversation, a rare feat with star interviewees, maintaining eye contact even through the shades.

The Artist's presence is calm and assured, an artist with no need for anti-stress pills. His voice is deeper than I had expected, pleasant and soft, with a slightly folksy twang to it that becomes more pronounced the more he relaxes. He is dressed all in white, a loose linen trouser-suit affair with a long shirt of the same material over it, a black scarf tied at the neck. He is, it must be said, prettier than his pictures. Clean-shaven, his hair cut in a neat, short bob with customary trademark sideburns curling down, he presents a sickeningly youthful 36-year-old.

Initially he doesn't seem in a hurry to do anything so I break the ice by presenting him with a copy of Hanif Kureishi's new novel, *The Black Album*, which shares the title with Prince's own bootlegged and later officially released work of the mid-1980s. He says 'Thank you' but seems slightly bemused, listening with the polite air of an adult dealing with a babbling child. It is only when I mention Kureishi's film, *My Beautiful Laundrette*, that he nods and says, 'Yes, I've heard of that.'

'Well,' I say. He does nothing. He stands like a dancer, his body balanced. I fidget and move towards one of the two sofas. We sit down and I notice his footwear: white, high-heeled boots. 'Thank you for coming,' he begins, that old showbiz conceit of thanking your audience, before he embarks on a lengthy statement about his legal troubles, an answer to an unasked question already scripted in his head. 'The reason I wanted to talk to you is so that it all comes out, everything. I want you to write everything, so that people can make up their own minds. If everything is known then people will understand.'

Some of this is slightly difficult to follow, like encountering Brando in his lair at the end of *Apocalypse Now*. 'Who are they to tell me what I can or cannot do? What if I don't want to sing "Purple Rain" every time I go on stage? The fans don't want that either. It's my music, they're my songs.' Although he is clearly quite worked up about this, interspersing his comments with 'But you gotta understand' and 'I gotta make this clear', he doesn't lose his good humour, the situation doesn't feel uncomfortable.

'Do you know how many of my songs I own?' he asks. 'Not a single one. Out of 16 albums, not a single one. They won't belong to my children. I won't be able to pass them on to my grandchildren. They belong to someone else. Why? It's my music.'

Is there an alternative? 'Do you know what a sense of freedom it gave me to release 'The Most Beautiful Girl in the World' on an independent label? When I released that I didn't have to give them the master, I could keep the master. I can release that record again next year if I want to.' (Interestingly, 'The Most Beautiful Girl in the World', the only new work the Artist released last year, was a critically lauded worldwide hit, his first, and last, for a while.)

Through layers of 'Well, you shouldn't have signed the contract, should you' cynicism, I start to see the man's point. 'I've been very upset with this,' he continues. 'I've gone to them when I've been physically ill and argued.' I try to comfort him with the thought that he's not the first that this has happened to. Frank Zappa, I remind him, had a similar problem with the same company. The tirade lets up. 'He was ahead of his time,' says the Artist. He offers more examples: 'The companies tried to do it with Miles, and with Duke.'

Has the controversy affected him artistically? Critics allege that not only has the Artist lost the legal plot, he's lost the musical plot as well. 'Did you hear "Letitgo"?' he asks, the minor hit from last year's *Come* album. I did. It was the best pop single of the year. His case is proven. 'But again it's the record company. If they don't want to promote a song, they don't make the effort to cross it over into other markets and the fans don't get to know it. It's the same with my albums. People say "Why did he drop Rosie Gaines after one album?" But I did three albums with her in between which nobody heard because the record company never released them. They're all in the vaults.'

Can he see any resolution? 'When I changed I felt reborn,' he says, his mood lightening as he speaks about his change of name.

I sense an opportunity to get him off his contractual troubles and on to the really interesting thing about him, his music. Is the new album, *The Gold Experience*, which will not be released thanks to the contractual problems, as good as word has it, 'his best work yet?' He laughs. 'I never said that, but it is good,' he says, and abruptly flops back on the sofa.

I focus on his boots, wondering if this would be the right time to ask for his autograph. 'I always have to wear them,' he says, interrupting my reverie. 'I went to see the Jackson Five when I was a kid and they all wore flat shoes and it didn't work.' I nod dumbly. 'Do you ever wear Timberlands?' I ask, trying to make sense of what's going on. The Artist finds this very funny, slapping his leg with glee. 'I did once, as a joke for a photo, and people were saying "There's something wrong, but we don't know what it is."'

'I grew up with Carlos Santana, and those crazy boots and his trousers rolled up,' he says. 'And now you go to see Eric Clapton with those big flat shoes, and you think, "Whoa there, Eric, what are you doing?"'

He is, it seems, disenchanted with today's young pretenders. 'Now there's no one to go and see. Where are the young ones coming along to whoop us up? Who is there to go and see? Fem 2 Fem?' The wronged voice of earlier has given way to jokey playfulness. He lolls back on the sofa as he talks about music and musicians, particularly his current band. 'Now that the record company isn't involved, we can play what we like on the tour. It's going to be much more like the after-show jams we used to do. It's going to be all new songs, with just a couple of old ones.

'You know I felt so annoyed and angry when you walked in,' he says. I change the subject, telling him that I had prepared a series of short questions, given that our interview was only for 15 minutes. 'They're from a questionnaire we do,' I say, 'but I'm not going to ask you all of them.'

'Thank God for that,' he replies. What is your idea of perfect happiness? I ask. 'Music,' he shoots back, laughing. 'What possessions do you always carry with you?' He pauses, shaking his head. 'Music,' he laughs.

'You're not going to catch me out.' 'How would you like to be remembered?' I try. 'Music,' comes the reply. 'What vehicles do you own?' Surely I've got him with this one. 'Uhh, uhh . . .' he sounds like John Turturro in *Quiz Show*. 'Lots,' he caves in.

Finally, I ask him what is the trait he most deplores in himself. 'My inability to communicate my music,' he says. 'I hear it but it has to go through someone else. That person may have had a bad day or may not think the same way I do. Why does there have to be a sound check? I don't have a song check. You don't have a clothes check . . .' Well, actually.

My time comes to an end and I make way for *Smash Hits*. On my way out after being played sections of *The Gold Experience*, a triumph of affirmative pop, I glimpse the Artist on stage, rehearsing. He is in character, in a pool of blue light, commanding the stage before an empty arena. ●

---

18 April 1995

Michael Billington
A Prince too far

What is happening to Shakespeare in this country? I'll tell you exactly what is happening. We are witnessing a constant narrowing of the main-house repertory so that the same dozen 'pop' plays are coming round with monotonous and excessive regularity. We are gradually reducing the canon of 37 plays to a soccer table with the Premier League way out front and the rest limping along behind.

You think I exaggerate? Let us look at the recent record of the RSC, which is bound by its charter to keep the canon alive.

Since 1984 on the main Stratford stage we have seen three productions apiece of *Hamlet, Macbeth, Romeo and Juliet, As You Like It, A Midsummer Night's Dream, The Merchant of Venice* and *Richard III*. In that same period we have seen no main-stage productions at all of *Timon of Athens, King John, Henry VIII, Titus Andronicus, Two Gentlemen of Verona, Pericles* and only one each of *Troilus and Cressida, Coriolanus, Antony and Cleopatra, Othello* and *All's Well*. Indeed, you can take the numbers game still further. There has been no main-house Stratford production of *Timon of Athens* since 1965, of *Pericles* since 1969, or of *King John* since 1974. In terms of large-scale exposure, these plays have virtually ceased to exist.

There are several obvious reasons for this. With the opening of the Other Place in 1974 and the Swan in 1986, the RSC has three Stratford venues to manage and can place the less obviously 'popular' plays in smaller spaces. I wouldn't deny for a moment that there is often artistic gain to be found in seeing Shakespeare performed in intimate conditions: witness Deborah Warner's overpowering *Titus Andronicus* or Sam Mendes's rhetoric-free *Troilus and Cressida*. But the existence of alternative spaces is no excuse for banishing certain plays for ever from large-scale presentation. I have a long enough memory to recall seeing *King John* at Stratford in the late 1950s: a thrilling affair it was too in that, under the chauvinist tub-thumping, one discovered a compelling study of a flawed hero. And anyone who remembers Scofield's brilliant performance in Schlesinger's 1965 *Timon of Athens* will wonder why this play is now deemed unfit for main-house production.

It is not just that we now have more studios; I also detect in this the deadening conservative hand of examining boards. All theatres keep a wary eye on syllabuses. I am told that the Shakespeare set-texts for key stage three – part of the national curriculum – are currently restricted to *Romeo and Juliet*, *Julius Caesar*, *A Midsummer Night's Dream* and *Henry V*: a limited choice. And while it is true that, at GCSE level, teachers can choose a Shakespeare play for course work, one wonders how many ever venture off the beaten track. As the Shakespeare syllabus constantly contracts, so the theatre tamely follows suit. Political correctness also plays its part in the reduction of the repertory: you don't see many *Othellos* these days for the obvious reason that it is considered offensive for a white actor to 'black up'. I too would much rather see a black Othello. But the logic of colour-blind casting, in which I believe, is that it should cut both ways.

Just as I wait impatiently to see a black Hamlet, Brutus or Timon, so I wouldn't banish the idea of a white actor playing Othello. As Jeffery Kissoon pointed out recently, we would all have been worse off for being denied Olivier's Moor.

The real problem, however, is the catch-22 tyranny of the box-office: one that applies not just to the RSC but to regional theatres everywhere. Certain Shakespeare plays can't be performed because they are unpopular; but, since they are rarely seen, we never discover how popular or not they are. I think it's all hooey anyway. If a great director or actor tackles an unfashionable play, it soon acquires box-office clout: I don't actually recall Brook's *Titus Andronicus* or Guthrie's *Henry VIII* emptying the main Stratford theatre.

What really worries me, however, is the disastrous artistic consequence of relying for ever on the same dozen Shakespearean 'golden oldies'. The more the same plays are repeated, the more directors are inevitably driven to discover quirkily 'original' concepts. But not every Shakespeare play is inexhaustible. After the shabby Shylock, the Venetian-ghetto Shylock, the City-financier Shylock, you begin to wonder what is left to say about *The Merchant of Venice*. And after the street-cred Romeo, the quattrocento Romeo and now the Victorian Romeo, one starts to feel it is time to vacate Verona for a while.

What I'm asking for is an acknowledgement of Shakespeare's range, diversity and abundance by theatres, audiences and bone-headed syllabus-setters. I appreciate that more people will always want to see *Hamlet* than *All's Well*. But that is no reason for turning the less fashionable plays into the theatrical equivalent of Gillingham or Hartlepool, languishing somewhere at the foot of Division Three. If we don't start re-exploring the whole canon on main stages, there is a real danger that playgoers will eventually get bored with yet another night in Venice or Verona and that the RSC itself will wind up as the Reduced Shakespeare Company. ●

26 May 1995

Andy Beckett
Eternally yoof

Two weekends ago a new face appeared in the News Analysis section of the *Sunday Times*. Between Norman MacRae dissecting tax on mortgage insurance and Peter Kellner exploring the dangers of Labour's municipal monopoly, there she was: a tumbling fringe, a sceptical pout, and thick-lined eyes staring out of the page. Her column was called 'Don't bend over backwards, girls', and she was called Julie Burchill.

After 19 years as a punk journalist, a polemicist, and a strange kind of public intellectual, from the *NME* and the music press to the *Mail on Sunday* and the mainstream press to the *Spectator* and the intellectual press, her salary matching her rise from specialist prodigy to ubiquitous media celebrity leap by leap, this is Burchill's latest incarnation. 'She's like an attractive woman walking into a men's club,' says the *Spectator*'s editor Dominic Lawson. 'Just be controversial,' said the *Sunday Times* to Burchill.

There was no need; she used her new column to dismantle an American feminist and to announce her new sexual orientation. Reader response was substantial and evenly split. Burchill has fired out thousands of volatile pieces like this, part unusual intelligence, part personal insult, part self-promotion. Her only consistency apart from her prolific output and her fierce, dense style has been her lack of interest and expertise in the traditional journalist's craft of interviewing and reporting. In April she had resigned as the *Sunday Times*'s film critic, complaining in print that watching two films a week for six figures a year was the worst job she'd ever had; two weeks later she had been promoted to the paper's High Table.

Three days before the new Burchill column appeared, a dapper man in a black shirt and an adventurous tie called Tony Parsons leant back in his BBC2 chair on live television and decided that 'ritual suicide is the only viable career option' for the Anglo-Japanese author Kazuo Ishiguro. His London vowels delivered the line flat and fast, his thin lips curled into a small smile, and the camera panned across to Oxford poetry professor Tom Paulin and the two other *Late Review* pundits laughing. Parsons delivers lines like this a lot, pithy and knowing enough for *The Late Review* to be recommissioned when its parent, *The Late Show*, is axed. He is also the rock critic of the *Daily Telegraph*, and is considered important enough by the Tory paper to star in its advertisements.

Like Burchill, Parsons was a pale young punk at the *NME* in the late 1970s; like her, he has gone from inky gig reviewing to glossy-paged columns to giving Middle England a whiff of danger; like her, he is courted by the media establishment now. Parsons calls the *Telegraph*'s editor Max Hastings by his first name. They have lunch every couple of weeks. 'When he takes me to his club,' Parsons says, 'I think, "Boy, here I am. I've made it" . . . It was the Lacy Lady in Ilford and now it's Brooks's.'

Burchill and Parsons used to be co-conspirators, tunnelling upwards together; they used to be married. Now he looks after their 15-year-old son in a light, modern Highbury house not far from Tony Blair's north London home. Burchill and Parsons's secret, besides their nimble ambitious minds, has always been youth: being young, sounding young to older editors and, most importantly, attracting the chimera of the modern press – young readers. Absurdly, at 35 and 42 respectively, youth is still their secret.

Ever since their arrival at the *NME* in 1976, a succession of increasingly important editors have offered Burchill and Parsons a deal. Give us your street credibility and your talent, they have said, and we will give you more money, more fame, more room to write whatever you want. For a time this was a deal that improved Burchill and Parsons and the newspapers and magazines they wrote for: their words eloquently carried the fury of punk to provincial teenagers for the *NME*, the implosion of the Left to the urban fashionable for *The Face*, the excess of High Thatcherism to the suburbs for the *Mail on Sunday*. But gradually, as Burchill and Parsons got older and their thoughts and words got diluted by the widening opportunities, the deal became more cynical. They started writing anything as long as it was controversial, editors bought anything as long as it was controversial, and readers read it all for a quick hit of attitude where before they had looked for insight. To different degrees, Burchill and Parsons became a new kind of columnist: pure, rootless controversialists, whose original dislikes were marketed and bloated into a random, and ultimately rather empty, aggression.

This sold; it still sells. But does it constitute a meaningful future for the rising stars of 1976 and seemingly every year since? Do Burchill and Parsons really stand for anything at all?

In the beginning, the role of Burchill and Parsons seemed clear: Before computer games, satellite TV and subcultures for sale on every high street, most young people thought pop music and the music press that propagated and translated it were important, life-changing even. But both were stagnating: 'Is Rock 'n' Roll an Old Man's Game?' asked a typical *NME* cover in January 1976; inside it read like a stale boys' changing-room. Then, over the summer, the *NME*'s rivals started writing about something new – the first stirrings of punk – and its editor Nick Logan knew things had to change. He advertised for 'hip, young, gunslingers'. The *NME* got 5,000 applications.

Novelist Sebastian Faulks sent one; so did cultural critic Paul Morley, but the first to get a job was a 22-year-old working at the Gordon's Gin distillery in Islington called Tony Parsons. He was just what they wanted, a spiky, meaty Essex boy who used to bunk off his night shift to go and see the Sex

Pistols at the 100 Club, the punk Mecca, but knew about Motown, too. More unusual was the second favourite, a 16-year-old Bristol schoolgirl called Julie Burchill.

'Julie looks like a fairly wild mutation,' wrote Peter York in *Style Wars*, the observation of London's 1970s subcultures he was compiling at *Harpers & Queen*. 'She's wonderfully pale and thin and looks like a bad girl *circa* 1963, which is to say totally 1976, with this bright red mouth . . .' Burchill sent a paean to punk poet Patti Smith as her application. 'I did it on bad school notepaper and shook ink all over it,' she says. 'It was incredibly drooly and libidinous and got their blood running . . . I was stage-managing myself even then.'

Nevertheless, when Burchill arrived she was terrified (she'd only been to London twice before). She smashed her telephone to avoid using it, stared at the floor and slouched silently against the office walls. This only increased her mystique for the older, still hippyish staff: 'They'd only heard of teenagers,' she says. Her writing was something else, too, pouring out of her in fickle enthusiasms for the new music, ecstatic as Kerouac, and hard schoolgirl insults towards her elders and (soon) enemies. Parsons was slightly more conventional, being six years older and knowing more about music, but just as furious a punk advocate – 'this ain't the summer of love' – and with apparently unique access to the 'fast, flash, vicious' bands with which the movement was scaring the tabloids.

The *NME* was soon selling as many copies as *The Times*, and to a narrow late-teenage demographic: Burchill and Parsons established a readership that would follow and age with them, even hire them later. They also established a partnership by getting married, the move of two isolated working-class people aspiring to more than the middle-class bohemia around them at the *NME*. Their under-age nervousness soon flipped over into terrifying arrogance (for her, this would become a modus operandi). Fortifying their desks into a 'Kinder Bunker' with broken glass and barbed wire, they poured scorn and missiles on to the other staff. 'Burchill-Parsons came on like a moral scourge,' wrote York. 'They want to be writers not rock stars, and they know the rock press is an elephant's graveyard.'

They had both quickly sensed the power of their youth and fierceness over their editors. She mocked the *NME* in print for hiring her; he wrote, 'trade on the fact that you are young' in his very first article. They were careful not to throw their advantage away: Parsons says he watched American punk star Johnny Thunders 'stuffing his life down the toilet' with heroin – and stuck to speed, 'an aspiration drug'. In 1978, as punk was fading, they rushed out their own paperback history of the movement, *The Boy Looked at Johnny*. Here, within two years, they were already revising their opinions, using and discarding the musicians who had given them their chance: Patti Smith, they wrote, was 'a silly old biddy', Malcolm McLaren an ageing chancer: 'John

Lydon of Finsbury Park slouched into Sex right on cue and zing went the strings of Malcolm's bondage pants.'

By the following year Burchill and Parsons were bored with the *NME*. But where could they go? Burchill could still barely conduct an interview, and few people had made it from writing about pop culture to writing for more mainstream publications (Nick Kent, the *NME*'s star of 1973, was still at the *NME*) since the mid 1960s breakthrough of Clive James and Germaine Greer. Punk, however, turned out to be a similar rapture in the cultural status quo. 'Punk won,' says Jon Savage, who wrote about it for a rival music paper: 'It was like hippie in America: it entered the mainstream.' In 1980 Nick Logan set up his own magazine, *The Face*, and took Burchill and Parsons with him, into a new glossy world of street fashion and style journalism which would become the decade's defining norm. Meanwhile, newspapers were beginning to take pop culture more seriously, partly because the Sex Pistols had made their news pages, and partly because of a need for cheaper entertainment-led pages. A demand emerged for young columnists: 'As newspapers found more space to fill, they filled it with faces,' says Paul Barker, editor of *New Society* at the time.

Burchill and Parsons did some of their best writing at *The Face* in the early 1980s. He prophetically unearthed old soul music five years before it became the adman's soundtrack, while Burchill's columns compressed bitchiness, eclectic polemic ('bring back Labour and bring back the death penalty'), and erudition ('at the end of 1917, 72 per cent of the Latvians voted for the Bolsheviks') into blaring state-of-the-world addresses. Fleet Street noticed the magazine's success: 'If you worked at *The Face*,' says Savage, who did, 'people would just throw things at you.' Burchill, styled as 'Mad, Bad, and Dangerous to Read', was particularly appealing. While dismissive of punk now, she had a punk credibility; she could write with the wit and density of Tom Wolfe; she was rough working class and still barely 20; and, most enticingly, she had some of the kind of opinions beloved but unsayable by conservative editors. 'She has retained an almost childlike purity of insight,' says Dominic Lawson. 'Men who've been to Oxford or Cambridge are reluctant to write in that way.'

With the kind of luck that plays like a motif through Burchill's career, Andrew Neil had just become editor of the *Sunday Times* and was keen to make the venerable, crusading paper younger and more right-wing. His special assistant was dispatched to woo her. 'I've always known what I've got,' says Burchill. 'Something they want.'

While she was negotiating a column over lunch, Parsons had started writing novels about power lunches. For both of them this move into the mainstream was less a betrayal of their punk roots than an accommodation with their deeper motivation: getting ahead. 'The underground is for losers,' Parsons wrote earlier this year. He was aspirational Essex working class, had been to grammar school ('you're constantly told how smart you are'), wrote for Jimmy Hill's *Football Weekly* aged 10, and sent a published novel, *The Kids*, as his *NME* application. Behind its laddish front, *The Kids* had some surprisingly straight themes (moral responsibility, pride in Britain) and one dominant one (making it); it sold 25,000 copies. Burchill's background was similar. Her communist father worked in a distillery, and wrote essays about Marxism for home study courses in the evenings. Like Parsons, she was far from the centre of things. 'I lie on my bed with the curtains drawn, reading Dorothy Parker,' she wrote. 'And I am mocked by muck-spreaders and scrumpy.' But she learnt one lesson young: 'You don't really exist until you see your name in print.

Burchill's columns were just what the *Sunday Times* wanted: attacks on pop music, on young people, on the working class for their 'tiny minds' *and* their failure 'to pull it all down' – in short, on all the things the *Sunday Times* wanted to cover but didn't like. But gradually her writing became dominated by this controversialist tic, to the exclusion of the other, less predictable thoughts her restless intelligence used to throw up.

Not all her stances were just stances – she supported Sara Keays against Cecil Parkinson loyally enough to get fired from the *Sunday Times* in 1984 – but she was indulged – the *Mail on Sunday* grabbed her straight away to write beside the professionally fuming John Junor; then the *Sunday Times* grabbed her back. Once editors had a hunch there was a market for Burchill they would take anything she gave them. Her voice remained that of a brilliant, indulged 16-year-old.

Parsons was losing his bite. He rushed out three thin would-be blockbuster novels in three years, thrown together from genre cliché, recycled music industry knowledge, and attacks on the music press. Like Burchill's columns, they were read, but not every word. 'Books were a dead end in a way,' he admits. 'If you're 25, 26 you can't just lock yourself away.'

In 1985 Parsons found a way out. Magazines were booming, and Sally Brampton, editor of the newly founded *Elle*, didn't want anyone to mistake the first edition for *Vogue*, so she commissioned Parsons to write a polemic. 'I wanted to show *Elle* was going to be classless, and he had that voice,' she says. 'He was still a hip young gunslinger.' Parsons's piece was called 'Stamp Out Sloanes', and was the first of many pieces he wrote for *Elle* and for Nick Logan's new vehicle *Arena*, a lifestyle magazine for punks who had grown up and made money, like Parsons.

His marriage to Burchill, which had grown increasingly 'claustrophobic', broke up nastily with adultery on both sides. Both of them seemed happy to write about it, having known no distinction between their professional and private lives since 1976. When Parsons moaned about women who drank and Burchill denounced 'Laddism' people knew who they meant. Parsons then expanded the range of his dislikes to cover anyone who made his uptight, ambitious self anxious. In particular, he went after the modern working class ('fat tattooed slobs') and beggars ('Street trash . . . my father would rather have seen us go hungry).

Predictability dulled Parsons as quickly as it had Burchill – but no matter. In the way that they have always been read by their next potential employer, television executives realised Parsons's polemics would make a lively half-hour on air. And he did turn out to be good on television: chippy but cheeky, saying his usual liberal unsayables in wide-boy trousers and a winning smile. 'Television has got a power that print can't match,' he says fondly.

No doubt to his satisfaction, Burchill failed to make the same transition. Tried as a guest controversialist, she lacked the safety of his predictability. She still looked like a sulky teenager on camera, and spoke like one, in a piping voice that leapt and giggled around the subject with rather less articulacy than the print version. 'Speech always felt like a shabby and badly mastered second language to me,' she wrote.

By the late 1980s, people began to think of her as an Old Punk. She recycled herself, and sometimes it worked. She constructed a hugely successful and sarcastic sex-and-shopping novel, *Ambition*, around her past, bulking it up with column-length speeches from characters about feminism ('to be ruthless, competitive and individualistic is the most rebellious thing a girl can do'). But the book didn't really say much except that Burchill was, well, ambitious. The follow-up, *No Exit*, was more grown up but less funny and bombed. Film scripts went nowhere.

By now, however, Burchill had enough fans for her current output not to matter; their reverence for her legend kept her rising. 'If you look at the features pages and the arts pages of newspapers they're full of the ruminations of people trying to be Julie Burchill or Tony Parsons,' says Barker; in 1991 some of them helped her start a journal about pop culture called the *Modern Review*. Its writers echoed her tastes and quoted from her *NME* articles; they carried her feud with Camille Paglia on the letters page; there was even an advertisement for her *Sunday Times* column on the back cover.

Her writing was partially reinvigorated by the flattery, rediscovering the sharp thinking about film and feminism and politics that her grandstanding had nearly drowned out. 'There's quite a lot of learning and hard graft worn lightly in Julie,' says York.

Parsons's past got himself a new job too. Mary Sackville-West, producer of *The Late Review*, had read him in the *NME*; his one-liners and his accent made him irresistible for a cultural panel show with populist aspirations. Like Burchill, he kept another, easier newspaper job going – politely explaining to *Telegraph* readers that unremarkable pop stars like Wet Wet Wet were 'exceptionally accomplished' musicians – and lived off the earning from a best-selling, undemanding book, his 1990 biography of George Michael.

Burchill and Parsons have a kind of power now. Many people will not talk on the record about them. The centre of other writers' attention at the

Groucho Club one night, Burchill 'went and asked Will Self to remove Stephen Fry from my table'. Parsons has a message from Nick Hornby on his answering machine and a request from 'Bowie' to do a book about him.

But it's easy to be disappointed. Paul Morley is: 'The two that broke through don't stand for anything; it's just success for its own sake. They just seem to drift . . .' Worries that his similar trajectory didn't match theirs may colour his opinion. His words resonate, though; for all the notoriety and ubiquity of Burchill and Parsons's work, its impact is fleeting. Books they published early this decade are out of print already. 'I don't remember reading a single column she's written,' says the *Telegraph*'s Comment editor Simon Heffer; most people can only remember their controversies and, as Parsons says, 'to be nothing but a controversialist is as limiting as writing about Thin Lizzy all the time'.

Maybe theirs is the fate of all pundits, and we should just admire their relentless chutzpah, their manipulation of supply and demand in the ever-changing media economy. But even this admiration fades when you think about how well *all* those late 1970s music press people have done: Danny Baker on the television, Jon Savage writing thick, acclaimed cultural histories, even Gary Bushell minting it at the tabloids. Parsons admits his is a 'jammy-git generation'; making a big splash in a media pond much smaller than today's, at a time when editors needed them.

So are Burchill and Parsons, at bottom, little different from Bushell? Maybe they fear that: both of them say they want a change, that they want to write a book people will remember. In the meantime they'll keep going famously — there will always be a Dominic Lawson ringing them up. Maybe Burchill will be asked to edit the *Spectator* one day. Just don't expect it to change lives like the *NME* once did. ●

Pass Notes

14 August 1995   Oasis

Age: Barely 18 months. Their first single, Supersonic, burst over an astonished world in April 1994.

Appearance: Moody, broody, pouty, swarthy, unshaven and hung over. Brothers Liam, who sings, and Noel, who writes the songs, Gallagher (both pictured) may sport black eyes and split lips from their latest bout of fratricidal fisticuffs. Noel scathingly refers to cantankerous Liam as 'Elvis'.

Occupation: The Stones to Blur's Beatles, even if Oasis nick bits from the Moptops at every opportunity. Oasis come from the north and are rough, gruff and tough. Blur come from the south and are wacky, cuddly and adorable.

Why should we care? Take those headphones off and pay attention. Oasis can take credit for putting a hobnailed boot up the bottom of a moribund British pop scene. Their public feud with Blur recalls the halcyon days of the sixties, when bands battled it out for column inches, the affections of young girls and the Number One slot.

How fascinating. It certainly is. Today, Oasis release their latest magnificent waxing, *Roll with It*. Playing their role to perfection, lovable pseudo-Cockneys Blur are releasing the eccentric *Country House* on the same day.

So do this Oasis make a revolutionary pop noise? No, they make a raucous rock 'n' roll racket, as a cursory blast of *Roll with It* will confirm. Liam sneers like a stroppy northern git, while brother Noel masterminds a backdrop of scowling powerchords. Champion!

My dear old thing, it sounds absolutely ghastly. Bring back the refined melodic sensibility of The Carpenters, I say. Obviously you know nothing about the contemporary pop scene. Oasis have single-handedly transformed British pop. They deserve a Queen's Award to Industry for sending all those dreary American grunge bands back to rainy Seattle where they belong.

But I thought you said Blur were the cuddly, lovable ones? Well, yes, they are, but . . .

So Oasis aren't the be-all and end-all, are they? If you like cartoon East Enders singing about transvestism and dog racing, then you'd better stick to Damon Allbran and his silly Blur. Leave Oasis for the real rock fans.

Right-oh. Give me a bit of music-hall knees-up over greasy old slob-rock any day. Noel Gallagher's songwriting has been hailed by critics for its historical scope and gritty authenticity. Here is a man who knows his pop history inside out and is brilliantly reshaping it for a new generation.

That's what they said about Kajagoogoo too. I must ask you to step outside.

Most likely to say: Liam: 'Want a kicking, you fooking Cockney twats?'
Noel: 'What number's the single this week?'

Most likely to do: Abandon hometown Manchester for somewhere with palm trees and low taxes. ●

Trafalgar Square David Sillitoe

Not forgetting . . .

9 November 1994

Michael Frayn
That having been said

I've been visiting the local Old Tropes Home.

I'm very concerned about what happens to expressions and metaphors in their old age. They start out in life so fresh and colouful, so full of humour, so eager to please. They're worked day in and day out over the years until they're exhausted — then they're brutally shoved to one side to make room for younger and more energetic expressions. I believe that they shouldn't have to eke out their last few years of life on the streets, taking any work they can get, spurned and abused. They should be looked after among their own kind in quiet and dignified surroundings.

In the place I've found the residents were obviously made very comfortable. Comfortable with and about everything, even the most appallling ideas and decisions. In fact they seemed particularly comfortable about Attila the Hun. There was a statue of him, placed somewhat to the left of the building, so that almost everything inside was somewhat to the right of him.

The Matron who showed me round spoke very reassuringly. 'I understand where you're coming from,' she said. 'So let me just bring you up to speed. We're very definitely state of the art here, and I don't need to tell you which art that is — it's the art of living. And if you're up at the sharp end then you've got to get your act together and show your street cred. That having been said, what gets up my nose is that people can't get their heads around this. I mean, what are we talking?'

I said it sounded to me like some dialect of English.

'We're talking serious money,' she said. 'We're talking megabucks. Because what are we looking at here?'

So far as I could see it seemed to be the ancient flagpole outside the window, up which things were run to see if anyone saluted them.

'We're looking at 10 grand a day,' she said. '10K — and I do mean K. Because, make no mistake, the sky's the limit. That said, you pays your money and you takes your pick.'

The social range of the residents was wide. As she showed me round, the Matron pointed out both the Poor Man, to whom many things here were said to belong, curiously enough, and the Thinking Man, who apparently owned much of the rest. But everyone there seemed to be terribly good value. Indeed, they were all getting increasingly better value. Because things in the Home don't just get increasingly whatever, or more whatever. They get increasingly more whatever it is. There seems to be an acceleration involved here which bears the fingerprints of the pace of modern living.

Some of the residents were in poor shape. Things had cost them an arm and a leg – often as a result of prices going through the roof, and the roof falling in, so that the bottom had dropped out of the market. Some of them looked as if they'd had a coach and horses driven through them.

A very decrepit old trope called Arguably buttonholed me in the corridor. 'In the last 20 years or so,' he told me, 'I have become arguably the most common word in the English language. I have arguably been responsible for making more unconfirmed statements possible than ever before in human history, and I've arguably saved writers and speakers more mental effort than the word processor and the dictating machine combined.'

He thought for a little, though not very hard.

'Then again,' he said, 'equally arguably I haven't.'

Couples are not separated in the Home. You can see them wandering along the corridors together, hand in hand, touchingly devoted. This Day and Age – they're still as much in love as ever. If you see First you're bound to see Foremost. Sick and Tired were being wheeled along in a double bathchair by Hale and Hearty. Care and Attention were being utterly devoted to all the Hopes and Fears. Though one of the Fears had left the family group and gone off with Trepidation. Now they've grown so alike that a lot of people can't tell them apart.

The old tropes are a remarkably lively lot, considering. 'We *have sex* a great deal,' one of them told me. I expressed surprise. 'Oh,' he said, 'we have it pretty well non-stop. Look through this keyhole. You see? People having every single variant of sex listed in the *OED*! Everything from (1) *either of the divisions of organic beings distinguished as male and female respectively*, through to (2) *quality in respect of being male or female* – even (3)*the distinction between male and female in general*!'My informant thumbed through a greasy copy of the *OED*. 'It doesn't stop there, either,' he whispered hoarsely. 'The *OED* says that this third usage is now often associated with a *more explicit notion.*' He licked his lips and bent closer towards me as he read it out. *'The sum of those differences in the structure and function of the reproductive organs on the ground of which beings are distinguished as male and female and of the other physiological differences consequent on these.'*

These torrid relationships and steamy romances raise the temperature and humidity of the Home so that everyone gets a little hot under the collar. The clouds of vapour given off by all this may be the mysterious *yonks* which so many people haven't seen each other for.

To take the inmates' mind off sex there is a playing field attached to the Home, and great efforts are made to ensure that it is a level one – though people are apparently always moving the goal-posts. Efforts to organise a piss-up in the local brewery have not yet been successful. The local vicar sometimes invites inmates to the original vicarage tea party. No one ever goes, though, because everything in the Home has been made to look like it already, even the steamiest sessions of distinction between male and female.

In the dining room residents were making a meal of it — and that was just for starters. Some of the dishes on the menu were out of this world. In fact they were to die for, and if they weren't to die for they were the kind of thing you'd kill to get your hands on. So, one way or another, by the end of meals a fair number of the residents tend to be out of this world as well. In other words, they'd had their chips, which was just as well, because when the chips are down there's no such thing as a free lunch. It's not a picnic here, after all — naturally enough, since some of the inhabitants are two sandwiches short of one. In the circumstances I was not surprised to be told that most of them were out to lunch.

The Home is organised along military lines. I talked to inmates who were proud to belong to the Gin and Tonic Brigade and the Blue Rinse Brigade. The Green Welly Brigade have a reputation for profligacy with the brigade colours — they are always giving things a bit of welly. I could hear the most alarming noises of protest in the background, but the Matron explained that this was coming from the 20th century, into which various things were being dragged kicking and screaming, entirely for their own benefit.

I asked why some residents were being made to stand in silence with their faces to the wall. The Matron said that they were members of the chattering classes — people who had had the temerity to talk about politics and other public matters that concerned them. She also pointed out a group of luvvies — actors and actresses who had ludicrously attempted to vary their slothful round of unemployment and awards ceremonies with some pretence at seriousness. They were being put down hard and sent up rotten.

In some of the rooms there was scarcely enough room to swing a cat — though this was impossible to check because, as the Matron explained, the cat was in hell, and it didn't have much chance of surviving. About as much as a snowball, she thought. Though, if the snowball managed to survive until hell froze over it would find itself in a whole new ballgame. They did have a handcart for going to hell in, said the Matron, if I wanted to go down that particular road, and she wished me the best of British. But before we could get the ball rolling all hell broke loose.

An inmate in bell-bottomed trousers staggered up and flung his money around. He was not, he explained, flinging his money around like a drunken sailor — he *was* the drunken sailor like whom everybody else flung their money around. Very difficult to know, in that case, I suggested, how he himself was flinging his money around. Was it, I asked, like money was going out of fashion? Not at all, he replied, it was like there was no tomorrow.

It was plainly crunch time, and the Matron cracked down hard, though she papered over the cracks as best she could. But no way could the crackdown be made to bite unless it was given teeth.

As I left I met a new arrival, still looking relatively fresh-faced. 'Political

Correctness,' he introduced himself. 'I feel I'm a bit past my sell-by date. And since the whole idea of a sell-by date has gone down the tubes itself some time ago, like the tubes it went down, I thought I'd join it in here, and we could all pop our clogs together.' Because that said, what's it all about, at the end of the day? What's the bottom line? Let me spell it out to you in words of one syllable – the bottom line is this. ●

Speak after the Beep, a collection of *Guardian* columns by Michael Frayn, is published by Methuen, £10.00.

5 December 1994
Peter Preston
Survivor's journal of a plague year

I have lived with it for 45 years and never written a word about it. After today, I hope and intend never to write about it again. My polio.

This fleeting break with silence comes because of a book – *A Summer Plague*, by Tony Gould (published by Yale University Press, £19.95). A book, and a launch party.

Dr Geoffrey Spencer, prime British expert on the treatment of poliomyelitis, tells us over white wine that we were victims of *the* great 20th-century disease. Aids is fledgling by comparison, really post-millennium stuff. But the publisher doesn't know whether that – the millions dead, the millions permanently disabled around the world – will mean many easy sales.

It *is* a terrific book; but we, like the survivors of VE Day, may be passing our sell-by date. We withered and perished in the 1940s and 1950s. Salk and Sabin, bringers of the miracle vaccine, drew a line under our experience. We aren't a growing threat. We aren't news. The last scythings of the glum reaper, a decade or three hence, will make us all history.

One summer day in 1949, in rural Leicestershire, my father had difficulty breathing and was rushed to the Royal Infirmary. Five days later, he was dead – and I was in an iron lung at Markfield Sanatorium, drifting back and forth across the edge of survival in a dreaming, fevered, but curiously peaceful way that, ever since, has made me feel a little less bad about dying itself.

I remember, when it was all over, waking up – as though from deep sleep – in a deserted hospital room. The sheets were tucked very tight. Overhead a fly buzzed around, then settled on my forehead. I tried to brush it away, then frighten it away. But my arms would not move. And my head would not be shaken.

The joy of Gould's research is that, almost for the first time, you realise you were not alone. He tells the scientific and political story: the epidemics which rocked America, Sister Kenny, Roosevelt, the March of the Dimes. But he sets it in a wider human context of remembrance.

David Widgery, the recently dead East End GP and saint of Socialist Workers, remembers 'the glorious era of physiotherapy, when there are all those beautiful buxom ladies with belts of different colours, like karate belts . . . sort of pushing and pulling'. And so do I, Miss Butters and Miss White. He remembers when 'we used to get issued with sweets and [because he was the only polio case on the ward] they used to throw the sweets at me – a sadistic sub-life on the children's ward'. I was the only polio on the ward, too, my plaster bed and encased arms protruding amidst a stretching line of TB hips. They didn't throw sweets, but they made me join in: so that, the sadistic sub-life night they raided teacher's cupboard and destroyed her hated musical instruments, I was asked to tear her tambourine to pieces with my teeth, the sole means of destruction I possessed. Sorry, Miss Bestwick.

A long road back. The feared excursions to the hot baths where, if you slipped, there seemed no way of not sinking into oblivion. The tottery challenge of walking again. The stairs you had to inch down on your bottom. The simple, natural struggle to become passably mobile.

Because (as I now see) there were common threads to this isolated experience, it all begins to make more sense. Infantile paralysis was a singular affliction. If you survived the first days of gasping for breath, if you stabilised, then there was a bedrock of debility to be built on. It wasn't progressive horror like MS. You could come back without remission. You were, literally, physically challenged. And, like so many in *A Summer Plague*, the wider challenge was to turn yourself into a different sort of personality, somebody who could forget what had been there before, and do the things you were able to do.

Such things, I now learn (courtesy of Dr Frederick Maynard and Sunny Roller of Ann Arbor, Michigan) are the normalities of abnormality. One may be a passer, a minimiser or an identifier: that is, to the naked eye, barely crocked, slightly crocked or totally crocked. And, sure enough, self-image is important. Are you still, as you were in the beginning, an obvious wreck? Or merely (as *Private Eye* once said) lopsided? Have you ceased, long since, to recall any better physical state than the one you have, which in longevity has become normality?

There is a sense – which Tony Gould pavilions in gentle regret – where the independence and isolation of the old polio sufferer is a bit of an affront. We're loners. Our battles are personal, inward-looking ones. We have disappeared (in our thousands) into the spread of the community so that we are neither a manifest problem, nor a reproach. Mrs Bottomley does not lie awake at night worrying about us. Perhaps it would be better if there were a problem. Some witnesses to the Summer Plague seem to hanker after 'post-polio syndrome', the possible mass infliction of lassitude and regression 30 or 40 years after the first event. If it exists, we can all be a Challenge to Society together and at last find the communality we skirted long ago.

But I rather hope, like Spencer, that there is no single syndrome – and that gradually country by country, continent by continent, the memory of poliomyelitis fades utterly. It was a bad deed in a fragile Western world of progress. It attacked and blighted children. But all the resource of America came back and defeated it. And now (even, retreating, in Asia) it is another name that today's children do not know.

Polio. Forgotten, like Winston Churchill. The Crippler. But also – on the testimony of Gould – the Tutor and the Challenger and the Invigorator. It's over; let it go. ●

....

10 May 1995

Matthew Norman
Diary

Cynics who have scoffed at his denial may have cause to apologise to Mr President. Reviewing a book about marijuana in the *Financial Times*, writer Christopher Hitchens slips in this little nugget: 'My Oxford contemporary William Jefferson Clinton (who never needed to inhale, by the way, because he baked his marijuana into cakes and cookies) . . .' Good Lord. After the usual mind games with International Directories ('The White House in Washington? Which country, please?'), a press officer snarls: 'If Hitchens is spinning some foolishness, we're not gonna comment.' But is it foolishness? Asked if she can recall him in an apron, weighing out the cookie mix, novelist and *Guardian* columnist Sara Maitland, an Oxford intimate of Clinton, is momentarily silent. 'No comment,' she says. Then she laughs enchantingly. ●

....

11 May 1995

After yesterday's report that President Clinton baked cannabis cookies while at Oxford (a culinary habit he may have found hard to break), the Diary has sought to give him the support he needs. Having consulted a counsellor on drug abuse from the charity Turning Point, I called the White House to relay the message. Anyone with a Touch Tone telephone can do this; just dial the White House, ask for the Press Office, press 1, then 2, and soon – certainly no more than 15 minutes after you began – a human voice will speak thus: 'The Presidential comments line. What do you wish to tell the President?' Remembering the counsellor's advice not to be too heavy-handed, the message went as follows: 'Mr President, we in Britain are concerned for you. I have spoken to a drug abuse expert on your behalf, and she says that, far from being safer than inhaling, eating it in cookies is hard to moderate and potentially more dangerous: after a bite you think you're fine, but by the end of the cookie you could well be out of your head. In the last 25 years, you may well have noticed one or more of these symptoms: loss of sex drive; lack of motivation; inability to hold down a responsible job. If so, please stop baking now. Your friends in Britain care about you, and wish you well. That's all.' 'Thank you sir,' said the voice. 'Your comments have been noted, and will be conveyed to the President. He sure will appreciate your concern.' Let us pray that he acts upon it. ●

31 May 1995

David McKie

Laying down the lore is a muggon's game

It's not often you see a superstition crumbling before your eyes, but it's happening now. Suddenly the streets are full of green cars. Once shunned by the average customer, they are now, according to the salesman who sold me mine, the most popular shade on the market – though his boss still won't even climb into one, which must make arranging test drives a bit of a problem. Perhaps buyers were never as wary as the trade assumed them to be; perhaps, imagining a level of superstition in the public which didn't really apply, the industry simply chose not to make them. I prefer to believe that one more irrational notion has been purged from the public consciousness – even if, in the way of these things, there will be another along in a moment.

Colours, like numbers and animals, have a particular potency for the superstitious. Green has always been rated unlucky, and possibly a presage of death. 'I never bought a green dress that I did not have to get a black one directly afterwards,' a woman in Shropshire was logged as confiding in 1883. 'If you wear green,' people said in Devon, 'you will soon after wear mourning.' As so often, the superstition attached with particular force to marriage. 'They that marry in green,' it was said in 18th-century Scotland, 'then sorrow is soon seen.' Green vegetables, especially kale, must not be served at weddings, it was taught in the north of England. The friendly colour was blue, which offered protection (see the book of Numbers, chapter 18, verse 35). The exception was the theatre, where blue, in common with almost everything else, was unlucky.

Theatres are temples of superstition. The destructive power of the Scottish play is well known, but it's not alone as a text that thespians fear. Never sing 'I Dwelt in Marble Halls' in a theatre. Don't even whistle it: whistling, from the stage to the green room, is dangerous practice. Don't take real flowers on stage, real jewellery, or even humble old knitting. A *Dictionary of Omens*, edited by Iona Opie and Mina Tatem, from which these illustrations are taken, quotes an actress, recorded in 1987: 'We went on tour with *Daddy Long Legs*, and it folded after six weeks. The older character-actress turned to me and said: "It's all your fault, you knitted at rehearsals."'

Yet superstitions do lapse. Does anyone now, for instance, believe that a barnacle broken off the side of a ship will turn into a goose? Or that hares change sex every year? Or that hummingbirds and lapwings can enter the mouth of a crocodile, without any risk to their safety, since it likes them to pick its teeth? Yet all were recorded by Brewer as once-potent superstitions, fallacies or delusions. Sometimes, apparent superstitions have at least the defence that they may have been based on long observation. That's the basis of country lore, some of which works. It is probably largely true that a red sky at night is a shepherd's delight and a red sky at morning a shepherd's warning – a contention advanced in St Matthew's Gospel (chapter 16, verse 2).

As for the rest, who knows? No doubt some aspiring Fish or McCaskill has examined the claim that rain on St Swithin's means rain for the next 40 days, but much of the country lore you hear in a rural pub has escaped academic scrutiny. There are simply not the resources to test the kind of proposition which asserts that 'if mugwort appears when the wind's in the north, it will snow and hail on September the fourth'. (I've made that one up, but it's no more inherently silly than some of what gets quoted.)

The same goes for cures recommended in old wives' tales. Some may work, since herbs may have therapeutic properties, as dock leaves do for nettle stings. Others sound rather more dubious. To get rid of warts, says Pliny, some lie in a footpath face upwards and fix their gaze on the moon, which must be at least 20 days old, rubbing the wart with anything handy. Not any more they don't. 'If a person suffering from whooping-cough asks advice of a man riding on a piebald horse, the malady will be cured by doing what the man tells him to do.' Even if it's 'naff off'?

It's just as much a mystery where some of these notions come from. We know why the number 13 is unlucky: because there were 13, one of whom was Judas Iscariot, at the Last Supper. (One version of this superstition is that the first to sit down when it's 13 at table is likely to suffer, another says it's the last.) When Charles Stewart Parnell arrived at Westminster he was allotted a room with the number 13. 'They are Tories, I suppose,' he said, 'and have done it on purpose.'

But the roots of others are simply untraceable. Like the Scottish superstition which tells of a funeral procession carrying a girl who had died prematurely down the banks of the Firth of Clyde. It was interrupted by a mermaid, leaping out of the water to utter the solemn warning: 'If they wad drink nettles in March and eat muggons in May, sae mony braw maidens wadna gang to the clay.' A bit late for this year, I'm afraid, since tomorrow's the first of June. ●

20 May 1995

Oscar Moore
The discreet charm of the pearl eye-patch

Accentuate the positive, accessorise the negative: this is my new spring season slogan. Having stumbled (those bloody platforms) out of Robert Altman's fashion extravorganza *Prat at the Party*, I feel it is my duty to strike a pose-tive profile and wear my accoutrements with pride . . . and there are several of them. On a daily basis my pockets have to accommodate two large plastic bottles, each containing a balloon full of medication that gradually deflates and pushes either foscarnet or ganciclovir up a tube, through a needle and into my Hickman line.

So far so efficient: except that the tube from the Intermate device (developed by Nasa for astronaut food, so don't tell me I'm not high-tech, cutting edge or space age) tangles with the wires of my Walkman, and the bottle gives my pocket a swollen bulge which I might use to effect if I had any libido left to exploit. But best of all is the Hickman line itself, which can bring Class 4B's swimming lesson at the Caledonian Road municipal baths to a changing room standstill.

Kids! Don'tcha love 'em? Don'tcha admire their natural curiosity and willingness to question? At Cally Pools, nobody batted an eyelid at the tube swinging from above my right nipple cluster . . . or at least not until after 2pm every Wednesday, when Class 4B invades the changing rooms.

'What's that?' said curious, energetic and unapologetic kid 1, pointing at the tube. (It is about10 inches long and does lead even me to wonder if I have become an android and this is my power supply outlet.) Being a sensibly brought-up and well-educated liberal, I dispensed with obfuscation (mind your own business) or euphemism (I am a robot and this is where I plug my battery pack) and went for the truth. After a sober but gentle explanation of my eye disease and the need to administer regular intravenous drugs, the boy looked thoughtful. For about 10 seconds. Then he shrieked at his classmates: 'Look at this bloke. He's got a tube for his eyes going into . . .'

With respect to Our Lord, I might paraphrase his wisdom: suffer the little children to stay in the schools-only changing room and not to come unto me until I have my shirt on.

But really, I'm not complaining about my new range of pumps, tubes, needles and valves. I have always had a penchant for paraphernalia. I just feel that the time is ripe for an entrepreneur with a sense of style to create a set of holsters, side-packs, front-loading flak jackets, syringe holders, stainless steel needle packs and matt black aluminium Thermoses for the litre and a half of mineral water I have to drink each day to stop the foscarnet polluting my kidneys.

Notwithstanding my bashfulness in the face of the Bash Street Kids of Cally Pools, I know some will say I am simply seeking attention. And others will say I always have done. There are probably still schoolfriends who remember my sudden sartorial blossoming with the arrival of punk rock in 1976 (well, 1977 really, but it's my history, I'll lie if I want to). I was not really a punk. I had no pierced body parts, hated cider and went to a 'posh' school. And, to be honest, I found the music a little noisy. But punk gave me the perfect cover-up (or Cover-Stick) for a fashion paroxysm that mingles drag, kabuki, glam-rock and too much neat gin. There is nothing quite like the buzz of stepping into a crowded carriage on a Saturday-night tube and bringing every conversation to a halt.

I have sobered up since those days. My wardrobe is discreet. My hair is untinted. My eyes clean, if blurred. I am not seeking attention but I am getting it. And suddenly, as a return of energy has brought with it a resurgence of confidence, I don't see why I shouldn't enjoy it.

It started with the eye-patch. This is not an affectation. The oedema in my right eye shrinks, implodes and telescopes the world, warping people, buildings and cars into the crazed reflections of a fairground mirror. Imploding heads may be amusing, but reading is hard work as my right eye superimposes a small and floating version of the newsprint page on top of the real-size one my left eye is quite happily reading. Given that my right retina has been so decimated by cmv that it delivers little more than a sense of perspective (the ability to reach for the salt and pepper without knocking over the flower display), I close it down with a black patch on tube and bus journeys and during solidarity lunches.

But necessity is the mother of pretension, and, while I travel London's transports in a discreet matt black patch with scarcely visible satin polka dots, I do have a party range, courtesy of designer-decorator-domestic artist Shaun Clarkson. Shaun has bequeathed me part of a dismantled optician's display: a white pearl swirl and a green and pink sequin spin with beaded tears. For more practical business and daywear (as part of his prêt-à-porter range) he is working on a Prince Edward check.

However, frivolity and facetiousness are close cousins and already I have had my new exuberance abused. Coming out to the opening of the London Gay and Lesbian Film Festival, I decided to don the pearl swirl. Unfortunately, my sartorial daring left me uneasy and off-balance. I had gone from victim chic to fashion victim and, moving through a cocktail crowd clutching a beer with a blind-side and no sense of perspective, I felt off-balance and off-colour.

Eye-patches – probably like toupees – are hot and cumbersome, but once you've started it's hard to stop without exposing yourself . . . to ridicule, that is. I only sneaked mine off once the film started rolling, and after it had finished I fled under cover of darkness to find a taxi. But I was not going to get away so lightly. Out of the invisible space on my right side lurched the definitive trainspotter: unkempt frizz, unbuttoned duffle, and overstuffed bag.

'You were wearing an eye-patch and now you're not,' he said in a revenge-of-the-nerd *cri de coeur*. 'What's the point?'

I don't know what I should have done. I know what I did. I stuttered something about partial vision and eye disease and finished with a limp 'And I really needed that', which attempted to reverse the sympathy of gathering bystanders back in my direction. Then I plunged clumsily into a door that wouldn't open, turning my victory for pathos into a failure for farce.

I haven't worn the pearls or the sequins since. I've just got to get my nerve back. Attention seeking is not for the lily-livered. Now there's an idea for a motif. ●

13 March 1995
Maggie O'Kane
Crash course tests Sarajevo sprinter

I t wasn't a serious crash. Denis, my driving instructor, took it well: he said it was the first time in 22 years that one of his pupils had crashed on the way to a driving test.

When I was 18, my father tried to teach me to drive. We had a Fiat 127 that had to be push-started by the five young O'Kanes between September and March. But after he made me cry twice for crunching the gears, we gave up. For almost the next 15 years, not having a licence was not a problem.

In 1989, as a freelance foreign correspondent, driving cars was not part of the package. Hire cars were what people from the big papers used, paid for with corporate American Express cards. They were the key to survival, and I was grateful for the lift. My job was to change the tapes, light the cigarettes and look unthreatening at hostile checkpoints.

In Dubrovnik in 1991 there were lots of abandoned cars as people fled on the ferries. The trick there was always to drive without lights, keeping the engine off going downhill in case the snipers heard. That was easy. Handbrake off, into neutral and away. No fiddly bits at the traffic lights; no worries about clutching on the corner.

When the *Guardian* gave me a job, I didn't say anything when the foreign editor announced we were going to get a bullet-proof car of our own for Sarajevo. Everybody had them, but ours was a lovely purple Peugeot with a tape deck that once belonged to a French cabinet minister. What was a girl to do? It was easy in Sarajevo. No one except journalists and the UN had petrol, so you could whiz up and down Sniper Alley in fourth gear knowing there was three inches of French glass between you and some bored Serbian sniper. I remember one bullet pinging off the frame of the driver's window and thinking: 'Jesus, it works.'

Outside Sarajevo it got more complicated. There were no trenches, no road signs announcing: 'You are about to cross the front line – take the next exit.'

In the three days before my test last Thursday, Denis fitted in 10 lessons. Sometimes the concentration lapsed and he explained calmly at a roundabout near Camden that I should be driving on the left-hand side of the road. He even got up at six on the morning of the test to teach me reverse-parking.

Denis's gentleness rubbed off on the examiner. When I crunched into the kerb on the reverse-parking, he said gently: 'Why don't you straighten her up?'

The worst part, though, was the Highway Code. Already deflated by the pavement crunch, I watched in horror as the examiner took out a pack of road signs and began flipping through them. The end, I knew, had come.

'No,' he said, showing me the sign for the end of a dual carriageway, that did not mean a fork in the road.

'Fog,' he said. 'What precautions have to be taken when driving in fog?' I said you have to drive 'really carefully following the car in front'. Would I follow the car in front into a ditch?

'No,' he said. 'The righthand lane of a motorway is not just for people who want to drive really fast.'

I thought about mentioning Sarajevo and the simple life without traffic lights, but I knew it was over for me.

Then he said he would give me the benefit of the doubt. I think he just felt sorry for me because I was 32½ and still didn't have a driving licence.

I thought briefly about kissing him as he wrote out the pink and green form that said I had passed – but he looked too stern and I wanted to save myself for Denis. ●

. . . .

27 December 1994

Derek Malcolm
The war hero, his wife and her lover

I found the book in a drawer of my father's bureau. It was called *The Judges and the Judged*, and subtitled 'An enthralling anthology of drama, scandal and sensation in court'. It was not the sort of tome he generally read and, browsing through the chapter headings on the contents page I read: Mr Justice McCardie tries Lieutenant Malcolm, page 33.

Not forgetting . . .

But there was no page 33. The chapter had been torn out of the book, which had been withdrawn from the local library the previous week. It didn't take me long to guess that Lt Malcolm was my father.

Without saying anything to him, I went out and bought the book, by the criminologist, Edgar Lustgarten. The foreword said: 'Covering a whole gamut of human drama and inhuman crime, Mr Lustgarten recreates, with his own unrivalled combination of forensic knowledge and literary skill, the impress of judicial personality, the cut-and-thrust of great advocacy, the revelation of minds and motives – all the elements that can hold the courtroom in a spell as binding as that of any theatre.'

It was in that luxuriant style that the chapter on my father was written. It began: 'Everybody wanted the prisoner to get off. The privileged and breathless company in court, gripping their precious seats from a subconscious fear of losing them; the unlucky and disappointed throng outside, unable to tear themselves away from the fortress they had failed to storm; the unseen multitude across the length and breadth of Britain devouring each edition of the papers, and then waiting in mingled hope and apprehension for the next – one and all devoutly wished Lieutenant Malcolm to go free. Even that granite prosecutor Richard Muir, whose thankless task it was to present this murder charge, momentarily disclosed the trend of his own feelings when he warned the jury: "Beware of sympathy."

'For what exactly had he done, this stalwart fighting soldier, to be snatched from the peril of death in the Flanders trenches and placed under the selfsame peril in the Old Bailey dock?'

I could hardly bear to read on. But by the time I came to the end of the chapter, I knew why my father had torn it out of the library book in case anyone should read it and identify him. Even some 45 years later, he couldn't bear to recall the case. He was an old man, trapped by the sudden revelation of an extraordinary past and unable to tell even his only son.

He had married my mother shortly before the war. He was the son of a rich Scots landowner who gave him a hefty sum at the age of 21 and told him either to go to university or travel the world. He chose instead to play rugby, go hunting and live the high life in London. There he met my mother, a beautiful society girl, the daughter of a Conservative MP who sang so well that Toscanini, on a visit to London, implored her to train for opera.

Instead she married Douglas Malcolm, a totally unsuitable match for both of them, since he cared little for things artistic and she dragged him off to concerts, the opera and plays. On one notorious occasion, he was so bored at a recital by the great French pianist Alfred Cortot that he shouted out during a particularly slow Debussy Prelude: 'Oh, get on with it, man' and had to be led by my mother from the hall.

He did, however, manage to teach her to ride sidesaddle to hounds, where once the Duke of Windsor apparently remarked: 'That's a very pretty horse, and a damned pretty rider sliding off it too.'

'Damned man,' my father was heard to observe, 'he can't ride for toffee himself. Go on, Dottie darling, jump the fence he funked.'

The two, married in some state, were soon to be separated. My father had volunteered for the trenches in August 1914 although his recent marriage had exempted him from conscription. In July three years later he won the Military Cross for gallantry ('I was only trying to save the horses,' he told me), was given a spell of leave and left for his home in London.

My mother wasn't there. She was staying with a friend named Mrs Brett somewhere in the Hampshire countryside. Hurrying there, he found Mrs Brett in the sitting room, much disconcerted by his presence. Without her permission, he went upstairs and found my mother and a man in the bedroom. Neither was fully clothed. The man said he was Count de Borch and, after a fight, let my mother go. She said he had kidnapped her, and my father, an innocent in these matters and very much in love, believed her. He wrote challenging De Borch to a duel – 'Pistols or swords, you can take your choice.' There was understandably no reply from De Borch.

But, once again on duty in France, my father did receive a letter from my mother. It said she was hopelessly in love with De Borch and wanted a divorce. Given a further spell of leave, he returned to London but could find neither De Borch nor my mother. So he went to Scotland Yard, who told him that Count de Borch was actually named Baumberg, was involved in prostitution and possibly spying too. My father's continued search eventually led to a Bayswater boarding house, where he entered carrying a riding crop, his Army pistol and a letter to my mother. It read: 'My dear, very own, darling Dorothy – I simply cannot stand it any longer. I'm going to thrash him until he is unrecognisable. I may shoot him if he's got a gun. I expect he has, as he's too much of a coward to stand a thrashing. If the inevitable has to got happen, I may get it in the neck first. I know I shall meet you in the next world.'

When he found Baumberg, who was alone, the tenant of the adjoining room heard a struggle and then a series of shots. My father immediately gave himself up to the police. Baumberg was dead.

He pleaded self-defence at the Old Bailey and hired Lord Simon, one of the most famous advocates of the day, to defend him. The contention was that 'the struggle in that little room became a matter of Baumberg's life or of his own.'

Baumberg did have a gun, which he had bought after the struggle at the cottage, telling Mrs Brett that if my father laid another finger on him he would use it. The gun was in an open drawer in Baumberg's Bayswater room. But it was still inside its leather case. Judge McCardie asked whether it could possibly have been fired without being taken from its case. The answer from the crown ballistics expert was that it could have been fired if the case was open so that the muzzle was exposed. If Baumberg had been trying to reach it, the case against my father might not be proven.

Unfortunately, Lt Malcolm refused to testify, though implored to do so by Lord Simon. And in his summing up Judge McCardie said: 'This man stands indicted with the gravest charge and offers not one word of testimony. He invites you to guess things he could have proved on the oath of a gentleman. The result is that there is no evidence from him that the dead man tried to get the pistol, that he ever threatened to use it, that the pistol was even in the room. The whole thing is simply left to conjecture.'

It was a summing up that tacitly asked for a guilty verdict. And everyone, including my father, expected it. But the jury retired for only 25 minutes before returning to pronounce him not guilty.

The papers said Lt Malcolm stepped from the dock amid resounding cheers, and was carried shoulder high down the steps of the building by a huge crowd. To them he was a war hero who had only done what many others might have been constrained to do under the circumstances. It was, said a leader, the first case of a *crime passionnel* treated in the British courts with an acquittal as it would have been in France.

Years after I had discovered the Lustgarten book, my father called me into his room one evening and, not knowing I had read it, and also having persuaded Lord Simon not to include the case in his memoirs, told me the story himself. 'You may not like what you're going to hear,' he said, 'and it's very difficult for me to tell you because I know you'll think very badly of me. But I once killed a man who was having an affair with your mother. I said it was in self-defence. But it wasn't. I meant to give him a good thrashing. I shot him instead. But please don't tell your mother I told you. She doesn't want you to know.'

All I could muster in reply was: 'Yes, I knew some time ago. But don't worry. If I'd had a gun, I'd have probably done it too. I think the same of you as I always did. There's no need to worry any more.'

He was a much relieved old man. But I harboured a grudge against Lustgarten, who, in one of his earlier books, had stated that he always gave false names to those whose cases he wrote about if he had ascertained they were still alive. In the case of my father and mother, he had made no contact at all.

Eventually I got my revenge. I was a reporter on a provincial paper when Lustgarten came to the town to deliver a lecture. It was called 'Famous Cases and the Criminal Mind', and I immediately offered to cover the talk. I sat in the front row and, thankfully, he didn't mention my father's case. But when it came to question time I put my hand up and said: 'Some of the people in these cases must be still alive today. Would you consider giving them different names in case they wanted to remain anonymous?'

'Yes,' said Lustgarten, in the same purple prose with which the book was written, 'I consider myself honour-bound to discover if any of these people are still living and, if they are, I do not write about their cases at all.'

'That's funny,' I said. 'Lieutenant Malcolm is still alive, but you made no contact with him before writing about the case in *The Judges and the Judged*. You made him pretty miserable. I know because I'm his son.'

There was a deadly silence in the room and poor old Lustgarten went very white and started to stammer. He said a mistake had been made and it would never happen again. There were no further questions put, and the meeting ended with some embarrassment on all sides except mine.

I didn't tell my father of the incident, and I didn't write it up in the local paper. But I did feel rather pleased to bite the biter just the same.

My father and mother never divorced, nor did they live separate lives. In truth, they lived together unhappily ever after, the mismatch of the century. My mother died before my father and I remember that he went into her bedroom, bent over her body and kissed her gently on the cheek: 'Well, Dorrie dear,' he said as he did so, 'we've been through a lot together. But it's all over now. Oh dear, oh dear . . .' ●

* * *

30 June 1995

Bel Littlejohn

Get real, guys – don't take this story for Granted

God knows, I love this paper, but why, I wanna know, did we offer such pitifully meagre coverage of the recent liaison between Hugh Grant and the LA prostitute?

The Grant Affair seems to me a matter of considerable and undeniable national and international significance, relating to such diverse topics as British/American trade sanctions, relations between the sexes in the mid-1990s, the nature of celebrity in the lead-up to the millennium, the English public-school attitude to women, the future of Hong Kong, the place of Britain in Europe and the soul of the Tory Party.

Yet the *Guardian*, in its high-minded way, has barely bothered to mention it. Yesterday, Grant received just a bit of coverage right at the bottom of the front page ('Disgraced Grant lies low'), a passing nod from Henry Porter in this space (facetiously titled 'Gee, if you wanna talk about it, Hugh'), another from Suzanne Moore in her characteristically brave and outspoken column ('in the great scheme of things I cannot see that he has actually done anything so terrible'), a police mugshot on the cover of G2, a cursory two-page piece by Ian Katz ('Hugh and cry'), a thoughtful but brief overview by Derek Malcolm ('it doesn't, in my opinion, confirm him as anything more than hopelessly naive and innocent'), a tiny advice column by Max Clifford ('in terms of public-relations opportunities, this is wonderful'), just a couple of quotes from Jilly Cooper ('the poor boy') and Cynthia Payne ('I feel a little cynical'), a passing political analogy in Simon Hoggart's sketch, a mere two letters to the editor ('Blue Hugh'), no more than a single item in Matthew Norman's diary and a passing reference ('Hugh Grant is not the only one who has betrayed his true love') in Niall Ferguson's right-wing overview of John Redwood. And no mention whatsoever of the incident in either the business or the sport sections. By my reckoning, that's barely more than a dozen items dealing at any length with the entire Hugh Grant case in a complete issue of the *Guardian*.

Why the almighty cover-up? Personally, I blame it on a failure of the British male intellectual class to recognise the broader, one-to-one human and emotional value-systems that are so often crushed by the narrow framework of events they deign to designate 'news'. But anything more personal, anything about the very real and very human dilemma of the individual set against the hand of providence, a providence at once tragic yet transforming – such as the Hugh Grant case – is to be strenuously avoided.

Do I make myself clear? In my years in voluntary exile from the *Guardian* (1986–95), I was employed by a wide variety of rival newspapers to force this new, essentially human angle upon their increasingly moribund world-view. My transformation of these newspapers was certainly evident in their coverage of the Grant Affair on Wednesday and Thursday. For instance, *The Times* (which I successfully revamped in '86) yesterday included a Hugh Grant Special Supplement, in which leading political experts such as Peter Riddell and William Rees-Mogg examined the impact of the arrest of Hugh Grant on Labour economic policy. 'It is, I think, fast becoming inevitable,' wrote Rees-Mogg, 'that Mr Gordon Brown will find himself addressing what might best be described as the Fellatio Option, whereby he must get into the same vehicle as a suitable stranger, and abandon himself to whatsoever might occur. I have long considered life to be a forgotten boulevard on some Los Angeles freeway, brightly lit in its reverential darkness, standing for what it stands for yet never entirely revealing its secrets, populated by buxom negresses, resplendent in high-heels and "hot pants".'

The *Daily Telegraph*, too, has obviously benefited from my spell as Special Adviser (1987–8). I was delighted to see that the *Telegraph* has hired the young lady in question, Ms Divine Brown, 23, as its Religious Affairs Correspondent, with her own column every Thursday. Their veteran reporter Bill Deedes placed special emphasis on the Grant Affair in yesterday's paper. 'Am I just being old-fashioned, or did it not use to be the case that one could expect a fair bit of change from a $100 note for oral sex with a known prostitute? Some things, I fear, have not changed for the better.' And, elsewhere in the *Telegraph*, in an exclusive interview with John Redwood, their veteran commentator Simon Heffer goes through the political niceties one by one ('Do you feel that capital punishment should be visited on everyone, or should it be restricted to known offenders?') before tackling the central issues: 'How much damage, in your view, has this latest incident inflicted upon Hugh Grant's career?' 'As an intellectual on the Eurosceptic wing of the party, how do you you imagine Liz Hurley is feeling?'

These were all imaginative, *empathetic* ways of dealing with a very important news event. Last week, I wrote about the crying need in contemporary journalism for far more soul-baring, truth-telling articles by leading column-ists such as myself. We must – my God, we must – break out of the patriarchal strait-jacket of facts, facts, facts. I am now embarking on an intensely personal tie-in piece on 'My Shame? The Day I Caught My Ex-Husband with a Prostitute'. Watch this space. ●

Sporting life

....

15 March 1995

David Lacey

Dawn swoops cast the game into darkness

English football faces its biggest scandal for more than 30 years. After a winter of sleaze it has now arrived at the brink of a cesspit of corruption. If the air had already turned sour it now stinks to high heaven.

Yesterday morning police investigating allegations of match-fixing arrested two Premiership goalkeepers, the girl-friend of a prominent Premiership player, and a London-based Malaysian businessman.

Finally they arrested the third player, John Fashanu, the Aston Villa and former Wimbledon centre-forward, a TV presenter and Unicef representative, a charming and articulate opponent, for those who have not encountered his elbows.

Four months after newspaper allegations of match-rigging arrived on football's doormat the dawn swoops on Southampton's Bruce Grobbelaar and Wimbledon's Hans Segers, followed by the apprehension of Fashanu, have taken football a significant step along the way to the sort of crisis it thought belonged to the murkier periods of its past.

The all-too-familiar caveat of everybody being innocent until proved guilty is hardly necessary. English football has been hearing little else of late. But all that has happened in the game this season pales beside even the thought of matches being bent by Far East betting syndicates. The Football Association is correct in leaving to the clubs decisions on whether those concerned continue to play. The FA cannot suspend players who have not been found guilty of breaking its rules. In the case of the injured Fashanu the point is academic.

Yet Lancaster Gate's reaction to yesterday's arrests still smacked of a rudderless body being borne along by events, and bore an uneasy resemblance to what was said in 1963 after three players had been found guilty of trying to fix a Third Division game.

'These are isolated cases,' said the FA then. 'The amount of bribery in existence is negligible compared with the great mass of football being played, which is free from any taint of corruption.' Yet another 10 players were eventually jailed for match-rigging and banned from football for life.

The game's public image has already been besmirched by the Premier League's on-going investigation into transfer deals and managers' bungs, and revelations of drug-taking by some players while others have been guilty of unseemly, unsociable behaviour. But it could live with all of this.

Until yesterday the worst news, as opposed to mere allegations, concerned events off the field. Even Eric Cantona left the arena to kung-fu kick his way into footballing history.

Match-fixing, however, is something else. It can destroy the game's soul. Nobody with any feeling for football wanted to believe Grobbelaar's guilt when the story first broke, not even after he had been charged by the FA with bringing the game into disrepute and accepting a consideration to influence the results of matches. It all seemed so unlikely, so out of character – and still does.

When news of Segers's arrest broke yesterday the mind's eye recalled the goal which last season kept Everton in the Premier League, and sent Sheffield United down, when Wimbledon lost 3–2 at Goodison Park after taking a 2–0 lead.

This may have been a simple error by Segers but, once a seed of doubt has been sown, suspicion, in retrospect, becomes rife and the game grows paranoid. So, to all appearances, did Fashanu the day after Grobbelaar was charged by the FA. Fashanu claimed that attempts were being made to stitch him up by linking him with the Grobbelaar allegations.

Recipients of Fashanu's largesse will be horrorstruck. Players such as Tottenham's Gary Mabbutt, whose face was shattered by a Fashanu elbow, and John O'Neill, whose playing career at Norwich was ended by a Fashanu tackle, may find it harder to shed a tear.

The irony is that Fashanu's own season has been ended by ligament damage suffered in a challenge on Manchester United's Ryan Giggs. This could turn out to be the least of his worries now.

Football's biggest fear must be that any new match-fixing scandal will drag on at a time, with the European Championship looming in 1996, when the English game is poised to present a bright, prosperous image to the world at large.

At the moment, however, it is threatened with being dragged into its muddiest hole yet by the game's lasting infatuation with the fast buck. Yet again football is in danger of standing the old saw on its head: where there's money, there's muck. And at the moment, in its higher echelons, there is more money sloshing around than ever before. ●

18 April 1995

David Ward

United's offside trap thwarts game of sardines

'When seagulls follow the trawler, it is because they think sardines will be thrown into the sea.' Eric Cantona, 31 March 1995

The seagulls swarmed around the Cliff yesterday in search of a crumb or two but were soon knocked off their perches by a professional scarer.

All they wanted was a glimpse of the great footballing sardine as he began his 120 hours of community service for kung-fuing a Crystal Palace supporter.

But Eric Cantona was playing hard to get, although he was briefly seen through a telephoto lens, clutching a bunch of bananas. The philosophical striker, whose gnomic quote has now been deconstructed by hacks as derogatory of their trade, turned up early at the Cliff, Manchester United's training ground in Salford.

The big brown gates closed firmly behind him as he prepared to teach 12 shamrock-shirted boys from Ellesmere Park Junior Football Club in Eccles the finer points of dribbling and scowling.

The photographers leant their ladders against the wall and peered over the top. They were shooed away from club property by a security official named Ned Kelly, wearing not a tin suit and bucket on his head but a Manchester United blazer and tie. The seagulls fluttered round the corner and settled on public land.

A Gallic type nestled on a branch beneath a bird box and talked to his mobile phone in French. Enterprising British specimens commandeered wheelie bins and hopped on top.

The reporter from *L'Equipe*, the French sports newspaper, rented a ladder for £30 from a local decorator.

Back at the big gates, Manchester United's manager, Alex Ferguson, came out, a man with a set of X-rays went in, and Marie Hassell, aged 13, loitered. She was decidedly miffed, despite having met the repentant offender. 'Eric signed my book, used my pen to sign everyone else's and then walked off with it,' she pouted. 'I prefer Ryan Giggs anyway.'

After two hours, the lads from Ellesmere Park emerged to tell of Cantona's latest humiliation: in the final six-a-side game, he had played for the Whites against the Reds, and saw his side go down 13–8. He seemed unable to halt the progress of diminutive Reds' star Jamie McDougall, aged nine, who scored five.

Paul Thompson, aged 12, tried to bypass linguistic problems by chatting in French. '*Je m'appelle Paul*,' he said. '*Ça va*,' said Eric. 'I'm going to use the skills he taught us,' added Paul (in English). 'He's my second best. I'm a Liverpool supporter.'

And to crown the day's coaching, Cantona told young Manchester United fans he had no plans to switch clubs. Liz Calderbank, of Greater Manchester probation service, pronounced herself satisfied with Mr Cantona's labours. 'The work is demanding in terms of time and restriction of liberty. It is not a soft option.'

Ellesmere Park's coach, Les Harris, was excited and delighted. 'I'd rather see these boys kick a ball than each other. He has taught them the tricks of the trade.'

Which tricks? Simon Croft, aged thirteen, ventured on to dangerous ground where even seagulls fear to tread. At the end of the session, he asked for advice about aggro on the pitch. 'Eric said: "If you think you're going to get a yellow card, don't argue with the referee. Walk away."'

Cantona now has more than 100 hours to consider his own advice. ●

24 May 1995
Richard Williams
The last roar of the Lion

The point about Nigel Mansell – and this was why you loved him or, just as probably, loathed him – was that he didn't fit. He was big and burly in a world of jockey-sized heroes, and the difference went deeper than the ultimately vexed question of double-D seat fittings.

Where Ayrton Senna and Alain Prost were rapiers, Mansell was a broadsword. And, in the end, just too damn cumbersome.

You could see it in the paddock, when he made his entrance at the start of a grand prix meeting. Most drivers are like Frank Sinatra, who developed the gift of being able to arrive on stage without being noticed: one moment he wasn't there, and the audience got on with their chatter; then, when they looked up, there he was, prowling about among the second violins. In racing drivers, the same gift allows them politely to avoid the autograph hunters and the snapshot takers who swarm around them without cease.

Stars like Michael Schumacher or Damon Hill can make it from the helicopter pad to the team motor-home without turning a head. Mansell couldn't do that, nor, perhaps, did he want to.

At Imola, in Italy, a few weeks ago, for what will probably turn out to be the penultimate race of his career, he arrived at the circuit late on the Thursday, the night before the first practice session. Intending to examine the new car that had been built to accommodate his oversized frame, he strode from the paddock gates to the pits, a distance of about 100 yards. At that time of day, the place was practically deserted. No anoraks. Just a few mechanics, to whom the arrival of a driver – any driver, even a former world champion – is an event long since purged of romance or excitement. But Mansell tore across the vacant tarmac as though he were the England front row trying to shake off the entire All Black pack: head thrust forward on its bull neck, face hardened, shoulders hunched.

He drove that way, too, which is why he won 31 of the 187 Formula One grands prix he entered, and – perhaps puzzlingly to outsiders – why he will not be among the starters in Monaco this weekend.

Mansell was a physical driver in a cerebral age. In the days when drivers went to work in strong-backed gloves, polo shirts and fibre helmets from Herbert Johnson of Bond Street, there was room for a chap to do his work, elbows flailing in the breeze as he sawed away at a giant wood-rimmed steering wheel. But by the time Mansell got into Formula One, there was barely room to breathe. A mechanic had to do up your safety belts, and you had to unclip the steering wheel if you wanted to get out. The actual driving was all in the wrists – or, when little switches under the steering wheel took over from the old-fashioned gear lever and when the clutch pedal disappeared altogether, in the fingertips.

That was when Mansell came unstuck. At its best, his driving had been a splendid demonstration of courage and brute force. Whereas Alain Prost, nicknamed the Professor, aimed to drive fast with the least possible fuss and bother, overtaking people only when he had to, Mansell regarded the whole thing as a sort of modern cavalry charge. He would slam his way into a corner, braking as late as possible and turning in at the last moment – a rough-and-ready technique that wasn't always the fastest way of getting round the circuit but was perfect for the sort of hand-to-hand fighting that crowds love.

And did they love Mansell. After Brands Hatch in 1985, when he crudely held off an attack by Nelson Piquet, his teammate, to win the grand prix, a certain kind of motor-racing fan loved him immoderately. With disdain in their voices, the paddock exquisites said that Mansell had brought football hooligans to the race tracks. There was some truth in that, in the sense that at Silverstone in subsequent years a Mansell defeat always carried the threat of a track invasion. But then Italian fans at Monza, supposedly far more sophisticated than Mansell's blue-collar army, had been doing that sort of thing for decades. And when Mansell went to America, in 1993, the crowd for the British Grand Prix was cut by perhaps two thirds.

So was the entertainment value. Reviled and despised as he was in the press room, and greatly though his gift for blaming all misadventures on his car irritated the hard-working and often brilliant engineers who provided his equipment, Mansell was a vital ingredient of Formula One during the years in which it captured a worldwide television audience measured in billions.

Senna versus Prost was a battle played in the mind: brilliance and ruthlessness pitted against brilliance and calculation. It ended with one dead and the other driven into retirement. Throw Mansell into the mix and you had the contrasting element: raw guts. His finest hour came during the Spanish Grand Prix at Barcelona in 1991, when he sat it out with Senna down the long straight, wheel to wheel at 180mph for what seemed like minutes, until the Brazilian, for the first and only time in his life, looked across and backed off, giving Mansell the race. If you wanted a single moment to justify his status, that was it.

The proof of his appeal to ordinary fans came in the readiness with which he was taken to Italian hearts during his two years with Ferrari. 'He's a bulldog,' the American driver Eddie Cheever once told me, but to the Italians he was forever *Il Leone*.

Always unlikely on paper, his relationship with the team ended in tears, thanks to the superior political skills of Prost, who joined the team and demonstrated the cunning of a Papal *consigliere* of the 16th century. But the fans have never forgotten the efforts Mansell made on behalf of their beloved team. They like to be able to see that a car is going fast and that the driver is doing something dangerous, and Mansell's ability to flirt with the limits of control gave expression to their desires. Opposite Mansell's pit at Imola a few weeks ago, a banner flew: '*Leone – Ruggisci Ancora Per Noi*,' it read. Lion, roar for us again.

His critics often accused him of showboating, of exaggerating the gestures of aggression during a race. But wasn't that half the fun? And didn't it put more on the gate than Prost's cold-blooded precision?

When his political maladroitness forced him to cross the Atlantic in 1993 to race Indy cars rather than defend his freshly minted Formula One championship, Mansell's presence reawakened a moribund series. 'Mansell Loathed by Many, Adored by Many More,' ran the banner headline in the *Indianapolis Star*. He never won the big one, the Indy 500, but he did win the overall championship, and the two titles back to back form an achievement that may never be equalled.

When a bad car discouraged him from completing his second season in America, he made what now seems an ill-advised attempt to reconquer Formula One. Times had changed and the cars no longer responded to his bullying style. Which, it could be argued, is the sport's loss as much as Mansell's, although there will be little mourning in the paddock by the harbour front under the Grimaldis' palace this weekend.

Socially, the Mansells never matched the Formula One stereotype. But Rosanne Mansell, entering the paddock a stride and a half behind her husband, provided another reason for cherishing the difference. Most drivers' molls conform as precisely to the regulations as a grid-full of Formula One cars. Take David Coulthard's girlfriend, the Canadian model Andrea Murray, who positions herself carefully in the pits throughout a meeting, never failing to greet or send off her man with a lingering and highly photogenic kiss. Georgie Hill, Damon's strong-willed wife, is an exception. But far more so was Rosanne Mansell, now 41, a mother of three who proved her loyalty when, as a newly-wed in the mid-1970s, she helped him scrape together the £15 for an introductory racing course at Mallory Park.

When they met, at Solihull Tehcnical College, he was a 17-year-old engineering student and she, a year younger, was studying home economics. Later he worked at Lucas as an electronics instructor while she gave evening demonstrations for West Midlands Gas. The aura of unpretentiousness stayed with them even 20 years later, when there were millions in the bank, they were living in a mansion on a Florida lakefront and her golf-mad husband was negotiating to buy an 18-hole course of his own.

Through it all, Rosanne appeared to remain the same woman who had put up with freezing dawns at Snetterton and Castle Combe, and had willingly agreed to sell their first home to pay for a crucial unsponsored season in Formula Three. They got £6,000 for the flat and spent £8,000. Mansell made up some of the difference by doing a spot of window-cleaning, while Rosanne made her own clothes and tried to improve the decor of the rented slum into which they'd moved. By the end of that season, they had run out of everything: money, patience, hope. Which was when, as legend has it, their luck started to change.

Now the luck has run out, too. But Mansell doesn't need it any more. His career as a top-line racing driver is over and he can content himself with developing his interests in golf and property. It's a pity that he didn't call a halt last November in Australia, when he picked up a lucky win after Michael Schumacher had driven Damon Hill off the track, but prudence was never among his defining characteristics.

Mansell will be remembered not for his Brummie whingeing, his lack of social graces, his melodramatic displays of exhaustion or his prodigious, pantomime-villain eyebrows and moustache, but for the fact that when you put him in a racing car his first instinct was to look for somebody to overtake. And there will be a few rich young men on the grid this Sunday of whom it would be hard to make that particular claim. ●

Pass Notes

30 November 1994   Shane Warne

Age: 25.

Appearance: Lobster in sunglasses.

Occupation: Leg-break bowler.

Sounds painful: For England, very. His 8–71 spun Australia to victory in the first Test in Brisbane. England's hopes are, you guessed it, in ashes.

Can you explain how leg spin works? Only with the aid of diagrams. But basically it's all in the wrist. The position of the hand and the way the wrist is flicked are varied to produce leg-spinners, top-spinners and googlies, always remembering of course that left-handed leg-break bowlers bowl googlies and chinamen.

I didn't think the Chinese played cricket: I fear you have missed the point.

And young Shane is good? A genius. Has almost single-handedly revived the lost art of leg spin in Australia, turning old-timers misty-eyed with memories of O'Reilly, Grimmett and Fleetwood-Smith, and reviving the interest of the young, who were being tempted by awful US sports like basketball.

Vital statistics: Has taken 145 wickets in 30 Tests. Bagged 67 in 1993 (a record for a spinner), including 34 against England, who got the usual drubbing.

Why are England so bad? Too old; too fat; can't play spin; can't play pace for that matter; Illy, Fletch and Athers unable to agree on time of day.

Did Shane enjoy a trouble-free rise to stardom? Far from it. As a teenager he had a reputation as a hell-raiser and was chucked out of the Australian cricketing academy. Spent a spell playing club cricket in Bristol, where his fondness for the local beer saw his weight increase by two stone. Nor did the cricket go too well: on his Test debut against India in 1992 he took 1 for 150.

That's bad? Look, perhaps you'd better stick to soccer's rather less sophisticated scoring system. I presume even you can understand a 0–0 draw.

But talent will out: Indeed, and the frequent series against England, where first-class leg-spinners are virtually extinct, has made life easier. Also helped by coach and master of euphemism Terry Jenner, who called him a 'non-conformist free spirit'.

Nickname: Warney to the unimaginative; Hollywood to his friends.

How come? His *Baywatch* persona, I guess. Blond locks, permanent suntan, shades, earring – Sir Donald Bradman he ain't.

He's *remarkably* blond, don't you think? Let's just say he doesn't lack bottle.

Useful headline: The Dumbfounding Blond.

Arcane fact: The googly was invented by B J T Bosanquet, father of newscaster Reggie.

Not to be confused with: Shane Ramsay in *Neighbours*; Shane Parrish in *Home and Away*; Australian swimmer Shane Gould; Australian rugby league star Shane Sheepshagger (just joking).

Most likely to say: 'Howzat' (about four times an over).

Least likely to say: 'Gee, Gatt, you've certainly got my flipper sussed.' ●

4 January 1995

Matthew Engel
Darren tricks Aussie villains

After weeks of savage criticism in two hemispheres, something happened yesterday that in a funny way was even more distressing.

England climbed off the floor, all right, and it was marvellous. But there was something thoroughly impertinent in the way the Sydney members applauded Darren Gough and the team into the pavilion. They were pleased for us. It was horrid.

'The Poms bowled very well, bowled a good line and length, kept us honest,' said Mark Taylor, all but giving us a pat on the head. 'England really fighting back here, which is good,' said the radio commentator Neville Oliver.

'Thank heavens we've got a competitive test match,' said Ian Chappell. It was as though Sri Lanka had batted jolly well at Lord's.

England, or possibly the English media, had brought all this on themselves by the response to the disasters of Brisbane and Melbourne.

There used to be something known as the Cultural Cringe. Australians assumed that if something artistic came from Britain it must be good. In the old days a second-rate Pommie actor or musician could be regarded here as a superhero.

The new version, in reverse, is the Cricketing Cringe, which assumes whatever Australia does must be right and that they could never be beaten until Britain is repopulated with strapping blond leg-spinners, with the rules, pitches and culture of the County Championship abolished in favour of whatever is done in the Sheffield Shield.

But in the short run it does not matter if county cricket is played over 45 minutes each way on the fast lane of the M4. All that was required was for the players to get off their knees and believe in themselves. They did it thanks to the nearest thing we have to a strapping blond leg-spinner: a strapping, barrel-chested, brown-haired fast bowler who is inventive enough to slip in the occasional leg-break.

The epidemic of renewed self-confidence spread from Gough's bat on Monday night, just as it did at the Oval in August when Gough's batting counter-attack with Phillip DeFreitas set the scene for Devon Malcolm's nine wickets. In the bar on Monday, Angus Fraser was sufficiently animated to be giving learned discourses on batsmanship, to be greeted by his team-mates with replies of 'Is that so, Bradman?'

The fast bowlers looked as if they meant business and their belief spread to the team; even Mike Gatting began running puppyishly around the boundary.

England started holding catches; Australia started dropping them. Australian commentators began to wonder if the right 11 men were out there and speculated on which players might be dropped.

It was like the moment when the beleaguered hero tricks the villain and grabs the gun; the added poignancy was the fear that the villain might, in this case, somehow grab it back.

But Gough is a marvel and a lesson to everyone. No academy can teach a cricketer to be hungry, to savour the big time instead of fearing it, to seize the moment the way he has done.

He swaggers around even in the hotel lobby. He is afraid of nothing and no one, which is why the comparison with a certain all-rounder, now better known for his pantomime appearances, is reasonably apt.

The Barmy Army loves him, and he does not shy away from that. But he understands history too. He went to see 90-year-old Harold Larwood before Christmas and yesterday Larwood rang him in the dressing room to say 'Well done', a gesture that re-established the thread with the great Ashes series of the past which seemed in danger of being lost.

But one fears for him, because English cricket's recent record of guarding its treasures is so dreadful. 'I've always had a bit of fun,' he said yesterday, 'always been open. No reason why I should change. I'm still Darren Gough.' You can almost see the line-up of demented Yorkshiremen, conservative administrators, fussy coaches, predatory agents and tabloid reporters all muttering, 'We'll see about that. We'll drag you down, son, don't worry.' Meanwhile, let him, and us, savour a very exciting moment. A few more days like this and the Aussies really will have to stop patronising us. ●

8 May 1995

Matthew Engel
The young person's guide to old fartism

On Saturday a Mr William Carling was removed from his post as captain of the England rugby union team for describing the game's administrators as 'old farts'. Some people may wish to know what an 'old fart' might be. I shall try to explain, though it may be necessary to invoke Louis Armstrong's reply to the lady who asked what jazz is: if you gotta ask, you'll never know.

The *Collins Dictionary* says a fart, aside from the definition every schoolboy knows, is also (noun) (taboo) (slang) 'a contemptible person'. But that is only the half of it. Anyone who has ever observed sporting administration will be aware that there is an entire set of beliefs – 'old fartism' – and skills – 'old fartistry' – involved here. (See also related subjects: nitpicking pedantry, overweening self-importance and sheer blithering idiocy.)

Fartists have been involved in running every sport. In soccer they would gravitate to the county associations, to exercise supreme power of a highly theoretical kind over all the football played in their domain.

The most stylish practitioners would occasionally threaten the local professional clubs with dire consequences under rule something or other if they did not field their entire first team against a park side in the first round of the Loamshire Cup. The real greats would try to invoke this the night before the league club were involved in, say, the European Cup final.

More humdrum operators would spend their time banning little boys from the game for life if they so much as passed the ball to a girl or, worse still, passed the ball to anyone on a Sunday. One county secretary stood in the centre circle to try to prevent a Sunday charity match going ahead. They played around him. Lower-grade fartists just collected their Wembley tickets.

In cricket they instinctively joined MCC. ('Whilst inside the pavilion, members and their guests should wear ties and tailored coats and acceptable trousers and appropriate shoes.') Jockey Club fartists maintained (until 1966) that women could not train horses. In golf they can still devote their lives to ensuring that blacks and Jews are kept out completely and that professionals and/or women are allowed to use only the back stairs. In tennis . . . but, no, that way madness lies.

And rugby union, ah, rugby union! This has to be the greatest of all sports for fartists because it is an organised hypocrisy and they have the chance to organise it. Its central tenet, amateurism, is a lie and has been for decades. In 1950 the Welsh Rugby Union banned a BBC commentator named Price from the Arms Park for claiming that some players in Wales actually received money for playing the game. The idea!

The Scottish RFU once refused to give an international called Jock Wemyss a new shirt on the grounds that he had had one last time he played. That was true but there had been a world war in between. He had lost an eye serving his country, as well as the shirt.

In the 1960s another Scot, Peter Stagg, put blacking on his legs to cover the holes in his blue socks. When the farts consented to let him have another pair they sent him a bill.

But for the true old fart there can be no greater moment than the one when you can claim to be insulted, and stand on your dignity and your high horse simultaneously. Thus the RFU and Carling. Fifty years on from the war (and what opportunities in the realms of pointless bossiness that gave the farts) sporting fartistry has reached its climax. It is also its death rattle, because crass stupidity is disappearing, to be replaced by crass commercialism. It is a pity not to have even a brief interval of honest common sense.

As the famously reverent British population emerged yesterday from Morning Service in their millions (all right then, ones and twos), some may have noticed new centres of worship opening up. For the first time on a Sunday it was possible to kneel at the shrines of St William on the Hill, Our Lady of the Coral and all the other chapels and presbyteries of the Church of the Immaculate Self-Deception.

It is an appropriate development in a country whose central belief system is now based on gambling, and gambling of a particularly boring and witless kind, ie the Lottery. Even as I made my oblation in the form of an each-way yankee and a loser in the 1,000 Guineas I felt rather sad.

Racing already goes on six days a week all year round. It seems to me that even the great races may soon blur into a background hum, like dog-racing. Gosh, I'm not turning into an old fart, am I? •

Anke Huber

Pass Notes

26 June 1995   Pete Sampras

Age: 23.

Appearance: Ronald Reagan's buddy in the WWII film *Hellcats of the Marine Catering Corps.*

Occupation: Wimbledon champion.

Theme-tune: Tap-tap-tap-whoosh-whack-bonk-clap-clap-40 love!

Irritating habits: Dog-like panting; beating more artistic players through sheer service power.

Nickname: Pistol Pete.

Pistol Pete? Is that really the best anyone could come up with? No, but Americans don't know what Daynurse is. And it reflects his identification with 'Rocket' Rod Laver.

The parallels are spooky? Laver was left-handed, 5ft 9in, 10st 10lb, and used wooden rackets. He could win on all surfaces. Sampras is right-handed, 6ft 1in, 12st 2lb, and uses graphite rackets. He is crap on clay, where rallies still occur.

So it's complete cobblers? No, they're both Leos.

This boring image – a trifle exaggerated? Even his own parents prefer shopping to watching him. And recall the *Guardian* reports on Wimbledon 1993 ('the one foolproof way of putting the ticket touts out of business: a final between Sampras and Jim Courier') and the 1994 Sampras-Ivanisevic climax ('a quite stultifyingly tedious final').

But surely less cynical publications are kinder? Nope: kindly *Tennis 95* calls him the John Major of tennis.

So you won't be entering the *Observer* draw to win free final tickets? Second prize: tickets for the final *and* the Sampras semi. No, I jest: this year will be different, if you believe the hype.

He's limiting himself to a single serve? No, but the Agassi revival encourages buffs to expect a classic duel of Cavalier and Roundhead.

A feud? Maybe in the past. Now they josh each other creepily. In the BBC's Wimbledon promos, Agassi calls Sampras 'a guy you'd take home to ma'.

The rascal! What does Pete say? 'I'll get you for that.'

Almost Wildean. But could you settle a couple of bets? Fire away.

Are those silly baggy shorts a present from a doting aunt? Yes, she's called Aunt Nike, and he gets £3 million for wearing kit that doesn't fit.

And the obsessive toying with racket strings: what's that all about? Adherents of the 'robot' theory contend that this is how he is controlled by his coach: either visual instructions appear on the racket, or he can actually be programmed via the string-finger interface.

101 uses for a Pete Sampras: Metronome; bird-scarer; child pacifier.

Preferable alternatives to watching Sampras: Catching up on Lords debates in *Hansard*; playing 20-disc *Best of Fado* CD; minding slow cooker.

Most likely to say: 'I was in a zone' [tr. 'playing well'].

Least likely to say: *No*, Barbra, I'm a born again *Christian*! Can't you just sit over there and sing 'People' again? ●

29 June 1995

Stephen Bierley

Canadian club holds the centre stage

The famous J F Kennedy declaration – 'Ask not what your country can do for you, but what you can do for your country' – is all very well, but first you have to choose your country.

Mary Pierce and Greg Rusedski were born within a year and half of each other in Montreal. Yesterday, with not a maple leaf or a Mountie in sight, they played back-to-back on Centre Court, one representing France, the other Britain.

Birth and place of birth are a mere accident. Pierce's mother is French; Rusedski's mum claims Dewsbury as her native home. But just as Pierce grew up a child of the United States, so Rusedski is Canadian through and through. Both have chosen to ply their trade with a European tag.

'The British tennis kettle was cold. What it needed was a bit of hot water poured in to make it boil, and Rusedski is just that,' Andrew Castle, Britain's former Davis Cup player, said yesterday.

Recently *Paris Match* published pictures of a bikini-clad Pierce, part of the never-ending quest to present her as something more than a mere tennis player. Much of what has been written about her has been equally alluring, but the essential points have remained covered up.

Those are that she is a pretty ordinary player – or an ordinary pretty player if you prefer the hype.

Those who expected her to lose comprehensively to Nathalie Tauziat of France (born, incidentally, in the Central African Republic) nodded knowingly as the first set drifted away. Others were in a muck sweat of apoplexy.

Pierce took the second set but even then was rubbing and flexing her right knee as if preparing herself for ultimate defeat. Thereafter she was really never in the match. There is, whatever the truth of it may be, the look of a poseur about her. Her weight of shot was obvious, albeit spasmodic, but too frequently her movement and anticipation are non-existent.

Tauziat broke Pierce's service three times in the final set and displayed a resolve beyond anything her opponent could muster. 'Yes!' Tauziat cried incongruously as she took a 5–1 lead, and within a couple of minutes Pierce's first Wimbledon was over.

Pierce plays for France because her infamous father, Jim, fell out horribly with the US tennis authorities. She must wonder if it really was the right decision, for yesterday there seemed no doubt that Tauziat was fired up with a little more than mere ambition.

Did she detect any French rivalry? 'Maybe. I tried not to think I was going to play against Nathalie.' But it must always have been in her mind, and will continue to be so.

There is little doubt that Rusedski, with the clear encouragement of his parents, decided to opt for these shores because being the British No. 1 will bring him a bundle more money than being Canada's top dog. He is, after all, following the same path as Robin Smith and Graeme Hick.

Like them he will find himself praised and lauded if things go well and blamed with that added edge of British hypocrisy when they go wrong. Yesterday, on his first visit to Centre Court, he was enveloped in adopted nationalistic fervour.

When Forget rushed through the first set it seemed it might indeed be an afternoon to forget. 'Take no notice of this Mr Nice Guy image Greg has been projecting during the past few weeks,' warned Castle. 'Deep down he's as mean as hell.'

Rusedski continued to club and volley his way back against the Casablanca-born Forget, who increasingly discovered himself to be in the wrong gin joint. Play it again – wham. So tight were things that the game hinged on only a handful of points. Essentially Rusedski won them all.

The expectations will now be huge, the sort of inflated expectations that have seen a succession of British players flag and wilt. But for Rusedski it all may be very different, simply because he is not steeped to the gills in false optimism, his mind uncluttered by a sequence of historical failure.

There will be those within the British tennis establishment, as there are some current home players, who will perhaps never take the Canadian to their hearts.

Fred Perry would have loved it. He always detested cant and frequently scoffed at the establishment. His hand would have been one of the first to grip Rusedski's and welcome him aboard.

Last night the British kettle was whistling happily on its Canadian hob. The French were in need of a little maple syrup. ●

· ·

27 June 1995

Richard Williams
Old echoes in South Africa's new anthems

Before all South Africa's games in the Rugby World Cup, the country's anthem was sung. Or rather anthems, since for this event a special medley had been devised.

The sequence opened with 'Nkosi Sikelel'i Afrika', the old ANC anthem.

then, seamlessly, it was followed by 'Die Stem van Suid-Afrika', the Afrikaner theme song. The Springbok players were expected to sing both, with hands on hearts, joined by the crowd.

At their quarter-final in Johannesburg, I was struck by how thin the rendition of the ANC song sounded, and how 'Die Stem' resounded from the grandstands with much more brio. The crowd was about 99 per cent white, and neatly confirmed all the prejudices with which I had arrived.

These were mostly to do with rugby union being the symbol of white supremacy, and with a suspicion that some elements within the rugby establishment might be using the event to reassert their old values. I came to South Africa with the memory of that dismal day at Twickenham two and a half years ago, when F W de Klerk was welcomed over the public address system with words from Peter Yarranton of the Rugby Football Union that could only be described, in the circumstances, as unduly fulsome.

Two weeks later, things look very different. You could put this down to transient euphoria in the wake of victory, or you could say that at last the nation had found something they could share. True, it wasn't gold, or diamonds, or adequate housing for the poor. But, thanks to astute and sensitive management, and to the wholehearted endorsement of President Mandela, the 15 men could fairly claim – in the words of François Pienaar – to represent all 43 million South Africans.

An editorial in yesterday's *Business Day*, the Johannesburg daily, reflected: 'For a nation with a long, dark history of division and conflict, and still frequently at odds with itself, unity of will is an unusual and thrilling experience.' Thrills, by definition, don't usually last long, but just as sport provided an effective non-violent means of expressing disapproval of apartheid, so it seems now to have helped the process of reconciliation.

Mandela took another step yesterday when he indicated his support for those who wish to keep the Springbok emblem and name, which seemed an unwelcome link with the past when South Africa emerged from isolation. The rugby authorities had agreed to follow the example of the cricketers by considering the possibility of replacing it with the Protea, a local flower, after the World Cup. Now even some former radicals are changing their minds, which suggests that symbols are less powerful than ideas and deeds, and that they can change their meaning before your very eyes.

But I can't forget something that happened on the way to England's semi-final in Pretoria, once the capital of the old Union of South Africa.

I had parked a few hundred yards from the stadium, in a pleasant street of whitewashed bungalows shaded by jacaranda trees. Towards me on the pavement came a boy and a girl, white, aged about 13 or 14, in neat green school uniforms.

The girl said something. I'm sorry, I said. I don't speak Afrikaans.

'Would you please buy a raffle ticket?'

Well, I won't be here after today.

'Then would you give us a donation, please?'

What's it for?

'It's to help children who can't pay their school fees.'

What sort of children?

'White children,' she said, and there was a half-beat pause while she saw some sort of reaction in my face. 'Not black ones,' she added, as if to reassure me.

'Not black ones,' the boy repeated. Their faces were eager.

Why? I couldn't think of any other way of saying it. Why white children?

They looked at each other. 'I don't know,' the girl said, shrugging.

I asked them who was organising this raffle, clearly targeted at rugby fans.

'Mr Labuschagne,' the boy said.

Their headmaster.

South Africa has a long way to go. On the other hand, it wasn't just my imagination registering that, as they were sung before the final at Ellis Park on Saturday, the decibels of 'Nkosi Sikilel'i Afrika' and 'Die Stem' had achieved equality. ●

....

4 February 1995

Frank Keating
Invasion of the veal eaters via Channel Tunnel

From mid-morning yesterday there was a sense and buzz of occasion in the Eurostar salon at the Gare du Nord in Paris and, by midday, a fair jostle of French rugby men – jaunty berets accentuating cauliflower ears – chorused a rousing *Bonne chance et Allez France!* as the first major international sporting team set off for a match by way of the Channel Tunnel.

All things considered, it would have been easier to fly as usual, but when the idea was mooted, the French Rugby Federation, with typical panache, went the whole hog and simply hired a special train for their first XV and hundreds of attendant alikadoos. There was not a seat to be had in first class. The mood was touched with the adventure of it and much jollity. To begin with, that is.

'*Sûrement, pas d'problème,*' the French captain, Phillippe St André, said when asked to say how confident he was for Twickenham today – but first he said he needed a couple of glasses of rouge by way of aperitif before lunch was served. Ah, yes, lunch. First things first, *Vive la France*. We edged softly out of Paris and the team tucked their white napkins into their oversized, already straining collars – then tucked in themselves.

For starters *Assiette Gourmande* – a stacked platter of bits and bobs from smoked salmon to caviare tart. Then a choice of fillet steak or (probably chosen in the circumstances to make a nice Gallic point to the Brits) *Mignon de Veau aux Morilles* – veal with morel mushrooms – and *haricots verts* and *carottes*, no cauliflower. Then trays of cheeses, *gâteau*, fruit, washed down with either or both of a 1990 Bergerac Château Plaisance or a Sauvignon 1993 Côte de Duras. Hey, steady, you guys, you're playing England tomorrow.

The charming captain and his two immediate predecessors, the clothes-prop Roumat and the legendary Sella, sat together, each fingering their designer stubble or their fashionable carelessly spiky Tintin hair, styled like it had been barbered with blunt scissors. They joshed each other, smiled at private in-jokes.

Suddenly, just like that, the meal was finished – at least they turned away Armagnac or any *digestif* – and simultaneously almost to the minute our 186mph flyer ducked with a whoosh into the darkness of the tunnel and the steward announced watches to be put back an hour.

At that stroke, the frivolity of the Paris farewell and the enjoyment of the meal was switched off. The hum of conversation died, the team became silent, focused, staring in their now solemn reverie at their own reflections in the windows and thinking of going over the top in less than 24 hours when England would be first teasing and then tearing into them at Twick. 'It's like playing 15 Cantonas,' the England vice-captain, Brian Moore, had said.

And no, *excusez-moi*, St André after all did not want to say anything about the morrow. At other extremities of the 18-carriage train, the wines were having a different effect on the supporters – and the 'Marseillaise' was sung slurringly as soon as, with a sense of occasion, we had burst out of the blackness under *la Manche* and into the slaty-bright afternoon light of Kent.

Of course, history keeps repeating itself. Well, in different ways. Almost 40 years ago, schoolboys of a certain age might remember Leslie Mitchell's golly-gosh tones of utter amazement on the Movietone newsreel reporting, wonder of wonders, that the England XV of 1956 were pioneers by actually flying to the match in Paris.

There they all were in grainy monochrome grinning sheepishly and standing in front of the stepladders alongside a tiny BEA twin-propeller aircraft with the couple of Nissen huts which then comprised Heathrow airport – Eric Evans in his first year as captain, Peter Robbins, Sandy Sanders and all, plus a lanky London Society referee who was to be touch-judge the following afternoon in the old Paris stadium at Colombes, one Denis Thatcher.

Yesterday was, in its minor way, an equally historic trip. Also an evocatively pointed one. The first rugby club ever to be formed in France was in 1872 when an Englishman called Longstaffe founded Le Havre RFC. Mr Longstaffe was the agent at the Channel port for Southern Railway ferries and boat trains. Not till 35 years later, in January 1907, did a French team first make the ferry journey to Dover for their first match on English soil — beaten 41–13 at the Richmond Athletic Ground. They had boarded the train at the Gare du Nord after taking Friday off work.

Not all that different from yesterday, really. Except that we did not arrive at Victoria station. Was there more of a resonant betting man's tip in the fact that for today's match the French arrived at Waterloo? ●.